TARPEIA

TARPEIA
WORKINGS OF A ROMAN MYTH

TARA S. WELCH

THE OHIO STATE UNIVERSITY PRESS
COLUMBUS

Copyright © 2015 by The Ohio State University.
All rights reserved.

Library of Congress Cataloging-in-Publication Data
Welch, Tara S., 1967– author.
 Tarpeia : workings of a Roman myth / Tara S. Welch.
   pages cm
 Includes bibliographical references and index.
 ISBN 978-0-8142-1281-3 (cloth : alk. paper)
 1. Tarpeia (Mythological character) 2. Mythology, Roman—History and criticism. I. Title.
 BL820.T38W45 2015
 398.20937′02—dc23
                              2015014963

Cover design by Mary Ann Smith
Text design by Juliet Williams
Type set in Adobe Garamond pro
Printed by Thomson-Shore, Inc.

♾ The paper used in this publication meets the minimum requirements of the American National Standard for Information Sciences—Permanence of Paper for Printed Library Materials. ANSI Z39.48-1992.

9 8 7 6 5 4 3 2 1

CONTENTS

List of Illustrations	vii
Abbreviations	ix
Acknowledgments	xi

INTRODUCTION		1
ONE	The Shape of Variety: Girl, City, Rome	19

PART ONE   Tarpeia, Ethnicity, and Being Roman in the Republic

TWO	Fabius Pictor's Greedy Girl: Not Yet *Tota Italia*	45
THREE	Tarpeia in Silver: The Denarii of the Social War	76

PART TWO   Tarpeia and the Caesars: From Republic to Empire

FOUR	Varro's Vestal Version: Tarpeia in Word and Stone	105
FIVE	Perspectives on and of Livy's Tarpeia	135
SIX	Elegiac Tarpeia (Who Won't Stay Put)	167
SEVEN	Valerius Maximus on Remembering Tarpeia's Memorable Deed	203

PART THREE   Tarpeia from the Outside In: Greek Sources and the Roman Empire

EIGHT	Hellenistic Tarpeia in the Elegy of Simylus	225
NINE	On the Edge of the Knife in Dionysius of Halicarnassus	239
TEN	Songworthy Athens, Invincible Rome: Tarpeia in Plutarch's *Romulus*	254

CONCLUSION   284

Appendix   289
Bibliography   293
Index Locorum   317
General Index   327

ILLUSTRATIONS

FIGURE 1 Denarius of L. Titurius Sabinus, 89 BCE, Tatius / Death of Tarpeia   77

FIGURE 2 Denarius of L. Titurius Sabinus, 89 BCE, Tatius/*Bigae*   77

FIGURE 3 Denarius of L. Titurius Sabinus, 89 BCE, Tatius / Rape of the Sabine Women   78

FIGURE 4 Basilica Aemilia in the Roman Forum   126

FIGURE 5 Basilica Aemilia relief sculpture, Death of Tarpeia   127

FIGURE 6 Basilica Aemilia relief sculpture, Edge of Tarpeia segment and wedding scene   128

FIGURE 7 Denarius of P. Petronius Turpilianus, 19–18 BCE, Augustus / Death of Tarpeia   166

FIGURE 8 Petronius Turpilianus' coin of Tarpeia and its re-use as a Mithraic token   285

ABBREVIATIONS

Beck   Beck, H., and U. Walter. 2001. *Die Frühen Römischen Historiker, Band I von Fabius Pictor bis Cn. Gellius (Texte zur Forschung Band 76)*. Darmstadt: Wissenschaftliche Buchgesellschaft.

BMC Italy   Poole, R. F. 1873. *A Catalogue of Greek Coins in the British Museum*. Vol. 1, *Italy*. London: Trustees of the British Museum.

BMCRE   Mattingly, H. 1923–62. *Coins of the Roman Empire in the British Museum*. 6 vols. London: Trustees of the British Museum.

BMCRR   Grueber, H. A. 1910. *Coins of the Roman Republic in the British Museum*. London: Trustees of the British Museum.

CIL   1893–. *Corpus Inscriptionum Latinarum*. Berlin: Brandenburg Academy of Sciences and Humanities.

CIMRM   Vermaseren, M. J., ed. 1956–60. *Corpus Inscriptionum et Monumentorum Religionis Mithriacae*. The Hague: Martinus Nijhoff.

FGrH   Jacoby, F. 1923–. *Die Fragmente der griechischen Historiker*. 3 vols. Berlin: Weidmann and Leiden: Brill.

FRH   Cornell, T. J. 2013. *Fragments of the Roman Historians*. Oxford: Oxford University Press.

HRR	Peter, H. (1906) 1914. *Historicorum Romanorum Reliquiae*. Leipzig: Teubner.
LSJ	Liddell, H. G., R. Scott, and H. S. Jones. (1843) 1996. *Greek-English Lexicon*. 9th ed. Oxford: Oxford University Press.
LTUR	Steinby, E. M., ed. 1993–2000. *Lexicon Topographicum Urbis Romae*. Vol. 1–6. Rome: Edizioni Quasar.
MRR	Broughton, T. R. S. 1951–86. *The Magistrates of the Roman Republic*. 3 vols. New York: American Philological Association.
OLD	Glare, P. G. W. 1968–82. *Oxford Latin Dictionary*. Oxford: Oxford University Press.
PColZen	Westermann, W. L. et al., eds. 1934. *Zenon Papyri: Business Papers of the Third Century BC Dealing with Palestine and Egypt*. 2 vols. New York: Columbia University Press.
RDGE	Sherk, R. K. and P. Viereck 1969. *Roman Documents from the Greek East*. Baltimore: Johns Hopkins University Press.
RE	Pauly, A. F. von, G. Wissowa, and W. Kroll, eds. 1894–1980. *Paulys Real-Encyclopädie der classischen Altertumswissenschaft, neue Bearbeitung*. Stuttgart: Metzler.
RIB	Collingwood, R. B, R. P. Wright, and R. S. O. Tomlin. (1965) 1990. *The Roman Inscriptions of Britain*. Oxford: Clarendon.
RIC	Mattingly, H., and E. A. Sydenham et al., eds. 1923–81. *The Roman Imperial Coinage*. 10 vols. London: Spink.
RRC	Crawford, M. H. 1974. *Roman Republican Coinage*. Cambridge: Cambridge University Press.
SEG	Hondius, J. J. E. et al. 1923–. *Supplementum Epigraphicum Graecum*. Amsterdam: Gieben and Leiden: Brill.
SIG	Dittenberger, W. ed. 1915–1924. *Sylloge inscriptionum graecarum*. Leipzig: S. Hirzel. 3rd edition.
TLL	1900–. *Thesaurus Linguae Latinae*. Leipzig: Teubner.
UPZ	U. Wilcken. 1927–57. *Urkunden der Ptolemäerzeit, altere Funde*. Berlin and Leipzig: De Gruyter.

ACKNOWLEDGMENTS

THIS BOOK has been long in the making. Its origin may be traced to my doctoral research on Propertius, and along the way it has met many friends and supporters. No enemies, though—for every single bit of criticism I received on parts or the whole was offered kindly, constructively, and in the service of a better project. It is difficult to offer fitting thanks to all those friends, but a pleasurable task to acknowledge and thank them here.

My colleagues at the University of Kansas have nurtured this book along in many ways. Tony Corbeill, Pam Gordon, Emma Scioli, and John Younger read many versions of many chapters. Those conversations—on paper, over coffee, in the hallway—are one hallmark of an outstanding department. As chair, Pam Gordon found many other ways to support my work, through amenable course scheduling to travel funding to funding for graduate research assistance. KU's Hall Center for Humanities funded a crucial semester's research leave early on in the writing, which KU augmented with a semester sabbatical; this year offered both time and opportunities to present my work to humanists in other disciplines.

Some of the best and most fruitful conversations I've had about Tarpeia have been with graduate students in KU's MA program in Classics, who merit their own paragraph. In addition to the rich atmosphere of the graduate seminars, in which Tarpeia always makes an appearance of some sort, I've been lucky to work with some of the best rising scholars in the field as research assistants. Jeffrey Easton, Lizzy Adams, and Stephen Froedge have left profound marks on this book. I am eager to return the favor.

Friends and colleagues beyond KU have been generous with their time and expertise. John Henderson read the whole manuscript at least once, expeditiously but with a great eye for detail. Allen Miller, Nita Krevans, Matthew Roller, Hans Friedrich Mueller, Nicholas Horsfall, Celia Schultz, Christopher Smith, and Lily Panoussi read and improved chapters. I am grateful for the excellent comments and lines of thought suggested by colleagues at conferences and talks; I single out audiences at Gustavus Adolphus, Baylor University, Yale University, and the Università di Trento for particularly fruitful input. My friend and colleague Gregory Crosby combed the typescript with an eagle eye for details and a gift for language. I recommend him highly.

Eugene O'Connor, managing editor at The Ohio State University Press, deserves special mention, not only for his patience but for finding extraordinarily helpful readers. These two anonymous scholars transformed a project into a book, and a much better one at that. I learned a great deal from them, and I thank them for being so generous with their time and expertise. With a light touch Eugene nudged along the process of revising this book. For this and for the confidence he showed all along, I offer thanks. Tara Cyphers saw the project to completion with patience, energy, and a meticulous eye. I am grateful for her participation.

Finally, to those whose support came in other ways—encouragement, babysitting, diversion—I offer my warmest thanks. Selene, Dan, Kate, and especially Kelly—thank you.

INTRODUCTION

WHEN THE SABINES were besieging Rome in the eighth century BCE, in response to Romulus's rape of the Sabine women, legend has it that the Roman maiden Tarpeia made a pact with the enemy forces: she would open the Capitoline stronghold to them, if they would give her what they wore on their left arms. The pact was sealed. At night, she showed the Sabines the entrance and they invaded. Then they killed her by heaping upon her their shields, which they bore on their left arms. She was crushed to death under their weight. The fighting that ensued between Romans and Sabines resulted in a truce that joined the two cultures into one and made the Sabine Tatius co-king with Romulus. Tarpeia's tale appears frequently in Roman literature, on coins, and in sculpture. These sources are always faithful to the core of her myth: that she opened Rome's stronghold and then died. Otherwise they show remarkable variety in the way they present and assess Tarpeia. She is usually a greedy girl, lured by the promise of finery to betray her city, but in some sources her motivation is love for the enemy commander. She might be a Vestal virgin, or just a girl with no special role in the state. She might look like a typical maiden, or look like an Amazon. Or—a shocking combination—she is a Vestal in love, and like an Amazon to boot. One author presents her as a double agent, patriotic at heart and trying to disarm the Sabines—until her plan backfires. In other sources, it was her father who was architect of the plan. Or, in one source quite unlike the rest, her deed opened Rome to the Gauls in the notorious sack of Rome in the fourth century BCE rather than the Sabines in the earliest days of Rome. Why this variety of tellings?

This book explores the uses and contours of Tarpeia's myth through several centuries of Roman history, from its first appearance in the mid-Republic (third c. BCE) to its fading in the mid-empire (2nd c. CE). In ten chapters, I examine the way her story functions for tellers who work in several genres of literature (history, poetry, biography, technical treatise, handbook) in both Latin and Greek, in silver coinage, and in marble. To understand these tellings of her myth, I invoke Rome's political and military history as well as its literature, law, art, topography, coinage, and ritual and religion. Throughout the book, I sustain the argument that Tarpeia's myth, set during a tense moment of Roman expansionism and war, and involving political and moral conflict at its core, was a complex tool that could be used by Romans and Greeks alike to explore their identity as part of the Roman empire, to consider tensions in their social and political ideology, and to scrutinize their relationships with each other and with other communities. This myth provides a powerful example of how literature, art, ritual, and topography all contributed to the Romans' self-perception.

Tarpeia's myth augurs rich findings about Rome's sense and projection of itself across these centuries. Sharing with Greek myth the theme of the traitorous female and involving Rome's violent absorption of a foreign culture, the myth of Tarpeia and its variations shed light on Rome's evolving views of gender and ethnicity, of the role of the individual in the state, and of the tension between private and public authority, all against the backdrop of Rome's development into an international power. By scrutinizing how Tarpeia's story is adapted to contemporary circumstances, we can recover some of the ways Romans conceptualized and addressed the problems raised when women and foreigners gained agency in society. This conceptualization in turn can illuminate the contours of Rome's self-perception as a pluralistic society—a society to which the contribution of women and foreigners is problematic, but necessary.

MYTH

It will be helpful at the outset to state what I mean by "myth." In this book, a "myth" is a traditional tale that houses truths or lessons for its tellers and their audiences. In this definition I follow a more or less standard understanding of Greek and Roman myth, which can be found in a variety of sources from the brief blurbs that introduce general textbooks[1] to the detailed parsing of specialists.[2] This definition draws attention both to the idiosyncrasy of a myth's manifestations and to its transcendent appeal. The case for idiosyncrasy is made forcefully by Claude Calame in his book *Greek Mythology: Poetics, Pragmatics and Fiction* (2009).[3] Calame argues that a "myth" does not exist at all apart from its utterance; rather, the context of its production and reception determines its meaning.[4] Borrowing the terminology of linguistics, Calame calls his approach "pragmatic." Pragmatics examine the way the context of an utterance determines its meaning—how it necessarily interacts with and even trumps semantics, which refers to the deep meaning of signifiers such as words: "Every version or formulation of what we call a 'myth' should be considered as the result of a particular and specific discourse production and discursive rendering that relates to a precise enunciative situation" (p. 54).

Calame's understanding of myth counters what he reads as the structuralist approach, a theoretical school exemplified by the anthropologist Claude Lévi-Strauss.[5] This approach understands systems such as language and myth to be expressions of universal and transcendent deep structures of human consciousness. An example of a structuralist interpretation of Tarpeia is that of Georges Dumézil. Dumézil, a scholar of ancient religions, argued that Tarpeia's myth displays the same triadic relationship among the sovereign (Romulus), the warrior (Tatius), and the commoner (Tarpeia) that he found in a number of other ancient societies and their stories.[6] Dumézil and other structuralists would admit that the deep structures manifest themselves in culturally specific ways; there is something Roman about the triadic pattern in the myth of Tarpeia, for example. So too Calame understands that "discourse production" and "enunciative situation" are broader phenomena than a momentary speech act. One must, for example, consider genre (whether literary or performative), a concept that cannot exist in the moment only but relies on the memory of patterns and structures established over time.[7] Though the structuralist

---

1. E.g., Powell 2012: 2; Morford et al. 2011: 25.
2. Burkert 1993; Graf 1993: 1–8; Bettini 2006; Wiseman 2004: 10–11.
3. Indeed it is made throughout his career; the 2009 book offers a lengthy, theoretical apology for the stance.
4. Calame 2009: 5–8.
5. Ibid., 7–8.
6. Dumézil strenuously denied that he was a structuralist (Dumézil 1973: 14 and see Littleton 1974), but others, even Lévi-Strauss, thought of him as one (see chapter 5 of Dosse 1997 for the intricacies of the relationship).
7. See also Calame 2011, esp. pp. 516–17: "In fact, if mythical discourse works, it is because

and pragmatic positions might be absolute in theory, then, neither is in practice absolute. The difference between them is one of strong emphasis.

The Calamian emphasis on context may be seen in a number of recent studies. Gumpert's book *Grafting Helen* (2001) traces the heroine's changes across several manifestations, from Homeric to modern. Blondell's *Helen of Troy: Beauty, Myth, Devastation* (2013) homes in on the Greek sources only. Clauss and Johnston's volume *Essays on Medea* (1996) looks at major iterations of Medea's tale and emphasizes its variability, as does Keike and Bartel's 2010 book *Unbinding Medea*. Loraux's *Tragic Ways of Killing a Woman* ([1987] 1991) examines a mythic story-type in the context of fifth-century Athenian tragedy. George Steiner's *Antigones* (1984) offers a widespread contextual treatment of the tragic heroine across centuries, genres, and cultures, followed by an exploration of what underlying structures of Western thought gave rise to her widespread appeal. The titles of these volumes (*Grafting . . . Ways . . . Antigones*) suggest plurality and mutability, rather than universality, of meaning. Yet in many we see also an attempt to grapple with the persistent popularity of certain stories across many contexts.

Tarpeia takes a Calamian stance and champions the idiosyncrasy of distinct manifestations of Tarpeia's myth. Nevertheless, my adopted definition of myth also recognizes the transcendent appeal that invites her presence in sources across time and space: "Myth is a traditional tale that houses truths or lessons for its tellers and their audiences." Tradition implies a handing down across time and space. As Wiseman quips, "if it matters enough to be *re*told, it is a myth" (my emphasis).[8] Perhaps "myth" does not exist beyond any one telling, but a myth certainly does. Yet this existence does not precede its tellings as it would in a structuralist approach. Rather, it is constituted by the sum of them.

ROMAN TRADITION AND ORIGINALITY

The word I use to describe Tarpeia's myth as the sum total of its tellings is "tradition." Tradition is relational and conservative in that it values a

---

of the strong relationship that narrative fiction and the world of text have with a world of cultural representations that corresponds to a universe of belief inscribed in space and time, and it is because of the poetic and practical, and usually ritualized, forms of communication that incorporate them in this universe. . . . Greek heroic narratives were active—in, and thanks to, their poetic form—within their particular ritual and cultural circumstances."

8. Wiseman 2004: 11.

shared past. Roman culture is deeply rooted in the concept of tradition. Roman behavior was shaped and upheld not by abstract laws or philosophies but by a system of precedents, examples of successful—or unsuccessful—Romans past. This system, the *mos maiorum* or "ways of the elders," championed certain values and behaviors not theoretically or abstractly, but precisely in concrete examples offered from Rome's past. Scholars of *exempla* recognize the delicate balancing act they perform between specificity, which renders them idiosyncratic and attached to a certain character, and universality, that is, adaptable to later Romans who would follow suit.[9] Like Tarpeia's myth, each *exemplum* has a set kernel of elements yet remains flexible to suit the needs of whoever is using it. Indeed, as we shall see below, Tarpeia is at times treated as an *exemplum*. Though few audiences would find themselves in her shoes, they can nevertheless glean something useful from her story. A similar combination of tradition and originality may be found in the uniquely Roman institution of declamation, in which orators-in-training were given a stock scenario (e.g., tyrannicide) or even a mythic crux (such as Helen's guilt) whose values and outcomes they would elaborate and debate. Mary Beard has even argued that declamation was a form of myth for the Romans, in that declamation exercised forms of imagination similar to those we might see exercised on the Athenian tragic stage.[10] To test this, we might apply the assertion to Tarpeia. Tarpeia never appears in the known declamatory corpus,[11] but split loyalties, problematic women, and just punishment do. The two intellectual milieus are similar. Beard made her bold case when skepticism about Roman myth as a valid category held sway; more recent work has largely overcome this skepticism, but Beard's analysis remains keenly relevant for two reasons. First, it insists that we treat Roman myth differently from Greek myth. Second, it identifies myth by its functionality rather than content. Myth and declamation do similar things in and for society.

Like myth, these broad cultural phenomena—*mos maiorum*, *exempla*, and declamation—suggest the Romans found and embraced a productive tension between tradition and originality. Maurizio Bettini has located this embrace in the Romans' very lexicon for myth: *fabula* and related words.[12] *Fabula*, a noun derived from *fari*, equivocates on the authority of the utter-

---

9. E.g., Langlands 2011.
10. Beard 1993: 44–64.
11. Never, that is, unless one considers Valerius Maximus's text to be closely linked with declamation (see, e.g., Bloomer 1992). My chapter on Valerius Maximus's Tarpeia takes a different direction.
12. Bettini 2006 and 2008.

ance. Since it originally seems to have meant "to divine," *fari* has shades of divine authority. *Fabula,* like *fari*'s other derivatives *fando* and *fama,* indicates not divine but social authority: that which has been said by the crowd. Social authority is powerful and, as Vergil notes (re: *fama*), gains strength by going.[13] It can, however, also be used pejoratively to indicate what other people, not the speaker, say or believe. Thus when a tale is called a *fabula* (as Tarpeia's is in Livy's narrative, for example; and cf. Propertius's use of *fabor*), its authority comes from both its tradition and its current speaker.

An appreciation for the value of Roman tradition as the material for originality goes some distance to quieting our skepticism about Roman myth as "secondary" or inauthentic. Nicholas Horsfall described Roman myth as "secondary," that is, literary and contrived, rather than truly mythic, which would refer to myth/s told around campfires or heard on the knees of nurses, which of course do not survive.[14] Greek myth as a category suffers less from the problem of idiosyncratic secondariness because of the visible blend of the oral and literate in the Greek epic cycle and because of the abundant, even overwhelming, presence of mythic scenes and characters in even the earliest Greek visual arts. The Roman collective and oral dimension is simply harder to recover. Nevertheless, Niebuhr was the great proponent of the oralist view of Roman myth. He theorized that Rome's most colorful traditional stories arose from preliterate, popular heroic ballads; we come rather close here to the campfire tales Horsfall so desires, but alas, none remain. Though the ballad theory was discredited as early as Mommsen (who preferred to find origins in annalistic records), a form of it was successfully revived by Zorzetti's work on early Roman banquets.[15] Zorzetti argued that, before Latin literature emerged in full force, *carmina convivialia* (banquet songs) served to preserve and transmit ancient stories.[16] One step further along the path from oral to literate is Wiseman's "drama theory," promoted in *Remus* and throughout his scholarly oeuvre.[17] Wiseman posits a form of origination for the Remus myth that combines popular culture and orality with literary structure and generic conventions: stage drama. Wiseman situated the earliest precise confluence of monuments and narrative about Remus—that is, the birth

---

13. *Aen.* 4.174–75.
14. This position is seen in Horsfall's introductory remarks in Bremmer and Horsfall 1987, in which he defines "original" and "secondary" myth.
15. Zorzetti 1990, 1991.
16. Cato attests to these (*Origines apud* Cicero *Tusc.* 4.3). For aitiologies of Latin literature, both historical and perceived, see Habinek 1998: 34–68; Goldberg 2005; and Sciarrino 2011.
17. See particularly Wiseman 1998, especially the first two chapters.

of the myth—in the political crucible of the late fourth and early third centuries. Niebuhr, Zorzetti, and Wiseman, in blazing a trail backward in time toward the birth of myths, are interested in mythmaking as much as myth itself. Exactly how does a myth arise and grow?

Many attempts have been made to locate the origin of Tarpeia's myth. Reinach posits that there was a pile of spoils of which Tarpeia was the tutelary deity. The heap was interpreted as a *tumulus* and the story of a human death and burial there arose. Finally, treason was assigned to her to explain her burial under armor.[18] Within the "spoils monument" possibility, varying dates are possible. Gansiniec also believes Tarpeia originated in a dedication of spoils, but she places this origin in the third century BCE. Nevertheless, she acknowledges (pp. 34–35) that this date does not allow much time for the military trophy to be forgotten, for the word τροπαῖον to morph into *Tarpeia,* and for the myth to emerge so as to be told by Fabius Pictor in the late third century. Horsfall sees aftermath of the Gallic sack (c. 390 BCE) as the period of Tarpeian mythopoiesis. The Romans, shamed by their defeat and by the treason of M. Manlius, transformed the details of his death into a new myth about treason on the Capitol; the rehabilitated Manlius took the surname Capitolinus.[19] Or, a century and a half later, the myth of Tarpeia is Fabius Pictor's fiction. This is the theory of A. Alföldi, who implies that Fabius Pictor all but made up the story, combining Alexandrian romance and tragic details with Roman moralizing tendencies so as to gratify the audience.[20] A further option is offered by Poucet and Semioli. Both scholars see the origins of Tarpeia's myth in the Sabine enfranchisement, Poucet the enfranchisement of the third century, Semioli of the fifth, though neither posits a specific moment of origin.[21]

I agree with this third possibility, but demonstrating it is not my aim in this book. Rather, this book confronts the symbiosis between the tradition of Tarpeia and the agency of its participants. Borrowing terms from Max Schiller's analysis of poetry, Matthew Fox describes this symbiosis as "sentimental," rather than "naïve."[22] The naïve (myth, or to Schiller,

---

18. Reinach 1912: 68–79.
19. Horsfall in Bremmer and Horsfall 1987: 63–75.
20. Alföldi 1963: 151–52. To Alföldi, Fabius also made up Sabine luxury to satisfy his personal antipathy to the Sabine Claudii, his political rivals. Momigliano's review (1967) does not mince words.
21. Poucet 1967: 114–16; Semioli 2010, based on the theme of Sabine riches; her conclusion is formulated concisely on p. 194.
22. Fox 2011. Schiller's original distinction, from "On Naïve and Sentimental Poetry," is about poetry: "Poets will either *be* nature or they will *seek* nature" (*Sie werden also entweder Natur sein, oder sie werden die verlorene suchen*).

poetry) arises spontaneously and is unself-conscious, whereas the sentimental is self-conscious and contrived. To Fox, myth's tellers are witnesses *of* which, rather than channels *through* which.[23] Here Fox situates the Roman predilection to list variants and sources; in Tarpeia's myth, we shall see this tendency outright in Livy's, Dionysius's, and Plutarch's treatment of Tarpeia's myth, and indirectly in Propertius's. Here too we may understand not only Livy's grudging admission in his preface of the use of *fabulae*, but even his Numa's exploitation of Egeria to foster religious piety among his people (1.19.5). Here is not only Dionysius of Halicarnassus's excursus on rationalizing and containing myth (2.18.3–2.21.1), but even his Romulus's paternalistic censorship of good myths from bad for his new citizens (2.18.3). As these examples show, the Romans themselves were quite sanguine about the coexistence of innovation and tradition in myth, just as they were sanguine in reworking Greek literary forms and even texts. Indeed, literary and mythic adaptation come together in several of the treatments of Tarpeia, in which the teller's creativity is restricted not only by traditional content but also by generic forms.

What follows looks at the myth in action as it plays out in the Roman imagination over five centuries. I am concerned with how the Romans used and tinkered with the tradition of Tarpeia's story: which elements they emphasized and which they downplayed, which elements they thought they could change and which remained steadfast. I am interested in the ways different media activate the myth, and what themes and nuances those media enable. As the readings herein will demonstrate, Tarpeia's myth is able to speak to a number of concerns, from the difficulties of an open society to Hellenistic dynastic succession, from ancient linguistic theory to the cultural angst of the Second Sophistic.

These concerns all center on belonging to and in Rome. Who is Roman and who is not? How does one become Roman? Who determines belonging and what belonging looks like? What is the perspective from the outside? The organization of the book recognizes that such belonging changes according to one's time and circumstances—indeed, one's context. The primary context within which I read instantiations of Tarpeia's myth is

---

23. Fox's designation recalls Horsfall's distinction between primary and secondary myth, a point about which Horsfall and Wiseman have exchanged many words, with Wiseman calling the distinction itself into question. Despite Horsfall's lament for the lost campfire stories and his focus on literary creation, Horsfall shares with Wiseman an interest in the hows and whys of mythic creation. See Horsfall 1993: 131–32 and in Bremmer and Horsfall 1987: 1–11; and Wiseman (1989) 1994: 23.

historical rather than generic (e.g., elegiac, antiquarian, numismatic). Thus the chapters are arranged in order of their appearance in the Roman consciousness rather than grouped by type. Also, though I do trace the myth chronologically, my interpretations are not diachronic; that is to say, they do not trace the evolution of Tarpeia's meaning over time. Rather, they are staunchly synchronic: looking sideways at the culture that surrounds the telling. In some cases the synchronic approach seems the only way to go: what else could we do with a very fragmentary source such as the history of Fabius Pictor? In other cases, it prompts a question about what sideways contexts are valid ones to invoke for interpretation; one source I treat at some length (the poet Simylus) is fragmentary and undated. Precise historical context cannot help, and so broad literary and cultural contexts must suffice.

STRUCTURE OF THIS BOOK

This book begins by locating Tarpeia within the broader mythological milieu of which she forms a part: the treasonous girl. Several mythic narratives, both common and obscure, rely on this figure to propel or explain heroic conquest. Some of these narratives dwell on the causes of her changed loyalty, while others focus on its aftermath. Some scrutinize her from within, that is, from the perspective of the people she betrays, while others judge her from without, from the perspective of those to whom she switches her loyalty. My first chapter places Tarpeia alongside Medea, Helen, and others to draw out themes that recur in her tradition, such as her flexible motive and the manner of her death. While it is the combination of these variables that shapes any one telling of her myth, the map of possibilities, when seen at once, renders more visible what is at stake in the selection of one detail over another. The chapter then turns to another context, broader than any one telling, in which her tradition operates: the Roman cityscape, in which many places share her name. Tarpeia's multifaceted presence in the *caput mundi* captures the themes visible in her mythic milieu, such as the blurry line between Roman and outsider and the simultaneous centrality and marginality of women in Roman society.

With these preliminaries in place, this book groups Tarpeia's appearances into three parts that recognize major shifts on the concept of belonging to and in Rome: the Republic, the transition to empire, and the empire.

Part One

Part 1 examines the ways the historians Fabius Pictor and Lucius Calpurnius Piso Frugi and the minter Lucius Titurius Sabinus exploit Tarpeia's potential to comment on ethnicity vis-à-vis being Roman. From its inception in a wolf's den on the Tiber, Rome grew steadily over the centuries to embrace first the towns of Latium, then the Etruscan territories to the north, followed by the Samnite-held mountains of central Italy and the fertile fields of Campania, and finally Italy's boot with Rome's defeat of Greek Tarentum. By mid-third century BCE Rome had control of the whole Italian peninsula and was recognized internationally as a power to be reckoned with. Nevertheless, the peninsula was by no means unified, and the wars with Carthage strained the Roman alliance to such an extent that several towns defected to Hannibal. The Tarpeia of Fabius Pictor, Hannibal's contemporary, launches this book just as it launches the dominant strain of her myth. Tarpeia in this first surviving telling responds to the pressures—moral, economic, strategic—that Hannibal's invasion placed on a unified Italy. This first part then follows Tarpeia through the aftermath of the Punic wars, in which a new and very positive Sabine stereotype arose in Rome while many other Italic states still considered themselves to be outsiders. Their differing opinions on belonging to Rome (different from each other's, and different from Rome's) erupted in a civil war across the peninsula. Part 1 ends with an examination of Tarpeia in the context of the recuperated Sabine in L. Calpurnius Piso Frugi's Tarpeia, and with the coinage from the war that carried Tarpeia's image all around Italy.

Chapter 2 examines Fabius Pictor, Rome's first annalistic historian who seems to have told Tarpeia's story at some length in his comprehensive history of Rome. The fragments preserved by Dionysius of Halicarnassus and confirmed by Livy show a preoccupation with Tarpeia's greed for Sabine gold and Tatius's deceit in killing her. As I argue, this version activates a perceived collusion between luxury and moral corruption/degeneracy/untrustworthiness that can be seen in contemporary sources and events, such as the passage of the *lex Oppia* restricting gold adornment and Hannibal's use of bribery to invite defection. Tarpeia's desire for gold and the Sabines' finery function within Rome as a way to explore elite self-control and the inherent dangers of an excessive desire for gold. This focus on greed also operates on a broader scale to explore the extent to which degeneracy, and indeed morality, is contagious. Tarpeia's vulnerability to foreign opulence represents a fear of incorporating outsiders who might contaminate native modesty. The discourse of corruption by a luxurious outsider was a core strategy of Greek historiography that had already been deployed in the shifting alliances among peoples in southern Italy. Pictor's history, written in Greek, would have had different force among the Greek speakers of southern Italy and their allies. The details of Tarpeia's story thus betray a deep uneasiness about Rome's fragile coalition against Hannibal. What is it to belong to and in Rome?

The third chapter jumps ahead a little more than a century. The second century BCE saw Rome's expanding jurisdiction over Greece and Asia Minor, Illyria, northern Africa, Spain, and parts of Gaul. The increased financial and military burden this expansion created led to social unrest within Rome and around Italy, prompting four decades of legislative back-and-forth about economic and citizenship rights, from 130 BCE and the land reform bill of Tiberius Gracchus to 90 BCE and M. Livius Drusus's proposal to enfranchise all Italians. This unrest exploded into civil war in Italy from 91 to 87 BCE. Tarpeia appears on a coin minted during this war, called the Social War: the obverse depicts King Tatius and the reverse shows her moment of death. Other coins in the same series by the same moneyer show Tatius and the rape of the Sabine women, and Tatius opposite a *bigae*, a two-horsed victory chariot. These coins, Tarpeia's especially, trigger the concept of ethnicity: through the cognomen *Sabin–* of the minter, through the first Sabine king on the obverse, and through the reverses' presentation of two core myths from the Sabine cycle. Once again the effects of this representation may be seen both within Rome, where Titurius advertised his ethnic difference in order to generate political clout, and outside Rome, where these coins with their ethnic markers found their way into the hands Romans, Sabines (and other Italian loyal allies), and rebels. The chapter first probes the benefits of boasting one's Sabinity within Rome. Interestingly, the Sabine reputation had reversed in the second century BCE, from deceitful and wealthy foreigner to austere and honest rustic. In an excursus within this chapter, I use this context of Sabine "belonging" to understand the version of Tarpeia's tale told by L. Calpurnius Piso Frugi, himself of Sabine descent. For Piso Frugi, Tarpeia was a Roman patriot trying to disarm the enemy Sabines through her ambiguous pact. Tarpeia was blameless, and the Sabines were guilty neither of luxury nor of deceit. The chapter then turns to the ways Titurius's Tarpeia coin might have spoken to people around Italy. At the core of my analysis is an understanding of the coin series— Tarpeia, Sabine women, *bigae*—as a set of images that probe three ways of becoming Roman: domination (the *bigae*), intermarriage (the rape), and joint society (the traitor). These three ways result in different sorts of belonging between and among the peoples so merged, for they imagine various levels of ethnic distinction or blending.

Part Two

The second part delves into the intense interest in Tarpeia that emerged in the last years of the Republic and the first years of the Principate. In this period too, belonging governs Tarpeia's appearance in Roman sources, but where the mid-Republican sources explore group belonging—what peoples belong, and how they do so—the Tarpeia tellers of the Augustan age focus more specifically on individual belonging: what does it mean to be a member of the community of Rome? The Republican model of elite participation in the state—competitive self-promotion within a framework of agreed-upon values, strategies, and goals—yielded to a new order whose rules and norms took some decades to evolve into a stable form of achievement through deference to the emperor.

Caesar's contemporary Varro inaugurates this portion of my study, and Valerius Maximus, writing under Tiberius, ends it. In Varro's text I see Tarpeia as a lens through which Varro contends with the problem of what to do—culturally, linguistically, and topographically—with someone or something that does not play by the rules. The artist of the Basilica Aemilia frieze, Propertius, and Livy invite us to look at Tarpeia as an individual grappling with (and against) her position within the community, especially as a woman operative in a man's world. The tension between individual and state and Rome's quicksilver gender roles are operative in these sources. At the tail end of this part, Valerius Maximus examines the fixity of Tarpeia's story as "tradition" and the correspondence of this fixity to the settling norms of the new establishment.

Chapter 4 takes Varro as its focus, whose *de Lingua Latina* includes Tarpeia at a prominent place. I argue that his spare telling juxtaposes features in her story that amplify rather than resolve its inconsistencies, such as the problematic connection between the girl and the Capitol. These inconsistencies undermine the categories by which Tarpeia is often evaluated: woman, Vestal, traitor, Roman. I connect this disjunction to the collapse of the codes and norms of the Republic, particularly with the threat posed to that system by Caesar. Personally, politically, and socially, Caesar proved uncontainable within the limits that had shaped the Roman elite for centuries. His existence and success gave those categories the lie. Tarpeia's awkward narrative fits within the context of Varro's linguistic theory of analogy and anomaly, which contrasts the anomalous (invented, one-off) with the analogous (regular, patterned); Tarpeia is an anomaly regularized in the punishment of traitors at the Tarpeian rock. Varro's narrative movement from *Tarpeia* to *Tarpeius mons* to *Saxum Tarpeium / rupes Tarpeia* is therefore a function of both language and statecraft, as she was subsumed to the state's needs yet conspicuous in her name-identity. Tarpeia is a puzzle: a central outlier whose very presence illuminates and even vindicates other central outliers in Rome. Like Caesar, Tarpeia belongs to Rome but not in Rome. So too is Tarpeia a central outlier on the Basilica Aemilia reliefs, a monumental figural frieze depicting scenes from Rome's foundation. This frieze, restored during the period 55–34 BCE and again in 14 BCE, portrays the maiden like an Amazon, breast bared as she sinks under a heap of shields; her death scene is watched by two men whose dispassion contrasts her frenzy and movement. The contrast invites viewers to consider how much they are touched by this manly woman and this violent event in Rome's past—that is, the degree to which those who belong can objectify, and therefore render external, Tarpeia and her fate.

Chapter 5 similarly explores the relationship between perspective and belonging. Livy's Tarpeia is familiar and follows closely the account seen in Fabius Pictor, but the broader context of the first book, which places her alongside other foundational women whose actions are problematic but who help shape early Rome, invites scrutiny of her as an individual within the family and community. Livy's foundational women are both objects available for differing assessment from several perspectives within and outside the text, and subjects who must negotiate their own process of discernment. Though this double role is difficult, both for the women who inhabit it and the men who must negotiate it, it is crucial to the knitting together of communities that constitutes Roman society. Livy's presentation of variants for her tale (Pictor's and Piso's, with Varro's Vestality thrown in for good measure) illustrates the clash of perspectives that she—or any women at that juncture—invites. In confronting the repeated meeting, confusion, and resolution of various perspectives, Livy's reader is witnessing a process of assimilation—of coming to belong—as much as an outcome. And this is the conclusion one takes from Livy's narrative of the Roman traitoress: more than a character in Roman myth, she is a process personified.

Propertius's rendering of Tarpeia's story, the subject of chapter 6, seems designed to shock. In elegy 4.4 Rome's premier love poet of the twenties and teens combines the Vestality that Varro added to her tradition with a motivation of erotic love for her betrayal.[24] Propertius further departs from tradition in giving Tarpeia a long and central monologue. The combination of Vestality, erotic love, and subjectivity brings multiple perspectives, loyalties, and agendas into collision. Not only is Tarpeia's love at odds with her priesthood, it speaks to the pull of individual desires against the needs of the state. Augustus had sought, through various measures including the moral legislation of 19–18 BCE, to establish guidelines and hierarchies for individual behavior so as to minimize the fragmentation and strife that had resulted from the unchecked liberty of the Republic's final decades. Propertius's Tarpeia is the site of a conflict between one person's idea of belonging to Rome and the way the state understands that belonging. The form of the poem, in which Tarpeia's monologue is embedded within the poet's own frame narrative, further represents the tension between her personal voice and the public assessment of her that surrounds it as Tarpeia's words and viewpoint are enclosed by and subsumed within the more judgmental, state-oriented narrator. This chapter concludes with an analysis of the topographical and chronological elements in the poem, which forge a relationship between Tarpeia's past and the reader's present-day experience. Propertius mentions the Tarpeian grove (*nemus*), grave (*sepulcrum*), and hill (*mons*), all of which overlap somewhat and bleed into one another in a muddled cartography. Likewise, Rome's past, its present, and Tarpeia's imagined future all bleed into one another. The spatial and temporal *aporia* mimic the contradictions that inhere in Tarpeia's myth more broadly. Where, when, and how does she belong?

Chapter 7 takes on Valerius Maximus, who, writing in Latin some thirty years later under Tiberius, moves Tarpeia's story in a new direction that responds to the new reality of a durable principate. Valerius locates the moral of Tarpeia's story in perfidy—not in greed, as Fabius had done, or lust (love), as had Propertius. Hers is the first example of this moral vice in Valerius's collection of exemplary tales, but despite the fact that this example follows the abstract definition of *perfidia* (perfidy), Valerius fails to pinpoint precisely the perfidy in the story, finishing instead with a *bon mot* about *proditio* (treason). Valerius's Tiberian age audience had a famous *proditor* in their midst, one that Valerius himself treats at great length as a vice to cap all vices: the traitor Sejanus, whom Valerius condemns in such strong terms that the dispassion in the earlier stories becomes evident. Sejanus, I suggest, is the reason for the bait-and-switch. Violence against

---

24. This erotic element is prevalent in Greek traitoress stories (discussed below), but was nearly invisible in the Roman tradition thus far. Pictor speaks of her "desire for golden bracelets" (*FRH* Pictor F7).

the emperor trumps all other vices; belonging to Rome has a new, and narrower, shape that reprioritizes moral values. In his dense paragraph about Tarpeia, Valerius gives us hearty food for debate about that reprioritization. This debate is one attempt to recover an opportunity for dialogue about the past at a time when writing history was a dangerous affair.

Part Three

If we can characterize part 1 as trading on the theme of "inside-out" and part 2 as focused on "inside-in," part 3 is distinguished by its approach to Tarpeia from the "outside-in." This part of the book examines Tarpeia's appearance in the texts of Greek authors whose texts betray an attempt to understand the interrelationship of Greeks and Romans under the Roman empire. The first through third centuries CE are rich in texts, monuments, inscriptions, works of art, and coins that all speak to the theme of "being Greek under Rome." The converse is also readily apparent: "being Roman in a broadly Hellenized world." The scholarly literature on this period is exceptionally fecund, in part because of the interplay of various modes of communication and in part because of our modern desire to dissect cultural transfer and definition between conqueror and the conquered. It is not so much that the break between the Republic and Empire in Rome caused a sudden rise in Greek pride and Roman respect for Greek culture as that the growing stability of the *pax Romana* enabled and made visible a cultural resurgence among Greeks under Rome. Greek rhetoric and philosophy flourished once again in what the Greeks themselves eventually called a "Second Sophistic."[25] All Greek elites could partake of the pride in this resurgence and reclaim some cultural uniqueness. Romans too, particularly outside Italy, could demonstrate themselves to be cosmopolitan and learned by embracing some of the elements of high Greek culture. Simylus (an elegist of unknown date), Dionysius of Halicarnassus, and Plutarch all find ways to exploit Tarpeia's story as a tool for understanding and embracing Roman culture and, more importantly, for understanding Roman culture's imperial embrace of their own native Greek culture. We shall see that here the Greek authors feel free to list many variants and choose among them; the menu of choices and the way these authors engage and evaluate them reveals something of their understanding of Roman culture.

---

25. Philostratus *Lives of the Sophists* 481, 507.

The poet Simylus, of unknown date but almost certainly Hellenistic, wrote a poem of unknown length in elegiac couplets that includes Tarpeia's tale. His poem is the subject of chapter 8. In his version, the fragments of which are quoted by Plutarch at *Romulus* 17, Tarpeia betrayed Rome to Gauls during their invasion of 390 BCE, and out of love for their commander Brennus. Her explicit desire to marry Brennus is thwarted by a thousand tribes of Gauls. The combination of marriage and ethnicity speaks to uneasiness among Simylus's Hellenistic, presumably elite audience about belonging in their own communities. The opening up of the world to travel and migration and the shifting gender dynamic that attended the new dynastic society placed new pressures on kinship and descent. The linkage of Tarpeia's tale to the Gallic sack of Rome under Brennus, moreover, brings Rome and Greece together in a shared set of concerns; the Gallic Brennus had sacked Delphi in 280 BCE. Other Hellenistic poems, by Callimachus and Butas,[26] similarly sought to understand and come to grips with Rome through Rome's history and myth. By blending the treacherous-girl motif with the Gallic sack, Simylus renders Rome more familiar to a Hellenistic Greek audience.

Dionysius of Halicarnassus's *Roman Antiquities* presents Roman history from the beginning to the present in twenty books. In addition, Dionysius authored a large handful of rhetorical treatises both abstract (such as *The Art of Rhetoric* and *On the Arrangement of Words*) and specific (such as the commentaries on Attic orators and on Thucydides). In chapter 9, I explore how Dionysius combines his interest in Tarpeia and early Roman history with his interest in language. In Dionysius's hands Tarpeia's story is a laboratory for investigating common language—as a point of intersection that can generate shared identity, or as a knife-edge that holds the possibility of cultural rift. Foremost in this exploration is Dionysius's use of words that convey several possible meanings, and even words whose meaning is "commonness of meaning." He also uses a varied lexicon to label elements of his story, a phenomenon that also evokes, in a different way, "commonness of meaning." The murky meaning of Tarpeia's verbal compact with Tatius mimics the girl herself, whose meaning cannot be pinned down precisely and who stands at a common point between Roman and Sabine. And both the pact and Tarpeia mimic Dionysius's *Roman Antiquities*, which also seeks to blur difference between Greeks and Romans by focusing on what they share, thus generating a mutual

---

26. Callimachus on Horatius Cocles (fr. 106 Pf.) and Butas on the Lupercalia (Plutarch *Romulus* 21.6).

and reciprocal sense of belonging, but one that retains the possibility of distinction.

My final chapter explores how Plutarch makes Tarpeia's tale meaningful in the context of Romulus's biography. Plutarch mentions many variations on the tale that dwell less on her treason than on the shrewd and savvy leadership—both Romulus's and Tatius's—that takes advantage of it. Musing about the ethics of benefiting from a traitor, Plutarch brings in examples of other leaders (Antigonus, Augustus) whose words or deeds are relevant to the subject. This invites a broader consideration of Rome as *caput mundi*: to what extent can those belong who have only a tenuous connection to Rome? Tarpeia is one such figure, as are Tatius and his Sabines, and also Rome's client kings and other subjects. My focus then broadens to scrutinize evocations of Tarpeia's story later in the *Romulus* and in the paired life, *Theseus*. Within the *Romulus*, Tarpeia's story resurfaces in a digression about Philotis, a double-dealing female operative of Camillus. In the paired lives her story resurfaces in the tale of the Athenian Amazonomachy. As in his treatment of Tarpeia's story, in these two instances women who belong, but not fully, illuminate dimensions of male leadership and hegemony. The Amazonomachy in particular is a fruitful partner to Tarpeia's tale, particularly vis-à-vis the monuments it leaves behind: Tarpeia leaves a grave and rock, and the Amazons leave no fewer than five burial sites that are contested in the sources Plutarch names. This pair of anecdotes mimics and highlights the project of the *Lives* as a whole, in which Rome emerges as a single force while Greece is seen as a plurality unable to be contained. Rome is *caput mundi* because, like Romulus, it skillfully manages those at its margins.

A brief conclusion to the book brings us to Tarpeia today. Why and how do *we* tell her story? The continuing vitality of Tarpeia's story illustrates the strength of Rome's legacy in the West: we champion the idea of our openness to the other, but we remain somehow jealous for the integrity of the self.

ON READING THIS BOOK

The chapters of the book are written so as to be accessible to the reader who picks and chooses. For this reason, some repetition is to be expected. This takes two forms. First, my analyses frequently loop back to earlier chapters and look forward to future chapters. Second, some scholars' work is outlined in more than one chapter. I hope any repetition of the arguments of these scholars will ease the reader's task and will show my great debt to their work. All translations are my own. But the chapters have more meaning for one who reads the whole. Readers of individual chapters will learn much about the needs and strategies of those who told her tale, but little about Tarpeia. Only by reading the book as a whole will a picture of Tarpeia emerge—but this will be a hazy picture of a girl whose meaning flickers and evanesces, and is not by any means fixed in stone.

CHAPTER ONE

THE SHAPE OF VARIETY
GIRL, CITY, ROME

THE PART of Tarpeia's myth that never changes is that she opened Rome's fortress to a besieging enemy who subsequently occupied the Capitol and killed her. Her provenance, her motive, the besieging enemy, and that enemy's motive for killing her are unfixed in the tradition. She shares the core of her story with a group of infamous women of Greek and Roman myth, and the variety within that group reflects exactly those elements in which Tarpeia's own myth varies. Through these diverse treatments, the prevalence of the core story—a woman who, in some unsanctioned way, mediates between two enemy cultures—helps us realize the use and popularity of the myth in a period that witnessed the growth and fall of two of the world's greatest empires.

Ancient literature is rich in stories of women like Tarpeia who for varying reasons ally themselves with an enemy commander to the detriment of their own kin and countrymen. My current tally is twenty-one such characters, some as famous as Medea and others all but lost from memory; an outline of these plus the sources in which they appear forms an appendix to this book. The details of their situations differ from tale to tale: at times the woman is fully in control of her situation, while at others, she is not. Her motivation for the betrayal might be political, or erotic, or pecuniary, or unknown. She may be already married, or widowed, or maiden. But her core function in the story is the same: she betrays her own, is rejected by her new ally, and suffers. Indeed, the consistency of this core pattern explains in some ways the brevity with which many of these women are preserved in our memory: they constitute a type, and a type can prevail independent of the baggage of contingent details.

Taken as a group, these women and their stories reveal the same set of concerns that can be seen in Tarpeia's myth. These concerns include the role and power of women over the health of the state, and a corollary to this, the intersection of women and *ktisis,* or urban foundation; women's agency, or lack of agency, as an element that requires management lest it pose a threat to the state (or any of its normative elements); and women as facilitators or symbols of change, whether of political structure or social makeup or even narrative unity. As I argue in chapter 8, some of these concerns come to the fore in Hellenistic literature, but the catalogue of treasonous women begins in Greece's earliest literary record and lingers past pseudo-Plutarch.[1] Not only do the stories span the history of ancient literature, but their heroines are also set across a wide spread of time, from the earliest heroic generation of myth to the Gallic invasions into Italy and Greece in the fourth and third centuries BCE. The geographical range of the stories is likewise quite broad.[2] The motif stretches from mainland Greece to Asia Minor to Ethiopia to Colchis to Rome.

The popularity of the "treasonous girl story" across space and time gives rise to the question of the universality of these themes. As I discuss above, in no way do I believe this set of myths, or this story type, means any one thing to all audiences at all times. Investigators of Parthenius's *Erotika Pathemata,* Parthenius of Nicaea's collection of tales of romantic woe (some of which involve treasonous women), have grappled with the tension between universality and cultural contingency of a mixed thematic group. In her commentary on Parthenius's text, Lightfoot notes that the temporal range of Parthenius's collection—particularly of his stories of treasonous girls—bears witness to "the seamlessness with which the mythical and historical periods blend, and the indifference with which folkloric motifs attach to them" (1999: 230). Indeed, as she notes, authors at times rationalize some of the more fantastic elements in their stories by explaining origins, offering realistic psychological portraits, and avoid-

---

1. Early: Pedasa in Hesiod fr. 214 MW, from the scholiast on Homer *Il.* 6.35. Late: Nadira in al-Tabari 2:47–50 (see Zakeri 1998).

2. I am indebted to Lightfoot's discussion of "mythography" (1999: 225–40) for noting the temporal and geographical spread of Parthenius's stories, and see also Francese 2001: 161, who attributes it to the Hellenizing influence.

ing *adunata* such as metamorphosis.³ Francese, who studied Parthenius's collection as an influence on Latin poetry, notes that "the local, contingent factors may be just as important in its (sc. the story type's) popularity as was ancestral tradition."⁴ The combination of myth and history in these stories is akin to the combination of transcendence and contingency. There are underlying themes that apply in a variety of historical, social, and cultural circumstances, and these coexist with details and contexts rooted in the specific circumstance of the telling. The maidens who are analogous to Tarpeia vary from one to the next, and even within themselves, when their story is told by multiple sources. The remaining chapters in this book aim to untangle Tarpeia's details and contexts; the sections below sketch some of the broader themes that the group of treasonous girls puts on display: woman as weakness, as unpredictability, as transformation, and as city itself.

SHE EXPLOITS A WEAKNESS / SHE IS A WEAKNESS

In her every appearance in this story type, the traitor exploits a weakness in her own community or family. This is, indeed, a traitor's job description, but I believe we can go further than this and explore why the hapless turncoat is so often a woman. Simply put, these women perform an extreme version of a function that characterizes Roman women more broadly—they are the insider-outsider.

Two analyses will help in our exploration. In a panoptic article from 1989, Judith Hallett juxtaposed two sorts of representations of Roman elite women that, on the surface, are antagonistic: the conception of women as the "other" (different at best, more frequently worse, animalistic, inferior, weaker) and the conception of them as "same" (potentially sharing the ideals and values of men and acting in ways that perpetuate or improve men's status). Hallett styles this combination as the Romans' "bipartite concept of women."⁵ She spends much more time elucidating the sameness; the otherness is easy to find in Roman sources. Such "same" women, Hallett argues, appear most frequently within a man's family; sisters, daughters, wives, and mothers behaving honorably could

---

3. See also Francese 2001: 100 on Parthenius's rationalizing in historical accounts and linking origins to practice.
4. Francese 2001: 162. For the contingencies themselves, Lightfoot 1999 and Dué 2002 are especially rich.
5. Hallett 1989: 59–60 and 67.

do great service to the prestige of their brothers, fathers, husbands, and sons. Hallett's analysis offers two points to consider in the context of the treasonous woman. First, the sameness of the elite woman within the family context draws attention to the gravitational pull of the family; blood can trump, or at least mitigate, behavior. The likeness of women to men, rooted in their androcentric behavior, acts of course to the benefit of men and their values. Second, Hallett argues, based on a reading of Sulpicia, that elite women may have held the same bipartite view of themselves; we need not assume they viewed themselves as lost and irredeemable (p. 72). The corollary begs to be stated: we need not assume they saw themselves as fully consonant members of their families and societies.

The combination of women's similarity and access to the world of men, coupled with their moral and physical deficiencies, makes them extremely dangerous elements of society. Victoria Pagán has drawn attention to women as crucial parts of Roman conspiracy narratives, both as conspirators or whistleblowers. Women have access to the plans of men through pillow talk and can convey information through channels unavailable to men. However, they cannot be trusted to keep that information confined to the right sources, even if their intention is to do so.[6] They are tokens of instability, therefore, and stand as symbols for conspiracy in general. To Pagán, the danger posed by women is contained by rhetorical strategies in the conspiracy narratives (and throughout Latin literature) with exaggerated praise of the "good" women and a literary obsession with the sordid details of the "bad" ones.[7] The woman conspirator is heinous and unique—so unique that it seems it could never happen again, and fears are thus allayed. Of course it does happen again, every time there is a conspiracy; the strategy of containment works only as long as it needs to. The problem she poses is never solved; it is just deferred. As Pagán concludes, "The dual subjectivity of women and slaves, as beings who are not only necessary and beneficial to society but also unpredictable and dangerous, makes them ideal participants in the duplicitous act of conspiracy."[8] We may easily substitute "treason" for "conspiracy"; let us return to the traitoresses.

---

6. Pagán 2004: 46–49 and 126.

7. Likewise, there are appropriate channels through which women can contribute to men's decisions. When they violate those channels—by speaking in the Forum, for example—the breach must be contained by horror and censure. For succinct statements to this effect, see Pagán 2004: 6, 44, and 126.

8. Pagán 2004: 126, and see also Parker 2004: 591–92.

The variety of her insider knowledge reveals a number of fears about the dangers of keeping an outsider on the inside. In many of the tales the actual act of treason is unspecified,[9] but there are some maidens whose treason involves undermining individuals. In the familiar Samson-scenario, the maiden cuts the magical lock of hair that protects her father, and therefore her kingdom, from invaders.[10] The cutting of the magical lock is a fanciful symbol of emasculation at the hands of a woman but also symbolizes the emasculation of the state. Scylla's case is emblematic. Her father Nisus heard a prophecy that, were his magical lock severed, he would lose his life or his kingdom (Apollod. 3.15.8).[11] In some sources for the tale he does die; in all sources his kingdom is lost. Not only does Scylla violate her strongest familial bond; Francese emphasizes the rift within the family that Scylla's "barberism" betrays.[12] This father–daughter rift occupies a large part of my analysis of Livy's Tarpeia in chapter 5. I wish here to draw attention to the metonymy of state and male body. She who has access to the one has access to the other.[13]

Then there are traitoresses who have some knowledge of fortifications or military weakness. Tarpeia, in all sources in which her actual act of betrayal is made explicit, exposed the path up the citadel to Tatius; in some she goes so far as to kill the watchdog. Peisidice also explicitly undermined her city's fortifications. Walls form a physical and metaphorical boundary of a community. They are a symbol of its discreteness from that which surrounds it and are closeable when necessary. Their integrity must be protected. How would these maidens know the ins and outs of the city walls?

Like the women, the walls mark the juncture between "self" and "other."[14] In most cases the meeting between the woman and her enemy ally is unspecified, but where it is specified—Tharbis, Scylla, and some versions of Tarpeia's tale—it arises from her presence at or on the city's walls. Teichoskopeia is a narrative device in which someone standing on the walls views and sometimes describes the scene on the far side of the wall. It is an opportunity for flashback and, more importantly, for the suggestion, or even inclusion, of perspectives other than the narrator's own—what narratologists call focalization.

---

9. Leukophrye, Arne, Nanis, Antiope, Demonike, and Tharbis simply betrayed their cities.
10. Comaetho and Scylla follow this pattern.
11. See Hollis 1970 *ad Met.* 8.5.
12. Francese 2001: 162.
13. Eriphyle's case is similar. She was bribed by Polyneices to convince her husband (= insider access) Amphiaraus to join the seven against Thebes. Dorcia and Pedasa used their insider knowledge to give the enemy a psychological edge.
14. Parker 2004: 568 makes the case that the Vestal virgins are coterminous with the city walls.

Helen's famous teichoskopeia in *Iliad* 3 offers a rich example of the complexity of the teichoskopeia as a narrative device. As the single longest narrative by a mortal woman in the epic poem, Helen's wall-speech offers the reader the perspective of a participant in the war that differs from the perspective of the heroes on either side. This difference exists for two reasons: she is a woman, and she has belonged on both sides.[15] From atop the walls she sees more than the soldiers below, yet cannot control their fate nor her own. As Scioli phrases it in her study of "women's transgressive gaze" in epic poetry, Helen "hovers at the threshold between observation and experience without actually crossing over" (2010: 232). She can only observe, crystallizing women's experience of war: to surrender to whatever man controls her at the time.[16] Fuhrer has come to a similar conclusion about Helen and other women wall-watchers: their observation reveals the problems and costs of war and yet they can do nothing to change war's outcome or to alter their own subordination to it.[17] The teichoskopeia opens other perspectives on warfare than that of the warrior, perspectives that are subsumed into the warrior's viewpoint. War retains its primacy as a vehicle for male glory despite the cost to others. Helen's famous self-blame (*Il.* 6.344–48) reveals how much pressure the male's perspective exerts on the woman's; Helen accuses neither Paris nor Menelaus of causing the war, but rather she shoulders the guilt they have assigned to her.[18]

In one of Tarpeia's appearances, an elegy by the Augustan poet Propertius, she sees Tatius from the city walls and then, sitting right at that boundary, utters a plaintive soliloquy akin to Helen's teichoskopic narrative. As we shall see in chapter 6, which examines that poem, Tarpeia's soliloquy shows her perspective to be divided, looking both inward toward the Rome to which she is loyal and outward to the enemy beloved with whom she would live. Like Helen, she blames herself. She is sitting on the city walls when she does this; then she betrays them. The traitoress who knows the boundary and is not bound to protect it—even prefers to go

---

15. Her self-blame for her involvement in the war, followed by her return to Paris's bed, also makes dramatic her conflicted loyalties and sense of belonging.

16. See also Hetzner 1963 and Burkert 1979: 176n32, who says, "In the background is the fact that the victors used to take over the women of the defeated."

17. Fuhrer 2012. Fuhrer locates one moment of true choice and empowerment for Helen: when looking from the wall she sees Menelaus defeat Paris in their one-on-one duel for her hand. She had just expressed regret for her presence in Troy and renewed desire for her husband Menelaus. Yet when fugitive Paris returns, despite her hostile words of greeting, Helen nevertheless follows him to bed. Her choice is really no choice.

18. Helen's self-blame gives a sense of agency (Blondell 2010), but in the end that agency is fictive, since it serves the male cause.

elsewhere—offers a challenge to the conventional wisdom that all roads lead to Rome.

Just as the leader stands for the state, the female traitoress links and even equates women with public and private weakness.

SHE HAS HER REASONS / SHE IS UNPREDICTABILITY

One concern that is prominent in this story pattern and its exemplars is what motivates a woman to betray her own. Some women seem to have acted for political reasons. Polycrite of Naxos is one such woman. Her story presents a twist: the besieging enemy commander fell in love with her, and she used this relationship to the advantage of her own Naxians, who then prevailed in battle. Alas, when the Naxians showered her with gold and other ornaments as a reward, she was accidentally crushed by the cumulative weight of them and died; the Naxians honored her by preserving her tomb as a monument. The Trojan priestess Theano, the Athenian Aglauros, and even the biblical Rahab of Jericho may be considered members of this category of women motivated by goals larger than or at least external to their personal rewards. In one version of her myth, Tarpeia's action was not intended as treason; it was intended to give the Romans a strategic edge in the war against the Sabines. In another version in which she is a Sabine girl, her action shows no disloyalty to her own.

Other women from the list took bribes to betray their countrymen. In most sources, Tarpeia is motivated by greed. The greed motif can be illuminated by an extreme example: Eriphyle of Argos, whom Polyneices bribed with Harmonia's magic necklace to convince her husband Amphiaraus to join Polyneices's cause, despite his foreknowledge of his death in that struggle. Her sons killed her to avenge their father. Eriphyle became thereafter a signpost for the greedy woman in both philosophical and literary discourse;[19] Cicero even uses her to demonstrate the universal greed of women, for "women are a greedy race, for Eriphyle sold the life of her husband for gold" (*mulierum genus avarum est, nam Eriphyla auro viri vitam vendidit, de Inv.* 1.94). Eriphyle's greed brought down her husband and led to the failure of the seven against Thebes.

Whereas men's greed in Athenian discourse was denigrated because it violated the fairness so crucial to Athenian democracy,[20] Eriphyle's greed

---

19. Plato *Rep.* 590a; Propertius 2.16.29, 3.13.57–58; Ovid *Ars* 3.13–14; Horace *Carmina* 3.16.1.
20. Balot 2001.

raises a different spectre: the danger of female adornment. Harmonia's necklace not only was extraordinarily beautiful but was endowed with a magic that would grant perpetual youth and beauty. Nevertheless, it brought only doom to many wearers.[21] The necklace, and the adorned woman, constitute a *kalon kakon,* the "beautiful evil" idea that stretches back to Hesiod and the first mortal woman.[22] Tarpeia's bribe consists of "what the Sabines wore on their left arms," namely, fabulous bracelets.[23] Alas for her, they also wore the shields with which they crushed her. Her reward was, like her, a *kalon kakon.* Tarpeia's greed and the allure of ornamentation are the focus of my second chapter, on Fabius Pictor's version of her story. As we shall see, that telling of her myth participates in a powerful anti-luxury rhetoric as Romans in Pictor's day grappled with their moral and social similarity—or dissimilarity—to other states in Italy and abroad.

In two sources (Propertius and Simylus) Tarpeia is motivated by love for the enemy commander, and she shares this motivation with the vast majority of mythic traitoresses. Peisidice is a close parallel to Tarpeia. She became enamored of Achilles when he was besieging her town Methymna on Lesbos. She offered to undermine Methymna's fortifications; after she had done so and Achilles had captured her town, the great warrior scornfully ordered her stoned to death. There are vestiges of several such raids preceding the Trojan War,[24] each involving its own local woman. While most of the women in the lover category are known only from brief or fragmentary sources, here fall the most famous exemplars of the type, who have merited and elicited their own studies: Medea, Scylla, and Helen. The love motif and its elaboration were especially popular in Hellenistic literature; my eighth chapter examines a Hellenistic Tarpeia. The motif found its culmination in the neoteric literature of Rome. The hapless and disaffected *innamorata* appears in Catullus's Ariadne, Parthenius's suffering lovers of the *Erotika Pathemata,* Scylla in the *Ciris* and in Ovid's *Metamorphoses* and indeed many other maidens in the *Metamorphoses,* and in most of Ovid's *Heroides.* Love is itself by no means a simple motive. One example from a rich tradition suffices to demonstrate the complexity of this element of the story.

---

21. Statius 2.265–305 describes its woeful history.

22. Hesiod's adorned Pandora: *Theog.* 560–612; *WD* 60–105. Hesiod's greedy wife, to be feared: *WD* 702–5.

23. The description comes ultimately from Fabius Pictor *apud* Dionysius of Halicarnassus 2.38.2 (= *FRH* Pictor F7) and is picked up by those who follow him: the bracelets appear in Fabius Pictor, Cincius Alimentus, L. Calpurnius Piso Frugi, Livy, and Plutarch. See also Rumpf 1951 on *armillae.*

24. See Dué 2002: 61–63.

Medea's story shows the strain a maiden's love places on her and on her community. One difficulty of the love motive that Medea's core texts exploit is the origin, and therefore responsibility, for her love. Euripides's *Medea* famously shows Medea claiming full credit for her behavior at Colchis, whereas Jason attributes it to Aphrodite.[25] Apollonius's *Argonautika* includes a long episode (3.1–266, 275–79) in which Athena and Hera plan Medea's love and enlist Aphrodite's aid; she then turns to Eros, her petulant son, to do the trick. Where does the buck stop in that chain of command? Medea in Apollonius's text is not aware of this divine activity, but she feels its effects, which are not entirely gratifying: she experiences first speechlessness, then sweet pain at the touch of "baneful Love" (οὖλος Ἔρως, 3.297). Later episodes in the book show that Medea is not comfortable with helping Jason out of love; she invents a pretext for her behavior, for others and for herself.[26] Ovid's heroine perceives a force from without: "Some god stands in my way," says Medea (*nescio quis deus obstat*, Met. 7.12). She then goes on to meditate the ethics and pragmatics of helping Jason or ignoring her love (7.11–71). Though she senses an external force, she still feels a sense of responsibility.

One of Tarpeia's tellers, the elegiac poet Propertius, likewise explores her degree of responsibility by blending the love motive with divine cause and ethical self-consciousness on the part of the maiden. This cluster renders her more sympathetic to readers than the greed versions do. As Francese notes, the greed motive in general in this story type lends itself to moralizing interpretations; the love motive—especially externally caused love—evokes sentimentality and pity.[27] My analysis of Propertius's Tarpeia in chapter 6 links the question of unclear responsibility with the further complication of blurred perspective: where in the poem do we perceive her thoughts, and where do we see her objectively, and therefore ignorantly of the gods' intervention or of her moral struggle? Yet even Propertius's rather sentimental treatment of Tarpeia (and the treatments of love-struck Medea, or Helen, or Scylla) reveals that a woman's love is a dangerous thing. It must be excused, deferred, and resisted lest it expose and exploit a weakness at home.

At the core, whatever her motive, the girl-in-the-middle explains and exonerates, to a degree, the losing side; the loss wasn't their fault. The girl can be blamed for the victory, whether martial or symbolic, of the outsider. The myth is therefore best understood as a self-serving one, perpetuated by

---

25. Medea says, "I saved your life" (ἔσωσά σ', Eur. *Med.* 477), while Jason counters "Aphrodite saved me" (ἐγὼ δ'Κύπριν νομίζω, 527–28).

26. *Arg.* 3.681–92, and cf. her shame in 3.648–64.

27. Francese 2001: 106–7.

the loser. If we expand this thought, it is an androcentric myth in which the failings of men are reassigned to women.

One set of women offers a twist on the notion of love as a motive for betrayal: those who were abducted and then fell in love with the abductors, a mythical equivalent of today's Stockholm syndrome. Herippe of Miletus is one such girl; she was captured by the Gauls, but by the time her husband came to rescue her she had already fallen in love with her captor. Helen may also be considered an example of this group; though she was vilified for her adultery by many ancient authors, some representations suggest she left with Paris unwillingly or, like Medea, at Aphrodite's compulsion.[28]

Briseis's situation illuminates some tensions inherent in this phenomenon. Briseis has a complicated backstory in the *Iliad,* in part because the epic poem conflates many other parts (some of them local), of the epic cycle into a pan-Hellenic narrative.[29] In her three core chapters, Dué describes how in the poem Briseis is at times a prize, interchangeable with other benefits of war; this is certainly Agamemnon's view. At other times she is a local girl, more closely associated with Achilles' mastery of her native town (see, e.g., 2.688–93). At other times she is a war widow, captive and now (to be) remarried to Achilles. Briseis never expresses affection for Achilles, but she does offer a poignant lament over Patroklos's corpse in which she tenderly describes her affectionate response to the protective kindness he showed her (19.282–300). As we saw above when describing Helen's teichoskopeia, a woman may comment on war but is unable to alter or affect war's outcome or her own; in her powerlessness she aligns herself with the man who can protect her. Briseis is the rare maiden on the list who is not blamed for her new allegiance (except perhaps by Agamemnon). She merely develops affection for the man who can protect her.

Roman myth also engages in this pattern in the myth of the rape of the Sabine women. This story is as rich as that of any of the women in our list in its variety, its fullness of detail, and the frequency with which it appears in ancient sources.[30] In the war launched by the Sabines to retrieve or avenge the seizure of the women, the Sabine women—now Roman brides—sued for peace between the opposing sides on the basis of mutual ties of love and kinship. Often in the Roman tradition the Sabine women are paired with Tarpeia to illustrate a number of points; their presence in the tradition feature prominently in chapters 3 on Republican coinage and 5 on Livy's presentation of Tarpeia.

---

28. See, e.g., the skyphos by the Makron painter, Boston 13.186.
29. Dué 2002.
30. See Miles 1995.

The very fact that the Sabine women are paired with Tarpeia suggests that Tarpeia's behavior is to be seen as occupying one part of a range of possible behaviors for women caught up in struggles between men. The very variety of women's motivations to betray suggests a few conclusions. Greed, love, ideology, and necessity are interchangeable in the tradition, not only in the group as a whole but even in individual cases, Tarpeia's included. Bremmer asks a relevant question when studying a similar group of interchangeable, but diverse, victims (scapegoats, a discussion that will be relevant below):[31] "Do these different *signifiers* perhaps possess the same *signified*?" Regarding our motives, the answer is "yes": from Plato on we see a discourse that treats greed and desire both as forms of acquisitiveness.[32] What is more, and more important, the variety suggests the inscrutability of women as agents. Who knows what prompts them to do what they do? At worst they are morally reprehensible; greed is considered a moral failing in both Greece and Rome. At best they are victims of war whose very weakness necessitates their complicity with their conqueror. Most often, though, their agency and morality fall in the murky area between villain and victim, the area of their own erotic desire. This desire can be styled as a moral failing or a force too strong for the women to resist. Wherever a woman falls on this spectrum of blame and agency, she poses a threat to the integrity of society. Her motives do not matter; in every case she must be contained, managed, and incorporated rather than deciphered. As I maintain throughout this book, Tarpeia in the Roman imagination is similarly inscrutable, so she may be placed on the moral and social spectrum where she is needed; were the conceptual problems she poses ever solved for good, she would cease to be interesting or useful.

WAYS OF KILLING A TREASONOUS WOMAN / TRANSFORMATION

The title of this section comes from Nicole Loraux's (1987) 1991 study of female deaths in Greek tragedy, *Tragic Ways of Killing a Woman*. Loraux examines tragedy's dying women as a phenomenon similar to the group approach I have taken here, looking for variety and similarity across a type to see what societal concerns they reveal. Loraux examines, in a chapter each, what sort of woman dies; by what means (and at whose instigation)

---

31. Bremmer 1983: 303.
32. E.g., Plato *Rep.* 580e2–581a1. See also Val. Max. 9.1.*praef.* (sc. *luxuria*) *iungatur illi Libido, quoniam ex iisdem vitiorum principiis oritur.*

she dies; and how exactly her body is represented in her death. Her study blends the anthropologist's eye for broader cultural themes with the philologist's inclination toward textual specifics. Athenian tragedy, a ritual community event, is the context in which Loraux sees thematized female deaths operating and gaining nuance. "What do spectators in the theater gain from thinking, in the mode of fiction, things that in everyday life cannot and must not be thought?" (p. 64). We might ask the same question of the way treasonous women in myth die. Loraux's answer, that the tragic deaths "gave the Athenian spectator the controlled pleasure afforded by an enjoyment of the deviant when it is acted out, reflected upon, and tamed" (p. 65), pertains to the Tarpeia types.

Women in the "treasonous girl" story type meet unhappy ends. This is to be expected, if order is to be restored. Yet one fascinating aspect of the unhappy ends of traitoresses is the way they meet that end. In most cases the treasonous woman is killed by the man she helped enter her city, not by her own people whom she betrayed. What is more, she is not stabbed or poisoned, but is crushed to death. In this section I explore what death by crushing might mean when attached to the story of the traitoress. First, however, it will be helpful to note the cases where the outcome is different.

A very few women in the doomed group live beyond their betrayal, but those who do are troubled and out of place, wherever they end up. Medea and Ariadne are two famous women who leave with the man for whom they helped win a sort of victory over their homeland. Medea finds herself an outsider in her new life with Jason, and unable eventually to live anywhere terrestrial. Ariadne is abandoned by her beneficiary Theseus and winds up first deserted and alone on Naxos and then taken by Dionysus in a divine marriage, to be human no more. Helen, even when she is back with Menelaus after the Trojan War, is nevertheless not at home; her relationship is strained and she and Menelaus are still struggling with divergent understandings of their past.[33] The key feature these women share is that, once they decide to help the outsiders, they become outsiders as well—everywhere. They cannot transfer their belonging.

Scylla is unique in the group of traitoresses in the end she meets. After being keelhauled by her would-be lover Minos, she undergoes a metamorphosis into a seabird (the *ciris*) as does, in some cases, her father, whose magic lock of hair she had cut in order to render him vulnerable. Scylla has

---

33. See Gumpert's discussion of Helen (2001: 10–13). Helen suffers displacement both within her hometown and in her new home; this plus the inability to pinpoint Helen's agency and motivations, both before and after her transfer of allegiance, led Gumpert to call Helen a metaphor for metaphor—something whose meaning is displaced meaning (pp. 19–21).

a rich tradition in ancient literature, and her unique outcome points the way to some themes that we may see in the rest of the maidens, those who died. In ancient sources, there were divergent interpretations of Scylla's transformation: she was transformed as punishment or continuation of punishment; or her transformation was granted out of pity, to save her from the keelhauling; and/or it was granted as an honor. *Ciris,* an Augustan-age epyllion of uncertain authorship, blends these three interpretations.[34] Is Scylla to be honored, condemned, both, or neither? Lyne suggests that the *Ciris*'s equivocality in this point is the result of a conflation of several of the author's literary sources; Lyne assumes vagueness in the tradition.[35] If so, the Scylla tradition refuses to settle on one "take-away" message. Lyne's solution for the poem is to explain away one of the inconsistencies (transformation as honor),[36] but this is to flatten the myth. What if the author of *Ciris* included those three interpretations in full awareness of their seeming contradiction? The rich result is even more suggestive of the richness of the maiden's legacy. The interpretation of her metamorphosis differs from moment to moment in the poem (punishment, *hanc poenam,* 48; honor, *honores,* 205; pity, *tale decus vexarier . . . non tulit,* 481–83). It also varies across perspective; Amphitrite sees the transformation as an act of mercy, but hers is an internal perspective unmatched by the poet's, who views it as punishment or honor. Interpret Scylla's metamorphosis however you will; in every case it is conversion.

More common for the traitoress is death by crushing. In those cases where the maiden's death is specified, she is crushed to death (in several versions she is simply killed by her beneficiary). Peisidice was stoned to death at Achilles' order, after she had helped him take her native Methymna. Demonike of Ephesus was crushed under the weight of the golden ornaments she had requested as her price for betraying her city. Polycrite of Naxos used her alliance with the foreign commander to have him undermine the enemy's capabilities. When her native Naxos won the battle, they gave her so much gold as a reward that she died beneath the weight of it. Tarpeia was crushed under the shields of Tatius's men, at Tatius's instigation.

The crushing motif spreads responsibility for the woman's death throughout the community, since no one person cast the fatal blow. The community participation in her death works a shared, even public cathar-

---

34. Lyne 1978: 48–49, and see also Hollis's discussion in his 1970 commentary on Ovid *Metamorphoses* 8: 145–46.
35. Lyne 1978: 9.
36. Ibid. *ad* 514–15.

sis that alleviates the anxiety she either caused or resolved. Larson, in her study of Greek heroine cults, connects this phenomenon to the idea of the *pharmakos,* a ritual sacrifice or expulsion—hence the desire to appease the victim's spirit with tomb-offerings thereafter.[37] Girard's seminal study of the scapegoat emphasizes the simultaneous guilt and innocence of the victim; the victim is both disease and cure. Here we might note the paradox of the patriotic traitors in the long list of Tarpeia analogues, those girls whose intervention into war was motivated by love for the country and yet resulted in death. An innocent Tarpeia found a champion in L. Calpurnius Piso Frugi, whose treatment of her myth is discussed in chapter 3.[38] Indeed Burkert, in his assessment of the scapegoat in ancient religion, calls Tarpeia a "scapegoat reversed," because she does not bring destruction to the enemy but enables his success.

Death by crushing as a punishment for treason was also similar to the punishment for Rome's Vestal virgins accused of unchastity, and we may usefully apply our understanding of shamed Vestals to our list of traitoresses. Guilty Vestal virgins were entombed alive with too little food or water to sustain them. Unlike crushing, which leaves bruises, this manner of death preserved the bodily integrity of the victim, even though the unchaste Vestal had presumably already compromised both her physical and the city's metaphorical integrity. Like a crushed maiden, no individual need claim responsibility for the punished Vestal's death. Plutarch (*Quaest. Rom.* 86.) wonders about the indirect manner of this death: it might be designed to keep the sacred fires of cremation free from her taint, or to keep her sacred body free from the taint of violence. The ambiguous taint and purity of the punished Vestal is similar to the ambiguous guilt and innocence of the crushed women and, like Greek worshippers at the cult of a crushed maiden, Roman priests, as Plutarch says, made death-offerings to the punished Vestal to expiate any residual guilt.

Following these threads, Holt Parker has labeled the punished Vestal as *prodigium, pharmakos,* and *devotio.*[39] As *prodigium,* or unholy anomaly, all traces of the shamed Vestal must be removed yet in such a way as to avoid incurring the pollution she presents; hence her burial alive, a death that gives secure responsibility to no individual. As *pharmakos,* or scapegoat, the guilty Vestal is ritually cast out or sacrificed to secure the common good.[40]

---

37. Larson 1995: 136. She mentions Tarpeia in passing, in part to draw attention to the fact that the crushed girl may be guilty like Tarpeia or not, like Polycrite.

38. See Burkert 1979: 76, with the fuller discussion of the virgin-scapegoat type at 72–77.

39. Parker 2004: 586–88.

40. Ibid. 585, and note the discussion on pp. 578–80 in which he argues, against Girard, that women can be the scapegoat. This relates to my discussion, in the main text above, of woman as

Parker notes how Vestal punishment sometimes preceded Vestal crime: in difficult times Vestals were accused and punished without full investigation or proof.[41] There was need to sacrifice a guilty party, so a guilty party was found. Parker's third category is the *devotio*, or self-sacrifice to secure a victory. Parker's range of ritualistic labels fits well the range we see within the punished traitoress type: *prodigium* (polluted), *pharmakos* (polluted and pure in one), *devotio* (pure).

From Varro on, Tarpeia was considered to be a Vestal virgin. Varro's assignment of Tarpeia to the Vestal priesthood was likely his attempt to rationalize the myth; she must have been a Vestal since she died like one. Nevertheless, as I explore in chapter 4, with this association Varro raises as many questions about her as the rationalization answers. For the purpose of my survey of crushed traitoresses, it is important to recall that "death by crushing" predates Varro and indeed predates Latin literature on Tarpeia, and that it is attributed to maidens far from the cult of Vesta, indeed far from Rome. Varro's rationalization fails, and the death and burial pattern has meaning external to any one maiden, or even one Roman maiden, or even one Vestal.

It also fits the range we see within the Tarpeia tradition, in which she is blamed securely in Livy's and Valerius Maximus's rather moralistic texts (chapters 5 and 7), exonerated as a self-sacrificing patriot (Piso Frugi, chapter 3), or left in between as both culpable and vulnerable (Propertius, for example, chapter 6). The manner of her death emphasizes her identification with the city. Like the unchaste Vestal who was buried within city walls, Tarpeia (and the other maidens) are pressed into the earth, thereby becoming part of it. The un-penetration of her death restores the un-penetration of the city she endangered. She enables the breach, she is the breach, she is what is breached, and she heals what is breached.

WOMAN AS CITY

We come to the final dimension I would like to probe within this group of traitoresses. Women in this story type are closely identified with places within the city or with the city itself. We have already seen how they often

---

insider-outsider. Bremmer's discussion of scapegoat rituals in ancient Greece (1983, see esp. pp. 303–7) emphasizes that usually, in the historical record, the scapegoat chosen is someone of little value to the community: slaves, animals, the deformed) who are considered, for the purpose of the ritual, to be valuable. In the mythic tradition, in which no concrete loss will be felt, the scapegoat can be someone of great value, such as a king or virgin.

41. Parker 2004: 587.

enter the story pattern from the city walls, where they are free to voice a perspective alternative to the norm. Like the walls that enable their perspective and their betrayal, they mark the meeting place of self and other. Their very position on and as "walls" allows them access to and a measure of control over the integrity of the city. In some cases our women even share their name with their city. Pedasa is the name of the woman and Pedasus is the town she betrays. Briseis, Nanis, and Arne are also toponyms.[42] In ancient Rome the debate raged whether traitor Tarpeia came first and gave her name to the Tarpeian rock and the *mons Tarpeius* (another name for the Capitol), or vice versa.[43] Varro, for example, says the hill and rock both derived their names from the girl (*DLL* 5.41, and see chapter 4). Whether the traitoress drew her name from the town or vice versa is immaterial for my purpose here; the one becomes the other in a discomfiting metonymy that ties treason into close association with a town's identity.

The story of a treasonous girl undermining a state's integrity all but erases the possibility of blaming men for a military defeat; the defeat was her fault. Yet, the story admits that the state was not in full control of its integrity. Not only was there someone for whom the state's safety was not a priority, but the state did nothing to suppress that perspective or to protect against it. Similarly, from the point of view of the enemy invader, the traitoress does not lend praise and glory to their victory; the enemy had unfair advantage. On either side—the state and the enemy—she is needed but not wanted.

The traitoress's ambiguity as a token for the city is matched by her presence in individual places and monuments, some of which are condemnatory and some of which are laudatory. Polycrite of Naxos, for example, was celebrated at a tomb in her hometown.[44] Helen was worshipped at tombs throughout Greece.[45] Antiope, says Pausanias 1.2.1, was depicted in a statue just inside the walls of the Athenian Piraeus; she had betrayed her kindred Amazons to go with Theseus and later died fighting either for or against

---

42. For Pedasa and Briseis, see Dué 2002: 3n10 and 59–62. See Huxley 1962: 160 for Arne, and Bremmer 2008: 269 for Nanis.

43. A similar question involves her father. She is sometimes said to be the daughter of a Spurius Tarpeius (e.g., Livy 1.11). We know nothing else about this man, but the Capitoline Fasti (Degrassi 1954: 30) cite someone of the same name as consul in the mid-fifth century BCE.

44. See Francese 2001: 84–88 for a cogent discussion. Her tomb was called, ambiguously, the "tomb of envy" (attested in Plutarch *de Mul. Virt.* 17 = *Mor.* 254, following Naxian chronographers). On p. 100 Francese notes that such monuments and their rites are ways society deals with the traumas that arise from problematic erotic love.

45. In addition to several sites at Sparta, Helen was the focus of a cult at Therapne. See Zweig 1999: 162–63 for a summary of sources.

him. In chapter 10 I discuss this statue and the tombs of the Amazons in Athens. Aglauros provides an interesting parallel from the foundation of Athens: this girl had violated Athena's injunction not to open the box containing the baby Erichthonius. She was honored in a cave shrine on the east face of the Acropolis, where every year ephebes swore an oath to protect Athens to the death if need be.[46] As a curious aside, the Georgians (site of ancient Colchis) erected a statue of Medea in 2007. One wonders what heritage and identity this marker projects in modern Georgia. Censure and honor sit side by side.

TARPEIA IN/AS ROME

Tarpeia is evoked in many places in the Roman landscape. She is recalled in the name of the Tarpeian rock and hill (*rupes Tarpeia* and *mons Tarpeius*). Literary sources also mention a tomb, annual rites, and a statue. She is also associated with the Porta Pandana, a symbolic gateway to the Capitol. The interplay of these monuments acts in a way similar to the way the group "treasonous women" acts: just like our maidens, the monuments did not arise from a single imagination or even at the same time. Above I suggested that Tarpeia herself was a sort of monument, or symbol for the city. In this section I outline those monuments in Rome that commemorate Tarpeia. Such an outline will be helpful inasmuch as these places figure from time to time in the chapters that compose this book, since some of the sources for Tarpeia's myth rely on the presence or interpretation of the monuments. Here taken as a group, these monuments offer another way of representing the "women as transformation" motif I outlined above.

The Tarpeian rock, called the *saxum Tarpeium* or *arx* or *sedes* or *rupes Tarpeia*, is the most notorious remnant associated with the myth of Tarpeia. Its precise location is unknown. Modern tradition places it on the southwest side of the Capitol near the temple of Jupiter, but a very persuasive case based on technical and ideological grounds has been made for the northeast edge of the Capitol near the *carcer Tullianum* and the *scalae Gemoniae*, in a sort of "topography of punishment."[47] From the rock, traitors were thrown to their death, but not all traitors; only the most heinous cases were resolved in this way, with other, lesser traitors merely exiled.

---

46. See Herodotus 8.53.1.
47. Wiseman 1979. The zone thus provides for detention (in the cell of the *carcer*) and execution (by the Gemonian stair or the Tarpeian rock). Wiseman's argument revives and supplements that made by Pais 1905: 109–116.

This punishment is attested from as early as the Twelve Tables in the early Republic and as late as the early imperial period.[48] Scholars are likely to think the name of the place came before the myth, which then grew up to explain it, but the ancient sources are (all but) unanimous that it is the other way around: the girl gave her name to the rock.[49] The *rupes Tarpeia* is not to be confused with *mons Tarpeius* or *arx Tarpeia*; these latter two are simply durable monikers for the Capitol and need not evoke punishment or betrayal. Plutarch is mistaken when he says that "the name of the Tarpeian hill died out except for the fact that even now on the Capitol they call the place where they punish malfeasants the 'Tarpeian rock'" (*Romulus* 18.1).

One mystery about the Tarpeian rock is why it was the form of punishment for treason when the first traitor did not die by being cast over its edge. This discrepancy is surely linked to the chicken-and-egg naming conundrum, and can easily be resolved by assuming the name of the hill came first, then the rock, then the girl. Nevertheless, ancient sources don't put it in this order and never wonder why her punishment differed from that of others traitors.

So far as I know, every known recorded traitor thrown from the Tarpeian rock was male.[50] Conversely, the "treason for love" motif focuses on

---

48. XII tables *apud* Gellius 9.18.8; Tacitus *Ann.* 6.19 and Dio 55.22.2 mention a Sextus Marius, condemned by Tiberius of incest and sentenced to death from the rock; Dio 55.15.3 mentions other unnamed victims of this punishment. The testimony of Josephus (*BJ* 7.153–57), despite popular belief, does not support that Simon ben Giora was executed by ejection from the rock; rather, like other triumphal prisoners, he was likely killed in the *carcer Tullianum*. See Beard 2007: 128–32.

49. One variant appears in Festus 364L, 343M saying the rock got its name either from Tarpeia or from L. Tarpeius. Lindsey's text is left, Mueller's restoration at right:

. . . [Sa-]	
xum Tarpeium appel[. . .]	xum Tarpeium appel [latam aiunt partem mon-]
tis, qui ob sepultam Ta[. . .]	tis, qui ob sepultam Ta[rpeiam ibi virginem, quae]
eum montem Sabinis pr[. . .]	eum montem Sabinis pro[dere pacta erat, ita]
nominatus est. vel[. . .]	nominatus est. vel [ab eo, quod quidam nomine]
L. Tarpeius Romulo[. . .]	L. Tarpeius Romulo [regi cum propter rap-]
tas virgines adversa[. . .]	tas virgines adversa[retur, in ea parte, qua sa-]
xum est, de noxio poena[. . .]	xum est, de noxio poena [sumpta est. Quapropter]
nolueruut funestum locum[. . .]	nolueruut funestum locum [cum altera parte]
Capitoli coniungi.	Capitoli coniungi.

(transl. of the restored text: ". . . they say that part of the rock was named the Tarpeian rock, which is so named because the maiden Tarpeia is buried there. She had promised to hand over the hill to the Sabines. Or it is named from this event: when a certain Lucius Tarpeius was opposing king Romulus because of the kidnapped maidens, punishment for his crime was exacted on that part where the rock is. Whereupon they didn't want the burial location to be associated with the other part of the Capitol.")

50. See David 1984, particularly 136–37 and 168–69. There is a record of women punished on the *scalae gemoniae* in Suet. *Tib.* 61.4. Seneca the Elder *Contr.* 1.3 presents for discussion a case of

the female.⁵¹ The lingering identification of punished treason with Tarpeia achieves two effects. First, it feminizes the traitor. As mentioned above, the worst traitors got this punishment; elite Roman men were normally exiled from Rome. Death from the more extreme casting-down served to separate the criminal from the community, while commemorating that separation in the most central location.⁵² "Central outsiderness" is familiar from the discussion above. Second, punishment from the rock recalls Rome's very origins, every time it is done. This temporal loop might have the effect of reminding both the criminal and the observers that Rome has withstood such threats from its very beginning. With both effects, the rock signifies punishment.

A second monument confounds the first one. Tarpeia's tomb appears first in L. Calpurnius Piso Frugi's account of the mid-second century BCE, discussed in chapter 3 in this volume. Dionysius of Halicarnassus (see chapter 8) preserves the relevant fragment (*AR* 2.40.3), which mentions an honorific monument at the place where she was buried on the Capitol, at which there were annual rites. Dionysius takes this information as confirmation of Piso's presentation of Tarpeia as a double-dealing Roman patriot. Dionysius himself probably did not know of the tomb or the libations, for he ascribes knowledge of these to Piso. Plutarch also refers to a tomb that Tarquinius excavated when he built Jupiter's temple (*Romulus* 18.1). Varro (*Lingua* 5.41) says Tarpeia was buried on the Capitol but does not mention a tomb or rites.⁵³ Since the tomb was not known to Dionysius except through texts, and autopsy is important to him,⁵⁴ we can conclude it was no longer extant at his time. There is no knowing whether any tomb was visible to Varro or even to Piso.⁵⁵ Since Tarquin is said to have excavated and moved it during the building of the temple to Jupiter, one wonders to what monument Piso could be referring.

The annual rite is attested by Piso alone, in the same fragment at which he mentions her burial. Dionysius's rendering of Piso has him using the present tense to describe the rites, suggesting that they were operative in his own day (καὶ χοὰς αὐτῇ Ῥωμαῖοι καθ' ἕκαστον ἐνιαυτὸν ἐπιτελοῦσι,

---

an unchaste woman hurled from the rock who survived; the execution of women seems fictitious. Tacitus *Ann.* 6.19 and 6.41 (the Sejanus affair) show men punished at the rock, and their female accomplices exiled.

51. Even when it is not the girl who is in love, she is the one remembered. Demonike's suitor is unnamed.

52. Though none of them comment on the gendering of the traitor, scholars have seen in punishment from the rock a form of ritual casting out. See David 1984.

53. The *monumentum* to which Varro refers is a memorial of her name, not her tomb (*huius nominis monumentum*).

54. Andrén 1960; Schultze 2000: 19 and 24.

55. All Piso said, according to Dionysius 2.40.2 and assuming with Forsythe 1994 *ad* F11 that this is a direct quotation, is that she was deemed worthy of a tomb where she fell.

Dionysius 2.40.3, "and the Romans perform libations to her every year"). If this is true, Piso must have known the location, but this information cannot be recovered. Dionysius believes such rites and the tomb to indicate that she was held in high esteem; had she been a traitor, he says, her grave would have been cast out. Reinach understands her as the epichoric deity of the place where there was also, coincidentally, a heap of dedicated arms; the story arose that it was a burial, but a sense of the sacred remained.[56] Burkert, following Girard's theory of the scapegoat, suggests that worship at the tomb of a villain would be just the combination of honor and rejection that one would expect with a scapegoat.[57]

Epigraphical evidence for the rite is tantalizing. Mommsen assigns this rite to the Parentalia, the annual rites to dead parents enacted in February, based on an inscription from the fourth-century CE Fasti of Philocalus: *VIRGO VESTA PARENTAT SENAT LEGIT* (The Vestal Virgin makes an offering to the dead by law of the senate).[58] Mommsen's assessment is a conjecture; in his comment (p. 309) he says, "*Initium fecerunt parentationis virgines Vestales testibus fastis Philocalianis; videntur autem eo die inferiae publice factae esse Tarpeiae* (Dion. 2.40), *quas ei utpote et ipsi virgini Vestali consentaneum est obtulisse Vestales*" ("The Vestal virgins made the beginning of the Parentatio, as attested by the Fasti of Philocalus; on that day, rites to the spirit of Tarpeia were done publicly [Dion. 2.40], which it is agreed the Vestals offered to her inasmuch as she is a Vestal virgin herself"). Degrassi agrees with Mommsen, but Latte's objections raise serious problems: Piso mentions no Vestality for Tarpeia; there is no tomb on the Capitol; and Tarpeia, being no one's parent, is not an appropriate target for the Parentalia.[59]

If an honorific rite to a patriot Tarpeia existed in Piso's day, it is possible that Fabius Pictor, Tarpeia's first literary source, ignored it. There is no trace of it in his fragments or in the sources, such as Livy, who followed him, and Dionysius, so keen to use the rite to attach meaning to the story (see chapter 8), ascribes it to Piso in contrast to Pictor. Another complication arises in Propertius's text; he says her treasonous act took place on the Parilia (Propertius 4.4.73–78; see chapter 6). The Parilia was an agricultural festival eventually associated with Rome's birthday; the Parentalia honors the dead.

---

56. Reinach 1912: 73–79.
57. Burkert 1979: 77.
58. *CIL* 1(2) p. 258.
59. Degrassi 1963: 409; Latte (1960) 1967: 111 with note 2 for a discussion of this debate. To be sure, the Parentalia need not be performed to one's own ancestors, but Tarpeia's exclusion from this category is still warranted.

The difference between these two and the freedom to omit the rite from narrative contexts leads me to suspect that the rite was not a strong element to her story. Wherever her rite, and whenever it fell in the calendar, and however imaginary it was, its meaning is potentially manifold.

The second-century CE grammarian Festus gives information about Tarpeia in Rome that exists nowhere else in her tradition. Festus's work redacts the *de Verborum Significatu* of Verrius Flaccus, an antiquarian and grammarian of the late Augustan period whose work remains in fragments only. Festus's text thus bespeaks a double interest (his and Verrius's) in connecting the present to the distant past, and in doing so with words. His snippet on Tarpeia makes reference to the Porta Pandana:

> Tarpeiae esse effigiem ita appellari putant quidam in aede Jovis Metellina eius videlicet in memoriam virginis, quae pacta a Sabinis hostibus ea, quae in sinistris manibus haberent, ut sibi darent, intromiserit eos cum rege Tatio, qui postea in pace facienda caverit a Romulo, ut ea Sabinis semper pateret. (496L, 363M)

> Some think the image of Tarpeia in Metellus's temple of Jupiter is so named surely in memory of the virgin who, having exacted a promise from the Sabine enemy that they give her the things they wore on their left hands, allowed them to enter (Rome) with king Tatius, who later in making a peace treaty sought from Romulus the precaution that it (Rome) would always remain open to the Sabines.

According to Festus, the Porta Pandana would remain ever open to Sabines, now Rome's allies.[60] Varro tells us that this gate used to be called the Saturnian gate; this comes at *Lingua* 5.42, right after he talks about the Tarpeian names for places on the Capitol. In chapter 4 I discuss Varro's presentation of these Roman places.

The Porta Pandana was presumably an entryway to the fortified Capitol, though its precise location is unknown.[61] Dionysius of Halicarnassus *RA* 10.14.1–2, discussing the Sabine commander Appius Herdonius's attack in 460 BCE, calls it the Porta Carmentalis, which confuses matters. Polyaenus 8.25.1 says the same compact was made between the Romans and Gauls

---

60. For sources and discussion about the variations in name, date, and function, see Coarelli in *LTUR*; Platner and Ashby 1929; and Richardson 1992 all s.v. *Porta Pandana*. The location of the monument is disputed; see Thien 2002 for possibilities.

61. Sanders 1904: 34–39 discusses at length the connection between the gate and the girl, and despite his careful reasoning, he can conclude little about it.

after the Gallic sack; this is highly unlikely, but reflects the Tarpeia myth in another way: a lost elegy in Greek by a poet named Simylus posits that Tarpeia betrayed Rome to the Gauls (chapter 8).[62] Further confusion arises when we recall that Manlius Capitolinus, defender of the *arx* from the Gauls in 390 BCE, was later thrown from the Tarpeian rock when convicted of treason.[63] The confusion of Gauls and Sabines, and of the exact location of the Porta Pandana, does not obscure the emphasis this monument places on openness—the inclusion of foreigners and thereby the enrichment of Rome. Tarpeia's tomb rites could celebrate the same thing—inclusion as the happy outcome of her crime—but with our current sources we cannot know the force and meaning of those rites. It should be noted also that the Porta Pandana was symbolic rather than functional; Tatius was already inside and joint ruler when it was so christened. What is more, the name means "open gate," which is exactly what Tarpeia was.

The interplay of these monuments—rock, tomb, and gate—suggests the extent to which Tarpeia in Rome encompasses seemingly irreconcilable ideas: the state's vigorous self-protection of its integrity *and* its openness to outsiders; its utilitarian ability to laud the end (assimilation of the Sabines) *and* its ideological intolerance for the means (treason); and its desire to commemorate the past without *really* pinning down what that past was or meant. Given this nexus of places, what were Romans to make of the grand relief sculpture of Tarpeia's death that adorned the frieze of the Basilica Aemilia, in the heart of the Roman Forum? Since the creation of this monument can be pinpointed fairly closely, I consider it as a telling of Tarpeia's myth situated in a historic context; my analysis of it can be found in chapter 4. Here it suffices to point out that the Basilica Aemilia places punished Tarpeia not on the ancient Capitol, but in the Forum—which was not yet part of Rome when Tatius and Romulus met in arms. In fact, it is where they fought it out.[64]

A final monument must be included. Festus's snippet quoted above also mentions an *effigiem,* presumably a statue, of Tarpeia in the temple of Jupiter Stator. This refers to the temple dedicated by Q. Caecilius Metellus Macedonicus after his triumph in 146 BCE, which stood inside the Porticus Metelli near the Circus Flaminius. Augustus would eventually convert this to the Porticus Octaviae. The site was a gold mine for famous art (Pliny *HN* 34.31, 36.40). Nothing else is known of this work of art, but if Festus's information comes here from Verrius, we can posit that Verrius drew

---

62. Fragments *apud* Plutarch *Romulus* 17.5.
63. Livy 6.20.1–12.
64. Livy 1.12; and see Jaeger 1997: 20–57.

attention to her origins and names. Verrius might in turn have gotten the information from one of his sources—likely Varro's *Antiquitates* (the extant *de Ling.* mentions no statue).

The text of the first phrase is awkward: *Tarpeiae esse effigiem ita appellari putant quidam in aede Jovis Metellina eius videlicet in memoriam virginis.* It is difficult to fit the two infinitives *esse* and *appellari* into a cogent Latin sentence. As Sanders says, though, "the sense is clear": there was a statue.[65] The phrase *quidam putant ita appellari,* however, and the nature of Festus's project and his sources, draws attention to the name of the statue. Festus says specifically that people attributed the name to the traitoress. He sometimes uses *quidam* in cases in which the word's attribution is disputed;[66] otherwise we see some formulation like *dicitur* in his text. This, coupled with the verb *putant,* implies that there might have been another attribution in circulation for the "Tarpeia statue." The name Tarpeia does appear elsewhere in the Roman record in instances not having to do with the traitoress.[67] Since "Tarpeia" is likely a local, Sabine spelling of "Tarqueia" (= Tarquinia),[68] it is not surprising that it is not unique to our traitoress. One must imagine that the name had become so associated with the traitoress that any others bearing that name were subsumed into her strong presence; a Spurius Tarpeius *must* have been her father, any Tarpeias *must* be the girl herself. So too, thought some folks (*quidam*), this statue *must* be of her.

One wonders what exactly the *effigiem* might have looked like. All remaining visual depictions of Tarpeia, all of which had appeared before Verrius, Festus's presumed source, wrote, show the moment of her punishment: the girl being crushed by shields.[69] If the statue showed the punishment, there would certainly be no lack of clarity about who its subject

---

65. Sanders 1904: 14–15.
66. E.g., *Tuscos: quidam dicunt . . . alii; tam: ut quidam perhibunt.* But cf. *trabs: proprie dicitur duo ligna compacta.*
67. One of Camilla's companions is a Tarpeia, for example at Vergil *Aen.* 11.656, as is, in Plutarch *Numa* 10.1, one of the first Vestal virgins; Plutarch does not connect this Tarpeia with the traitoress at *Rom.* 17, though our traitoress becomes a Vestal in parts of her tradition.
68. Modern analysts have seen in her name Etruscan roots (= Tarquinia), transformed into our familiar form "Tarpeia" by the common switch of *–qu* to *–p* when Etruscan language meets Oscan verbal habits. This theory is widely held. See most recently Negri 1992: 236; with Devoto 1940: 75; Poucet 1967: 91–93; Dumézil 1947: 281; and Pais 1905: 105. This derivation would bespeak a meeting of Sabine and Etruscan in Rome. Poucet suggests the fifth century BCE, with its influx of Osco-Umbran forms and its apogee in anti-Etruscan sentiment; this combination would provide the best context for such a change.
69. These include two coins (*RRC* 244.2a–c and *BMCRE* 1.29–31) and a sculptural relief in the Basilica Aemilia, discussed in chapters 3, 4, and 5.

was. Perhaps, then, it depicted some other moment or facet of the myth and required explanation. The image's presence in a place of leisure—the museum-like portico, a place with no particular civic or religious function[70]—coupled with the need to clarify the name of the portrait's subject, suggest that it was largely aesthetic rather than politically or ethically forceful. I imagine, fancifully, a spectator leaning closer to scrutinize details, or discussing the image with a friend. I am not inclined to read this *effigiem* as indication that Tarpeia's moral message is everywhere, at work and at play. Rather, I see it as an indication of the fundamental openness of her story and of the opportunity she offered Romans for conversation.

---

70. See the discussion of porticoes in Jenkyns 2015.

PART ONE

TARPEIA, ETHNICITY, AND BEING ROMAN IN THE REPUBLIC

CHAPTER TWO

FABIUS PICTOR'S GREEDY GIRL
NOT YET *TOTA ITALIA*

WAS IT FOR love or money? Was she a traitor or patriot? Regal or Republican? Priestess or layperson? Did she admit Sabines or Gauls? If these questions do not immediately evoke Tarpeia in our minds, it is because of Q. Fabius Pictor, the Roman senator during the Second Punic War whose annalistic history, written in Greek, chronicles Rome's progression from Monarchy to Republic to a power that could defeat Hannibal, Carthage's formidable army commander. Pictor's *Annales* marks the crucial moment in the history of the myth of Tarpeia when the tale enters Rome's literary imagination. Pictor's account of the legendary maiden's treason when she opened Rome's gates to enemy forces is the first in extant Roman literature, and it would become the core version adopted by Cincius Alimentus, Livy, and Plutarch, among others. Though Pictor no doubt inherited a flexible and rich tradition about the girl whose action left the Capitol vulnerable, his choice of details was the one that would eventually stick. Pictor's Tarpeia was motivated by greed, not love. She was not a priestess but rather a maiden with no official role in the state. She, a Roman, opened Rome up to invasion by the Sabines, not the Gauls, and her action was not at all patriotic but rather treasonous, even apolitical, in its very disregard for the state.

This chapter explores the cultural and political factors that give meaning to the details of Pictor's version. Broadly speaking, Pictor's version of Tarpeia—like his history in general—participates in the dynamics of Roman self-positioning in a diverse and changing milieu. This milieu includes Rome itself, the center of decision making for the growing power; it includes Italy, a conglomeration of different peoples brought under Roman rule and providing the base of Rome's military manpower; and it includes a broader international community, particularly the Greek and Carthaginian powers that were Rome's rivals in power and scope of empire.[1] This approach to Pictor aligns with a growing consensus that his work was aimed both at his senatorial peers in the Curia and at an audience, Greek speaking and not, far away from the seven hills.[2] Tarpeia's story is responsive to local Roman elite politics. Her greed, one of the clearest features of Pictor's Tarpeia and the legacy his narrative left to tradition, speaks directly against elite rapaciousness and competition at a time when Rome was adjusting to its new role as an international power. Faced with the threat of Hannibal, with eroding alliances in Italy, and with growing antipathy abroad, Romans struggled to preserve unity both within its citizen population and among its allies in Italy. Tarpeia's greed functions as a way to explore elite self-control and the inherent dangers of excessive desire for gold. As we shall see, laws passed in Rome during the Second Punic War indicate that the financial burden of resisting Carthage placed additional pressure on the already-strained social tensions caused by uneven access to opportunities for income. The *lex Oppia* in particular, a sumptuary measure passed in 215 BCE, restricted displays of wealth by elite women and thereby standardized behavior and reduced competitiveness. In this context, Tarpeia's greed is a powerful cautionary tale, and fits part and parcel within the strongly moralizing tendency we can see in Pictor and in other early Roman histories. In *The Politics of Latin Literature,* Habinek links early Roman historiography's moralizing tendency with the socially charged ritual practices that gave rise to Latin literature: "Roman historiography . . . starts out and remains moralizing and hortatory because the conditions on which it draws are created and recreated as a means of assuring group identity and enforcing the authority of one sector of society over another."[3] This chapter explores a snapshot of this tendency in action.

Tarpeia's story is responsive to the needs of Rome as head of Italy at

---

1. The last fifteen years have seen three excellent and influential books on cultural politics of the emergence of Latin literature: Habinek 1998; Goldberg 2005; and Sciarrino 2011. Though none treats Pictor, and Sciarrino's study focuses on the novelty of Cato's *Latin* prose (my emphasis), each book is acutely valuable for assessing Pictor's contribution to Rome's literary tradition.

2. Dillery 2009 offers a summary of the consensus and proofs of Pictor's self-positioning among Roman elite and his outreach to Greek readers.

3. Habinek 1998, quotation from p. 54.

a troubled time. Her avarice in Pictor's account is complicated by the emphasis Pictor gives to the Sabine presence in the story. It is their gold that inspires her misdeed. The detail of Sabine opulence sits uncomfortably against the later characterization of the Sabines as an austere people. Indeed, the Gauls or Etruscans would better lend themselves to the accusation of luxury that Pictor levels against the Sabines—and both Gauls and Etruscans lurk in the background of Tarpeia's tradition as possible alternatives to the Sabines.[4] Pictor, in contrast to later tradition, does not valorize Sabine austerity. On the contrary: he censures them not only for their own duplicity in accepting Tarpeia's help and then killing her, but also for displaying luxuries to tempt the Roman girl—a fault corroborated elsewhere in Pictor's history, in which the historian says the Romans learned about riches from this people. The contagion of Sabine opulence and the blame game Pictor plays in this story meditate on deeper questions of Roman identity in Italy, such as how alike are those peoples in Italy who are knit together under Rome's power?[5] What does it take to belong to Rome, and to what extent must new members of the Roman state adopt Roman *mores*? What is the moral and practical cost of expansion?

Tarpeia's story is responsive to the dynamics of Rome's emergence as a power on the international stage. Here Pictor's Greek comes strongly into play. Pictor's text served to acquaint the Greek-speaking world with the distant and recent history of Rome, a relative newcomer on the international and literary stage. The historian's use of Olympiad dating, of Greek measures and coinage, and even of some Greek etymologies for Roman names suggests a work designed in part to market Rome around the Mediterranean world.[6] Such Hellenic touches would render Rome more familiar to Greek and Greek-acculturated audiences.[7] Pictor's Greek language history may be read as a response to, or at least in dialogue with, existing pro-Carthaginian and anti-Roman histories circulating at the time.[8] The

---

4. One version of the myth positions Tarpeia's treason at the time of the Gallic sack of Rome (Simylus *apud* Plutarch *Romulus* 17; see chapters 9 and 10); Devoto (1940: 75 and 1958) suggests an Etruscan derivation of Tarpeia's name, and Fabius Pictor's own account mentions the Sabines as Etruscan-like in their tempting opulence.

5. See Curti 2001: 21–2, who argues that Pictor puts Rome at the center of Italian history such that other peoples appear not as equals in the peninsula, but as eventual Romans.

6. Olympiads: Dionysius of Halicarnassus 1.74 = *FRH* Pictor F8. For coins, measures, and names, see Frier (1979) 1999: 281 with note 70. See Dillery 2005 and Goldberg 2005: 81–83 for recent statements of Fabius's Greek aims.

7. We know from the Taormina inscription (*SEG* 26.1123), which mentions Pictor, that he was read in Greek-speaking territories.

8. For Fabius's apologist stance, see Polybius 1.14 with Walbank's 1957 commentary *ad loc*. See also Gelzer (1933) 1964.

history was thus "an extension of diplomacy,"⁹ and should be read with an eye to the ways it positions Rome within its widening world.¹⁰ The rhetoric of modest homelanders tempted and corrupted by the opulence of a foreign people was a staple of classical Greek historiography. Readers of Herodotus and Thucydides could understand military conflict in just such moral terms. Pictor's history brings that understanding into play and presents Roman dominion to a Greek audience in ways designed to resonate with that audience. Greek sympathy at the time of Pictor's writing was crucial, as Greek communities in southern Italy were faced with Hannibal at their gates and were presented the opportunity to defect, and as Carthage was seeking to draw Philip V into the Punic wars as a way to distract Rome. Tarpeia's greed for Sabine luxuries thus trades not only in the internal dynamics of social class at Rome, but on the dynamics of Rome's fragile coalition against Hannibal.

Set during a tense moment of Roman expansionism and war, and involving political and moral conflict at its core, Tarpeia's myth became in Pictor's hands a vehicle Romans used to explore their own identity, to consider tensions in their social and political ideology, and to scrutinize their relationships with each other and with other communities. She thus speaks to the very heart of the construction of Roman identity, and how the Romans promoted this identity to themselves and to others.

PRELIMINARIES: ON USING FABIUS PICTOR

Fabius Pictor's Tarpeia is preserved for modern readers by Dionysius of Halicarnassus as part of the Romulus cycle in the second book of his *Roman Antiquities*. Brunt has rightly cautioned against trusting overmuch fragments quoted by later authors, whose own style and purpose in quoting might distort the source text.¹¹ Brunt is especially wary of using fragments to assess the style of the source text, since paraphrase so easily conforms to the style of the paraphraser. Even where content is concerned,

---

9. Rawson 1985: 218 and cf. Curti 2001: 20–21.
10. Pictor's participation in the embassy sent to Delphi after the defeat at Cannae is a similar instance of Rome's "self-positioning"; while the mission surely had diplomatic and intelligence motives (such as to gauge Philip's response to Hannibal's presence in Rome), it is important to note that Rome sought out and followed Apollo's advice, thus emphasizing Roman affinity with the Greeks. Details of the embassy and Pictor's participation can be found in Livy 23.11; Plutarch *Fabius* 18.3; and Appian *Hannibal* 27. For motives and results of the mission, see Gruen (1990) 1996: 10, 30–31 and 1992: 231, 242; and Frier (1979) 1999: 235–36 and 265.
11. Brunt 1980.

distortion might be mitigated or exacerbated by the purpose of quoting. Schepens uses the phrase "cover text" to capture the way the quoting text (the cover text) protects the quoted text from the loss of time, obscures its meaning by severing it from its original context, and envelops it with a new context.[12] Walbank notes, for example, that Polybius most often names and quotes prior authors in order to disagree with them (2005: 1–3); this antagonistic stance at the very least puts the source text in an unintended dialogue with Polybius's text—and in a position of inferiority in that dialogue. Or the cover text might put two or more source texts in dialogue with each other. Comparison presents its own set of challenges and opportunities for the critic. Cover texts that excerpt a source for the purpose of comparison might be trustworthy in terms of the bare content of the comparison, but the act of comparing overemphasizes the detail of the comparison over its context or importance in the source texts. Let us consider a case such as "X said this, whereas Y said that." We might trust that X and Y did disagree in such a way, but the details might have been a large part of X's original text and only a small note in Y's; or X might have been written to buttress one audience's clout and Y another's; or X and Y themselves used different sources; or even, though it might be unlikely, the larger unquoted text of Y could have contradicted Y's detail, thus: "We certainly shouldn't believe *that*." As a final nuance, where independent authors quote the same source similarly, there is more cause for trust.

For the Tarpeia story, Dionysius quotes Fabius Pictor in comparison to the version of Lucius Calpurnius Piso Frugi. This is in an overall exegesis of her tale which moves back and forth between citing the differences between the two historians' accounts and narrating the common parts, for which Dionysius says such things as "Thus far everyone is in agreement."[13] For this reason I think it is possible to separate the Fabian content from the Dionysian content.[14] In other words, Dionysius seems to take pains to distinguish between Pictor's voice, the Fabian tradition, another historian (Piso), and his own views. This gives some comfort in interpreting this set

---

12. Schepens 1997; the idea is further nuanced in Walbank's introduction to Schepens and Bollansée's 2005 volume, *The Shadow of Polybius* (and probed in the essays therein). More recently Berti has presented a typology of fragmentary reuse (2013) to describe the various relationships the cover text might establish with the source text. Indeed, the scholarly dialogue about quotation (or paraphrase) in historiography (e.g., Marincola 2010 and 2011) has demonstrated that textual co-presence in this broad genre is no less nuanced or problematic than in poetry.

13. E.g., 2.39.1, μέχρι μὲν δὴ τούτων συμφέρονται πάντες οἱ Ῥωμαίων συγγραφεῖς.

14. Jacoby does as much in his foundational *Fragmente der griechische Historiker* (*FGrH*) by printing all of Dionysius's text, but using larger type to indicate quotation of Pictor, tiny type for what he understands as purely Dionysian, and intermediate-size type for paraphrase. Cornell at *FRH* Pictor F7 does the same with boldface type.

of fragments as fairly true to Pictor's text. The shape of Pictor's account as preserved by Dionysus is also corroborated by Livy, Dionysus's contemporary.[15] Independent corroboration further strengthens the case for reading through Dionysius's presentation to recover Tarpeia's story as Pictor told it.

It is a core purpose of this book to read the myth of Tarpeia in the context of its telling. One such context is historiography; it would thus be possible to assess Tarpeia in historiography and consider Pictor together with Dionysius and Livy. To do this, however, is to prioritize literary genre over sociopolitical and cultural context, and to seek likenesses in the texts rather than differences. This would be a valid approach in some cases, but I am interested in separating Pictor out of Dionysius's account precisely because Dionysius explicitly disagrees with Pictor in key respects. Given my understanding/position that myth has meaning in the telling, that it is alive at those moments when it is instantiated, the contextual priority is reversed, and sociopolitical and cultural context—the "horizontal" context, if you will—rises to the fore over the ("vertical") literary context of genre. This is not to say that genre does not matter; the historians were certainly more constrained to follow their sources than the poets. Yet I find in this book that Pictor, Livy, and Dionysius—despite them all writing histories, and even citing each other from time to time—all do very different things with Tarpeia that have to do with how they write, and when and to whom. Chapters 5 and 9 scrutinize, in part, what Livy and Dionysius do with the material from Pictor, but this is in the context more broadly of what they do with Tarpeia's narrative as a whole.

GREED

Dionysius draws attention to Fabius's authorship at the precise point at which Fabius's version differs from other remnants of the early tradition (notably, Piso): that point is Tarpeia's motive. Dionysius is specific in attributing the greed motive to Fabius's account:[16]

παρθένος τις ἀπὸ τοῦ μετεώρου κατεσκόπει θυγάτηρ ἀνδρὸς ἐπιφανοῦς, ᾧ προσέκειτο ἡ χωρίου φυλακή, Τάρπεια ὄνομα; καὶ αὐτὴν, ὡς μὲν Φάβιός τε καὶ Κίγκιος γράφουσιν, ἔρως εἰσέρχεται τῶν ψελλίων,

---

15. Champion (forthcoming) explores how Livy and Dionysius independently use the same source to construct very different narratives about Scaevola and about the Horatii and Curiatii.

16. I take the text from the new compendium *FRH = Fragments of the Roman Historians* (2013) edited by T. J. Cornell and refer periodically to Jacoby's *FGrH*, Peter's *HRR*, and Beck's *Die Frühen Römischen Historiker*.

ἃ περὶ τοῖς ἀριστεροῖς βραχίοσιν ἐφόρουν, καὶ τῶν δακτυλίων; χρυσοφόροι γὰρ ἦσαν οἱ Σαβῖνοι τότε καὶ Τυρρηνῶν οὐχ ἧττον ἁβροδίαιτοι.
(2.38.2–3 = *FRH* Pictor F7)

A certain maiden looked down on them from above, the daughter of a distinguished man, to whom was entrusted the responsibility of guarding the place. And on this maiden, as both Fabius and Cincius relate, fell a desire for the bracelets, which they wore on their left arms, and for their rings. For at that time the Sabines used to wear gold, and were no less decadent than the Etruscans.

The description of greed takes a curious form: desire, ἔρως, for bracelets. Dionysius's choice to emphasize Pictor's authority in just this place in the text, with the phrase "as Pictor and Cincius say" leads us to imagine that ἔρως is Fabius's word, not Dionysius's gloss.[17] If this is so, then Pictor's choice of wording might betray the presence of the Greek traitoress-in-love tradition in the background. It is even possible, but not at all demonstrable, that Pictor inherited a tradition about Tarpeia in love and changed it to suit his purposes. In any event, after ἔρως the delayed genitive object "bracelets" (ψελλίων) might have come as a surprising punch. To be sure, the Greek word ἔρως, while it normally designates erotic desire, can also flag other, more material forms of desire.[18] But, as I explored in the first chapter, greed and love can be considered two sides of the same coin, each stemming from desire and each impossible for a woman to resist, each inscrutable and ineluctable. Indeed, Greek thinkers had grappled with desire's collusion with greed, either as its instigator or as a companion to it. In a recent study on greed in Greek discourse, Ryan Balot probes the philosophical, political, and theological discussions of greed in Greek letters that describe it as an internal failing, a violation of natural boundaries, and a problem in and of itself independent of its social ramifications.[19] Tarpeia's greed marks her as this sort of natural aberration.

More importantly, she is a social aberration. As we shall see, in Pictor's account Tarpeia's desire for bracelets isn't so much of interest for its

---

17. Cincius Alimentus was a contemporary of Fabius Pictor and seems to have followed him in the particulars of his history of early Rome, differing only when his text turned to more recent times, a difference explainable by their very different experiences of the Hannibalic war—Fabius Pictor's as a senator, Cincius Alimentus's as a prisoner of war. See Forsythe 2006: 60–61.

18. ἔρως can also indicate love or desire of an object: *LSJ* s.v. ἔρως, 695 def. 1–2.

19. See Balot 2001: 158–59 for the collusion between greed and other forms of desire. For a discussion of fourth-century discourses on the psychology of greed, see pp. 31–39. On greed and love as two (of several) identified motives for the treasonous mythic girls, see the discussion in chapter 1.

psychological dimension as for the threat it poses to society. Greed attends competition, too much of which can undermine a society's cohesion. In Balot's formulation, greed stands at the crux of a complex value system that prizes competition and individual achievement on one hand, and communal belonging and responsibility on the other.[20] Excessive acquisitiveness privileges the former over the latter, disturbing their delicate balance and leading to social disorder. The discourse of greed, Balot argues, comprises its operation within the radical Athenian democracy where equality of citizens is a must; within the coalition of city-states that formed to resist Xerxes' invasion; within the clearly authoritarian Delian League that promised to keep the peace; and within the oligarchic movement that unseated Athens's democracy for a time and shadowed it thereafter.[21] Though the political systems differed between the Roman Republic and democratic Athens, the same balance between individual achievement and communal belonging pertained. Prestige among Rome's elites was a zero-sum game; the impetus toward competitive display of status was high. Yet competitive display could go too far (indeed, in a sense the Republic eventually crumbled because of it), and the Republican political system depended on at least loose cooperation within the senatorial class and between the senatorial class and the lower orders.[22]

Greedy Tarpeia is out of step with the notion of belonging to a community. It is my broad thesis that Fabius Pictor's story about Tarpeia, as it purports to explain Rome's past, also is shaped by and helps shape its present. We know that Pictor wrote his history sometime in the last decade of the third century BCE.[23] At that particular moment in Rome's history, when Hannibal threatened its very existence, greed spoke strongly to Pictor's audience in Rome. Things were dire for Rome and its allies. Hannibal had been in Italy for a decade or more, had laid waste to the southern countryside, and had devastated the Roman army at Lake Trasimene in 217 BCE as well as at Cannae in 215 BCE. The war with Hannibal, like so many of Rome's wars during the Republic, strained Rome's domestic order. The his-

---

20. Balot 2001: 12–14.

21. These are (not explicitly) the subjects of Balot's fourth, fifth, and sixth chapters.

22. The starting point for a conversation about this cooperation is Polybius's description of Rome's tripartite constitution in book 6 of his *Histories*. A useful conspectus of scholarly trends about the Roman sociopolitical order may be found in Ward 2004.

23. Frier (1979) 1999: 237–46 argues that Pictor's composition makes most sense in a climate of "cautious optimism"—optimism after Marcellus's capture of Syracuse and Pulcher's of Capua, and caution because Hannibal remained in Italy. Pictor's accusation of the Barcids rather than broader Carthage also, to Frier, constitutes an apologia for the senate's policies that makes more sense during than after the war (p. 246).

torical narratives record a sharp divergence in senatorial opinion about how the war should be prosecuted, with Fabian caution pitted against Scipionic daring.[24] Legal activity of the period marks not only the financial crisis caused by fighting Hannibal (as can be seen in the various appropriations passed during the war)[25] but also the strain this crisis put on the delicate harmony of social class at Rome. By and large, these laws sought to curtail elite opportunities for income at the expense of the lower classes. For example, the *lex Claudia de navibus,* passed begrudgingly in 218 BCE, limited senatorial opportunities for large-scale maritime commerce.[26] The *lex Cincia* of 204 BCE and the *lex Publicia* of perhaps 209 BCE restricted gifts to patrons from their clients.[27] These laws suggest that elite acquisitiveness, in light of the scarcity of resources, was beginning to be a problem.

An examination of the *lex Oppia,* passed in 215 BCE in the wake of the Roman disaster at Cannae, reveals that Romans were struggling to maintain a similarly delicate balance between competitive and cooperative values.[28] The *lex Oppia* restricted luxurious display, particularly by women. Women were not to own more than a half ounce of gold, nor to wear purple clothing, nor to ride in carriages within the city.[29] It is possible that this law masks an appropriation of assets from women to help defray the enormous

---

24. See Livy 28.40–44 for a debate that encapsulates the two positions; the recorded debates are complicated by the bias of the historians (e.g., Pictor's pro-Fabian stance; see Frier [1979] 1999: 234–35 and 279n65; Peter [1906] 1914 *HRR* 1: xlvii–xlviii) and the presence in the background of Athenian politics of the Peloponnesian war.

25. Scullard 2002 points out that the financial burden of the Second Punic War compelled the Roman senate to take drastic measures: *triumviri mensarii* (finance officers) were appointed and the treasury reduced the weight of the *as* (216 BCE); the annual citizen tax (*tributum*) was doubled (215 BCE, Livy 23.31.2); the state appropriated cash and jewelry directly from citizens (210 BCE); endowments to widows and orphans were seized by the state; and military officers were refused pay. Frank 1933 provides plausible estimates of expenses and receipts from the Hannibalic war (p. 81, and more broadly pp. 76–97). See also Lazenby 1996: 93–94. Livy 23.48.4ff. claims that Roman commanders in Spain sought cash and supplies directly from local cities. Zonaras 8.26.14 may record the debasement of silver coinage in 217 BCE.

26. Livy 21.63. See Harris 1979: 67–70 and cf. 62–67 (for the senate's unwillingness to limit their own opportunities); David 1996: 50 suggests that the senate approved the law in order to appear disinterested in profit on the eve of war); Vishnia 1996: 48 offers a rather pleasant view of the social harmony produced by this law. See also Harris 2004: 23–24; Gruen (1984) 2004: 34–36 and 41–42n43. Cassola 1962: 216–17 argues that the *lex Claudia* was meant to exclude businessmen from the senate.

27. On the *lex Cincia* see Zimmerman 1996: 482–84; Livy 34.4.9. On the *lex Publicia* see Vishnia 1996: 94–95nn164–65.

28. To be sure, the Greek examples understand communal responsibility in terms redolent of Athenian democracy, and the Roman concerns cannot be perfectly parallel. As we shall see, however, the Roman system, too, blended individual and collective achievement.

29. Livy 34.1–8, corroborated by Tac. *Ann.* 3.34; Valerius Maximus 9.1.3; Aulus Gellius 10.23 and 17.6; Oros. 4.20; Zonaras 9.17.1; and *de viris illustribus* 47.

cost of the war against Hannibal. During the war, bereaved women had certainly become wealthier, and the state needed money. The following year the property of wards, widows, and single women was transferred to the state treasury, lending support to a possible practical motive for the *lex Oppia*.[30] Yet measures passed over the next decade reveal that women retained more property than the *lex Oppia* allowed, casting doubt on an exclusively economic interpretation of the law.[31] In order to resolve this difficulty, one recent scholar has suggested that the law was prophylactic and aimed to protect women from squandering their new resources in case the state should need them.[32] It would thus sit more comfortably against later measures that "repeat" the initial confiscation.

Some light may be shed on the *lex Oppia* in its historical context by the debate about its repeal twenty years later. Livy presents speeches against the repeal by the conservative Cato, consul for 195 BCE, and in favor of the repeal by the tribune L. Valerius. Livy's account is anachronistic at points and is certainly infused with ideas of his own day about luxury and female probity,[33] but Cato's speech matches his sentiments on luxury and gender preserved elsewhere,[34] and Valerius's and Cato's arguments taken together present a powerful case that the Oppian law addressed the same socioeconomic concerns about elite materialism and social (im)mobility as did the *lex Claudia* of 218 BCE. The tribune is explicit about the fact that the law was a safeguard against public and private emergency (*praesidium*, 34.7.4) and, as it was intended as a temporary measure fit for the wartime context only (34.6.16), it has a shelf life (*mortalis*, 34.76.5). Valerius's arguments lend some small support to the interpretation of the law as an emergency economic measure (cf. his word *praesidium* at 34.7.4), but more pertinent to the present argument is Valerius's attitude toward the

---

30. Livy 24.18.13–14; cf. 34.5.10 and 34.6.14, in which Valerius lumps together the restriction of display and the transfer of property. Zanda 2011: 51 distinguishes the *lex Oppia* from other laws that involve feasting and, because of its abrogation, she considers it a war measure, i.e., a tax. Pomeroy 1975: 177–81 sees the law as both practical (there being newly rich women during the war) and ideological (to encourage a decorously somber attitude in such difficult times). See also Culham 1982: 786–93 and Johnston 1980: 145.

31. Culham 1982: 786–93, particularly 787–88. Gruen (1990) 1996: 143–44 argues that the *lex Oppia* was not meant to alleviate the economic strain of the Hannibalic war, but rather was simply a sumptuary law intended to curb lavish displays of wealth among elite Roman women. He points to evidence that Roman women apparently retained much of their wealth but did not display it publicly.

32. Vishnia 1996: 91.

33. For emphasis on the Livian elements in the speeches, see Moore 1993 and Mastrorosa 2006: 501–3.

34. Robert 2003: 377.

law's symbolism. Answering Cato's claim that adornment leads to undue competition between women (34.4.14–15), Valerius responds that adornment is a natural and appropriate benefit of peace (34.7.1). Now that the crisis of war has passed, says Valerius, display has resumed for men—even the lowest-ranking among them (*infimo generi,* 34.7.2)—and should for women as well. The jealousy that would strike men who were constrained to hide their own honors would hit women all the harder for their weak nature (34.7.7).

Valerius's speech shows that he considers adornment to be a means to display rank and to jockey for position—for men, for women, and for men via their women—for, if it were repealed, men may choose to limit their wives' and daughters' accouterment or not (34.17.13). Indeed, female ornamentation was an effective way for Roman men to display their own status in society.[35] The *lex Oppia,* restricting one type of display of status, would thus indirectly reduce competition among the elite men, via their wives, in a time when unity of this class was an absolute necessity.[36] Support for this interpretation has been found in Plautus's plays. *Aulularia* (500–503 and 526–31) and *Epidicus* (226–28) reflect the connection between female adornment and the erosion of aristocratic unity.[37] In both passages, men lament that adorned women broadcast the wealth of their families, thus making it apparent that the upper classes were devoting money to their own consumption that should have gone to the war effort. Private financial comfort so visibly displayed during the war against Hannibal—when even prisoners weren't ransomed because of the great cost (Livy 22.61.3)—drew attention to the disparity of motives and means among Romans in the war effort. The law strove to create the appearance of Roman unity.[38] Cato agrees with this symbolic interpretation of the law and favors its preservation precisely because of its equalizing power: at 34.4.14 he imagines a rich woman complaining about it: "Why am I not conspicuous as a notable woman in my gold and purple? Why does other

---

35. Culham 1982: 792. The classic example is Scipio Aemilianus's gift to his impoverished mother Aemilia; her trappings became a visible testament to his status and decorum. See Poybius 31.26–27 and Rei 1998: 99.

36. Gruen 1990 (1996): 69–71 and 1990: 144–46.

37. Culham 1982: 790–91.

38. Cf. Gruen 1992: 69–70 on the *lex Oppia* and on sumptuary laws in general as ideological gestures rather than practical measures: "Its (sc. The *lex Oppia*'s) promulgation doubtless served to *demonstrate* state solidarity in the darker days of the Hannibalic war" (p. 70; my emphasis), and "the measures were generally ineffective, loosely enforced, and designed more as an *advertisement* of aristocratic conscience than as authentic reform" (p. 69; my emphasis). Also see Gruen (1990) 1996: 143–44.

women's poverty lie hidden under this facade of law?" (*cur non insignis auro et purpura conspicior? Cur paupertas aliarum sub hac legis specie latet?*).

Livy's Valerius adds the detail (34.7.6) that the Roman women were jealous of women in allied Latin towns who remained unrestricted, as if imperium lay in those women's towns, not in their own (*tamquam in illarum civitatibus, non in sua, imperium sit*). This detail suggests that elite competition was not simply a problem within Rome but also jeopardized harmony within Italy—again, when harmony was paramount. The *lex Oppia* thus might have aimed at helping Romans present a more humble face to their nearby allies, who were providing troops and money for the war effort without, perhaps, reaping any of the benefits of a wartime economy. Like the *lex Claudia*, then, the *lex Oppia* responded to concerns about the perceived iniquity of the economic burden of war as well as social (im)mobility. In restricting the Roman ruling class's behavior, these laws helped disarm critics of that class's apparent greed.

As an interesting aside, both Cato and Valerius were of Sabine descent, the latter tracing his family's presence in Rome back to the very war in which Tarpeia earned her fame.[39] For now, the point I want to make is that, in the context of Hannibal's threat, greed was seen as a major danger that faced Rome from within its own ranks and threatened to undermine Roman security and unity. It is especially noteworthy if we can ascribe to Pictor the description of Tarpeia as the daughter of a distinguished man (θυγάτηρ ἀνδρὸς ἐπιφανοῦς)—a representative of the elite class, desirous of rings and bracelets.[40] Tarpeia's desire represents exactly the sort of behavior the *lex Oppia* sought to moderate—especially since it led her to look outside Rome for its fulfillment and drew her away from her nation's cause. To press the matter further, the Sabines' display of gold ornaments was what inspired Tarpeia's desire, an idea to which we return below. Adornment leads to emulation, which in turn leads to competition that threatens to undermine Rome.

---

39. The *gens Valeria* was also philoplebe in the fifth century BCE (see the *leges Valeriae* of 449 BCE, Livy 3.55.67). For this *gens*, see Wiseman 1998: 78. Furthermore, Farney 2007: 190 writes, "Cato was most likely Sabine himself," adding, "we know that Cato grew up on a family farm in Sabine territory and that he admired the life-style of the people there and emulated their demeanor and manner of living." Cato had also risen through the *cursus honorum* from plebeian roots.

40. The phrase "daughter of a distinguished man" is not explicitly assigned by Dionysius to Pictor, but its placement in Dionysius's text just before the Pictor citation does not exclude the possibility, and Livy, who follows Pictor's version until he cites variants, calls her the daughter of the man who was in charge of the citadel (1.11).

GREED'S PARTNER: GENDER

While Tarpeia's story explores the greed that was perceived as a regrettable motive of Roman political policy and as a threat to internal cohesion, it also explores contemporary concerns about gender roles in the late third century BCE. Pictor's era showed a tremendous rise in the influence and independence of Roman women, and a concomitant concern over the social disorder enabled by this change. Trasimene and Cannae left 60,000 Roman men dead or captive, and countless rich widows and daughters in Rome.[41] As these women remarried or married, the larger dowries that accompanied them shifted the power dynamic within Roman families.[42] The comic plays of Plautus, who, like Pictor, wrote in the late years of the war against Hannibal, are replete with well-dowered wives who shrewishly keep their randy husbands on a short leash.[43] It's a funny stereotype, to be sure, but these on-stage wives must have made Roman male audiences a little uncomfortable.

Indeed, the period of the Hannibalic war boasts a remarkable amount of legislation concerning women and their activities and also events in which women played a prominent role. In 218 and 217 *matronae* made dedications to Juno Regina—in 218, of a bronze bowl (Livy 21.62.8) and in 217 of whatever they could spare (22.1.17–18). Freedwomen were to offer a gift to Feronia (Livy 22.1.18). In 216 BCE Livy tells us that the annual rites of Ceres were canceled because there were too few women available to perform them; the missing women were in mourning for their dead husbands and were thus ineligible to perform rites.[44] This led the senate to restrict the period of mourning to thirty days (Livy 22.56.4–6). Since mourning was also a way to display status, the senate's injunction, like the *lex Oppia* the following year, also had the effect of regulating female influence at a tricky time.[45] Also in 216 two Vestal virgins were found guilty of unchastity; one was put to death in the traditional way of live burial, and

---

41. Livy 22.7.1–3 cites 15,000 Roman dead at Trasimene, and 22.49.15 says the Romans and their allies suffered over 48,000 killed at Cannae (*quadraginta quinque milia quingenti pedites, duo milia septingenti equites, et tantadem prope civium sociorumque pars, caesi dicuntur*). The figures for Cannae are roughly corroborated by Appian *Han.* 109.1 and Plutarch *Fab. Max.* 16.9, while Polybius 3.117.4 records the outrageous total of 70,000 Romans and allies killed. See also Hoyos 2007: 66 and Pomeroy 1975: 177 for the effect of these casualties on women's freedom.

42. Rei 1998: 92–96.

43. Rei 1998: 99–104.

44. Livy claims that this mourning was so loud and prevalent that it caused public disturbance (22.56.4).

45. Culham 1982: 789.

the other killed herself before she was punished (Livy 22.57.2). Livy tells us in this chapter that this calamity was so great that an embassy—including Fabius Pictor, our historian—was sent at once to consult the Delphic oracle, and special and brutal expiatory rites called for by the Sibylline books were performed: the live burial of humans, a pair of Gauls and a pair of Greeks, one male and one female each. Still, in 216 BCE, when the senate was deliberating the fate of Hannibal's Roman prisoners from Cannae, Roman women joined the public entreaty to the senate to ransom the captives (Livy 22.60.3). They did not succeed, and it is worth noting that money played a part: Livy cites the state's concern about delivering so much money to Hannibal as its reason for denying the chance to purchase the prisoners' freedom (22.61.1–4). In 215 the cult of Venus Verticordia ("Changer of Hearts," presumably toward greater virtue) was initiated in Rome (Valerius Maximus 8.15.1; Pliny *HN* 7.120; Solinus 1.126). The *lex Oppia* was also passed in this year. Next, in 214 BCE the state borrowed the money of widows, single women, and wards of the state when the holders of these funds deposited them in the state treasury for safekeeping (Livy 24.18.13–14). The following year minor magistrates tried and exiled some matrons on charges of adultery (Livy 25.2.9–10). After some extreme prodigies in 207 BCE—the birth of a huge child and a lightning strike on the temple of Juno Regina—priests ordered virgins to sing a hymn throughout the city, and married women in Rome and nearby towns to propitiate Juno with a gift paid for out of their dowries (Livy 27.37.9–10). Finally, in 204 BCE, in response to another prodigy (rain of stones), the Sibylline books demanded the importation of the Magna Mater. She was received by Roman matrons led by Claudia Quinta and passed from hand to hand among them until she reached her new home on the Palatine (Livy 29.14.5–14; Ovid *Fasti* 4.179–372).

Three themes emerge from this list: the involvement of women in the affairs of the state, through demonstrations, contributions, and religious activity; the importance of female propriety; and the connection of the (female) body to social status and order.[46] A concern that runs through all three of these themes is the extent to which women act appropriately when left to their own devices. Their activities vis-à-vis Juno and Cybele suggest that women may be entrusted with managing important affairs; the *lex Oppia,* the limit to mourning, the exile of adulteresses, the punishment of the Vestals, and the importation of Venus Verticordia suggest

---

46. For the implications of Rome's domestic affairs of the late third century BCE on the body, see particularly Resinski 1997 and Rei 1998: 92; more generally, see Richlin 1997: 18.

that they may not. The tally of events leads to a negative conclusion about women's participation: they are more dangerous than useful, or are useful only when carefully monitored and regulated. What is more, of the twelve instances named above (offering to Feronia, restricted mourning, unchaste Vestals, plea for ransom, *lex Oppia,* Venus Verticordia, transfer of funds, persecution of matrons, three donations to Juno, and Magna Mater), eight involve questions of money (*lex Oppia,* plea for ransom, transfer of funds, limit to mourning, and three donations to Juno and one to Feronia).

The combination of female cooperation, material resources, and (im)morality explains the potential interest of Tarpeia's story to Fabius Pictor and his Roman audience. The Romans saw female morality as intimately connected with the threat Rome faced from foreigners. The *lex Oppia* in particular reflects a fear of women themselves and the power that women with resources might wield. Domestic events of 218–202 BCE show Romans struggling to control and regulate Roman women through official channels, revealing mistrust in the efficacy of private means of exerting gender control.[47] Tarpeia's legend not only addresses Romans' concerns about greed and its corrosive effect on state unity, but more pointedly it acts as a parable about the dangers women pose when they are uncontrolled. If we return to Pictor's text with this context in mind, two details stand out. First, Tarpeia's greed is styled as ἔρως τῶν ψελλίων, a collocation that combines material acquisitiveness and bodily desire. I mentioned above the problems with this combination as an indication of Tarpeia's flawed nature. Here I wish to stress that the implicit identification that ἔρως draws between her flawed nature and her female body. Second, Tarpeia is a passive reagent to the desire that befalls her. Greed does not come from Tarpeia, but rather it happens to her (αὐτὴν ... ἔρως εἰσέρχεται) and the result is Rome's defeat at the hands of a foreign invader. All the greater, thus, is the need for the state to protect women from falling prey to the dangers around them. The state regulates women and other individuals for their own good, as well as its own. Because of its combination of Tarpeia's passivity and proclivity, Tarpeia's myth validates increased political paternalism and moral conservatism in times of foreign threat. Such are the workings of empire.

---

47. Resinski 1997: 4–5 explores how the repeal of the Oppian Law in 195 BCE did not permit the Roman woman to display her wealth again so much as it placed her more firmly in the control of her paterfamilias. See also Mastrorosa 2006: 595–96, 602, and 608–11 for the sum total of the pair of speeches as explaining and justifying the subordination of women.

TARPEIA LOOKING OUTWARD: MORAL CONTAGION

Tarpeia is (as a woman) victim to the visual pull of golden ornaments. As such, she is to be protected as much as censured, and that protection was one of the aims of the various forms of legislation during the Hannibalic war. If it weren't for the allure of Sabine finery, we are to presume Tarpeia wouldn't have let her judgment lapse.[48] In drawing attention to the enemy's luxurious ways, Pictor's story participates in a mode of ethnic characterization long operative in Greek culture. Luxury had a rich past in Greek letters as a trope describing and marginalizing the dangerous foreigner. But it could also indicate the sort of sophistication that distinguishes Greeks from more rugged barbarians. As I shall argue, Pictor's soft Sabines insert Rome firmly within the intellectual and cultural milieu of his Greek audience, working on a broad level to foster a sense of cultural kinship between the Romans and Greeks—both powers that have grappled with the dangers posed by a rich invader. The discourse of soft Sabines resonates in an even more immediate way with the Greeks in southern Italy, who struggled to define themselves and their Greekness against their own "barbarian" neighbors: the various Italic peoples—including Sabines—with whom they traded, fought, and allied. But like the trope of luxury itself, Rome's self-positioning in this context is neither simple nor straightforward.

To begin, it is worth revisiting Pictor's description of Sabine luxury:

> καὶ αὐτήν, ὡς μὲν Φάβιός τε καὶ Κίγκιος γράφουσιν, ἔρως εἰσέρχεται τῶν ψελλίων, ἃ περὶ τοῖς ἀριστεροῖς βραχίοσιν ἐφόρουν, καὶ τῶν δακτυλίων· χρυσοφόροι γὰρ ἦσαν οἱ Σαβῖνοι τότε καὶ Τυρρηνῶν οὐχ ἧττον ἁβροδίαιτοι. (Dionysius 2.38.3 = *FRH* Pictor 13)

> And on this maiden, as both Fabius and Cincius relate, fell a desire for the bracelets, which they wore on their left arms, and for their rings. For at that time the Sabines were golden-clad, and were no less decadent than the Etruscans.

It is possible that the comparison with the Sabines is Dionysius's and not Pictor's, since the idea of rich Sabines certainly would need explaining in Dionysius's day when the stereotype of this people as austere had taken a

---

48. The desire for golden ornaments is a contagion that is spread not from possession, but from display: Nenci 1983: 1026.

firm hold of Roman imaginations.⁴⁹ While we can only be certain that the first sentence comes from Pictor, Dionysius clearly understands Pictor as depicting Sabine wealth, even highlighting it. In this case the comparison with the Etruscans will have underscored not only the excess of their riches, but also its antiquity.⁵⁰ Indeed, Pictor emphasizes the quantity of Sabine gold elsewhere in the tale:

> οἱ δὲ περὶ τὸν Φάβιον ἐπὶ τοῖς Σαβίνοις ποιοῦσι τὴν τῶν ὁμολογιῶν ἀπάτην· δέον γὰρ αὐτοὺς τὸν χρυσόν, ὥσπερ ἡ Τάρπεια ἠξίου, κατὰ τὰς ὁμολογίας ἀποδιδόναι, χαλεπαίνοντας ἐπὶ τῷ μεγέθει τοῦ μισθοῦ τὰ σκεπαστήρια κατ' αὐτῆς βαλεῖν, ὡς ταῦτα ὅτε ὤμνυσαν αὐτῇ δώσειν ὑπεσχημένους. (Dionysius 2.40.2 = *FRH* Pictor F7)

> But the Fabian tradition attributes the fraud in the performance of the agreement to the Sabines; for they had to hand over the gold according to the agreement, just as she demanded, but they, angered at the magnitude of the reward, threw their shields upon her, heaping them on her as if they had sworn to give her these.

We return to this part of the story later; for now it suffices to note not only the emphasis on Sabine wealth, but the fact that the explanatory phrase is clearly taken from Pictor, and, like the Etruscan comparison, is connected to the main thought only with the connective γάρ. A third snippet of Pictor's text, as yet unplaced, seems to confirm Pictor's authorship of the rich-as-Etruscan Sabines. Strabo preserves the following proof that Pictor drew strong attention to Sabine wealth:

> φησὶ δ' ὁ συγγραφεὺς Φάβιος Ῥωμαίους αἰσθέσθαι τοῦ πλούτου τότε πρῶτον, ὅτε τουτουτοῦ κατέστησαν κύριοι. (Strabo 5.3.1 = *FRH* Pictor F24)

> The historian Fabius says that the Romans then for the first time understood wealth when they became masters of this people.

---

49. Dench 1995: 88. Austere Sabines became popular in the second century as a way to anchor moral value in Italy's countryside, in contrast to the excesses of the urban elites. Austere Sabines are not, however, necessary to understand the comparison with the Etruscans.

50. See also Farney 2007: 105–8 for a slightly different version of my argument; Farney accepts the sentiment as Pictor's, arguing that in the historian's day the Sabines had already become austere, being stripped of their resources by the Romans who now controlled them. The texts of Jacoby (*FGrH* 809.4) and Peter (*HRR* Fabius Pictor 8) support (with type size) a Fabian reading of the second sentence, without comment. Beck (10) does not comment, and Cornell (*FRH* Pictor F7) indicates that the sentiment about luxurious Etruscans is Dionysius's own.

This description could be part of Tarpeia's story (with which it fits very well) or it could come from Pictor's description of the Roman conquest of the Sabine territory in the early third century. Whether the annalist in this fragment is referring to the regal period or the more recent conquest does not matter here. Pictor's Sabines are wealthy, and the preconquest Romans—a category that would include Tarpeia—are not.

The language of luxury, framed as τρῡφή/ἁβροσύνη/χλιδή and the like, was familiar to Greek audiences from the time of Homer. While these terms seem to be interchangeable (and in any case a word was not necessarily needed to convey a people's luxury), the choice of ἁβροδίαιτοι (if it is indeed Fabian, as I believe) gives rise to some interesting nuances regarding his Sabines. As Lombardo's survey of the term "ἁβροσύνη" reveals, what began as a neutral, even positive characterization of elite success within a community was transformed, in the context of the Persian wars, into a marker for a dangerous and foreign moral lassitude one saw in others.[51] Thus, whereas Sappho 140.1 can describe Adonis as a refined gentleman (ἁβρός), Aeschylus's Agamemnon warns Clytemnestra not to turn him soft (μὴ ... ἐμὲ ἄβρυνε) by making him walk on purple (*Ag.* 918–19). Lombardo posits that the beginnings of this shift in the attitude toward refinement can be seen in the conflict between the elites of the prosperous Greek cities of Asia Minor and the rich Lydians further inland. Thereafter the trait was attached to any Persians, or to the whole lot of them, if need be: the descriptor was equally apt for whole communities, with the similar double edge of sophistication on one side and excess on the other. Thucydides, equating Greece's unsophisticated past with its barbarized present, famously describes the Athenians themselves as "luxuriously living," (ἁβροδίαιτοι) in contrast with the simple and rugged Spartans, but Aeschylus cites soft living (again, ἁβροδίαιτοι) as a particularly Lydian trait at *Persians* 41.

This last pair of examples uses the same word Pictor uses to describe the Sabines in a concise example of self-positioning within a broader milieu. Like the Athenians against Sparta, the sophisticated Sabines operate against a rugged and primitive Rome, as yet unacquainted with the finer things that progress and peace bring. But Pictor seems to tilt the balance toward the other, more dangerous sort of softies: the Lydians. He likens his luxurious Sabines to those most decadent of all Italian peoples, the Etruscans—long thought to be Lydian in origin.[52] As Lydians, Pictor's

---

51. Lombardo 1983, esp. pp. 1078–79.
52. Herodotus 1.94 and see Briquel 1991: 62 and 108n60 for the origins of the trope (in Lydian

luxurious Sabines thus take the shape of the alluring but dangerous barbarian, and their very presence casts Rome as a Greek pristine self—more specifically, Greeks yet uncorrupted by Eastern contact. All this is set in Rome's distant past, lending Rome—the newcomer on the Mediterranean stage—a history not only contemporary in antiquity to Greece's "golden age" but comparable in experience. Rome faced the same challenges the Greeks did, and it faced them even earlier. In this way Pictor's Tarpeia offers a conceptual linkage between Greece and Rome similar to that produced in the myths of wandering Odysseus, Hercules, and Aeneas—myths that were also emerging in the mid-Republic to anchor Rome's presence in the wider world.[53] Unlike those figures, though, Tarpeia is locally grown. The version of her myth that Pictor relates might represent one of Rome's early forays into this mythic dialogue about Greece and Rome.

Pictor's comparison of the Sabines to the sophisticated Etruscans anchors Rome in the local arena as well, to an audience more closely acquainted with Rome, the Sabines, and the Etruscans than readers in Athens or Alexandria might be. Synthesizing epigraphic, literary, numismatic, and archaeological evidence, Emma Dench has explored the way Greeks and non-Greeks in southern Italy used the language of the decadent other (and its corollary "the austere self") to negotiate the shifting and complex alliances they forged and fled from in Hellenistic southern Italy, now playing the civilized self to align themselves with Greek communities, now playing the barbarian if that served their purpose.[54] Pictor's opulent-as-Etruscan Sabines thus act to align the Romans (by implication, the uncorrupted, simple ones) to their immediate Greek neighbors. Fabius's effete Sabines, Dench argues, "find close parallels with fifth-century Athenian images of Persia: wealthy, decadent, but also with a dangerous edge. I would suggest that this is the kind of imagery by means of which enmity and subsequent conquest were explained and, perhaps, justified."[55] Dench does not mention Pictor's follow-up to the Tarpeia episode, but it is especially relevant to the larger point she makes. After describing

---

political necessity) and its evolution and dissemination.

53. For example, Polybius 12.4b = *FGrH* 566 F36 records that Timaeus found traces of Trojan ritual at Rome. For Odysseus's connection to Rome see Gruen (1990) 1996: 84–85. Pictor himself lists Hercules as Rome's first founder (*SEG* 26.1123, the "Taormina inscription"). Additional examples may be found in Dench 1995: 71–72, Gruen (1990) 1996: 11–20, 32–33, and 85 and 1992: 6–51 on the development of the Aeneas and Odysseus legends in Italy.

54. Dench 1995: 45–46 and 2005a, esp. p. 300–303.

55. Dench 1995: 89, and see more broadly pp. 85–94 for traditions about the Sabines. In contrast, Martini 1998 sees Pictor's Tarpeia as explaining to a Roman audience the incorporation of Sabines in their state.

Tarpeia's death in Piso's and Pictor's accounts, Dionysius preserves an important detail from Pictor's narrative about the Sabine character:

> ἔπειτα πάλιν ὁ μὲν Πείσων φησὶ τῶν Σαβίνων τὸν χρυσὸν ἑτοίμων ὄντων διδόναι τῇ κόρῃ τὸν περὶ τοῖς ἀριστεροῖς βραχίοσι τὴν Τάρπειαν οὐ τὸν κόσμον ἀλλὰ τοὺς θυρεοὺς παρ' αὐτῶν αἰτεῖν. Τατίῳ δὲ θυμόν τε εἰσελθεῖν ἐπὶ τῇ ἐξαπάτῃ καὶ λογισμὸν τοῦ μὴ παραβῆναι τὰς ὁμολογίας. δόξαι δ' οὖν αὐτῷ δοῦναι μὲν τὰ ὅπλα, ὥσπερ ἡ παῖς ἠξίωσε, ποιῆσαι δ' ὅπως αὐτοῖς μηδὲν λαβοῦσα χρήσεται, καὶ αὐτίκα διατεινάμενον ὡς μάλιστα ἰσχύος εἶχε ῥῖψαι τὸν θυρεὸν κατὰ τῆς κόρης καὶ τοῖς ἄλλοις παρακελεύσασθαι ταὐτὸ ποιεῖν. οὕτω δὴ βαλλομένην πάντοθεν τὴν Τάρπειαν ὑπὸ πλήθους τε καὶ ἰσχύος τῶν πληγῶν πεσεῖν καὶ περισωρευθεῖσαν ὑπὸ τῶν θυρεῶν ἀποθανεῖν. οἱ δὲ περὶ τὸν Φάβιον ἐπὶ τοῖς Σαβίνοις ποιοῦσι τὴν τῶν ὁμολογιῶν ἀπάτην· δέον γὰρ αὐτοὺς τὸν χρυσόν, ὥσπερ ἡ Τάρπεια ἠξίου, κατὰ τὰς ὁμολογίας ἀποδιδόναι, χαλεπαίνοντας ἐπὶ τῷ μεγέθει τοῦ μισθοῦ τὰ σκεπαστήρια κατ' αὐτῆς βαλεῖν, ὡς ταῦτα ὅτε ὤμνυσαν αὐτῇ δώσειν ὑπεσχημένους. (Dionysius 2.40.1–2 = *FRH* Pictor 7)

Then again Piso says that, when the Sabines were ready to hand over to the girl the gold they wore on their left arms, Tarpeia requested from them not their adornment but their shields. But Tatius's bravado emerged at this ruse (ἐξαπάτη), and a strategy of not breaking the agreement. He decided to give her the weapons just as the child demanded, but to do this in such a way that she would not be able to benefit from them. Stretching out with all his might, he threw it at her as forcefully as possible and ordered the others to do the same. And so, being assaulted on all sides by the number and force of the blows, Tarpeia fell died, buried under the shields. But the Fabian tradition assigns to the Sabines the fraud (ἀπάτην) in the performance of the agreement; for they were bound by the agreement to give her the gold, just as Tarpeia had asked, but they begrudged the size of the payment and threw their shields at her, as if when they made their oath they had undertaken to give these to her.

Piso's Sabines are the ones deceived (they suffer ἐξαπάτη), but they recover through Tatius's cleverness: they keep but neutralize their vow by killing Tarpeia before she could use the shields (or their nakedness) to Roman advantage. Fabius's Sabines are the opposite: they are the perpetrators of deceit (ἀπάτην). They renege and find a way to keep the letter, but not the spirit, of their compact. In this respect they engage another discourse of the moral self-identification operative especially in mid-Republican southern Italy: the discourse of keeping faith (Latin *fides*, Greek πίστις).[56] While deception and oath-breaking had played a part in the Classical discourse about foreigners, it, like luxury, flourished in the increasingly complex politics of the Hellenistic era. *Fides* was styled as an especially Roman virtue that shaped not only her internal relationships (both symmetrical such as *amicitia*/friendship and asymmetrical such as *clientela*/patronage)[57] but her external relationships as well.[58]

Literary and archaeological sources alike reveal the extent to which Roman *fides* was at play in third-century diplomacy in southern Italy. A few examples will suffice. Sometime in the third century, probably just after the Pyrrhic war, the Locrians produced a coin depicting Pistis crowning Roma, perhaps to ensure their continued protection.[59] Polybius describes the Romans' desire to restore their reputation for πίστις after some of their Campanian allies massacred the population of Rhegium in 281 BCE, which was under Roman protection at the time (1.7.8); he later famously cites Roman πίστις as their primary reason for resisting Hannibal's movements in Spain (3.29.8 and cf. Livy 21.19.5).[60] As Diodorus relates, Hiero's complaint that the Romans trotted out πίστις in their decision to intervene in the Mamertine affair in 264 BCE was just a pretext (32.1.4).[61] In the 250s BCE the Romans dedicated a temple to Fides on the Capitol (Lucretius *de Nat. Deor.* 2.61), on whose walls were displayed international agreements (Cass. Dio 65.17.3; Julius Obseq. 128). It is worth noting that the Romans later ascribed the introduction of the cult to the Sabine Numa—an attribution which probably reflects the same second-century rehabilitation that left them beacons of old-fashioned austerity rather than luxury.[62]

It is interesting in this context to note how *fides*, like luxury, was attached or denied to non-Romans as a way of claiming them as (potential) allies or enemies. Against Roman *fides* two enemy "others" stand out:

---

56. I am treating *fides* and πίστις as equivalent in purpose, despite their potential difference in the perceived equality of the participants.

57. Burton 2004: 212–23 and 235 provides numerous examples from Plautus, with extensive bibliography. Verboven's 2011 article on *amicitia* is a useful overview of the extensive dialogue about Roman sociopolitical friendships.

58. Freyburger 1986.

59. Crawford 1985: 33 fig.8 = *RRC* 724–25 = *BMC* Italy 365:15. For nuances and date, see Gruen 1984: 321 and Dench 1995: 69.

60. Gelzer (1933) 1964: 163–66 suggests that Pictor's recurring interest in *fides* as a theme reflects the senate's preoccupation with it.

61. Harris 1979: 34–35 sees πίστις in this case as a justification for expansion.

62. Numa and *fides*: Dionysius 2.75.3; Livy 1.21.4; Plutarch *Numa* 16.1; Florus 1.2.3.

One was the cunning Greeks, visible on nearly every Plautine stage and in the negative depiction of Odysseus's trickery that held sway in early Roman representations of him.[63] Franko's 1995 analysis of one counterexample in Plautus illustrates the usefulness of the concept as an ideological tool in this era. In *Captivi,* Plautus stages Aetolian characters (normally the worst of cheats in Roman literature) who discuss *fides* and strive toward it, and who display the virtue truly and deeply.[64] Since the Romans were at war with the Aetolians (or on the verge of it) when the play was performed, Franko asserts (p. 174) that Plautus's play "boldly showed the inclusion of Aetolia in the world of Roman moral and political values" in characters that "uphold specifically Roman codes of behavior. Plautus offers a story in which characters can achieve a happy ending only when they embrace Roman virtues rather than cling to native Greek vices." The other "other" contemporary to Pictor's deceitful Sabines are the Carthaginians themselves, those ultimate tricksters.[65] So thorough was the Roman characterization of them as oath-breakers that the phrase *Punica fides* entered Roman idiom as a calque for "double-dealing."[66] Livy would take the portrait to the extreme, citing Hannibal's *perfidia plus quam Punica* ("treachery beyond Punic," 21.4.9) and describing even his elephants as duplicitous (*anceps,* 27.14.9). One crucial feature of this triad—faithful Rome, clever Greece, cheating Carthage—is that these three powers are the "big three" of Pictor's day: states jockeying with each other for control of smaller, more vulnerable communities. The suggestion that Rome was a more trustworthy ally and protector than Greece or Carthage might have enabled the spread and stability of Roman authority. Good faith was something Rome projected that she could offer that the other two could not.[67]

Pictor's attribution of deceit to the Sabines works toward several purposes. First and most simply, it tags the Sabines as tricky barbarians, and so participates in the same sort of ideological positioning that we saw in

---

63. Champlin 2006: 9–10. "The impression of him in Greek tragedy and in much of the *Iliad* is that of a treacherous, cold-blooded schemer, and this negative image is carried over into Roman drama, the public vehicle through which most ordinary people would know him." Stanford 1982: 4, an interpretation of the earliest development of the schemer persona, mentions Odysseus's "perpetual execration among the Romans."

64. See Franko 1995: 167–69 for the Aetolian reputation.

65. On *Punica fides,* see Isaac 2004: 329–35 and 349; Waldherr 2000: 211; Thiel 1994: 129.

66. See, e.g., Sallust *Jugurtha* 108.3; Cicero *Pro Scauro* 19.42 and *de Officiis* 1.38.

67. Of course, Rome emerges as the native soil of good faith because it is Roman sources that survive; see Thiel 1994: 130, who writes, "we have practically no inside knowledge of Carthage. The sources for the Punic Wars at our disposal are for the major part Roman and hence biased."

operation with respect to their luxury. In this respect it bears mentioning that the Carthaginians were also reputed to be notorious bribers (Dio 14.24; Nepos *Hamilcar* 32.3.3), and to bury their enemies waist-deep before burning them alive (Cato the Elder *ORF* (4)8.193). The Sabines' treatment of Tarpeia might have activated stereotypes about Carthaginians, perhaps triggering the fear that lay behind those stereotypes.[68] Tarpeia's story, in a sense, thus warns Rome's allies in the war against trusting the rewards offered by the enemy at their gate; that trust will not be repaid. Second, Sabine deceit absolves Tarpeia of some of the shame of her own treason. Despite her action, which runs against Rome's interests and flies in the face of patriotism, she is the trustworthy one in this story, the party to the agreement who keeps her end of the bargain. In contrast to her, the Sabines willfully misconstrue the terms of the agreement. Tarpeia presents an odd model of Roman *fides,* to be sure, but perhaps Pictor's account thus recuperates what it can for Tarpeia and the Romans from the bits and pieces of a tradition that is in part hostile. Third, the Sabines' own motivation in shirking their agreement balances Tarpeia's fault, in this respect: they resist paying the girl's price out of their own reluctance to part with their gold—in short, because of their own greed. Where it exists, greed is not uniquely hers.

LUXURY, GREED, EMPIRE, AND ROME

The Sabines' tempting display of gold, their deceit in breaking their pact, and their own greedy reason for doing so place Tarpeia's desire for golden trinkets in a context of other faults that makes it difficult to see her or her action in an entirely negative light. Her greed does not exist in a vacuum within the story, nor is it independent of other factors external to the story. Even as the Romans were promoting an ideology of their own *fides,* they were fighting the perception, abroad and in the peninsula, that their expansion was motivated by greed for material goods. This criticism, usually uttered by Greek voices, leaves traces in the historical record. In 264 BCE, for example, the Romans conquered Volsinii, a rich Etruscan city north of Rome, and returned with magnificent plunder. The accusation spread in Greek mouths that Rome had only moved against Volsinii for

---

68. To be fair, there is evidence of Romans burning half-buried prisoners, but it is described as barbaric. At Cicero *ad Fam.* 10.22, for example, Asinius Pollio describes as monstrous the punishment meted out by Caesar's lieutenant Balbus.

the spoils.⁶⁹ A letter by Flaminius to the Thessalian Chyretienses in 190 BCE defends Roman intervention there, stating that the Romans never wish to take action for gain's sake; this line of defense assumes a Greek attack on Roman motives.⁷⁰ Historians are still ardently debating the truth of these Greek allegations.⁷¹ For what it is worth, I believe that material gain was only one, and not the biggest one, of many Roman incentives toward expansion. What interests me more, and what is more relevant to Tarpeia, is that Roman greed was a key part of the public discourse about Rome's growing empire and that the Romans' own entries into this discourse surround Roman greed with other factors that render it impossible to condemn *tout court*.

The complexities of greed can be seen even within the single text of Pictor's history. Pictor doesn't elide the linkage between material gain and Roman warfare. On the contrary: the annalist seems to confront greed in many forms throughout his history, as if to reveal the situation as more complex than may be perceived among foreigners. For example, Pictor's account of the beginning of the First Punic War, an account preserved in Polybius's narrative, asserts that the Roman assembly was persuaded to aid the Mamertines in 264 BCE by the consuls' promise of spoils to be won.⁷² Pictor here acknowledges Roman acquisitiveness while putting it into the hands of the people, not the senate.⁷³ Or, when the Romans met the Gauls at Telemon in 225 BCE, Polybius—again following Pictor, who had fought in that battle—recounts that the Romans' fear was overcome by their wonder at and desire for the Gauls' exotic golden accouterment—specifically, their necklaces and bracelets (χρυσοῖς μανιάκαις . . . περιχείροις).⁷⁴ In this case, a tendency toward materialism inspires courageous action against a fierce foe—a dynamic not unlike the beneficial rivalry promoted by display in Valerius's speech on the *lex Oppia*, as discussed above. Such episodic

---

69. Preserved in Pliny *HN* 34.34, put in the mouth of Metrodoros of Skepsis—a Greek.

70. Cf. Flaminius's letter to the Thessalian Chyretienses in the 190s, that the Romans never wished to take action for the sake of gain: τελέως ἐν οὐθενὶ φιλαργυρῆσαι βεβουλήμεθα (*RDGE* 33.1.12 = *SIG*.3.593 line 12). See Harris 1979: 57 and Dench 1995: 69.

71. Gruen 2004: 30–46; Badian 1968: 16–29 and 76–92; and Rich 1993: 38–68 provide a good analysis of Harris's recent argument that Roman expansion was driven by a hunger for glory and economic gain. See Harris (1971) 2004 for a reassertion of his influential argument, including a note on nonaristocratic attitudes toward expansion.

72. Polybius 1.11.2 with Walbank's 1957 commentary *ad* 1.11.1–15, and cf. 1.20.1, in which the senate, delighted at their victory, presses their advantage further. See also Forsythe 1994: 153–54 with note 117.

73. Walbank 1957 *ad* 1.11.

74. Polybius 2.29.8 with Walbank 1957 *ad loc*. For Fabius's involvement in that battle see Orosius 4.13.6.

rapaciousness on the part of the Roman people is balanced in Pictor's history by chronic Carthaginian greed, particularly within the Barcid family that brought forth Hannibal. Polybius's famous criticism of Pictor's analysis of the causes of the Second Punic War bears witness to this: Pictor, says Polybius, blames the war on Hasdrubal's love of power and his greed: πλεονεξίαν καὶ φιλαρχίαν (3.8.1).[75]

Earlier in this chapter I examined Tarpeia's greed as a personal failing that renders problematic her membership in the Roman community. Greed also has a broader dimension in ancient literature as a medium through which to consider both personal and collective acquisitiveness and their effects on forms of government, imperialism, and social harmony.[76] In visiting greed's various forms, Pictor not only contributes to that tradition but also taps into Greek modes of articulating the dynamics of a powerful state made up of powerful individuals. Tarpeia's story similarly engages the complexities of greed and its relationship to state and empire. The difficulty of assigning a moral to her story in Pictor's version lies exactly in these complexities. For example, to what extent does it matter to an external audience that Tarpeia is female, and a member of the elite class? Pictor's version hedges: her identity as an elite casts some blame on Rome's decision makers, but her gender distances her and her action from those in power. Moreover, to what extent is Tarpeia responsible for her greed, to what extent the adorned Sabines? It is relevant to note here that Tarpeia did not meet Sabine gold abroad, but at the very heart of her city; the Sabines were the aggressors, not the Romans. Further, given the fact that Tarpeia's action resulted in the assimilation of Sabines into the Roman state, one could say that her desire for gold, like that of the Romans at Telemon who coveted Gallic gold, had a similarly positive result. The paradox of Tarpeia's deed as a *felix culpa* lies at the heart of several treatments of Tarpeia's myth, from Dumézil's 1947 identification of her as an Indo-European figure of fecundity to Martini's 1998 examination of her as a parable of Sabine

---

75. The words are Polybius's; they are not in the extended quotation from Pictor that he here offers, though we cannot know if Fabius used them. Polybius's criticism is that Pictor's emphasis on Carthage's disavowal of Barcid greed rings counter to reason; had the Carthaginians in general opposed the rapacious policy they would have recalled its proponents. Walbank 1957 *ad* 3.8.1–9.5 attributes Fabius's error (for he believes it is an error) to the annalist's reliance on anti-Barcid sources emerging from Carthage at Hannibal's expulsion. Such propaganda "would be useful propaganda in Greece, where, otherwise the Roman policy towards him in 195 might have been regarded as rancorous."

76. Balot 2001: 22–57, and 67–68 on this concept in Aristotle's *Politics* and Homer's *Iliad* and *Odyssey*.

synoikism, the incorporation of Sabines into the Roman state.[77] Another facet of the "beneficial Tarpeia" possibility is latent in the Pictor fragment discussed above that identifies the Sabine conquest as the moment when Rome first "became aware of wealth." The fragment is morally neutral and makes us wonder whether that awareness was considered to be a moment of cultural progress or moral decline. Finally, is her desire for material rewards more or less important than her *fides*?[78] Tarpeia's greed is a rich medium through which Pictor could, in front of a Greek audience, explore the tension between empire's causes and its results.

THREADS IN THE TAPESTRY

To see just how implicated Tarpeia is in the contemporary language of cultural self-definition in Italy and beyond, I would like to trace four threads in this tapestry that add nuance to Tarpeia's story, all of which start with Tarentum, a prosperous Spartan colony at Italy's southernmost tip, and end in Rome via the themes of Tarpeia's story. The first involves Tarentum's reputation among outsiders. While there is some evidence of a positive reputation for Tarentum because of its mixed and stable democracy, the general picture that emerges from the literary sources is that Tarentine prosperity had given way to the bad sort of luxury and profligacy.[79] These excesses led to hubris, which in turn invited Tarentum's downfall. Clearchus of Soli, for example, notes that the Tarentines, drawn into arrogance because of their luxury, were induced to attack the Iapygians in 473 BCE, to whom they lost. Polybius, surely reading earlier sources, echoes this sentiment in the context of the Tarentine war. For him, Tarentine luxury (εὐδαιμονίας) led to arrogance (ὑπερήφανον), which led to the need to call in Pyrrhus (8.24). This Tarentine vicious cycle (luxury → overreaching → loss of autonomy) seems replayed in Tarpeia's story, with the Sabines playing the part of the wealthy people whose overreaching (attacking Rome) leads, inevitably and justifiably, to their eventual subjugation. The Sabines' luxury provides the Sabines' own undoing. Enter Rome.

The second thread involves how the Tarentines answered their reputation as luxurious: they denied it. Tarentum's embrace of Pythagoreanism

---

77. Dumézil 1947: 249–50; Martini 1998: 33–34.

78. Freyburger 1986 makes the sustained case for *fides* as the perhaps most important of all Roman values.

79. See Aristotle *Pol.* 6.3.5, 1320b for praise of the democracy, and Athenaeus 12.522d–f for lament of the decline (a lament he attributes to Clearchus). See the thorough discussion in Barnes 2005: 21–29, esp. 27–29.

broadcasts a tendency toward the simple life, and Tarentum was home to both Archytas and his biographer Aristoxenus. Two relevant patterns emerge from the evidence. First, the literary tradition surrounding south Italian Pythagoreans suggests that the Tarentines "exported" Pythagoreanism to non-Greek communities in southern Italy as an arm of diplomacy. Cicero, for example, preserves memory of a dialogue about virtue and temperance between Archytas and the Samnite Pontius Herennius in which Herennius comes off as enlightened (*de Senec.* 39–41), and Aristoxenus discusses Pythagoras's influence all over Italy.[80] Second, epigraphic evidence reveals that communities all over southern Italy, but Tarentum in particular, prided themselves on the virtue and chastity of their unadorned women.[81] In this they followed the injunctions of Pythagoras himself, in his discourse to women on proper Pythagorean behavior:

ἀναγκαῖα δὲ μὴ ἡγεέσθω εὐγενηίην καὶ πλοῦτον καὶ μεγάλης πόλιος πάντως γενέσθαι καὶ δόξαν καὶ φιλίην ἐνδόξων καὶ βασιληίων ἀνδρῶν· ἢν μὲν γὰρ ἔῃ, οὐ λυπέει· ἢν δὲ μὴ ἔῃ, ἐπιζητέειν οὐ ποιέει· τούτων γὰρ δίχα φρονίμη γυνὴ ζῆν οὐ κωλύεται. κἢν ἔῃ δὲ ταῦτα ἅπερ λελάχαται, τὰ μεγάλα καὶ θαυμαζόμενα μή ποτε διζέσθω ψυχή, ἀλλὰ καὶ ἄπωθεν αὐτῶν βαδιζέτω· βλάπτει γὰρ μᾶλλον ἐς ἀτυχίην ἕλκοντα ἢ ὠφελέει. τούτοισι γὰρ ἐπιβουλή τε καὶ φθόνος καὶ βασκανίη προσκέεται, ὥστε ἐν ἀταραξίῃ οὐκ ἂν γένοιτο ἡ τοιήδε.
(Thesleff 1965: 143, 28ff.)

But let her not think that noble birth, and wealth, and being from a great city are necessary things, and reputation and the friendship of respected and regal men. If these things happen to be true it doesn't hurt, but if they aren't, it doesn't accomplish anything to seek after them. Absent these things, the wise woman is not hindered from living, and if she should be such a woman as is grasping, let her soul not seek out great and wonderful things. For these harm more than they help, dragging one into misfortune. Plots and envy and malice cling to them, such that a woman like this would not be in a state of serenity.

Pythagoras here spells out the linkage between wealth and greed. Wealth in itself is not an evil (ἢν μὲν γὰρ ἔῃ οὐ λυπέει), but desire for it is, for two reasons: the fruitlessness of that desire, and, more importantly, the psychological toxins that accompany it. These toxins not only infect

---

80. See Dench 1995: 58–61 for these stories and others.
81. For female virtue in Pythagoreanism, see Thesleff 1965: 151–54 and Dench 1998: 134n37.

the greedy woman; they infect her household as well, and woman's primacy within the household might be the reason Pythagoras gave her extra behavioral injunctions.[82] The public advertisement on stone of women's modesty in Tarentum and elsewhere, especially in light of the privacy and containment normally required by Pythagorean ethics, suggests that a healthy home had social value (particularly, perhaps, in Tarentum, which had to counter its reputation for luxury). Ironically, then, publicly displayed lack of concern for status became a public mark of status. As we saw above, the emphasis on female modesty—particularly adornment—as a gauge of elite male self-control works in Tarpeia's myth through the girl's desire for golden baubles and her status as a member of the elite class. The Tarentine example shows that, well beyond Rome's walls, women and their adornment were avenues through which communities could express their own health. Tarentine Pythagoreanism thus also adds a new dimension to Rome's passage of the Oppian law; beyond the message it communicated to Rome's own elite and their rivals in nearby cities, the *lex Oppia* also aimed Rome's ruling class closer toward the advertised Pythagorean values of Italy's Greek south. Indeed the Romans had, during the Samnite wars, dedicated a statue of Pythagoras in their own Forum.[83] The threat posed by Sabine finery would resonate all the more among an audience attuned to the cultural value of unadorned women.[84] Even though she gives into the temptation for gold, Tarpeia's punishment indirectly confirms Pythagoreanism's tenets and subtly aligns the Romans with their powerful neighbors to the south.

The third thread involves the Tarentines' attempt to define other communities in their environment. When in the late fourth century BCE they faced war with Syracuse, a wealthy Corinthian colony whom they styled as decadent,[85] they secured and justified their "soft" use of Samnite mercenaries (already the move of a people softened by comfort) by claiming a kinship with the Samnites, an Oscan-speaking people from the central southern Apennines. The Samnites, the Tarentines

---

82. Lambropoulou 1995: 122–34, and esp. pp. 125 and 133–34.
83. Pliny *HN* 34.26.
84. Dench 1998: 137 locates this sort of advertisement-through-women in monumental painting as well; in fourth-century tomb paintings of Paestum, a Greek colony in Lucanian territory that fell to Rome after the Tarentine victory, women appear weaving wool and riding in mule carts (the *lex Oppia*'s restrictions about transportation come to mind here), whereas in Campania they tend to be depicted attending to their appearance or relaxing.
85. See, for example, Aristoxenus fr. 50 *apud* Athenaeus 12.545a, in which Archytas argues against the Syracusan Polyarchus about pleasure; Archytas warns against it, while Polyarchus defends it. For a discussion, see Dench 1995: 58 with notes.

claimed, were (like the Sabines) descended from the rugged Spartans.[86] The poverty of the (Spartan) Samnites stands against other images of them as wealthy and refined. For example, Livy describes them as wearing golden and silver armor over chain mail, with complementary clothing underneath (9.40 and cf. 10.39). The Samnites indeed appear on contemporary vase paintings wearing patterned clothing into battle.[87] Golden Samnite armor leads to a famous Roman story about them as the "luxurious other" that threatens to undermine Roman values. Like the golden Sabines, they resort to bribery, offering to buy off the Roman commander M.' Curius Dentatus, who rebukes them.[88] Dentatus is Tarpeia's alter ego in a number of ways. Most broadly and importantly, he resists the temptation to take gold and thus advertises Roman austerity in the face of foreign luxury, while she submits. Also, in her story, Rome is the defender against the foreign aggressors, while in his story Rome is already the victor; her story thus meditates on greed as a cause of military action, while his meditates on greed as a potential result. Dentatus's pithy comment that he prefers to rule the wealthy rather than to be wealthy draws a neat boundary between imperialism and materialism. It is also noteworthy that he is male, while Tarpeia is female. Her weakness and her femininity explain each other, as do his self-control and his masculinity. It is worth mentioning also that this same Dentatus would conquer the Sabines in 290 BCE (indeed, they are sometimes named as his resisted bribers), and that the Sabines would later be equated with the Samnites, both as noble offspring of Sparta.[89] The proliferation of alternatives—austerity or wealth? Samnites or Sabines? Dentatus or Tarpeia?—reveals both the list of key ingredients used in cultural identity formation (behavior, ethnicity, gender) and the dynamic nature of that identity in third-century Italy. Two of the three key ingredients—ethnicity and gender—are biologically determined.[90] Behavior is not necessarily so. Thus Plautus's *Aetolians* can be oath-keepers, showing themselves worthy of being in the fold; on the flip side, luxury, for better or worse,

---

86. Strabo 5.4.12. See also Dench's discussion at 1995: 53–61, 63, and 184.

87. See also Dench 1995: 100. For a catalogue of Campanian vases depicting Samnite warriors, see Schneider-Herrmann's (1996) chapter on the image of the Samnite warrior (pp. 3–76 with corresponding plates), and in particular pp. 4–15 for a survey of Samnite tunics.

88. Valerius Maximus 4.3.5, and cf. Ennius *Ann.* 209 Skutsch 456 and Pliny *HN* 19.87. Samnite bribery also appears in a contemporary account preserved by Dionysius 15.5ff., when the Samnites bribed Neapolitan council members to let the assembly decide whether Naples would ally itself with Samnium or Rome. See Dench 1995: 102.

89. Dench 1995: 56–58; Dionysius 2.49.5.

90. Hall 2002: 9–19 on ethnicity as a relationship of kinship, not simply of shared identity.

is also contagious.⁹¹ As a woman Tarpeia perhaps couldn't resist the allure of gold like her male counterpart Dentatus could, but she is still able to keep her bargain. The pair of stories locates women's weakness rather precisely in the behavioral spectrum; her danger comes from her inability to resist finery, not her inability to keep her word.

The fourth thread takes us inside Tarentum during the Second Punic War. In 209 BCE Q. Fabius Maximus was besieging Tarentum, then under Hannibal's control, when a curious incident turned the tide of the siege. A Tarentine girl, beloved by the Bruttian commander whom Hannibal had left in charge of the walls, engaged in a complicated plot with her brother, a soldier under Fabius Maximus, to induce the Bruttian to turn coat against Hannibal and betray the gates so that the Romans could enter and regain the city. The story is told most elaborately by Livy and also appears with minor variations in Plutarch's *Life of Fabius*, Appian's *Hannibal*, and perhaps Polybius's *Histories*.⁹² Their source remains unknown, but the favorable picture the anecdote paints of Roman rule (Tarentines and Bruttians are fine with it), and especially of the daring and clever Quintus Fabius Maximus Verrucosus Cunctator ("The Delayer" who exploits the girl's position and designs the stratagem) suggests strongly that the source was pro-Roman. Q. Fabius Pictor, the Delayer's cousin and Rome's first historian, is a likely candidate.⁹³

The Tarentine girl's story is a dense encapsulation of the complicated and shifting allegiances that pertained during the war with Hannibal. The Tarentines were Rome's ally before the war, then defected in 216 BCE to neutral status, then fell to Hannibal in 212 BCE before they were retaken by the Romans in 209 BCE. The alliances and enmities are further complicated in that they are not merely bilateral; here, Romans and Carthaginians, Tarentines and Bruttians all take part in the elaborate dance of belonging and control. Attendant to this complexity is the assumption of an already pluralistic Roman identity; not only is the girl's Tarentine brother serving Fabius Maximus's army even though she and other Tarentines remain under Hannibal's control, but the relationship between the girl and the Bruttian commander is never questioned as impossible or even

---

91. Nenci 1984: 1026.

92. Livy 27.15.4–16, Appian *Hann.* 49; Plutarch *Fab.* 21; Zonaras 9.8; Polyaenus 8.14.3; and Polybius fr. 70; see Walbank 1957 *ad loc.* for a discussion of the difficulties of assigning the fragment to the episode in question.

93. Frier (1979) 1999: 240–46 argues for a relatively early date of composition for Pictor's *Annales*, during the cautious optimism that followed the successes in southern Italy in the late teens. Others argue for a date after the end of the war (Vishnia 1996: 11–12).

odd. On the contrary; in Livy's account she brags to her brother about her familiarity with a rich and respected man (*de nova consuetudine advenae locupletis atque inter populares tam honorati*, 27.15.10). An elaboration of this position appears in Plutarch's narrative, through the voice of the girl's brother (the Tarentine serving under Rome's eagle). The brother's ulterior motive (cementing the relationship and so the treason) does not obscure the commentary on Romanness:

> εἰ γὰρ εὐδόκιμός τίς, ὥς φασιν, ἀρετῇ καὶ λαμπρός, ἐλάχιστα φροντίζει γένους ὁ πάντα συμμιγνὺς πόλεμος· αἰσχρὸν δὲ μετ' ἀνάγκης οὐδέν, ἀλλ' εὐτυχία τίς ἐν καιρῷ τὸ δίκαιον ἀσθενὲς ἔχοντι πρᾳοτάτῳ χρήσασθαι τῷ βιαζομένῳ. (*Fabius* 21.2)

> "If someone is well-respected, as they say, and eminent in virtue, war—that mingler of all things—doesn't care a whit what country he's from. Nothing is shameful in necessity. Rather it is a blessing, in a time when right is weak, for the one in power to behave gently."

The story of the Tarentine girl, however passing an episode it might have been, gives a complicated picture of identity as permeable—both positively and negatively—at sites of loyalty, conquest, and intermarriage. But whereas the nobility of the Bruttian commander makes marriage with him possible—even desirable—for the Tarentine girl, no such alliance is yet possible with Pictor's Tarpeia and her Sabine tempters. Only when Italy had been redefined as *tota Italia*; when Sabinity, and for that matter Romanness, were no longer contested in the Italian peninsula; and when opportunities to control the meaning of Rome's past were available to fewer and fewer men, would Tarpeia be able to fall in love with her Sabine challenger.

CHAPTER THREE

TARPEIA IN SILVER
THE DENARII OF THE SOCIAL WAR

IN 89 BCE Lucius Titurius Sabinus, as *triumvir monetalis,* issued a silver denarius depicting Tarpeia's punishment (fig. 1). The obverse shows the profile portrait of King Tatius, the Sabine beneficiary of Tarpeia's treachery. Near his chin is a laurel branch, and above his head is the mark "APV," for *argento publico,* "made from the public treasury." In back of his head is the legend "*Sabin.*" On the reverse is Tarpeia with arms outstretched, buried up to her waist in shields, while two soldiers, one on each side, thrust their shields toward her. She is frontal, and a crescent moon and star appear above the scene. The moneyer's name Lucius Tituri sits *in exergue,* that is, below the image around the curve. That same year Titurius Sabinus's coinage included two other denarii: the same Tatius obverse but with a reverse of Victory driving the two-horsed *biga* chariot and Titurius's name just under the *bigae* (fig. 2), and a Sabine Women denarius: same obverse, but the reverse shows two men each holding a woman aloft, again with the name "L. Tituri" *in exergue* (fig. 3). At that time Titurius also minted two bronze coins: an *as* with Janus on the obverse and a prow and his name on the reverse, and a *semis* with Saturn on the obverse and the same reverse as the *as*.[1]

---

1. Crawford *RRC* 344.1–7. See also Babelon *Monnaies* 2.167.1–4 and Grueber *BMCRR* 1.2322–66, pp. 297–300.

FIGURE 1. Denarius of L. Titurius Sabinus, 89 BCE. Tatius / Death of Tarpeia. Photo courtesy of the American Numismatic Society.

FIGURE 2. Denarius of L. Titurius Sabinus, 89 BCE. Tatius/*Bigae*. Photo courtesy of the American Numismatic Society.

FIGURE 3. Denarius of L. Titurius Sabinus, 89 BCE. Tatius / Rape of the Sabine Women. Photo courtesy of the American Numismatic Society.

This is the first overt, selective partnering of Tarpeia with the Sabine women.[2] Certainly they appear together in Rome's earliest annalistic histories (Fabius Pictor; *FRH* Pictor F7; Cincius Alimentus *FRH* Cincius F3) as part of the Romulus cycle. Because of the fragmentary nature of these sources the correspondence between the stories is difficult to assess, but one presumes they sit together in those accounts by reason of historical contiguity, and they are not presumably to be distinguished as a pair from other Romulean episodes. The tales would appear together in later narrative histories such as Livy's, Dionysius's, and Plutarch's, but again as part of a larger narrative complex. There is plenty of evidence for the independent treatment and use of these two stories: Tarpeia's tomb, the rock named for her, her annual worship, Propertius's and Simylus's elegies, and Valerius Maximus all sever Tarpeia more or less from the Romulean cycle and treat Tarpeia independently, whereas Ennius's play *Sabinae,* the names of the thirty voting curiae—according to tradition taken from the raped women's names (Cicero *de Rep.* 2.14)—and the narrative at Ovid's *Ars Amatoria* 1.101–34 focus on the Sabine women as a stand-alone story. Interestingly, the only other instance of a selected coupling of the two stories, isolated from the rest of the Romulus cycle, is in another pair of coins, minted in 19 BCE and to be discussed later.

---

2. The set is die-linked (same obverse die used with different reverses).

The Basilica Aemilia relief, also to be discussed later, combines Tarpeia and the Sabine women in a larger mythological context that is difficult to pin down.³ Since the image on Titurius's coin, the later coin, and the Basilica Aemilia relief all show the same scene—the moment of Tarpeia's death—it is tempting to suggest, as does Toynbee, that the frieze copied the design on the coin,⁴ or indeed that both frieze and coin followed a yet earlier image, some monument or representation of Tarpeia's death. If this is so (and there is no way to prove or disprove it), the fact remains that here on Titurius's coins, the images of Tarpeia and of the Sabine women are paired and isolated from the historical context of their activity for the first time, and are linked with an additional image—victory, via the third denarius of Titurius Sabinus.

There is something about the currency of coins that activates this cooperation between Tarpeia and her numismatic partners, the Sabine rape and the victory chariot. By currency I mean the literal running about, the portability and exchangeability of coins. Coins pass through many hands, literate and not, Roman and not. For this reason, the archaeological context for the coins is paramount. Titurius's coinage was found in hoards all over Italy from the Social War period, from Liguria to the Marche to Campania.⁵ Slight variations within the types and control marks for Titurius's issue reveal that this set of coins was minted frequently and for wide distribution, perhaps to pay soldiers during the Social War.⁶ Because of this currency, the coins must speak quickly and simply, impressionistically. Without the scaffolding of narrative context the images are distilled to totemic moments in the story that somehow convey broader themes, even to an audience only lightly acquainted with the stories, in the same way that clasped hands indicate concord or a dagger bespeaks tyrannicide.⁷ In the case of Titurius's issue, those totemic moments are Tarpeia's

---

3. The Basilica frieze includes identifiable scenes from Romulus's ascension and reign and religious and civic scenes that seem to have no particular historical context. See chapter 4 for a discussion of Tarpeia on the frieze.

4. Toynbee 1956: 223.

5. Lockyear 2013 is the most thorough research tool for the Republican hoards and allows data searches in a variety of criteria. Crawford 1969: table XII and pp. 92–93. Some hoards have Titurius's coinage as their last included issue, and so most clearly locate immediate circulation of the coins. These hoards are at Luni and Fiesole. Interestingly, hoards with closing dates within eight years of Titurius's coinage were also found in Greece, Portugal, and Romania. See Elkins 2009: 42–43 for an impassioned plea to consider archaeological context of coins.

6. Crawford 1974: 75–77. Crawford posits as many as 251 dies for the obverse of the Tarpeia coin and 279 for the reverse.

7. For coins as semantic vehicles that convey broad ideas and themes with single details, see Elkins 2009: 39–41.

death, the rape of the Sabines, and the victory chariot, which was already a very common coin type.

This chapter focuses on ethnicity as the distillate to which these stories are reduced. The coins trigger the concept in multiple ways. The legend "Sabin" on the obverses, the bearded portrait of the first Sabine king Tatius, the name of the moneyer "L. Tituri" on the reverses (whose *cognomen* was "Sabinus" and whose *gentilicium* "Titurius" also evokes the Sabine king), the iconic stories from the Sabine cycle all bring Sabinity to mind—especially Sabinity as it relates to Romanness. The images further bring the notion of gender to bear on ethnicity. Tarpeia and the Sabine women are the first known nonmythical women to appear on Roman coins.[8] Historical (or considered historical) mortal women on Titurius Sabinus's coins explore how ethnicity functions in real time and with real people.

In this chapter I argue that ethnicity was a fluid and contentious concept in Titurius's time. This is hardly surprising in itself; the coins were minted during the Social War between Italy and her former allies who were demanding full citizenship rights or independence. The Gracchan brothers in the 130s and 120s BCE had sparked tensions in Italy with their controversial legislative programs of land redistribution and citizenship extension. Marius's settlement of veterans on confiscated land added fuel to the fire of Italian resentment of Roman privilege. Drusus's proposed citizenship law in 90 BCE detonated the Italian rebellion, and the politics of the early 80s were a delicate game of increasing personal authority, demagogic policies, attempted reconciliations and concessions, and *novi homines,* new men from unproven families, entering the political class by gaining positions along the *cursus honorum.* What does it mean for Titurius to boast of a personal Sabine heritage within this climate? Why two different images of assimilation, one resulting in intermarriage and the other emphasizing the resolute separateness of the people involved? How could the distilled images of the coins speak to spenders, be they Roman or Sabine (with all the polyvalence operative in those categories) in the city or in the (rebellious or loyal) countryside?

Even among rebellious states, motives for fighting Rome surely differed. Some people wanted full access to the benefits of citizenship; others wanted the legal protections citizenship would offer them; still others might have been lured into the war by the rallying cry for independence. In 1965 Peter Brunt painted a complex picture of the diversity of opinion among the rebels—especially given the differing sentiments in 120 and

---

8. Severy 2003: 28; Cocchi 2004: 47.

90 BCE.[9] Brunt's analysis, however, concerns the *principes* rather than the lower classes, who "would for the most part be ready to follow the lead they (sc. *principes*) gave" (p. 92). In a recent article entitled "*The First Italia*," Mark Pobjoy has made a convincing case that the rebels' alleged desire for citizenship is a byproduct of the bias of the Roman sources for the war.[10] Rather, he argues, independence was their goal, and the name the rebels adopted for their federation, *Italia*, markets it as such to a Greek audience. As Pobjoy notes, however, "there is no way of telling whether the rebels intended *Italia* to provide the foundation for a more lasting political structure in the event of winning the war" (p. 205). I find it difficult to see unanimity of purpose in any war effort, even when (as is not the case for the Italian rebels) there is an expressed single aim for fighting. In the absence of a clear "exit strategy," the Italian aims become even more difficult to pin down. There was not one "non-Roman" response to Rome, not even one Paelignian or Samnite or Oscan or Campanian or even Sabine response. How, in this particular context, does the third of Titurius's set, the familiar victory denarius, fit in?

These coins offered their holders images and symbols through which to explore what ethnic or regional identity was, and how that identity should interface with the identity marker "Rome." Williamson, in a 2005 volume dedicated to *Coinage and Identity in the Roman Provinces*, usefully defines identity as "concepts of belonging" within a series of overlapping domains which are always contextual and historically contingent, even though they do not feel contingent to the individuals who negotiate them. Williamson notes the difficulties in identifying differing perspectives in a system with a clear center such as Rome, in which expansion is "described variously as conquest (legions with swords), cultural assimilation (governors with big ideas), or elite self-acculturation (local elites keen to follow Rome's cultural and political elite)" (p. 21.) As Williamson concludes for local, imperial coinage, I believe that Titurius's Social War coins can illustrate much about the interaction of "concepts of belonging" and about authorized ways of expressing difference within a larger, homogenizing identity. In particular, I explore the coins' proposition of various ways of becoming Roman: through subjugation, through intermarriage and children (the melting pot model), and through side-by-side assimilation (the mosaic model). These questions are of the greatest importance if we are to understand responses to Roman expansion, and

---

9. Brunt 1965. See also Gabba (1973) 1976 and (1994) 2008.
10. Pobjoy 2000; and see Hexter 1992 for a contemporary Roman expression of the sentiment "of course non-Romans want to become Roman."

if we are to seek in history ways of thinking about our own world, in which ethnic identities butt heads with other forms of self-identification in often violent ways.

THE COINS AND THEIR MINTER

Little is known about the minter Lucius Titurius Sabinus other than what may be gleaned from the coins themselves.[11] Foremost, he is or presents himself to be Sabine. The *cognomen* "Sabinus" on the obverse of the coins is the clearest marker,[12] but the images from Sabine-Roman history add to the depth of the evocation, as does the *gentilicium* Titurius, for Tatius is said to have given his name to the tribe Tities (Varro *de Lingua Latina* 5.55; Livy 1.13.8). There is nothing to link this moneyer to a Sabine heritage outside of the coins.[13] Two younger relatives bear the *cognomen*. An inscription mentions a Titurius Sabinus, perhaps a son or younger relative of the moneyer (*CIL* 6.67988 = Dessau 8302),[14] and one Q. Titurius Sabinus appears frequently in Caesar's *Bellum Gallicum* as one of his legates who was killed in battle (and cf. Sallust. *Hist.* fr.2.94). But inscriptions that might relate to the family have been found in Aquileia, Ateste, and Brundisium—not one of which is in Sabine territory (Evans 1992: 125).

The coins are our only evidence for Titurius's ethnic affiliation. Farney traces the prevalence of Sabine ethnic markers appearing on coins of the time.[15] Wiseman identifies most of these ethnic identities, including Titurius, as spurious—the families weren't Sabine at all (1971: 258). They simply claimed Sabinity in order to reap the benefits of the identification. Cicero calls one such candidate on the ruse; in a letter to C. Trebonius, Cicero ridicules a candidate who spuriously adopted the *cognomen* as a strategy for success (*ad Fam.* 15.20.1). Sabinity clearly added value to the

---

11. *MRR* 2:454.

12. It is common enough for the *praenomen* and *nomen* to appear on one side and the *cognomen* on the other; see, e.g., *RRC* 214–16.

13. Lily Ross Taylor (1960: 260) goes furthest in pinpointing the Sabinity of Titurius, assigning him to the Sergia tribe since she assumes him to be from the same hometown as Tatius (Cures). It is tempting but impossible to locate Titurius that precisely. See Forsythe 1990: 297 with note 17.

14. The tablet includes two unconnected inscriptions; the stone seems to have been reused. Regarding Titurius: *hoc monimento L. Titurius Sabinus se vivo donavit L. Salvio Symphoro mancu / pavitque sestertio nummo uno* (Lucius Titurius Sabinus, while living, bestowed this monument to Salvius Symphorus, and he surrendered it to him for one sestertius).

15. Thirteen out of 43 issues that refer to the ethnicity of the moneyer refer to Sabinity. See Farney 2007: 82.

new man seeking to establish himself among the elite ranks of the ruling class.[16] One obvious pathway to respectability is Sabine antiquity: a *novus homo* could co-opt for himself a presence and cooperation in Rome's distant past. The antiquity of the images on Titurius's coins functions in this way, since they place the moneyer alongside one of Rome's first kings (and early gods, if you count the bronze issues). Gruen lists the Titurii among the *novi homines* of the period.[17] The persistent use of the *cognomen* "Sabinus" asserts the claim of this ethnicity for this family, which was participating in lower levels of the Roman *cursus* in the early years of the last Republican century. Whether the moneyer sought his office as a rung on his own incipient *cursus honorum,* or in order to circulate the family name in preparation for a relative standing for higher office, the appearance of establishment would help.[18]

In the case of the Sabines, mere antiquity worked together with the particulars of the Sabine past at Rome to offer a more targeted political message to Titurius's audience. Later in this chapter I discuss the Sabine integration, and Tarpeia's participation in it, as a broader message for Italy beyond Rome; for now I would like simply to draw attention to how the images on these coins might further Titurius's own political agenda with the Roman electorate. Tatius was one of two kings, established on the throne alongside Romulus in the first great political compromise of Rome, one which, whenever it was imagined, may be understood as a precursor to or doppelganger for the double consulship, that institution of checks and balances.[19] Because of this imagery, and the focus on a period of Sabine-Roman integration, Rowland has seen Titurius as a partisan of Cinna, the erstwhile compromiser between Sullan antipathy and Marian openness to the Italian cause. Treading lightly between the two extremes (at first at least), Cinna was seen as a champion of equestrian order and of new men,

---

16. Dench 1995: 85–94 and 2005b: 25–27, 172–73. The 1995 selection explores the particular value of the noble Sabine; the 2005 book discusses the tension the newcomer places on an open society, which then has to find more subtle ways of restricting access to power, lest chaos reign: "What we do not see here is any unchallenged belief in the benefits of an open society and a plural society, but a complicated set of questions about who is who, with varying emphasis on kinship and cultural affinity" (p. 25).

17. Gruen (1974) 1995: 115.

18. Cocchi 2004: 48–49; Wiseman 1971: 148–49; both connecting the passage of the *lex Gabinia* of 139 BCE, which made elections private, with the appearance of names and family images on coins as a form of propaganda. New men would benefit most from both developments.

19. Mommsen 1886: is a champion of this view. It is generally agreed that Rome's narratives of its early monarchy are at best contaminated with the views and needs of its later (Republican) political order, but see Smith 2011 for ways to recover some historical truth from tales of Rome's legendary kings without necessarily embracing the idea of the seven monarchs *tout court*.

who rushed to him.²⁰ Even before flipping the coins over to see the reverses (which are examined below), Titurius's Sabine coins might thus advertise his ability to compromise.

In contrast to Titurius's coin we might note that coins of the Italian federation minted in this period name leaders of the resistance, if they name anyone at all other than the federation's name *Italia*.²¹ The appearance of minor magistrate Titurius's name on all his coins, even when minted and distributed around Italy, functions as a phenomenon of Roman coins, not simply of coins. Even during the war Titurius could campaign for the future; the Italians were careful to promote unity in the cause (*Italia*) and respect for their commanders (named on the coins). Their coins do not yet look toward inclusion in the Roman state; members of the Italian aristocracy needed to gain legitimate avenues for inclusion, such as citizenship, before they could attend to their reputation and name-recognition for elections.

SABINITY DEFINED: LUCIUS CALPURNIUS PISO FRUGI AND THE TARPEIA TRADITION

By Titurius's time Sabine heritage meant more than partnership and antiquity. When we last met the Sabines, in Fabius Pictor's history, they were luxurious at best and decadent and deceitful at worst. The second century BCE was kind to the Sabine image in Rome, for two key reasons: first and foremost was the development of an "anti-luxury" rhetoric in response to the influx of foreign wealth that Roman imperialism sparked. Second was the fortunate existence of two great rhetoricians, both Sabine, who rehabilitated the Sabine reputation from one of luxury to one of austerity by promoting the image of the rugged simple Sabine as a foil to the newly corrupt *nouveau riche* of Rome.²²

Cato the Elder did perhaps more than anyone else to rescue the Sabines from the dangerous reputation for luxury they had during the fourth and third centuries.²³ Born in Tusculum and raised on a Sabine farm, Cato

---

20. Rowland 1966.

21. Burnett 1998: 169. Italian coins do at times name the two Italian head generals, Q. Silo and C. Papius Mutilus. See, e.g., Sydenham 1952: 640–41. That the legends are often in Oscan also suggests that Italian coins do not aim to market to Romans, except to market the alternative they pose to Latinity.

22. The transformation of the Sabine reputation is treated with nuance and force in Dench 1995: 67–111 and 2005b: 61–69 (esp. 64–65) and Farney 2007: 78–124.

23. See especially Farney 2007: 105–11.

championed the cause of Sabine austerity and moral uprightness; indeed it is from Cato that the "Sabine = Spartan" lineage began to take hold. The second great Sabine champion in Rome was Lucius Calpurnius Piso Frugi, an illustrious scion of the plebeian *gens Calpurnia*. Piso claimed, for the Calpurnii and for many other Roman families, descent from king Numa himself.[24] This man wrote a Roman history that includes Tarpeia, so it is worth lingering for a time on the man, his background, and his depiction of the legend.

The *gens Calpurnia* seems to have come from the northern edge of Sabine territory, where it borders Etruria.[25] The earliest known Pisones held Roman administrative posts in that territory from the late 200s BCE.[26] By the mid-second century the Pisones had split into two branches, the Frugi and the Caesonini, both of which asserted themselves on the Roman political scene and both of which began at that time to assert their Sabinity.[27]

Lucius Calpurnius Piso Frugi was tribune of the plebs in 149 BCE, when he passed a law criminalizing provincial extortion, the *lex Calpurnia de pecuniis repetundis*. He was consul along with M. Scaevola in 133 BCE, the tumultuous year when Attalus III, king of Pergamum, died and bequeathed his wealthy holdings to Rome, and when Tiberius Gracchus as tribune of the plebs proposed a set of financial and political reforms that would weaken the aristocracy. Our Piso opposed the Gracchan reforms. He became censor in 120 BCE, just a year after Tiberius's brother Gracchus, who had also urged radical social and political reforms, was driven to suicide rather than be killed on the Senate's decree. Sometime after his censorship Piso wrote an annalistic history of Rome in seven or eight books, of which some fifty fragments remain. These are preserved mostly by historians, a fact which demonstrates that Piso was of interest primarily for his historical rather than his literary qualities. And he is of historical interest. Frugi's Tarpeia is radically different from the Fabian tradition that would become dominant. In the censor's version, preserved by Dionysius of Halicarnassus, Tarpeia is a patriot trying to give the Romans the upper hand by tricking the Sabines out of their shields:

---

24. Forsythe 1990: 297n14; Forsythe 1994: 203ff., 184–85. Cf. Plutarch *Numa* 21.2.

25. Forsythe 1990: 296 finds evidence in linguistic (the *-urn* root is typically Etruscan) and epigraphic evidence (inscriptions in Etruscan letters, mentioning the family). See also Holleman 1984 for an Etruscan identity for the Calpurnii, countered by Farney 2007: 127–29.

26. Forsythe 1990: 297.

27. Ibid. 297n14 remarks the claim to Sabinity, citing coins and literature. Descent from Numa: see Plutarch *Numa* 21 and Forsythe 1994: 184–85. See Farney 2007: 22–25 and 114–15 for the Sabinity of the Pisones.

ὡς δὲ Πείσων Λεύκιος ὁ τιμητικὸς ἱστορεῖ, καλοῦ πράγματος ἐπιθυμία γυμνοὺς τῶν σκεπαστηρίων ὅπλων παραδοῦναι τοῖς πολίταις τοὺς πολεμίους . . . Πείσων γὰρ ὁ τιμητικός, οὗ καὶ πρότερον ἐμνήσθην, ἄγγελόν φησιν ὑπὸ τῆς Ταρπείας ἀποσταλῆναι νύκτωρ ἐκ τοῦ χωρίου δηλώσοντα τῷ Ῥωμύλῳ τὰς γενομένας τῇ κόρῃ πρὸς τοὺς Σαβίνους ὁμολογίας, ὅτι μέλλοι τὰ σκεπαστήρια παρ' αὐτῶν αἰτεῖν ὅπλα διὰ τῆς κοινότητος τῶν ὁμολογιῶν παρακρουσαμένη, δύναμίν τε ἀξιώσοντα πέμπειν ἐπὶ τὸ φρούριον ἑτέραν νυκτός, ὡς αὐτῷ στρατηλάτῃ παραληψόμενον τοὺς πολεμίους γυμνοὺς τῶν ὅπλων. τὸν δὲ ἄγγελον αὐτομολήσαντα πρὸς τὸν ἡγεμόνα τῶν Σαβίνων κατήγορον γενέσθαι τῶν τῆς Ταρπείας βουλευμάτων . . . ἔπειτα πάλιν ὁ μὲν Πείσων φησὶ τῶν Σαβίνων τὸν χρυσὸν ἑτοίμων ὄντων διδόναι τῇ κόρῃ τὸν περὶ τοῖς ἀριστεροῖς βραχίοσι τὴν Τάρπειαν οὐ τὸν κόσμον ἀλλὰ τοὺς θυρεοὺς παρ' αὐτῶν αἰτεῖν. Τατίῳ δὲ θυμόν τε εἰσελθεῖν ἐπὶ τῇ ἐξαπάτῃ καὶ λογισμὸν τοῦ μὴ παραβῆναι τὰς ὁμολογίας. δόξαι δ' οὖν αὐτῷ δοῦναι μὲν τὰ ὅπλα, ὥσπερ ἡ παῖς ἠξίωσε, ποιῆσαι δ' ὅπως αὐτοῖς μηδὲν λαβοῦσα χρήσεται, καὶ αὐτίκα διατεινάμενον ὡς μάλιστα ἰσχύος εἶχε ῥῖψαι τὸν θυρεὸν κατὰ τῆς κόρης καὶ τοῖς ἄλλοις παρακελεύσασθαι ταὐτὸ ποιεῖν. οὕτω δὴ βαλλομένην πάντοθεν τὴν Τάρπειαν ὑπὸ πλήθους τε καὶ ἰσχύος τῶν πληγῶν πεσεῖν καὶ περισωρευθεῖσαν ὑπὸ τῶν θυρεῶν ἀποθανεῖν . . . ἔοικε δὲ τὰ μετὰ ταῦτα γενόμενα τὴν Πείσωνος ἀληθεστέραν ποιεῖν. τάφου τε γὰρ ἔνθα ἔπεσεν ἠξίωται τὸν ἱερώτατον τῆς πόλεως κατέχουσα λόφον, καὶ χοὰς αὐτῇ Ῥωμαῖοι καθ' ἕκαστον ἐνιαυτὸν ἐπιτελοῦσι (λέγω δὲ ἃ Πείσων γράφει), ὧν οὐδενὸς εἰκὸς αὐτήν, εἰ προδιδοῦσα τὴν πατρίδα τοῖς πολεμίοις ἀπέθανεν, οὔτε παρὰ τῶν προδοθέντων οὔτε παρὰ τῶν ἀποκτεινάντων τυχεῖν, ἀλλὰ καὶ εἴ τι λείψανον αὐτῆς ἦν τοῦ σώματος ἀνασκαφὲν ἔξω ῥιφῆναι σὺν χρόνῳ φόβου τε καὶ ἀποτροπῆς ἕνεκα τῶν μελλόντων τὰ ὅμοια δρᾶν. ἀλλ' ὑπὲρ μὲν τούτων κρινέτω τις ὡς βούλεται.[28] (Dionysius 2.38.3–2.40.3 = *FRH* Piso F7)

But as Lucius Piso the Censor writes, it was desire of doing a great deed: to hand over to her own countrymen the enemy forces, now stripped of their defensive weapons. . . . For Piso the Censor, whom I mentioned before, says that a messenger was sent out of the place by Tarpeia at night, who would disclose to Romulus the agreement that the girl had entered into regarding the Sabines, that she would demand their defensive arms, misleading Tatius through the indistinctness of

---

28. The text is Cornell's *FRH*; the translation is mine.

the agreement, and that she thought Romulus should send an additional squadron up to the guard-tower that night, so that he could receive the enemy with their leader, stripped of their weapons . . . but the messenger deserted to the commander of the Sabines and turned traitor on Tarpeia's plans. . . . Then again Piso says that, when the Sabines were ready to hand over to the girl the gold they wore on their left arms, Tarpeia requested from them not their adornment but their shields. But Tatius's bravado emerged at this ruse, and a strategy of not breaking the agreement. He decided to give her the weapons just as the child demanded, but to do this in such a way that she would not be able to benefit from them. Stretching out with all his might, he threw it at her as forcefully as possible and ordered the others to do the same. And so, being assaulted on all sides by the number and force of the blows, Tarpeia fell and died, buried under the shields. . . . It seems that the events that followed these render truer the assessment of Piso, for she was given the honor of a tomb where she fell, holding the most sacred peak of the city, and the Romans carry out libations to her every year. I am saying what Piso writes. But if she died while betraying her fatherland to the enemy, she would have received none of these honors, neither from those she betrayed nor those who killed her. On the contrary: if there had been any remains of her body, they would have been dug up and cast out over time, out of fear and also as a protective measure for any others who would do something similar.

But regarding these matters let each decide for himself as he thinks fit.

Dionysus's treatment of and preference for this version are discussed in a later chapter. Here I consider why Piso might wish to exonerate the treasonous girl. The traditional view is that Piso is a nationalizer and a rationalizer;[29] that is, he aims to solidify and elevate the idea of Rome, and to explain things in such a way as makes sense. Piso's Tarpeia narrative serves both these aims. It not only erases an embarrassing moral blunder from Rome's traditional aristocracy (the description Dionysius gives of Tarpeia as θυγάτηρ ἀνδρὸς ἐπιφανοῦς, "daughter of an eminent man" probably belongs to Pictor), but it makes sense out of the observable practice of her annual worship.

Yet the particular forms of Piso's changes in the story act beyond those aims. In Piso's version Tarpeia was not swayed by the allure of foreign

---

29. Poucet 1967: 248.

luxuries. Though the theme and thrust of Piso's fragmentary history is impossible to assess, his caution against luxury is visible in the remaining fragments and in the events of his life preserved in the historical record. Indeed it seems to have been one of the central planks of his political career. Recent events had given fuel to this fire. With the victories over Carthage and Greece, and the expansion of Roman hegemony to wealthy lands further out, Romans had opportunity for profit. A turning point was seen in the triumph celebrated in 187 BCE by C. Manlius Vulso over the Asians. In one fragment preserved by Pliny the Elder, Piso lists the luxuries Manlius imported at this triumph: brazen dining couches, sideboards, and pedestal tables (*triclinia aerata abacosque et monopoda*; Pliny the Elder *HN* 34.14 = Forsythe 1994 F44).

Like any contagion, it got worse from there. Another fragment also preserved by Pliny the Elder (*HN* 17.244 = *FRH* Piso F36) places the breaking point of Roman morality at 154 BCE, during the censorship of Cassius and Messala, in which the spontaneous growth of a fig tree on a sacred spot marked that chastity had been toppled (*pudicitiam . . . subversam*). Valerius Maximus preserves an anecdote in which our Piso was caught up in an opportunity for moral lapse and personal gain through victory in combat (4.3.10). His son had behaved admirably in battle in Sicily, and Piso awarded him a golden crown of three pounds weight—made not with gold taken from the treasury, mind you, but with gold taken from Piso Jr.'s own patrimony, "so that he would get the honor publicly from his commander, but the prize privately from his father" (*ut honorem publice a duce, pretium privatim a patre reciperet*). There would be no hint of illgotten gain among the Pisones. Piso Frugi would solidify his reputation as Censor in 120 BCE, and his monikers Frugi and Censorinus would stand as a marker of his upright morals.[30]

In this climate of war and gain Piso expressed his anti-luxury stance in his *lex de pecuniis repetundis* of 149 BCE. Cicero calls this law the first law against provincial extortion (*Brut.* 27.106; 2 *Verr.* 3.84.195, 4.25.56; *de Off.* 2.21.75). It was certainly not the last: the *quaestio de repetundis* would become one of the fiercest battlegrounds of the last generation of the Roman republic.[31] Piso's law set up a permanent jury of senators, under the *praetor peregrinus,* for trials against provincial governors. This law recognizes prior transgressions by governors abroad, and creates a legal forum for discussing luxury. In other words, it marks the codification of

---

30. Farney 2007: 115 with sources.
31. Gruen (1974) 1995.

avarice as a trope,[32] and as an accusation to be used against one's political opponents.

It is important for understanding Piso's version of the myth to recognize that luxury—and its bedmate, greed—were seen to have come to Rome from abroad. Luce, studying Livy's realization of this trope of foreign luxury, calls this the "senatorial version" of corruption at Rome, a version espoused in the second century by Piso, Polybius, and Cato.[33] The "senatorial version" is that greed is a contagion that came to Rome from without, and was linked therefore to cross-cultural contact. It is a learned vice that depends on cultural contact. In the second century Rome was rapidly becoming more diverse, and more like the Hellenistic Greek society it was conquering, a phenomenon that would be summed up in Horace's famous saying *Graecia capta ferum victorem cepit et artes intulit agresti Latio* ("Greece, when captured, captured its fierce captor and brought arts to rugged Latium," Hor. *Epist.* 2.1.156–57). Cross-ethnic contact was seen as a potential medium for moral contamination and a veritable hotbed for the growth of moral disease. In this context Piso writes about a Tarpeia who is not seduced by Sabine luxuries, if indeed there were any Sabine luxuries. The pristine time of Rome's forebears threatened no such contagion, and blood purity and moral purity remain intact after Tarpeia's unfortunate act.[34]

Her annual worship therefore need not be inconsistent with Piso's moral outlook and its interpretation of the past. What is more, if Tarpeia is not guilty of greed or treason but remains a loyal Roman, then Sabine Tatius is not guilty of anything either, not of breaking his pact or of disregarding the life of someone who had helped him—that is, not of the native treachery of his race that Pictor had exploited. Instead, he killed an enemy and took care not to break the sanctity of an oath.

Perhaps more important is the way Piso's version clears Tatius of carrying the contagion of luxury to Rome. In the previous chapter I noted the passage from Fabius Pictor, preserved by Strabo, saying that "Romans first perceived wealth from the Sabines" (Strabo 5.3.1 = *FRH* Pictor F24). Whether this fragment is to be placed in Pictor's Tarpeia episode or at the

---

32. For various interpretations of the aim of the law (anti-avarice, provincial protection, self-policing, etc.), see Richardson 1987; Rosenstein 2010: 375–76.

33. Luce 1977: 275–77. See also Dench 2005b: 89. This point is made by Freeble 2004: 84, who notes the contrast between the "corrupting outsider" notion and Sallust's belief that corruption sprang from within Roman hearts.

34. An interesting point of comparison is Piso's interest in the restraint of the first Roman king. Forsythe 1994 F13 is an anecdote about Romulus's modest drinking vis-à-vis other Romans, who overindulge. Piso elevates the Roman king.

moment of the Roman conquest of the Sabines in the early 200s BCE, it blames the Sabines equally. Not so in Piso's account. His Sabines are not the ones who introduced the contagion of wealth to Rome. Of course, Piso benefits more directly from a Tatius with scruples, and from an early moral high ground for Sabines and Romans.

BACK TO THE COIN

In the pro-Sabine climate that evolved in the second century, the Sabines of Titurius's day could enjoy the benefits of the stereotype of them, whole cloth, as upright, frugal, sober, and disciplined people, immune by birth and habit to corruption or personal indulgence, and, to boot, apt to improve moral health by contagion as had their forebears the Sabine censors of the prior century.[35] It is small wonder that so many families, the Titurii included, sought to advertise Sabinity for themselves in the late Republic.

To return to the coins, Titurius's chosen imagery taps into the stereotype in interesting ways. Tatius is rugged looking, with strong features (straight nose especially) and a robust, curly, chunky beard. Tatius's portrait is, as Bieber 1973 describes it, "expressionistic and geometric," reflective of the Italic style—not as refined (e.g., Hellenistic, classicizing) as numismatic portraiture would become later in the first century.[36] Unruly hair is one visual and verbal indicator of old-fashioned ruggedness—of Italian vigor rather than Roman urbanity, of martial valor rather than political savvy, and of honesty rather than polish. Art, including coinage, was very much a site in which various ways of being a good Roman were contested, and which values constituted (or should constitute) being Roman. The chunky beard could even, in these 90s and 80s, point to a Marian ideology in as much as Marius styled himself a rugged champion

---

35. The faux-Sabine of Cicero's letter had a modest-enough face and constant-enough speech, which seemed to have a certain something of the character of the Cures (*ad Fam.* 15.20.1, *etsi modestus eius vultus sermoque constans habere quiddam a Curibus videbatur*).

36. Bianchi Bandinelli (1970 and 1971) assigns the dichotomy rugged/polished to two competing and early modes of representation, the (common, local) plebeian and the (elite, philhellenic) patrician; the former's usefulness for newcomers ensured its continued presence. See also Brilliant 1973 and the contextualization for Bianchi Bandinelli's work within numismatics by Elkins 2009: 35–43. The idea of plebeian art has been nuanced, rather than entirely challenged, by the essays in De Angelis, Dickmann, Pirson, and von den Hoff 2012; Holscher's contribution is particularly constructive. In any case, I see rugged Tatius as a marker for Sabinity rather than for plebeian status.

of the Italians.³⁷ Love poets would later adopt the image of the rough and rugged forebears as a foil to their own Hellenistic polish.³⁸ Rough Tatius was literally and figuratively muscling into a position of Roman authority. Titurius's amply bearded Tatius situated him politically, morally, and ethnically with the noble savages outside Rome—and yet, or perhaps therefore, he had made it in Rome, too, with a minor but influential post as *triumvir monetalis*.

THE COINS AND THEIR USERS

However the Tarpeia coin positions Titurius in the context of other Romans, as a man with a solid, recognizable, and respectable past to facilitate his new entry into Rome's circles of power and influence, its circulation all over Italy suggests a message beyond one directed solely to Rome's electorate. Scholars have focused on the ethnic images on the coin, and its partner the Sabine women coin, with an eye for what it might have conveyed to a broader Italian audience during the Social War.

Opinions range the gamut. On one extreme is the "pro-Roman" coin idea expressed by Evans (1992: 125): "Titurius' type would serve to remind the allies in revolt that just as the earlier traitor to Rome had been severely punished, so would modern-day traitors. But it also would remind the Roman people that the city had suffered through occasional military defeats earlier in its history (even to the point that the population was besieged on the Capitoline Hill), yet the Sabine king had been defeated by divine intervention. Titurius saw the glory of Rome, though it could be temporarily dimmed by traitors, as enduring."

On the other side are those who see the coins' "Sabinity" as an assertion that challenges Roman hegemony. Gansiniec's argument that the coins constitute a "renascent current of Sabine nationalism" (1949: 25) is perhaps the strongest formulation of this perspective.³⁹ In this view, the coins might inspire the Sabines to take advantage of the shifting power structures of the Social War and reposition themselves vis-à-vis Rome. Though it seems unlikely—the Sabines remained loyal throughout the war—this view is not to be dismissed outright, especially given the diversity of responses to the conflict within communities. Members of the Sabine lower classes might have appreciated the nod to what made them distinctive.

---

37. Wiseman 1971: 113.
38. See Propertius 4.1.61, 4.4.28, 4.9.49, 4.10.20; Ovid *Tr.* 2.259, 2.424.
39. See also Morel 1962.

I wish to suggest not only that both these interpretations might be true, depending on the beliefs and attitude of the person holding, earning, or spending the coin, but also that between these two extremes there is important common ground: "us" versus, and vis-à-vis, "them." Whether the "us" is the Roman or the Sabine matters little; the coins simultaneously join and individuate Roman and Sabine identity. Why? How? For whom? To what end? Addressing these questions means accepting that these coins are an act of communication—that they constitute a discourse.

That discourse is about ethnicity.

Of course ethnicity is also a discourse. Rather than an intrinsic, objective, uncontested marker of identity that applies no matter the circumstances, ethnicity is subjective. Certainly various agents recognize something like objective ethnicity—the U.S. Census Bureau is one such entity, asking respondents to put themselves into categories such as "Latino," "Native American," and "White." The Census Bureau calls this "Race," but the categories "Race" and "Ethnicity" clearly elide,[40] and the assignment of individuals to categories is overtly subjective in that respondents are asked to locate themselves in one or more categories.

Ethnicity is thus a way people talk about and identify themselves (or others), and as a concept it relies on difference: difference from other ethnic groups, or from some non- or pan-ethnic megaculture such as the United States or ancient Rome. Ethnicity is almost always a marker of a subordinate or minority rather than dominant group. Sometimes the distinction might be useful, at other times not. Does my own Italian descent matter when I apply for a driver's license? Not so much. At the local international food festival? More so. At a family party? Absolutely. When I vote? Not at all. If I were to run for office? Perhaps. It depends on whether and how this identification matters in the context. To illustrate further: in each of the above scenarios ethnicity takes on a unique cant, and evokes, for me, my physical abilities and habits (which are to me independent of my Italianness), my culinary heritage, my notions about Italian family structures and values, political leanings (which have little to do in my mind with my Italianness), and finally a sense of the history of Italian immigrants and their descendants in the United States.[41]

---

40. Moving boundaries: what is "Latino"? The Census Bureau equivocates about whether "Latino origin" should be marked as ethnicity or race; the 2010 solution was to ask them separately, but without using the label "ethnicity." See <https://www.whitehouse.gov/omb/fedreg_1997standards> and <http://www.census.gov/2010census/about/interactive-form.php> (both accessed 3/14/15); and Nobles 2000: 187–90.

41. A similar point is made by Williamson 2005: 25.

Sabines had come to be understood in various ways by this point in Roman history. Sabinity operated on various axes such as shared ancestry (Titurius and Tatius, Piso and Numa), common morality that may or may not be encoded in one's blood (genetic austerity or the trickiness that springs from luxury), territorial identity (poor honest highlanders vs. rich tricky lowlanders), political experience (joint rule with Rome), and more. By contrast, *Romanitas* is not generally considered to be an ethnicity but is rather a culture that transcends ethnicity,[42] a pan-ethnicity or anti-ethnicity, in the sense that being Roman always involved secondariness and plurality of which Romans were resolutely proud. Secondariness means that Romans always already came from somewhere else. Roman mythology and history as far back as Aeneas—even Saturn—present a more distant past that must be left behind. As Dench formulates this feature of Roman identity, the Romans place heterogeneity at the very beginning of their understanding of themselves.[43] To this extent heterogeneity is a defining feature of the Romans, and it is this core of otherness that drives the Romans' (current and always) valorization of plurality. Not only did they consider their plurality a strength, but they also did not seem to limit the ways ethnicity could be perceived or exercised.

Titurius's coins, read together, explore the flexibility in ways of understanding ethnicity in a pluralistic society. Recall that all three of his coins present Tatius on the obverse with the legend "Sabin," and all three reveal L. Titurius's name on the reverse. These features combine Sabinity with an individual who asserts his belonging to that ethnic identity marker. The coin with the victory *bigae* suggests conquest as one way of giving rise to a pluralistic society, a model that preserves distinction and hierarchy of some groups over others. The Sabine women coin suggests intermarriage and ethnic blending—a melting pot model in which ethnicities would eventually disappear. The Tarpeia coin puts forward a mosaic model of pluralism, in which participant ethnic groups retain their identities and yet become part of a bundle of diverse identities. I am aware that these descriptors of cultural contact are coarse, and that subtler metaphors are available. I choose them precisely because their extremity delimits a scope of possibilities Romans and non-Romans might find to describe themselves.[44]

---

42. Hall 2002: 22–23; but *contra* see Dench 2005b: 3–5.

43. Dench 2005b: 11–25.

44. I am also aware that this model obscures other us-and-them factors such as socioeconomic class, gender, or language, but I do not see these as the core discourse of the coins except

CONQUEST / MELTING POT / MOSAIC

The Victory-in-*bigae* coin seems the most obvious type in the context of the Social War. Though it was very typical of Republican coinage in the years leading up to the Social War—enough so to have become commonplace—its context amid intra-Italian strife, and amid its unique partner coins, suggests additional nuance. Such generic patriotic images as this, we may imagine, might generally inspire courage among the Romans by celebrating recent battles won and by looking forward to the successful completion of others. In active wartime the message might seem more acute. The other issues from the Social War suggest a similar desire to inspire. The coins of the other Social War moneyers, L. Calpurnius Piso Frugi (descendant of the Censor), C. Vibius Pansa, M. Porcius Cato, and Gn. Cornelius Lentulus, boast various combinations of Mars, Minerva, and victory chariots.[45] Slight variations in type and diverse control marks suggest multiple stamps of these coins, presumably also intended for soldiers in the field. The encouraging message for soldiers is not hard to identify.

Yet let us prod this feel-good result a bit. The massive issue of this coin type and its distribution in finds around Italy suggest the coin was stamped to pay soldiers in the field. Titurius's name on the coin—a feature with local Roman importance, and potential meaning in his hometown, but not elsewhere in Italy—might yoke that imperialistic pride with his, or his family's, ascendancy in Roman politics. We must immediately qualify this, however, because it is impossible to say what the Roman goal might have been in fighting the allies in the first place. The outcome of the war was assimilation of Italians into the institutions of Roman government. Was this the goal of victory? Or was the goal rather to keep Italians out? Or to incorporate some Italians but not others, or to compromise on the rights received, or simply to bring peace again to the peninsula? The intricate and shifting party politics of the 90s and 80s suggest the answers were many to the question "What does victory mean?" In an open society such as Rome's, there evolve other ways to control or restrict access to positions of power. Status was an effective way in Rome, though as many texts of the era reveal (e.g., *pro Archia*), even status is a multifaceted and slippery thing. For a Roman audience in Rome and around Italy, therefore, Titurius's silver victory *bigae* wasn't necessarily monologic. War and its objectives are not always straightforward. This is not to suggest the *bigae* is somehow anti-

---

(as in the case of gender) insofar as they relate to ethnicity.

45. *RRC* 340, 342, 343, and 345 respectively. Q. Titius, moneyer in 90 or 89 BCE, stamped coins with Liber on the obverse, and a Pegasus opposite (*RRC* 341).

imperialist; far from it. I simply suggest that the shorthand image on the coin might have spoken about victory and its implications for Italy to different Romans in different ways.

Two features of Social War coinage[46] suggest that this coin was also often in the hands of Italian rebels as well. The first is the fact that, though the Italian federation minted its own coins during the war, they used the same denominations, materials, and iconographic schemes as the Romans. Thus Italian coinage did not aim to supplant Roman coinage but rather to supplement it. Second, the same hoards include types from Rome and from the Italian federation, which proves that the coins did circulate together. An Italian juggling this coin in his purse might resent the presumption of Roman victory—especially if this Italian was one of the lower classes who saw little to gain and much to lose by Roman enfranchisement. Or he might long to become like Titurius, an active and successful, self-professed non-Roman participating in Rome's inner circles, who had managed to retain, and could still boast, some non-Roman identity; thinking about Tatius, the Italian might wonder what that victory would look like—a stalemate that results in joint leadership, or a triumphal procession in which a similar chariot might play a real part. It is important to note here that he who gazes at the coin gazes upon the moving *bigae* rather than drives it. The coin, by the forced economy of its scale and its representational strategy, makes the holder an onlooker rather than a participant.

The *bigae* coin links ethnicity to victory, that is, to an outcome that retains a sense of "us" and "them" and places them in hierarchy, which is, next to hostility, the strongest expression of difference. This is what Mitchell and Greatrex describe as "true ethnic solidarity," a self-identification that has an impact on everyday life, and may even involve risk.[47]

CONQUEST / *MELTING POT* / MOSAIC

The coin depicting the Sabine women, in contrast, asserts a moment in which the distinction between "us" and "them" is about to be blurred. Rape casts a multiethnic society as a melting pot within which pure bloodlines become alloyed to others. Dougherty, exploring actual documented rapes in the recent ethnic war in Bosnia, describes this dynamic as a sort of biological imperialism in which the conqueror spreads his bloodline

---

46. Both in Burnett 1988.
47. Mitchell and Greatrex 2000: xvi n. 7.

into the victim's very body and descendants.[48] Rape as metaphor for conquest (that is, rape of women standing for occupation of fertile territory) and rape as an actual artifact of war thus elide and explain and reinforce each other. Ethnically mixed children complicate and problematize the concept of ethnicity, in general and for individuals.[49] Narrative accounts of the rape of the Sabine women fixate on the crisis of ethnic identity the rape produces for the parents and grandparents—the Sabine women, their Roman husbands, and even the Sabine elders who had lost daughters in the rape.

In this way alloyed children redefine and recontextualize even those who are not in the melting pot.[50] As a discourse and the product of (perceived) relationships, ethnicity will, as Mitchell and Greatrex advise, never reveal an individual personality. Nevertheless, like imagining real rape behind the image on the coin, we can easily imagine the consequences of recontextualization for individuals.

Who are we, then, as we hold the coin?

Before turning to this question, we might probe the coin's presentation of the rape as the totemic image from the episode. This choice raises fascinating interpretive avenues about the Sabinity it espouses. The fact that this instance of rape is recorded, remembered, and circulated suggests that the Sabines adopted it as a core element of their identity (by "the Sabines" I mean, "some Sabines, and enough of them for the story to stick"). The story is highly unflattering to the Romans, and Roman authors are at pains to defend the Romans' behavior, from plan to execution, and to attribute some fault to the Sabines themselves.[51] If this is so, having been raped became one of the core ways Sabines understood themselves, in the same way that secondarity was a feature of *Romanitas*.

This image speaks about the outcome of assimilation—literally, incorporation—to a variety of audiences in a variety of stances regarding Rome.[52] The mixture in the pot that results from incorporation might be considered stronger than the ingredient parts. The Romans themselves thought this was the case, and they embraced their plurality and elevated it as one

---

48. Dougherty 1998; for rape as biological imperialism, see esp. p. 278.

49. See recently the essays by Eula Biss (2009). While Biss focuses on race and even dismisses it as a sound rubric, she recognizes the elision between race and ethnicity in modern American culture.

50. The tangle of Aeneas, Lavinia, Ascanius, and Silvius demonstrates an analogous complication of identities brought about by a rape. See Servius *ad Aen.* 6.760 = *FRH* Cato F8.

51. For example, had the Sabines not been hostile to intermarriage in the first place, Romulus need not have resorted to rape: Livy 1.9. See also Cicero *Rep.* 2.12; Dionysius 2.30.5.

52. Cocchi 2004: 51–52 sees the image as a symbol of Concordia, the idealized harmony within families, within communities, and among communities. To me, the rape seems to stress "not yet."

of the reasons for their success on the world stage.[53] Some spenders in 89/8 BCE will have been a part of the Roman melting pot for a long time and might view their belonging in just this way. Others not yet in the cauldron might be longing for exactly such an opportunity to join themselves to "the Roman" in ways that would make them practically indistinguishable from other Romans. Still others might see the rape as an act of imperialistic violence, and would prefer to retain an identity independent of Rome. The Samnites, for example, strongly resisted Romanization, and they fought long after other communities had capitulated and accepted a place in the Roman state through citizenship via the *Lex Iulia* and the *Lex Plautia Papiria*.[54]

It is worth noting here what sort of community the Italians promoted on their own coinage during the war. I have already mentioned that the Italian federation chose Roman denominations, media, and styles. Thus the federation did not distinguish itself as an entirely different sort of being from the Rome which it opposed. Some of the coins minted by the Italians had legends in Latin, others in Oscan. Far from being a linguistically distinct identity or ethnic unity, the Italian federation was, in its diversity, more like than unlike its enemy. The name Italia, moreover, while it had been used by non-Romans in a variety of contexts with a variety of meanings, does not seem to have caught on as a consistent self-descriptor of the (inhabitants of the) peninsula.[55] Samnites, Etruscans, Bruttians, and Atellans did not call themselves Italians before the war against Rome. The pluralistic moniker engineers a shared identity among these peoples. This shared identity was seen by the federation's officers to be a crucial component to a successful resistance to Rome. In order to resist Rome, it was seen as necessary to replicate, symbolically at least, the plurality of Rome's culture. The Romans felt the need to destroy Italian coinage after the conclusion of the war; not only might the symbolism on the coins have been vexing (the wolf gored by a bull, for example), but

---

53. For inclusivity as a virtue, see Dench 2005b: 5–6.

54. When viewed from the distance of time passed, the gravitational pull of Rome on the Italian peninsula would seem inevitable and beneficial, both to Romans and to those incorporated. Velleius Paterculus's "centripetal history" reveals this outlook; his family came from Aeclanum, fought bravely against Rome in the Social War, and then joined Rome to its improvement and theirs. See Gabba 2008: 118 and Dench 2005b: 119 and 166. The centripetal perspective, a byproduct of colonialism, is pervasive in Roman letters; see, e.g., Hexter 1992 on Dido.

55. Dench 2005b: 157–73. Though Strabo (5.1.1) gives a linear account of the expansion of the name (and the idea behind the name), Dench urges caution, p. 158: "We might rather want to emphasize the existence and co-existence of conflicting traditions on the limits of Italia." Italia did not signify ethnic harmony. See also Burnett 1998 on the use of the term "Italia" in Social War coinage of the federation.

they might have been anxious at the possibility of a pluralistic identity other than their own on the peninsula. Unified Italy would only be appropriate on coins when paired with Rome.[56]

But in 89/8 BCE, with much of the peninsula battling over questions of how different "Roman" and "Italian" identities were, Titurius's coin speaks volumes. Its depiction of the rape on the reverse posits an ethnic identity that is about to thin. Yet on the obverse, it presents a strong and pure Sabinity in the portrait of Tatius, and a lingering ethnic identity long after assimilation, in the cognomen Sabinus. When we hold the coin, we look at one side or the other. Gazing at the obverse we are reminded of a strong ethnic identity. Watching the rape on the reverse we see that ethnicity in tension with another; "Sabin" on the reverse emphasizes the tension in identity that the coin's two sides offer.

We are on the sidelines of this particular struggle, neither participants (already Roman) nor victims (about to become Roman). Seeing this image we must choose who we will become in the context of this ethnic reconfiguration. Titurius can still boast to be a Sabine, descendant of a mixed marriage, and is now enough an insider to assert himself on the Roman political scene. To press the melting pot image, he is enough "ingredient" to stand out, and enough "alloy" to fit in. The coin distills into one handheld artifact the before and after of the melting pot, in its best-case scenario. For Titurius, the "after" worked out pretty well. His Sabinity, however, functions purely symbolically—available to be invoked when helpful, yet relegated to a cognomen and a coin.

CONQUEST / MELTING POT / *MOSAIC*

On Titurius's third type, the Tarpeia reverse depicts the girl in the center, a pile of shields rising to her midriff. Her arms are up as if to supplicate or to ward off a fresh attack.[57] Her hair is long and loose, and shows some disarray. On either side of her stands a soldier, advancing toward her with bent knee, holding aloft and toward her a shield as if to cast it upon her. A star-in-crescent hovers over the whole scene.

It is remarkable how much detail the designer was able to include in this tiny medium, and what he chose to represent. The most arresting detail is Tarpeia's frontality. Not only are images on coins almost always

---

56. E.g., Crawford *RRC* 403/1 of 70 BCE, with a reverse of Italia and Roma shaking hands.

57. Not, as Reinach 1912: 71 and Babelon *Monnaies* 2.167.4, p. 498, suggests, separating the two warring parties. Pais 1906: 111 sees the two soldiers as a Roman and Sabine. Contra, Morel 1962: 34.

profile, but the girl's position and direction has her looking at me, the viewer of the coin. My choice of the first-person pronoun is calculated; every viewer who looks at, and is seen by, Tarpeia at the moment of her death is brought into a very intimate relationship with her and the story.[58] On the reverse of the rape of the Sabine women, spenders see the scene obliquely. Tarpeia's direct gaze makes us participants in her story. Her gaze keeps us separate but locked together. We confront each other directly, identify each other, and are defined by each other. We can know what we make of her, but can we know what she makes of us? What are we, in her eyes?

This coin does not grant Tarpeia subjectivity in the same way Propertius's poem would some decades later; in Propertius's treatment, as we shall see in a later chapter, Tarpeia is allowed to speak for herself. The coin does, however, prevent her from being only an object, or perhaps it prevents her from being the only object, since the viewer is also granted this role by her gaze. The linked separation between Tarpeia and the viewer encapsulates a third way of understanding ethnicity in a pluralistic society: the mosaic model.

The mosaic model imagines a pluralistic society in which diverse elements retain their distinctiveness. The model became a popular way of describing Canada, in reaction to what was perceived as a faulty American melting pot model: the pot's tendency to erase cultural difference, and more dangerously to blend everyone into the mold of middle-class whiteness.[59] In 1971 Canada adopted a national multiculturalism policy, further defined in 1988's National Multiculturalism Act, which affirms the right of minority groups to retain their language and culture.[60] The second law demonstrates the profound difficulty of finding and maintaining a balance between unity and distinctiveness.

Tarpeia's story reveals this difficulty. It retains the distinctiveness of Sabinity and Romanness (such as it is) while bringing them together into unity, albeit uneasily. Tarpeia and Tatius are on opposite sides of the conflict, and—unless one follows Piso and exonerates her from blame—her intention was to admit Sabines into her city. To what end we can never know, but we must recognize that in part she knew her action would lead to Romans and Sabines mingling together, as quite distinct (here

---

58. See chapter 4 for further discussion of this relationship operative in the Basilica Aemilia relief sculptures.

59. Gibbon 1938.

60. Text available at http://laws.justice.gc.ca (accessed 10/21/10). The literature about the mosaic and melting pot is vast and spans academic disciplines, from philosophy to sociology to economics and law. A good primer may be found in Wong 2008.

hostile) entities. This mingling might model an Italy allied with Rome; Strabo uses the same word (κοινωνία) for both phenomena (Strabo 5.3.2, 4.2). The further outcome of this together-yet-distinct pairing was the eventual joining of Roman and Sabine into a mixed state, each group having equal powers. It is interesting that this mixed state was ultimately brought about by the image of the blended Roman-Sabine children; the polity sparked by the melting pot myth was not a true melting pot, and for several generations the Sabines retained resolutely distinct identities. Otherwise historians would not have called Numa and Ancus Martius "Sabine" kings.

Consider Tarpeia's punishment, so carefully focused on the coin, and the totemic image for her story. She is crushed to death by shields—the very devices used to protect the integrity of the body. The Sabine soldiers use (the armor of) their own bodily integrity in order to kill Tarpeia in a way that leaves her body unpenetrated. This is opposite to her counterpart, the Sabine women, whose bodies will be penetrated by men who also open their own bodies to mixing.[61] Tarpeia's story preserves bodies intact and distinct just as it preserves ethnicities intact and distinct. Yet Tarpeia's intact body leads to further violence back and forth, and to stalemate, a cycle that would repeat for centuries until the dissolution of the Latin league in 338 BCE.[62] Distinctiveness runs that risk. One criticism of the modern mosaic model of diverse societies is precisely the way it encourages "ghettoization."[63] Sabine Numa seems a good example of this, the prioritization of one's former identity over one's new identity. Though a Roman king, he remains Sabine. One might consider here the difference between the urban legacy of Tarpeia and the Sabine women. She became a place of punishment, while they became the names of the voting units for fully enfranchised men.

The continued ghettoization of the Sabines is reinforced by later events

---

61. In a paper I hope to see published, William Short discusses the gender orientation of the Tarpeia–Sabine women pairing: the rape of the Sabine women retains the femininity of the ethnic "other," while Tarpeia's admission of Sabines into Rome's walls enacts a Sabine "rape" of Rome that reverses the usual ethnic–gender association (Short 2005).

62. For a very different reading of Tarpeia on Titurius's coin, see Cocchi 2004, for whom Tarpeia functions as a symbol of and agent for fertility and Concordia, and therefore betokens the lasting health of the Roman state (*aeternitas*, emphasized by the moon and star). Tarpeia's virginity-unto-death, which would become Vestal virginity one generation after Titurius's coin, seems to belie this.

63. Sociologists have described this phenomenon (also called "fragmented pluralism") as a "vertical mosaic," in which diverse components of society have access to different levels of socioeconomic success. See Porter 1965. Another danger of the mosaic model is moral relativism, keenly felt as a threat in the post-9/11 world.

in Roman history. There was a gate on the Capitol called the Porta Saturnalia (Varro 5.42) until Romulus, now joint king with Tatius, renamed it the Porta Pandana (Festus 246L, 296L) to indicate that it would always be open (*pateret*) to the Sabines. This was the promise of diversity, and we might recall that Saturn was himself a god of diversity, exiled from the Greek pantheon and welcomed into his new home in Italy. Despite the open message of the Porta Pandana (and the primacy of Tatius, Numa, and Ancus), Roman history has the Sabines storm through this gate and besiege the Capitol again under Appius Herdonius in 460 BCE (Dionysius of Halicarnassus 10.14). Thereafter the Sabines were in turn insiders and outsiders until, after much fighting, they were enfranchised in the 290s. It does not matter whether any or all of these events were historical. The fact that these episodes coexist in the Roman imagination points to an understanding that the mosaic, too, is not a perfect model for a pluralistic society.

This exploration into the mosaic model of pluralism might lend some support to one explanation of the star-in-crescent-moon motif that appears on the coin. This motif has been explained in many ways: as a symbol of *aeternitas*, a visual clue that the episode happened at night, a driving force behind Tarpeia's madness, or proof that Tarpeia was a moon divinity.[64] Some suggest that the moon symbol might evoke the Latin cult of Luna/Diana.[65] This last suggestion is pertinent to my argument if we imagine the coin's primary symbolic work to be focused on ethnicity. Varro credits Tatius with introducing the cults of Luna, Lucina, and Diana at Rome (Varro *de Lingua Latina* 5.74; and cf. Dionysius of Halicarnassus 2.50.3); Varro earlier says that some call "Luna" "Diana" (*de Ling.* 5.68). These three are at heart the same goddess, or parts of the same goddess, with Luna and Lucina being aspects of the larger, more complex deity Diana. Luna had a temple on the Aventine, just below Diana's great temple there. The latter temple was said to have been dedicated by Servius Tullius in an attempt to galvanize a Latin federation which had Rome as its head and heart (Livy 1.45; Dionysius 4.26; cf. Varro *Ling.* 5.43). Though her cult center at Aricia remained the heart of the Latin league (and this league

---

64. Evans 1992: 123nn8–9 lists theories and their proponents. The following includes but adds to her list. *Aeternitas*: Cocchi 2004; Alföldi 1957: 36. Nighttime episode: Evans 1992: 123; and cf. Propertius 4.4, refuted conclusively by Cocchi 2004: 52. Madness: Cesano, *BMCRR* 1:297n2. Moon or nature divinity: Babelon *Monnaies* 2.167 introduction (pp. 497–98); Picard 1957a: 109–17 and 1957b: 184.

65. Momigliano 1938: 24–25. See also Morel 1962: 38–45 and Evans 1992: 12n9; see also *BMCRR* 1:297n2; Sydenham 1952: 699; Belloni *Monete* xlvii. Cocchi 2004: 49 notes the importance of divinities and mythical characters as "reservoirs of symbols characterizing a locale."

remained hostile rather than subject to Rome), Diana became a fixture of Roman religion.

The adoption of a foreign cult—notably, not through *evocatio*—links diverse people under a common religious umbrella.[66] According to Livy (1.19), Numa saw the wisdom in religious development as a calming and uniting force.[67] As a religious symbol, the moon goddess might overcome ethnic differences. Social War minters recognized the unifying aspect of religion when they placed Apollo on their coinage; Apollo was a god for everyone: nonpartisan—indeed egalitarian, a savior, himself multiethnic and willing to travel.[68] Diana seems to have been even more connected to the theme of ethnic amity. The *lex arae Dianae in Aventino,* which does not survive except in later descriptions, establishes rules for ritual dedication for people with potentially conflicting allegiances,[69] that is, those not fully Roman nor fully not-Roman. The moon and crescent, if seen as shorthand for Diana/Luna, offers a bridge between peoples who are in relationship with each other but remain distinct. This is the message Tarpeia's coin might have sent around Rome.

It is ironic that the episode considered most scandalous to all parties involved might speak most respectfully about cultural and ethnic union, for, like Diana's moon and the altar and law the goddess represents, the totemic moment of Tarpeia's death suggests a process rather than an end point, and it recognizes—and preserves for all time on the coin—a moment of difference in which the newcomer (the Sabine) not only retains his identity but has the upper hand. It is a flight of fancy, but a powerful one, to imagine the coin striker in the process of striking Tarpeia's coins. Free or slave, in either case a servant of the Roman cause,[70] every time he lowered the hammer the striker became a Sabine, crushing Tarpeia anew to the service of a pluralistic Rome.

---

66. Similarly, Gabba 2008: 113, who discusses an oath sworn by Italian leaders to Rome and Drusus, a religious act recognizing the value of generating religious ties among diverse people.

67. It is telling that Livy's Numa saw religious activity, including new cults, as a tonic against the dissipation that prosperity would generate. Even then Sabine Numa was combating the virus of luxury.

68. Rowland 1966: 418 and cf. Luce 1968: 28 and 34ff. for whom Apollo is a Marian factional symbol. Wiseman supports the view that Apollo betokens anti-Sullan sentiment by harnessing evidence for the archer god's interchangeability with anti-optimate Veiovis in the 80s BCE (2009: 72–78).

69. Green 2007: 95–96.

70. Based on production quantities and control marks, workshops were quite large and were composed of skilled craftsmen, apprentices, and workmen. Of the latter, one would wield the hammer while the other would position the heated flan onto the die. See Witschonke 2012 for an overview of the Roman minting process and for an assessment of practices to mitigate fraud.

PART TWO

TARPEIA AND THE CAESARS
FROM REPUBLIC TO EMPIRE

CHAPTER FOUR

VARRO'S VESTAL VERSION
TARPEIA IN WORD AND STONE

TWO RENDERINGS survive from the last years of the Roman Republican age: the scholar Varro's mention of Tarpeia in his linguistic treatise *de Lingua Latina*, published in the 40s BCE, and the new frieze decorating the Basilica Aemilia, sponsored by Caesar and erected between 55 and 34 BCE, in which Tarpeia appears as an Amazon. Both renderings can be attributed to the period's fierce interest in Roman antiquities, an interest sparked perhaps by the spread of Greek scholarly trends but fueled by the Romans' desire to understand their native Roman/Italian identity and to root it deeply in the past.

Varro is the first extant source to name Tarpeia as a Vestal virgin. This chapter explores Varro's addition to Tarpeia's story and some of its implications for our understanding of the myth, the Vestal priesthood, and the historical context of the telling. I argue that Varro's new focus on Tarpeia's gender identity relates to the collapse of Rome's ruling aristocracy at the end of the Republic. Recent scholarly work has confirmed that the Vestal virgins embody gender confusion and instability, combining elements of virgin and wife, even male and female. A Vestal Tarpeia confounds even this confusion in that she is a traitor to boot, another sort of marginal figure who at once embodies self and other. In her refusal to be easily mapped onto a stable set of behaviors and identities, and in her ability, moreover, to embody seeming opposites, a Vestal

Tarpeia acts as an analogue for the political and social crisis of the end of the Republic.

What is more, Varro connects Tarpeia explicitly to several locations named for her at the center of Rome; like her gender identity, her topographical identity is multiple and vexed. In the second half of this chapter, I situate Tarpeia in the landscape much as Varro does: by exploring the words associated with her. Varro's treatise on language, rich as it is with information on Roman words and echoes of Rome's past, is often mined for details that illuminate and enrich other, less fragmentary or less overtly informational sources. I have used Varro for this purpose in my own work.[1] Several recent studies expose the pleasures of reading Varro's text for its own sake (rather than using it) as a richly nuanced and purposeful work with a compositional strategy that goes beyond the encyclopedic. Hinds and Wallace-Hadrill, among others, make an impassioned case for Varro the artist.[2] Here I adopt this outlook and connect Varro's fussy details about Tarpeia's words to a view of the work—and the world—that is deeply political and ideological. The brief chapter on Tarpeia is full of gems for the ancient linguistic theorist, with at least three instances of word invention from scratch (*Roma, Tarpeius, a, um, Capitolinum*) and a window onto the process of how new words become regularized in language. Just as Varro's linguistic theory takes an outlier word, "Tarpeia," and makes it a comprehensible and containable feature in the language, so too does his narrative take the historical figure Tarpeia and make her comprehensible and containable within Rome. Thus I read this brief Tarpeia narrative as an encapsulation of how an anomaly such as Tarpeia is accommodated within the community and within the narrative history that configures that community.

I conclude with a brief look at the Basilica Aemilia relief, Caesar's own entry into Tarpeia's evolving story. The traitoress's appearance at the heart of this civic project illustrates a paradox of Varro's treatment: namely, that while a Vestal Tarpeia destabilizes the ease with which her myth can act as a moral *exemplum*, Varro's focus on this unstable figure normalizes that very instability, making it possible for the myth to remain vibrant throughout the violent changes Rome was about to witness at the beginning of the age of the emperors. On the relief Tarpeia is even more an anomaly than in Varro's text, for she is styled as an Amazon and poised to interrogate the viewer's sense of self and Rome. As a result, the Basilica leaves us strangers in our own land.

---

1. Welch 2005: 37, 121.
2. Wallace-Hadrill 1997: 18; Hinds 2006: 8–15.

THE NOVELTY OF THE VESTAL

Sources prior to Varro do not call Tarpeia a Vestal. Rather, they refer to her as a παρθένος (virgin, Pictor), θυγάτηρ (daughter, Antigonus), or κόρη (girl, Piso). To be sure, hints of Tarpeia's Vestality can be found in the early tradition. For one thing, Piso records that her grave was on the Capitol where she fell; unlike other people, even other priests, Vestals were buried within the city's sacred boundary, the *pomerium*. For another, when Tarpeia's death is described in the early sources it is by crushing (Pictor and Piso). Other, later traitors were thrown from the Tarpeian rock, then buried outside the city's walls, but Vestals found guilty of unchastity were buried alive with a tiny amount of food within the tomb as a safeguard against divine rancor, as Plutarch tells us in the *Numa* (10), "as though they [sc. the Romans] wished to avoid the pollution (sc. of the starving to death) of one who had been consecrated with such holy ceremonies." Tarpeia's unpenetrated death mimics Vestal punishment and, indeed, Vestal life.

Yet Pictor's account in particular, given the time of its composition, points toward the conclusion that Vestality was not a part, or at least a secure part, of the tradition about Tarpeia that he inherited.[3] As many scholars have noted, guilty Vestals pop up in the Roman tradition at times of political and social crisis, such as in the midst of external wars and times of plague. The most recent explanation for this coincidence posits that the Vestal virgins' bodies were metonymic for the health of the state; intact Vestals reflect and perpetuate a healthy state, while violated or guilty Vestals accompany and generate calamity.[4] During the Second Punic War, when Rome faced perhaps its most dangerous foreign threat ever in the person of Hannibal, and when Fabius Pictor was writing his version of Tarpeia's story, one Vestal virgin was executed for *incestum* (unchastity), another was accused and committed suicide, and a third was scourged for letting the sacred fire go out.[5] Surely Tarpeia-as-guilty-Vestal would have appealed to Pictor. She either didn't exist in his sources or, if she did, her

---

3. Martini 1998: 26–35, arguing that Tarpeia's story emerged in the mid-Republic to reflect its own concerns, calls her a "*Vestalis ante litteram,*" a "Vestal before the name was invented."

4. Parker 2004: 568. Martini 1998: 31–32 seems to me to be alone in suggesting that a Vestal's *incestum* always accompanies and achieves a moment of internal transformation in Romanness. Parker and others maintain that Vestal sacrifice seeks to maintain the *status quo*.

5. Parker 2004: 593–94 conveniently catalogues and gives sources for all Vestal shame. He adds to his catalogue related accusations and drastic measures, such as human sacrifice (more than four attested during the crisis of the Second Punic War), matrons accused of adultery and exiled, sumptuary laws passed, and temples to feminine virtues vowed and dedicated.

Vestality was less interesting to him than her greed when faced with Sabine gold.

So, where did Varro get the idea? Given his wide learning and his access to sources now lost to us, it is possible that the scholar uncovered some detail about Tarpeia's history that remains elusive to us. For example, Plutarch names a Tarpeia as one of the original four Vestal virgins (*Numa* 10); his source might have been earlier than Varro. Indeed Sanders posits that this is the case: that Varro conflated the existence of a Vestal Tarpeia, known to him from the historical record, with the Tarpeia traitoress of the myth.[6] Or Varro might be rationalizing from a number of details that point to Vestality without naming it. If her annual worship convinced Piso (and later Dionysius, who endorses Piso's version)[7] that she was no simple traitor, might it not convince Varro of her sacrality, especially in light of her burial within the city? This is Martini's underlying assumption.[8] Varro's general approach to myth was to rationalize it, as Rawson notes, "which simply strips tradition of the obviously fabulous, without asking what its real nature or value is."[9] Varro's intention might well have been a movement toward reason, but the result, Tarpeia the Vestal, causes more problems than she solves, and it is to these—Rawson's "real nature or value"—that we now turn.

It is highly ironic that the man whom Vitruvius holds up with Cicero and Lucretius as enduring learned voices, and whom Cicero claims as Rome's savior from its own ignorance, should remain so obscure to modern readers.[10] Marcus Terentius Varro was a man of great learning and literary output; of the seventy-four titles known to us, only two survive in any length: the short treatise *De re rustica* (On Agriculture), complete in three books, and some six out of twenty-five books of the *de Lingua Latina* (On the Latin Language).

The loss of Varro's works is all the more keenly felt by modern readers in that he was witness to and participant in the tumultuous events of the Republic's fall. Born to a wealthy family in Reate in Sabine territory in 116

---

6. Sanders 1904: 9–10. This is similar to Tarpeia's own conflation in Propertius's poem (4.4.39–40) of two Scyllas.

7. Dionysius of Halicarnassus 2.40.3.

8. Martini 1998.

9. Rawson 1985: 245 refers specifically to Varro's *De gente populi Romani*, a text about Rome's origins, but her conclusion applies equally well, if not better, to the *Ling*.

10. Vitruvius 9.17; Cicero *Ac.* 1.9. The irony was not lost on Petrarch, who calls Varro "*il terzo gran lume Romano*" (*Triumphus Fame* 3.38) despite the fact that Varro had already lapsed into his dark age.

BCE,[11] Varro was a friend of Pompey and fought with him both in the external wars of the 60s BCE and in the civil wars against Caesar in the early 40s BCE. Pardoned and promoted by Caesar, Varro was named librarian-to-be of Rome's first public library, but Caesar was assassinated before progress could be made on the project. Varro fell into ill favor with Antony and was proscribed, but he survived under the protection of Octavian. The rest of his life was spent writing, and he died in 27 BCE at the age of eighty-nine.

Varro's *Ling.*, dedicated at least in part to Cicero,[12] is a treatise in twenty-five books on the history and forms of the Latin language. The work contains an introductory book and four sets of six books each: the first set on the origins of words, the second on words derived from other words, the final two sets on syntax. Each set is further divisible into two halves: the first theoretical, the second applied. Tarpeia's story falls in the second (applied) half of the first set, on word origins:

> Ubi nunc est Roma, Septimontium nominatum ab tot montibus quos postea urbs muris comprehendit; e quis Capitolinum dictum, quod hic, cum fundamenta foderentur aedis Iovis, caput humanum dicitur inventum. Hic mons ante Tarpeius dictus a virgine Vestale Tarpeia, quae ibi ab Sabinis necata armis et sepulta: cuius nominis monimentum relictum, quod etiam nunc eius rupes Tarpeium appellatur saxum. (5.41)[13]

> Where Rome now is, used to be called the "*Septimontium*" (Seven Hills), from that same number of hills which the city later enclosed within its walls. Of these hills, the Capitol is so named because here, when the foundations were being dug for the temple of Jupiter, it's said that a human head (*caput*) was found. This hill used to be called the Tarpeian Hill from the Vestal virgin Tarpeia, who was there killed by the Sabines with their armor and buried. A reminder of her name is left behind in that even now its cliff is called the Tarpeian rock.

It is striking that Varro, born in Sabine territory, does not draw undue attention to the Sabine element of the story. Neither the context of the myth in the Sabine wars, nor any patriotism on Tarpeia's part, be it Sabine (*à la* Antigonus) or Roman (as in Piso), nor the Sabine national character

---

11. For Varro's life see Dahlmann *RE* Suppl. 6 (1935) col. 1172–84.
12. *Ling.* 5.1.1; and cf. Cicero *ad Fam.* 9.8, *ad Att.* 13.12.3. See Stroup 2010 introduction and chapter 6 for broad discussions of literary dedications among what she calls a "society of patrons," including Varro's reciprocal dedicatory exchange with Cicero.
13. I use Kent's Loeb edition of 1938.

(luxurious as in Pictor's history, austere elsewhere), nor the resulting assimilation of Sabines and Romans make the cut in Varro's tale. Nor, indeed, does the displacement of Sabine shrines from the Capitol during the excavations for the temple foundations (see below). But the scholar does name Tarpeia specifically as a Vestal virgin.

Though Tarpeia in the earlier sources negotiates the space between (Roman) self and (Sabine) other by working out through example the extremes of loyalty, Varro's Vestal Tarpeia has no such function. Since she is consigned to virginity throughout her fertile years, her potential as a woman to bridge the gap between families or communities is erased. Nor does she express or display any allegiance one way or another, or any motive for that matter. Indeed, her Vestal-style death and burial are the only things that suggest her culpability at all.[14] What is more, that same Vestal death and burial suggest that she alone was considered guilty; as Parker points out, guilty Vestals are held completely and solely responsible for their putative lapses: "A feature, usually unnoticed or unremarked by ancients and moderns, is the entirely optional presence of a man . . . Vestals always sinned willingly."[15] Thus whatever motive or mitigating circumstance we might imagine for Tarpeia (and some authors such as Piso did imagine such things), she is nonetheless culpable. So profound, in fact, is her condemnation in tradition that, despite Piso and Dionysius who exonerate her, she is not a known subject of *declamatio*, that genre of overt ethical hair-splitting. Declaimers did not avoid various permutations of the guilty Vestal. The elder Seneca's collection of speeches includes sets of speeches (e.g., *Cont.* 1.2.23) wondering what constitutes virginity sufficient for Vestality: can a former prostitute now virginal be a Vestal? What if she was forced into prostitution? If she was, is that some indication of a natural blemish or unchastity, or predilection to *impudicitia*?[16] To what extent is she responsible for her own lapses? Given the freedom declaimers had in inventing details, it is possible to imagine a rhetorical defense even for a guilty Tarpeia.[17] She is never given that defense.[18]

---

14. See chapter 1 for a general discussion of Tarpeia's death as analogous to Vestal punishment. Though there are other analogies to her death (stoning in particular), I here single out her Vestality since Varro does.

15. Parker 2004: 581–82. In some cases of Vestal prosecution men are named; some of these might have been politically motivated accusations. Parker's more material point is that in most cases no man is mentioned.

16. Langlands 2006: 253–64.

17. See Roller's (1997) comments about wholesale invention permissible as *color* in the rhetorical tradition.

18. Indeed, as I argue in chapter 7, the most declamatory of authors who treat her story—

As a Vestal buried in the manner fitting for *incestum,* Varro's Tarpeia is thus a crime in and of herself. Her problem—like her sacrality—stems from her inherent ambiguity as a priestess of Vesta. Modern studies of the Vestal priesthood were long dominated by an attempt to understand its origins: was she originally or symbolically a daughter of the state, ever the virgin, or a wife tending the public hearth? Mary Beard, in a short but seminal article in 1980, turned these questions on their head.[19] Why choose? Beard argued that such attempts to place the Vestal virgin neatly onto the grid of sanctioned, even censured, Roman gender roles, however that grid is understood, are doomed to fail since the Vestal is always an amalgam of the feminine roles "virgin" and "mother." Holt Parker in 2004 complicated Beard's proposed ambiguity by adding the antitypes "whore" and "stepmother" to the mixture, as well as the combined femininities of the "Madonna" and "witch" figures.[20] We can't stop there; Beard had even suggested that Vestal virgins were understood, in some senses, as men; they sat with men at the games, for example, and were allowed to testify in court.[21] While other scholars express caution about this last claim,[22] it is undeniable that Vestal virgins enjoyed some of the prerogatives of men.[23] Perhaps a way to a solution lies not in understanding the Vestals to be both men and (various kinds of) women, but rather to see them as neither men nor women, but something else.

What else? That question, said Beard in an equally famous (deconstructionist) retraction of her first (structuralist) article, is the point. In the later piece,[24] Beard notes that what fascinates the Romans most about the Vestals is the various circumstances and permutations of their transgressions (Seneca the Elder's declaimers are among the star witnesses for this

---

Valerius Maximus—condemns her despite gaps in the evidence for her culpability that he includes in his text.

19. Documented by Beard 1980: 13–15. See also Parker 2004: 565–67 for a cogent argument against the limitations of the "paleontological approach."

20. Parker 2004: 569–70 and 582, based on Mediterranean anthropological studies. The Madonna combines the virgin and mother, and the witch combines the whore and stepmother.

21. Beard 1980: 17–18.

22. Particularly scholars of Roman law, such as Gardner 1986: 24, for whom a Vestal cannot be a man since (a) she only has some, not all, legal prerogatives; and (b) even a complete set of prerogatives doesn't equal maleness. Takács (2010: 82) notes the Vestals' subordination to the Pontifex Maximus, though this is in a general discussion of their uncategorizability. Cf. Dumézil 1970: 587, who calls their virginity "an intermediate stage between femininity and masculinity; not mythologically, as elsewhere, but juridically, as one might expect at Rome."

23. For Parker 2004: 574, these prerogatives do not attend their masculinity but rather their independence from typical female family subservience.

24. Beard 1995.

understanding). Rather than participating in the categories of femininity (virgin, wife, whore, slave, viper), Beard's Vestals thus function to test those categories and their limits, tapping constantly against their edges so that their shape may be discernible. Hersch's recent study of the Roman wedding suggests the same understanding about the destabilizing effect some figures have on traditional categories of belonging. The example of Tarpeia proves that virginity and moral rectitude are not coterminous.[25] For Hersch, Tarpeia's married corollary is Tullia, the viper whose sexuality, though sanctioned and contained within marriage, nevertheless runs out of control and gives rise to other transgressions. If they cannot predict or generate behavior, categories such as "virgin" and "matron" mean nothing.

Varro's Vestal Tarpeia is likewise not a solution but rather a puzzle not to be solved, one whose insolvability calls into question the very categories she seems to transgress. Though his account of her and her urban legacy might appear to be a rationalized combination of disparate tidbits, she cannot escape the irrationality that arises from understanding her in Varro's text as a Vestal virgin. If we return to his text we note these three features, prominent because his narrative is stripped of other details. First, she gave her name to the Mons Tarpeius where she was buried, later renamed Capitolium for a head found there. Second, she also gave her name to the Tarpeian rock (*saxum Tarpeium*), well known as the punishment place for traitors. Third, she was killed and buried on this site, within the *pomerium* as/like an unchaste Vestal. Questions proliferate from the combination of these givens. Why and how did a skull trump her name as moniker for the hill? Was it her skull, and if so, why the name change? Why, also, is the name change only partial to some of the hill, while other parts or functions retain her name? More broadly, what part of identity remains through a name change? Since Varro does not mention the treason per se, is her Vestality, with her Vestal-like intramural burial, more closely linked with the place names than her ambivalent sense of belonging to Rome?

Tarpeia as Vestal, replaced as eponym but still present in the placename, invites Roman audiences to consider how the Vestal's gender ambiguity works in conjunction with other questions of category and identity. In this she participates in a growing trend visible in late-Republican sources of layering vexed gender identity onto other aspects of murky

---

25. Hersch 2010: 64, who notes that the overlap of categories (virgin traitor, married viper) gives rise to further category-destabilizing thoughts: is general depravity independent of sexual desire, or does one cause the other? If so, which way does causality work?

or shifting categories as a way to explore and understand the upheaval of identity that attended the changing political order. While the literature is vast, a familiar example will make the point. Julius Caesar—the man whose refusal to conform to political and social norms undermined them to the breaking point—was styled in Republican sources as a catamite, mistress, queen, male prostitute, seducer of noble women and yet divorcer of his own wife when (perhaps) cuckolded.[26] In short he was, as Curio's famous jibe goes, "a man for all women and a woman for all men."[27] Catharine Edwards's 1993 study of the politics of immorality in ancient Rome argues that such accusations "were implicated in defining what it meant to be a member of the Roman elite."[28] Anthony Corbeill, in his 1996 book *Controlling Laughter*, probed both the means and the limits of this mode of (self-)definition; jokes and invective attempt to limit aristocratic excess, but the system fails when the butt of the jokes embraces rather than refutes the claims. Caesar did exactly this, all but calling himself a queen in one speech to the Senate (Suet. *Iul.* 22.2). As Corbeill notes, "By embracing the charges that have been leveled against him, Caesar openly asserts his power over the traditional, elite standards that this type of humorous mockery supports."[29]

Like Caesar, Varro's Tarpeia resists efforts to control her by assigning her to a category. Varro's text places the anomaly metaphorically at the heart of Roman religious institutions,[30] and literally at the front and center of his city. Here it is worth noticing where Varro mentions Tarpeia and the monuments that commemorate her. Book 5 begins Varro's section on applied etymology; its first forty chapters deal with generic place names such as "vineyard" from "vine" (5.37), or "cavern" from "cavity," which itself derives from "chaos" (5.20). Tarpeia's story represents the very first etymology of a specific place-name in Rome: the now-outdated *mons Tarpeius* and its lingering offshoots, the *rupes* (sc. *Tarpeia*) and *saxum Tarpeium*. While Varro does give an etymology for the proper place-name *Capitolinum* (from *caput*, head), he does not offer any etymologies for Tarpeia's name, even though other ancient authors do and there are additional possibilities out

---

26. Suetonius catalogues most of these jibes and their authors at *Iul.* 49–52; to his catalogue, which is corroborated in later sources, must be added Catullus's invective poems such as 29.

27. Preserved by Suetonius, *Iul.* 52.2: *omnium mulierum virum et omnium virorum mulierem.* The polyptoton adds to the joke.

28. Edwards 1993: 12.

29. Corbeill 1996: 197, and see pp. 189–209 for other examples of Caesar's use of humor to undermine rather than shore up categories of behavior and identity.

30. For this function of the Vestals see Parker 2004.

there.³¹ It seems as though for Varro the name itself was the meaning.³² Tellingly, in Varro's text the Tarpeian rock is a monument—a reminder—not of her deed but of her name, which is her identity: *cuius nominis monimentum*.³³ It is a nice if unintended illustration of the gendered conundrum she poses that Roman topography preserves, and Varro uses or implies, Tarpeia's name/adjective in all three genders: *mons Tarpeius, virgine Tarpeia* and *rupes* (sc. *Tarpeia*), and *saxum Tarpeium*.

The problem of Varro's Tarpeia spreads to other tellings of her myth and makes visible and untenable any attempt to use her as a moral example. Her rock and her tomb just do not make sense together. Some other ancient authors recognized this. Piso, whose exoneration of Tarpeia is based on the known sacrality of her tomb, does not account for her rock.³⁴ Antigonus erases her treason by making her a Sabine, which would explain the rock—but why then would the Sabines kill her, or if they didn't, why would the Romans bury her so centrally? Propertius, whose Tarpeia is a Vestal guilty as much for love as for treason, accounts for her grave, her grove, and her mountain—but not her rock (*Tarpeium nemus et Tarpeiae turpe sepulcrum*, 4.4.1; *a duce Tarpeia mons est cognomen adeptus*, 93). Festus must also reassign the hill's name (364L). And Pictor and Livy (1.11), two authors who would present Tarpeia as a negative example, ignore her tomb altogether. Modern interpreters face similar problems reconciling her guilt and her honor. For example, Poucet sees in Tarpeia's myth the combination of two different myths about the Sabine synoikism, or amalgamation into Rome, one pro-Roman and another Sabine in origin.³⁵ Georges Dumézil considers the tension between love and greed in her tale, but ignores the impact of her Vestality and concludes that Tarpeia repeats an older and more universal Indo-European type in which she is both traitor and nourisher.³⁶ Her quest for Sabine gold to enrich herself is (sort of) a good thing

---

31. Propertius 4.1.1 (*turpe*, shameful; see Boyd 1984) and P. Petronius Turpilianus, who connects Tarpeia with his own family name on a coin, *BMCRE* 1.29–31 with plate 1.16 (see Wallace-Hadrill 1986: 77). For other etymological possibilities, see Gansiniec 1949: 36–37 (Greek τρόπαιον, "trophy"); Sanders 1904: 46–47 (Indo-European –*trp*–, "satisfy" or the town name "Tarpe" on the Apennines); and Devoto (1940) 1991: 75 (Etruscan "Tarquinia," and cf. Poucet 1967: 91–93; Dumézil 1947: 281; and Pais 1905: 105).

32. Cf. Corbeill 1996: 73, which argues for *cognomina* as both old and as having semantic value.

33. For the equation of a concept and its name in Stoic linguistic theory, see Rawson 1985: 117–18. Cf. Balbus in Cicero *DND* 2.69, for whom Venus (a cosmic given) is the anomaly who gives her name to *venustas* rather than the reverse. See Hinds 2006: 6.

34. Dumézil 1947: 280 also points out that she can't have been Roman, a daughter of Romulus—because the Romans had no women before they kidnapped the Sabine women.

35. Poucet 1967: 120–21; see also Krappe 1929.

36. Dumézil 1970: 68–69 for this quick assessment; his extensive 1947 treatment, in which he

in its focus not only on accretion of resources but on the accretion of people into Rome.

Varro's version avoids the problem of Tarpeia-as-*exemplum* by refusing to make Tarpeia an example, positive or negative. She just is, without motive or judgment. But so great is Varro's authority[37] that Tarpeia's Vestality hijacks the tradition, despite the problems it creates for interpretation. Livy, for example, even adds the detail that she was performing rites to Vesta when she met the enemy (1.11; see chapter 5); her Vestality, though, goes uninterpreted. Propertius alone seems to press the implications of the Varronian tradition. By painting Tarpeia as a patriotic Vestal in love, this elegiac poet writing under Augustus makes even more problematic the gender tensions inherent in service to Vesta (Elegy 4.4, and see chapter 6).

VARRO'S VERSION: INTELLECTUAL CONCERNS—LINGUISTICS

The legacy of this one detail demonstrates a broader phenomenon that scholars are beginning to explore in greater detail: that antiquarianism, even if it eschews the sort of moral agenda always visible in exemplary discourse, nevertheless is not apolitical.[38] Wallace-Hadrill explores the mechanism whereby scholarly work becomes political during Rome's "cultural revolution": seemingly neutral scholarly treatments of a variety of topics became fair ground for what might then be considered unimpeachable or unmotivated appropriation.[39] Not only were the "neutral" topics themselves in flux, but so, more importantly, was the locus of cultural authority shifting from the *nobiles* to the scholars, whose work and/or methods could be co-opted by various parties. Wallace-Hadrill notes the prime example offered by Caesar, whose linguistic work *de Analogia*, written in the down moments of the Gallic wars, intermingles military imperialism

---

makes the case for her role as "nourisher" (one of the three parts to just about every ancient myth, along with the "ruler" and "soldier"), does not discuss her Vestality.

37. Scholarly attention paid to Varro seems to be turning in this direction (see, e.g., Baier 1997 and Pasco-Pranger 2002), perhaps because it is so difficult to study "Varro" in light of the loss of so many of his texts. Baier's study, tracing Varro's influence within his lifetime and living memory of him, gives some sense of what we are missing.

38. Rawson 1985: 102–3, 233–49; see also Baier 1999.

39. Wallace-Hadrill 1997. Thus, for example, a Varronian chronology probably lay behind Augustus's decision to host the *ludi Saeculares* in 17 BCE, even though they were not yet due.

with the cultural imperialism of language rules.[40] Cicero did not approve of this linguistic turn and generally valued usage over strict rules.[41] One can hardly defend a reading of the linguistic differences between Cicero and Caesar as neutral or purely scholarly.

Varro's *Ling.* partakes of the very same contemporary and touchy debate in linguistic theory that vexed Cicero and Caesar: analogy versus anomaly. Simply defined, analogy is a prescriptive approach to words, in which new words arise according to strict rules. Anomaly, on the other hand, is a descriptive approach that favors usage. Neither Cicero nor Caesar were dogmatically extreme in this debate, though they stay perhaps on either side of the moderate line—Cicero on the side of anomaly, Caesar closer to analogy.[42] Varro explores this debate and its related phenomena in books 8 through 11, but this narrowly disciplinary debate has large implications for our Tarpeia narrative. Perhaps I have put the cart before the horse in discussing the narrative stripped of this linguistic debate before introducing the debate and its terms, but Varro has done so as well by delaying his technical discussions. As we shall see, Varro's Tarpeia narrative raises questions that, like Tarpeia's Vestality, probe the contours of the opposing categories "analogy" and "anomaly" by showing them as inextricably linked in a process of linguistic change.

Language,[43] says Varro, is made up of two sorts of words: those that can beget other words (*genus fecundum*), and those that are barren (*genus sterile*):

> Causa, inquam, cur eas ab impositis nominibus declinarint, quam ostendi; sequitur, in quas voluerint declinari aut noluerint, ut generatim ac summatim item informem. Duo enim genera verborum, unum fecundum, quod declinando multas ex se parit disparilis formas, ut est lego legi legam, sic alia, alterum genus sterile, quod ex se parit nihil, ut est et iam vix cras magis cur. (8.9)[44]

---

40. Wallace-Hadrill 1997: 19, based on Fronto 221N: *scripsisse inter tela volantia de nominibus declinandis, de verborum aspirationibus et rationibus inter classica et tubas.*

41. *Brutus* 258.

42. The bibliography is extensive. For starters, see Cavazza 1981: 136–37, Ax 1996, and Rissanen 1997.

43. General studies abound. Anglophones may consult Taylor 1974; Langendoen 1966: 34–35 with caution; Colish 1985 (1990): 321–23; Frede and Inwood 2005: 1–13. All these rest on the studies of Collart 1954 and Dahlmann 1932.

44. Goetz and Schoell 1910 read *eam* (daggered) in the first line, and *vix cras* reads daggered as *vixerat*. Emendations include *vix cras* and *vix sat*.

The reason why they declined these [sc. forms] from the names that had been imposed is as I have shown. It follows that I should likewise show, class by class and summarily, what forms they wanted or didn't want to be generated by inflection. There are two categories of words: one fertile, because it begets many different forms from itself through declension, such as: "I read," "I have read," "I will read," and others like it; and the other category is the sterile type, because it begets nothing from itself, such as "now" "scarcely" "tomorrow" "more" "why."

Analogy and anomaly have to do with the *genus fecundum* in that they theorize how language expands beyond an initial set of words, and how words are understood. Beyond an initial set of signifiers, which are given (the analogy–anomaly debate does not really concern itself with word origins), analogy posits that words beget other words under the guidance of a set of rules understood by all speakers of that language. These rules, understood by the collective, make a language learnable and infinite from a finite set of original words. Varro calls this *declinatio naturalis*. Though Varro does not delve into the philosophy behind this position, it is connected with those who view the universe as the fixed manifestations of a constant physics. The "physics" of language is, however, not universal across all languages but is consistent within a language. The analogist position can also be seen as collective and participative in that all language users understand and operate by the same rules. To put this in practical terms, the genitive of *puella* is *puellae* because we Latin learners agree that this is how genitives operate in the first declension. Varro associates *declinatio naturalis* with words such as *constantia, ars,* and *ratio*.

Whereas the analogists espoused a language of rules, logic, and reason, the anomalists validated usage. "Anomaly" is the creation of new words that do not follow a set of rules but rather spring from the mind of the individual speaker. I might therefore, knowing the word *puella*, make up a new word, *puellitas*. However this new word might itself be subject to analogy (*puellitas, puellitatis, puellitati* and the like), the original coinage is my own and anomalous. In a purely anomalous language, in which each word is *sui generis*, language acquisition would be impossible. The philosophical underpinnings of linguistic anomaly lie in Stoic physics, in which the universe is a composite of unique and unpredictable events. Varro mentions Chrysippus and Crates as the titans of anomaly theory (9.1, and see Colish (1985) 1990: 321–23). Varro calls anomaly *declinatio voluntaria*, and associates it with the words *impositia, inconstantia, voluntas, consuetudo,* and *historia*. Varro contrasts the two modes, analogy and anomaly, in a lovely and clear simile in his eighth book:

> Duo igitur omnino verborum principia, impositio <et declinatio>, alterum ut fons, alterum ut rivus. Impositicia nomina esse voluerunt quam paucissima, quo citius ediscere possent, declinata quam plurima, quo facilius omnes quibus ad usum opus esset dicerent. (8.5)

> There are therefore two sources of words—invention and derivation, the former like a spring, the other like a river. Invented words should be as few as possible so that they might be able to be learned readily. Great is the number of derived words, since everyone who needs to use them can recite them.

Varro straddles the line between these two and, though he leans toward analogy (as did Caesar), he admits that both modes exist in Latin, anomaly generally giving way to analogy as a spring might lead to a stream. His moderate position is prudent in the intellectual battle zone of the last days of the Republic, where not only did this debate lead to some subtle barbs and defensive language among Cicero, Caesar, and Varro,[45] but it also touched on issues of class and elite power. The political aspect of Varro's linguistic theory is addressed in Diana Spencer's forthcoming book *Varro's Guide to Being Roman: Citizen Speech and de Lingua Latina,* where she argues that analogy espouses and relies upon collective agreement on and public performance of the rules of language, a consensus that polices linguistic boundaries and maintains a status quo (or subverts it in the collective's interests). Anomaly, in contrast, is individualistic and allows each and any speaker the power to affect change in language. Anomaly represents a breach in concord and can be the source of factionalism, autocracy, and discord, or representative of democracy in its basic sense as "institutionalized uncertainty."[46] The tension between analogy and anomaly could be mapped onto the contemporary political struggles between the senatorial conservatives, on one hand, and Caesar, on the other. Wallace-Hadrill sees the equation the other way around: *consuetudo* (unregulated usage) was the purview of the people and their elite, and *ratio* (rules and structures) was the grammarian's domain; Caesar appropriated, even became, the latter.[47]

---

45. Sample barb: Cicero *Brutus* 258 and defensiveness: Varro *Ling.* 7.1. See Rawson 1985: 121–23.

46. Spencer (forthcoming): chapter 1. The phrase "institutionalized uncertainty" is from Przeworski 1991: 14.

47. Wallace-Hadrill 1997: 19.

If the overlap of linguistic theory onto politics is not clean and precise, it is no surprise: neither was the reality on the ground. It is Caesar again who messes things up: while he may himself be an anomaly, his own *de Analogia* urges that rules and regularity be imposed onto current practices. In other words, he embraces anomaly (usage, *consuetudo*) so as to convert it to analogy (rules, *ratio*), but this time the authority for the rules resides not in consensus or the elite collective, but in one man.[48] The categories themselves fail to apply to Caesar, and therefore themselves fail, analogous (sorry) to the challenge Vestal virgin Tarpeia poses to categories of gender and national identity. With these aspects of words in mind, we return to the language of Tarpeia in the *de Lingua Latina*:

> Ubi nunc est Roma, Septimontium nominatum ab tot montibus quos postea urbs muris comprehendit; e quis Capitolinum dictum, quod hic, cum fundamenta foderentur aedis Iovis, caput humanum dicitur inventum. Hic mons ante Tarpeius dictus a virgine Vestale Tarpeia, quae ibi ab Sabinis necata armis et sepulta: cuius nominis monimentum relictum, quod etiam nunc eius rupes Tarpeium appellatur saxum. (5.41)

> Where Rome now is, used to be called the "Septimontium" (Seven Hills), from that same number of hills which the city later enclosed within its walls. Of these hills, the Capitol is so named because here, when the foundations were being dug for the temple of Jupiter, it's said that a human head (caput) was found. This hill used to be called the Tarpeian Hill from the Vestal virgin Tarpeia, who was there killed by the Sabines with their armor and buried. A reminder of her name is left behind in that even now its cliff is called the Tarpeian rock.

The nuanced and elegant analysis of this passage in chapter 5 of Spencer's *Varro's Guide to Being Roman* sees here Varro's concealment of discord. Not only is Tarpeia's treachery not mentioned directly (p. 215), but other sources of discord are swept under the rug, so to speak. For example, Spencer notes (p. 215) that Varro fails to mention the Sabine presence on the Capitol in the form of shrines dedicated by Tatius during the hostilities against Romulus, which were removed when Tarquinius Superbus continued construction on the temple of Jupiter (Livy 1.55). Plurality is there but not there, and Tarquin the Proud marks a high point in Roman autocracy. What is more, Spencer (pp. 215–16) draws attention to the fact that Varro ignores the enticing detail, found in Propertius, that Tarpeia's

---

48. Wallace-Hadrill 1997: 18–19.

event happened on the Parilia—Rome's birthday, and not coincidentally also the day in Varro's recent memory on which Caesar's victory at Munda was announced in Rome.[49] Caesar's victory was the inauguration of a new Rome and a new autocracy. Spencer concludes that "Varro's brief treatment here might already have seemed omissive, or at least to be surprisingly laconic. Instead of Tarpeia's treachery (or tragedy), or talk of refoundation, Varro headlines an admonitory etymology: don't betray your city; don't wield power tyrannically; keep the collective in mind" (p. 216). In this way Varro also erases, in his text, what was erased in history at these moments of momentous change.

We may add to this his passing over of the meaning or origin of the name "Roma." Later in the text we find that "Roma" is one of Varro's prime examples of anomaly, since Romulus invented the name:

> Ego declinatus verborum et voluntarios et naturalis esse puto, voluntarios quibus homines vocabula imposuerint rebus quaedam, ut ab Romulo Roma, ab Tibure Tiburtes, naturales ut ab impositis vocabulis quae inclinantur in tempora aut in casus, ut ab Romulo Romuli Romulum et ab dico dicebam dixeram. (9.34)

> Quae in eas res quae extrinsecus declinantur, sunt ab equo equile, ab ovibus ovile, sic alia: haec contraria illis quae supra dicta, ut a pecunia pecuniosus, ab urbe urbanus, ab atro atratus: ut nonnunquam ab homine locus, ab eo loco homo, ut ab Romulo Roma, ab Roma Romanus). (8.18)

> I consider derivations of words to come from the will (voluntary)[50] or from nature (natural). The voluntary are the ones for those things for which men establish certain words, like "Roma" from "Romulus," "Tiburtes" from "Tibur." The natural are the ones which are declined, in case or tense, from those established words, like from "Romulus" comes "Romulus's" and "(toward) Romulus," and from "I say" comes "I was saying" and "I had said."

> In those matters, the things which are derived externally, such as "horse-pen" from "horse," "sheepfold" from "sheep," and others follow suit. These

---

49. This detail is given first by Propertius (4.4.73–78), another major innovator in the tradition.

50. Langendoen 1966: 35 with note 6 argues for "spontaneous" rather than "voluntary." I hope my "to come from the will" gives a clearer sense.

are the opposite of the things I spoke about above, like "moneyed" from "money," "civilized" from "city," "black-clad" from "black." Like sometimes a place is named for a man, a man may be named for a place, like "Rome" from "Romulus," "Roman" from "Rome."

Varro twice uses *impono* to describe Romulus's naming of the city, and Romulus's rule over the language results in all Romans taking their name, ultimately, from this first autocrat of the seven hills. Like the omission of the obliterated Sabine shrines, the ignorance of Tarpeia's treason, and the refusal to mention the Parilia, the elision of Rome's first autocrat Romulus in 5.41 leaves the city's foundation free from discord—for the moment.

I would like to press this analysis further. *Roma* is an anomalous word, imposed upon the collectively and descriptively named "Seven Hills." The Capitolinum is also an anomalous word (as was the *caput* on which is it based), since someone made a decision, upon finding the head, to rename the hill after that head. So too is the name Tarpeia anomalous, and it gave way to the analogist adjectival forms *Tarpeius, a, um,* which appear in the relics of her name (*nominis monumenta*) that Varro mentions, *mons Tarpeius* and *saxum Tarpeium*. Varro's text makes apparent the way Tarpeia, anomalous in the broad rather than strictly linguistic sense of the word, gave way to a regularization of her semantics into the regular, predictable, and reproducible forms of an *us, a, um* adjective. The anomaly she represents has now been subsumed and tamed by the collective into a comprehensible and reproducible form: the name given to the place for punishing traitors. The Tarpeian rock, Tarpeia's analogous relic, relies on and buttresses the sense of collective shared identity that holds Rome together and pushes other anomalies out.

Consensus on the Tarpeian places—the collective, normative interpretation of these places—may be found in Varro's very grammar. No active verbs are applied to the etymologies in this section. No one calls a place X, or says a place is named Y, or gives the name Z. I reproduce the passage here with the passive verbs in boldface and active verbs underlined for ease of assessment:

> Ubi nunc <u>est</u> Roma, Septimontium **nominatum** ab tot montibus quos postea urbs muris <u>comprehendit</u>; e quis Capitolinum **dictum,** quod hic, cum fundamenta **foderentur** aedis Iovis, caput humanum **dicitur inventum.** Hic mons ante Tarpeius **dictus** a virgine Vestale Tarpeia, quae ibi ab Sabinis **necata** armis et **sepulta**: cuius nominis monimentum **relictum,** quod etiam nunc eius rupes Tarpeium **appellatur** saxum. (5.41)

All the place names are passively assigned, without any agency. Indeed the one ablative in the passage that could indicate naming agency turns out to be an ablative of origin, and that is our antiheroine: *dictus a virgine Vestale Tarpeia*. For contrast Varro assigns agency and means in the very next sentence, but not with a verb of naming: *ab Sabinis necata armis et sepulta*. It is noteworthy, too, that Tarpeia morphs from an ablative of origin to a passive subject, acted upon. The erasure of linguistic agency follows suit with the exploration above: the anomaly, or linguistic intervention, is smoothed over by the practice and consensus of the many nameless speakers. Passive verbs and participles of naming are common in Varro's text, to be sure, but are generally interspersed with some active intervention into the language. The two chapters adjacent to Tarpeia's chapter show the contrast, again, with passive verbs in boldface and active verbs underlined.

> Prata **dicta** ab eo, quod sine opere **parata**. Quod in agris quotquot annis rursum **facienda** eadem, ut rursum capias fructus, **appellata** rura. **Dividi** t<am>en esse ius scribit Sulpicius plebei rura largiter ad <ad>oream. Praedia **dicta**, item ut praedes, a praestando, quod ea pignore **data** publice mancupis fidem praestent. (5.40)

> Hunc antea montem Saturnium **appellatum** prodiderunt et ab eo Lati<um> Saturniam terram, ut etiam Ennius appellat. Antiquum oppidum in hoc fuisse Saturniam **scribitur**. Eius vestigia etiam nunc manent tria, quod Saturni fanum in faucibus, quod Saturnia Porta quam Iunius scribit ibi, quam nunc vocant Pandanam, quod post aedem Saturni in aedificiorum legibus privatis parietes postici "muri <Saturnii>" **sunt scripti**. (5.42)

Meadows (*prata*) are named from the fact that they are prepared (*parata*) without any work. Because the same things have to be done again and again (*rursum*) every year in the fields so that you can harvest the crop, those are called fields (*rura*). Sulpicius, though, writes that it is the law that the *rura* of the people be divided up with public beneficence (*largiter*) as merit-payment for soldiers. Estates (*praedia*) are so called, and also bondsmen (*praedes*), from "providing," because these, given publically with a pledge, offer a guarantee of the property transfer.

They say this mountain used to be called the Saturnian Mount before, and from it, Latium has been called the Saturnian land, as Ennius calls it. It is written that Saturnia was an ancient town in this region. Three traces of this remain even now—that there is a shrine of Saturn *en route*, that there was a Saturnia gate which Junius writes about, which they now call the Pandana Gate, and that behind the sanctuary of Saturn, in the laws about buildings for private persons, the rear walls are called Saturnian walls.

Note how Ennius, Junius, and Sulpicius are given status as individual speakers, and in the second passage anonymous speakers, collectively at least, actively exert their voice (*prodiderunt, dicunt*). In Tarpeia's passage, Rome is the only active agent: *Roma est, urbs comprehendit*. Rome emerges as the entity that converts anomalous interventions (Romulus whose naming act is unremarked, Tarpeia who gives way to the adjective signifying "treasonous") to collective usage, just as it brings seven hills together into one polity. The *caput* is also subsumed; as Spencer says (p. 216), "Here, the essentialist and anomalous qualities of the *caput* are (like Tarpeia's treachery) regularized and given meaning within the Roman system, right at the beginning of the trauma that would generate the new Republican order." The following schema might help imagine the sequence, with the middle (anomalist) column transforming into the column of comforting names on the right:

Former name	Intervention	New name
Seven Hills	Romulus intervenes	Roma
Unnamed hill	Tarpeia intervenes	Mons Tarpeius
Mons Tarpeius	*caput* intervenes	Capitolinum
Rupes Tarpeia	*caput* intervenes	Saxum Tarpeium

If Tarpeia's is the head they found while digging the temple foundations, my interpretation gains strength and resonance. The juxtaposition of head and girl in the text, one image abutting the other, makes possible the interpretation that it is or at least could be her head. The girl then cedes twice—once to a skull, emphasizing her death, and again to the names *Capitolinum* and *Saxum Tarpeium*, which together assert Rome's control over dissenters. The Parilia connection gains meaning here as another way to order disorder: the death of the traitor becomes the birthday of Rome.

Tarpeia would die again and again and again in the next few decades—in Livy's text, in Propertius's, on the Basilica and on an Augustan coin, in the history of Dionysius of Halicarnassus, and in Valerius Maximus's compendium of great moral tales. Her repeated death in Roman arts and letters in a way ritualizes the violence of her story, making it comforting, even sacrificial.

A dozen years ago Stephen Hinds wrote about the Varronian tendency of Augustan poets to etymologize. His argument was that the poets thereby engaged neither in cute aesthetics nor in scholarly pedantry, nor (I would add) in some odd Alexandrian combination of the two. Rather, Hinds understood Varro's words on words to be indicative of his culture's habit of etymologizing as a way to understand the world.[51] Varro's text, focusing as it does on the very words and names of her story and how those words and names came to be, shows the process whereby an anomaly: *one treasonous girl* becomes an analogy: *all traitors are punished*. It is a ritual of language and statecraft. This is not to say that Varro served a particular political agenda in writing his *de Lingua Latina*, even less so that Caesar or other contemporary gender or political aberrations lay behind his Tarpeia. My more modest claim about Tarpeia is that, as a puzzle now prominently and unapologetically placed at Rome's heart, she naturalizes other such central puzzles. The "myth of mythlessness" that is the result of rationalizing antiquarian inquiry emerges, in this argument, as deeply mythic in the sense that it powerfully unites human concerns with cosmic structures and proposes a worldview that is just yet must be processed and regularized. Language, politics, religion, philosophy, gender, personhood, and the very physical world around us are, to Varro, all part of one coherent system in which Tarpeia is both a threat and a linchpin.

IN THE FORUM ROMANUM

Varro's multidisciplinary impulse to comprehend Rome's past, in both of the word's core senses—to understand, and to hold together—led to Cicero's famous compliment in the text the orator dedicated to Varro:

> Nam nos in nostra urbe peregrinantis errantisque tamquam hospites tui libri quasi domum deduxerunt ut possemus aliquando qui et ubi essemus agnoscere. (*Acad.* 1.9)

> For when we were travelers abroad in our own city, wandering around like strangers, your books led us home, as it were, so that we could know who and where we were.

---

51. Hinds 2006: 11.

I find it fascinating that Cicero says "who and where," joining identity and place. Another cultural artifact from Varro's age reveals the same juncture of identity and place: the Basilica Aemilia, with its glorious frieze depicting scenes from the Romulean foundation of the city. The best-preserved of these sculptures shows Tarpeia at the moment of her punishment. In what follows I suggest that Tarpeia's position in the Basilica Aemilia performs a function similar to the one she performs in Varro's text: as I called her above, she is a threat and a linchpin, a conundrum at the heart of Rome that is to be embraced and cast out at once.

The Basilica Aemilia lies in the northwestern portion of the Roman forum, between the Curia and the Regia (see fig. 4). It was constructed in 179 BCE by M. Fulvius Nobilior and M. Aemilius Lepidus in commemoration of their tenure as censors; it appears in Varro's text as *Basilica Aemilia et Fulvia* (*de Ling.* 6.4). In 78 BCE, M. Aemilius Lepidus, *consul*, decorated the building with shields; this restoration appears on a coin minted by his son of the same name (*RRC* 419.3). From 55 to 34 BCE—a period encompassing the publication of Varro's *de Lingua Latina*[52]—the Basilica underwent a massive restoration at the hands of another branch of the *gens Aemilia*. L. Aemilius Lepidus Paullus began the project and another basilica opposite it to the southeast across the Sacra Via; Caesar added financing; and Paullus's homonymous son completed and inaugurated it.[53] Thereafter it is called in the ancient sources the *Basilica Paulli*.[54] The building burned and was restored in 14 BCE by Augustus, who added a portico to his grandsons Lucius and Gaius. It burned again and was restored in 22 CE. The building whose remains are now visible in the Roman forum is the Augustan restoration and the Tiberian rebuilding.

The frieze exists in several fragments now housed in the Palazzo Massimo alle Terme in Rome. It was long thought to be a continuous composition, but the Freyberger group now excavating posits that it was intended as a series of individual panels placed lower in the central nave so as to facilitate viewing.[55] The fragments show scenes from the life and rule of Romulus: in addition to the punishment of Tarpeia at issue here, fragments reveal the rape of the Sabine women, wall-building, Romulus and

---

52. Though we can never know if the whole text was published at once, *Lingua*'s dedication to Cicero sets a likely *terminus ante quem* at 43 BCE, the year of Cicero's death.

53. See Cicero *Att.* 4.16.8 for the elder Aemilius's restoration (and Wiseman 1998: 106–20 for a full discussion). Plutarch *Caesar* 29.3 mentions Caesar's involvement (cf. Appian *BC* 2.26); and Cassius Dio 49.42 covers the dedication by the younger Aemilius.

54. At Tacitus *Ann.* 3.72, it is called *basilica Pauli Aemilia monumenta*.

55. Ertel et al. 2007: 120.

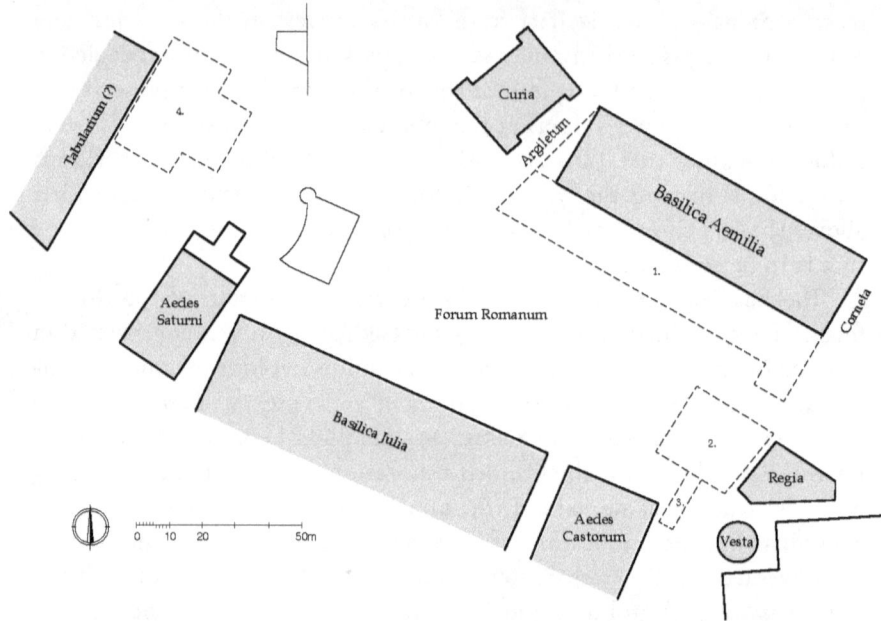

FIGURE 4. Basilica Aemilia in the Roman Forum. Plan courtesy of Philip Stinson.

Remus, and a marriage scene, perhaps the first Roman marriage following the rape of the Sabines. Because of the paucity of remains from the Basilica Aemilia frieze (only 10 percent of the whole remains),[56] it is impossible to know what is missing. It is possible that, like the roughly contemporary painted frieze of the tomb of the Statilii, the missing parts displayed elements of the Alban cycle, or even, like the Forum Augustum would later, the Aeneas legend.[57] It is also possible that some of the lost scenes came from later in Rome's foundation; one scene of a duel between two warriors could be Romulus versus Acron or the Horatii and Curiatii.[58] The figure of Tarpeia occupies the largest extant fragment (fig. 5). She stands at the center of the panel against a rocky background, buried to her waist with

---

56. Roughly twenty-two meters out of a hypothesized 185, according to Carettoni 1961: 8–9. If the frieze is not continuous, what remains represents a larger percentage of the whole.

57. Evans 1992: 15–18 has a good description and brief discussion of the tomb paintings; see more recently Holliday 2005 and Borbonus 2014; the latter includes many plates and thorough analysis.

58. For the dueling pair as Romulus vs. Acron, see Albertson 1990: 807; as the Horatii vs. Curiatii, see Carettoni 1961: 36–39. Simon 1966: 838–39 sees the frieze as entirely Romulean.

FIGURE 5. Basilica Aemilia relief sculpture. Death of Tarpeia. Photo courtesy of Philip Stinson.

FIGURE 6. Basilica Aemilia relief sculpture. Edge of Tarpeia segment (l) and wedding scene (r). Photo courtesy of Philip Stinson.

shields. Her arms are outstretched and she faces the viewer. Her mantle swirls around her head, and her tunic has slipped off one shoulder, revealing one breast. She is flanked by soldiers on either side, who are poised to add their shields to the pile at her midriff. Further out on each side are bearded men watching her—one with his foot perched on a rock, the other half kneeling and resting his chin in his hand. This scene is adjacent to a marriage scene (fig. 6). The frieze was part of the Augustan restoration of the Basilica, but its original date of composition is under dispute. Carettoni argued that the frieze was designed and executed for the rebuilding of the Caesarian period; when this building burned, the designers of the replacement of 14 BCE reused the relief.[59] His arguments are fourfold: (1) Some panels are extraordinarily thin, suggesting they have been recarved to fit a new housing. (2) The frieze is Pentelic marble, whereas the Augustan trabeation for it is in Luna marble. Pentelic marble was popular in the Caesarian period before the quarry opened at Luni, and the different materials at any rate suggest reuse. (3) There are indications of different hands and techniques on various panels, suggesting reworking and adaptation to a new context. (4) The spatial proportion of the frieze to the rest of the architectural elements of the Augustan basilica is taller than usual, suggesting it was designed for a differently proportioned structure. Most scholars follow Carettoni's dating for the frieze.[60] Kampen, in contrast, has suggested that the frieze's iconography better fits the Augustan restoration, when the moral legislation reoriented myths toward social patterns and gender roles, and when interest in the foundation was perhaps at its highest (cf. the Ara Pacis reliefs).[61] The Freyberger group, in charge of the current excavation, dates the frieze to the Augustan era for iconographical and technical reasons.[62]

I follow the reuse theory. The frieze no doubt resonates in its Augustan context; I have discussed this resonance previously (Welch 2005: 58–62). Here I would like to make a case for Tarpeia's ideological resonance in the Caesarian context, particularly vis-à-vis the dynamics of "central anomaly" maintained in this chapter. As Wiseman convincingly argues, the Paullan restoration was part of the dynastic posturing of the troubled decade

---

59. Carettoni 1961: 5–7 and 64–65; see also Arya 2000: 306–11, who emphasizes more than did Carettoni the variety of attachment techniques used.

60. He is followed by Albertson 1990; Arya 2000; Bauer 1988 (who comments more generally on the decorative elements); Holscher 1988: 380–82; Richardson 1979: 209–15; and Zanker 1988: 206 does not commit but leans toward reuse.

61. Kampen 1991; Kampen 1988: 15.

62. Tomei 2010; Freyberger et al. 2007: 505; Ertel et al. 2007: 118–22.

before the civil wars between Pompey and Caesar.⁶³ Pompey had dedicated his monumental theater complex in 55 BCE; Caesar was away in Gaul, and planning his own extensive projects—the *Atrium libertatis*, the Saepta, and of course the Forum Iulium; and Paullus (brother to the future triumvir Lepidus) was in Rome positioning himself as a player in this grand dynastic game. Paullus was aedile in 59 BCE and would gain influence as praetor in 53 and consul in 50. In a letter to Atticus in 54 BCE (4.16.8), Cicero mentions Paullus's designs to edge the Forum with two basilicas bearing his name—one a restoration, the other a grand new building. During Paullus's consulship Caesar gave 1,500 talents of silver to complete the project; fifteen years later Paullus's son dedicated the remade Basilica Aemilia, and the second basilica was dedicated in 46 BCE, unfinished. It came to be known as the Basilica Iuli. With this money Paullus, initially a dynast with his own pretentions, had become Caesar's partisan.

These basilicas mark an important stage in the process of transformation of the Forum Romanum (fig. 4) from a landscape of rivalry to a landscape of coherence.⁶⁴ Caesar was squeezing the Republican life out of the Forum with pressure on two sides. The Tabularium / *Atrium Libertatis*⁶⁵ on the Capitol slope would make three sides, and, after Caesar's death, the temple to his new godhead would complete the noose. The Forum Romanum was becoming a tribute to anomaly at Rome's center. Consider the Basilica's ideological and physical position in the Roman forum. Originally a reception hall and diplomatic space for Greek monarchs and their representatives,⁶⁶ the Basilica occupies the space between the political seat of the Republic, the Curia (Senate House) and the seat of Rome's former monarchy, the Regia (the King's House, which is itself next to the Vestal complex). It was a sort of central and useful transitional space.

In the Julian context, the frieze of Rome's foundation sets Rome's new dynast in the context of her first monarchic founders—Romulus (here building walls) and Numa alike, since Tarpeia's *felix culpa* (fortuitous lapse) led to the Sabine partnership in Rome that made Numa's kingship possible, and Numa is an ancestor to Julius Caesar via the latter's grandmother Marcia. This is Grimal's reading of the frieze,⁶⁷ and while I believe

---

63. Wiseman 1998: 114–20.
64. Favro 1996: 130; Zanker 1988: 81–82.
65. Purcell 1993 identifies the missing *Atrium libertatis* as what we have called the Tabularium.
66. K. Welch 2003; to Welch, the Basilica Aemilia represents an updating of the original diplomatic functionality of the Atrium Regis, also in the area, and the slightly earlier Basilica Porcia.
67. Grimal 1951: 212–14 sees this connection operative in Propertius's poem as well and reads the poem as laudatory of Augustus, but the Sabine–Numa connection is more applicable to the Julian use of the legend.

the Numa connection is not the most ready to hand, the pointer toward monarchic imagery is fruitful. One possible resonance of this imagery is its connection of royalty to the calendar.[68] The frieze depicts religious observances, and many of its events are connected with Roman festivals. Caesar was keenly interested in the calendar. Another possible interpretive avenue opened by consideration of the frieze as monarchic is its focus on women; Tarpeia, the Sabine women, and the bride on the frieze would thus meditate on the role of women in dynastic succession, be they mothers, daughters, wives, allies, or even enemies.[69] The important and uppity women of Rome's monarchic period (Tarpeia, Tullia, Horatia) had given way to the more traditionally circumscribed women of the Republic, even the famous names such as Veturia, Verginia, and Cornelia. In Caesar's day the politically subversive woman resurfaced in Fulvia and of course Cleopatra VII, and in the artistic sector, where they remained firmly entrenched throughout the imperial period. The presence of these women in a public, monumental space represents, to Kampen, a confusion between public and private.[70] Given the women depicted, it also represents a confusion of gender.

Traitor Tarpeia appears next to a bride and near rape victims. The confluence of resistance, force, and cooperation on this one frieze reveals the breadth of the category "woman." The fact that the Roman and Sabine men are dressed alike on the frieze—distinguishable only by their narrative context—suggests that the frieze itself is not a meditation of ethnicity.[71] This throws the gender differences into higher relief (sorry). Tarpeia's panel is especially rich in its engagement with conceptions of gender.

Tarpeia's left breast is bared like an Amazon's. In this she resembles Greek sculpted Amazons and their Roman copies, rather than the exotically dressed Amazons of Greek vase painting. This choice strips Tarpeia of

---

68. As Albertson 1990 notes, the frieze as a whole seems to celebrate not only Romulus as an ideal king, but also Rome's evolving calendar—both themes that were pertinent to Caesar's rule. See also Arya's (2000: 312–15) suggestion that the frieze alternates scenes of action and ritual in a meditation on Rome's festivals. In this context Arya connects Tarpeia to the Parentalia, a connection he supports by reference to Piso's "offerings at Tarpeia's tomb" (Dionysius of Halicarnassus 2.40.3). There is much discussion about this possibility, first advanced by Mommsen (*CIL* 1(1) p. 258.) and refuted convincingly by Latte 1960: 111n2. Albertson connects her to the Matronalia based on the adjacent wedding scene (1990: 807–8). See the discussion in chapter 1.

69. Glinister 1997.

70. Kampen 1991.

71. The statues of easterners that adorned the upper story of the Basilica add a layer of otherness to the whole building; Schneider situates these within a late-Republican trend to link Rome to the East, which paradoxically becomes, in iconography, Rome's ancestor and subject (Schneider 2012: 114–20).

the barbarian aspect and, like the indistinguishable clothing worn by the men, leaves her gender rather than her ethnicity as the focal point. As an Amazon—a woman who lives apart from civilization, who does not marry, and who adopts masculine activities—she is marginal and hostile to the natural order. In a way, the Amazon is a fitting model for Tarpeia, who as a Vestal is also segregated from society and does not marry, and as a traitor enters the masculine world of warfare. Yet she is central to the composition, its focal point, held there by the two soldiers that press in on either side. Her status as an Amazon (a woman nonwoman) finds echoes in her action, a treason that requires female weakness plus male initiative, and in her location, as a woman appearing in a public, male, political space.

The concept/goddess *Virtus* was sometimes styled as an Amazon in Roman art.[72] This connection allows the personification, feminine because the Latin language dictates it thus, to be warlike, and says something about the Roman concept of *virtus*.[73] It also says something about the Roman conception of the Amazon. Though foreign and dangerous, she was still able to be the icon for that most Roman of traits. More provocative is the fact that the goddess Roma was also styled as an Amazon, this time, like Tarpeia, with a pile of weapons at her feet.[74] The wide circulation of these images in coins and sculpture around the Graeco-Roman world indicate something about the way Romans positioned themselves within the world they had conquered, and the way their presence was received locally.[75] I am not suggesting that Tarpeia looks like these figures or could be confused for Roma or *Virtus*, or vice versa. Rather, these two figures together demonstrate Rome's ability to embrace an enigma—a grammatically feminine noun signifying manliness or an embodiment of the state represented by a manly woman. In this they are like Tarpeia, whose myth is crucial to Rome's foundation story, whose rock **is** the Capitol in Varro's text, and whose monumental face in stone gazed down on the Basilica Aemilia's many visitors, in the heart of the Roman forum.

Flanking Tarpeia and her attackers, who are focused on her, the frieze depicts two men who contemplate the scene impassively. These two men

---

72. E.g., *RRC* 329, a denarius of P. Cornelius Lentulus Marcellinus from c.100 BCE.

73. See McDonnell 2006: 146–49 for the Amazon likeness (which speaks to martial glory) and 161–68 for the discomfit of virtue and the feminine.

74. E.g., the denarius of M. Fourius Philus from 119 BCE (*RRC* 281), and Amazonian Roma appears as well on the Boscoreale cup, for which see the discussion at Kuttner 1995: 19. Vermeule 1959 remains a good starting point.

75. Gergel 2004 discusses the cluster Amazon-*Virtus*-Roma in Greek breastplates in the context of Hadrian's philhellenism or imperialism. The foreign and imperial contexts of this self-fashioning place them outside the scope of this study, but they draw attention to the fact that, rather than appearing outside Rome, the Basilica's Tarpeia is fixed in Rome's center.

face inward and frame the Tarpeia tableau, as it were. Elsner (1996) has emphasized the Roman fixation on viewing practices by noting the presence and importance of internal viewers in Roman art. These internal viewers present us, the external viewers, with models to emulate even while they complicate the process, for they present multiple perspectives and objects of attention.[76] Here, the attackers look only at Tarpeia, the framing men look at the attack, and we look at Tarpeia, the attackers, and the witnesses (the bride and groom in the contiguous panel aren't interested in Tarpeia's story at all; see fig. 6). The witnesses strike poses of contemplation, the one on Tarpeia's far right with his foot on a rock, a common Hellenistic conceit. His gaze at once objectifies Tarpeia and her attack, and yet it also holds him in her thrall. Looking at her gender-vexed image, her central otherness, this viewer and his partner on Tarpeia's left are problematized as active interpreters of her story and as passive objects of its force.[77] These witnesses are variously identified as Tatius on her right (the Sabine king) and Romulus/Mars on her left, but no one can be sure with the current evidence.[78] Tatius makes sense as a witness to her death, but Mars and Romulus raise questions. If the figure is Mars, does his witness sanction her deed, or her punishment? If it is Romulus, why is he there, and what would it mean that his calm reaction and Tatius's are the same? The frieze would have been above eye level. In the absence of labels of some sort that identify the frieze's images, how likely is it that a viewer could identify these figures securely? If we don't know who they are, how are we to view their viewing?

Meanwhile, Tarpeia looks directly at us. Her frontality poses a challenge to the viewers, for, whatever we make of the relationship between the men attacking or watching the attack and Tarpeia, viewers locking eyes with her image have a different relationship. Frontality is one feature of epiphanic images of the gods, and as Verity Platt has argued (2011: 117–19), it places viewers in a worshipful stance vis-à-vis the image. Her swirling mantle also nudges viewers toward an aweful response to her, for *velificatio* often distinguishes goddesses in relief sculpture.[79] Platt draws a distinction between viewing a frontal image, as visitors to the Basilica do, and viewing it obliquely, as the embedded onlookers do; the former have (or seek) to encounter her, while the onlookers have (or seek) a narrative

---

76. Similar is the inclusion of builders in monumental art, such as the wall builder on one of the frieze panels. See Reitz 2012.

77. For the gendered ambiguity of the erotic gaze, see esp. Kampen 1996: 20–21.

78. Carettoni 1961: 28 identifies the figure on Tarpeia's right as Tatius, and on the left as a soldier bringing heavier arms.

79. Rehak 2006: 111.

reading of her (Platt 2011: 119). With epiphanic statues of the gods, there results a theological tension between the image as god and as artifact. This particular tension does not pertain in Tarpeia's frieze, yet the ontological problem her image poses is just as acute, for she is divinely appearing yet also in the process of dying, engaging the impotent viewer and ignoring her onlookers/interpreters.

Her arms are raised high, palms forward. It is possible to see in her a posture of resignation, one of martyrdom, or one of defiance.[80] Like all the narrative sources (save Propertius) that don't allow her a voice, we can never know what she is thinking. We can only see her and interpret her, as do the sculpted watchers. Though her image is one of movement and action, she is stationed and stationary in the Basilica, even as diverse viewers walked around the vast interior of the building for manifold purposes and caught various glances of her. To me, this viewing dynamic resembles her myth. She is the enigma at the center—of the Forum, of the foundation myth, of the sculpted panel—and we, as we pass by her, see her differently. As is also the case with Caesar: we cannot recover what exactly he is; we can only recover what others thought he was.

---

80. Her outstretched arms might indicate openness or a lack of modesty (cf. Europa), and her upturned palms could be construed as a hostile gesture. Carettoni 1961 opts for resignation (p. 29, "un gesto di rassegnato fatalismo," and p. 31, "conscia del suo destino, non intenda fare alcuna mossa per sottrarvisi ed attenda impassabile la fine. Il suo gesto è di aperta offerta, non di raccolta difesa") verging on martyrdom (p. 31, "è l'eroina romana che offre il corpo in olocausto alla patria, e tale ferma decisione è espressa nel volto"). In this he argues that the scene follows Piso's patriotic account. For an interesting account of Giotto's possible use of this image as the basis of his "Inconstantia" in the Scrovegni chapel in Padova, see Grassigli 2002. That her image is apotropaic is another possibility; Platt 2011: 113 sees frontal Pandora on the base of Phidias's Athena Parthenos as an apotropaic doublet of the gorgon on the *aegis*. Like Tarpeia, this sculpted Pandora is flanked by onlookers who do something to her; beyond the relief, like Tarpeia, Pandora remains silent and blamed.

CHAPTER FIVE

PERSPECTIVES ON AND OF LIVY'S TARPEIA[1]

LIVY'S TARPEIA is generally the first Tarpeia that modern audiences meet, either as a short example of a "famous Roman woman," or as part of the cycle of colorful stories that makes up early Rome. In this chapter I explore these Livian Tarpeias in turn: how Livy constructs (or deconstructs) Tarpeia as "exemplary," and how he frames her example, such as it is, in the broader context of his first book to explore the role of women in early and contemporary Rome both as objects available for differing assessment from several perspectives within and outside the text, and as subjects who must negotiate their own process of discernment.

Nevertheless, the double role is crucial for the knitting together of communities and identities that constitutes the rise of Rome and ensures its growth. Women, born into one family and then married into another, function as objects in the marriage transaction enacted by men and as subjects in those relationships who may perceive their matronage differently. Tarpeia's story is one of the less tidy vignettes about Rome's growth, not because she is a traitor (and thus an embarrassment to Rome, though this did not stop them from telling her story), but because the process of incorporating outsiders is itself cluttered with various irreconcilable perspectives.

---

1. This chapter appeared in *EuGeSta* 2 (2012). I am grateful for the readers and editors for their extremely fruitful comments.

Horatia's story offers a particularly rich point of comparison, for there the outcome is much more comfortable. In contrast to Tarpeia's story, in which no one is heroic, Horatia's story is full of commendable behaviors.

In both episodes, Livy exploits the language of seeing and seeming so as to frame the latent questions about identity that these foundational stories explore. Unfortunately, the distance of time and the panoramic view Livy offers in his first book do not help the reader of either tale come to a firm conclusion about the moral lessons these stories offer. Rather, like the actors within the stories, we are faced with a fragmented and fragmentary picture that makes it difficult for us to label as good/imitable or bad/inimitable. What we do perhaps have that Livy's characters lack is the realization that our perspective is partial and that we are studying a process of assimilation as much as an outcome. And this is the conclusion one takes from Livy's narrative of the Roman traitoress: more than a character in Roman myth, she is a process personified.

BETWEEN HISTORY AND HISTORIOGRAPHY: THE *EXEMPLUM* AND ITS REQUIREMENTS

Livy's famous preface announces that history is a useful moral tool:

> Hoc illud est praecipue in cognitione rerum salubre ac frugiferum, omnis te exempli documenta in inlustri posita monumento intueri; inde tibi tuaeque rei publicae quod imitere capias, inde foedum inceptu foedum exitu quod vites. (*praef.* 10)[2]

> In understanding (past) events, this especially is salutary and beneficial: that you can see records of every sort of example set on display in this illustrious monument, from which you can take for yourself and your country both that which you should imitate, and that which, being shameful from start to finish, you should avoid.

This statement makes clear Livy's goal of moral instruction, but this is no simple goal nor is it a simple statement of that goal.[3] The natural reading is to take this as a generalizing statement about history, but the words themselves give rise both to general and to more specific interpretations.

---

2. The text is Ogilvie's Oxford edition (1974).
3. Ogilvie 1965 *ad loc.* notes the ease of understanding the general sense but the difficulty of locating the "precise force of these words."

Livy's specific wording in this passage links history with historiography as partners in moral instruction, and draws in his audience not only as impressionable moral agents but also as readers and learners. On one level we can simply say that the events of the past (*rerum*) are full of examples (*exempli*) for moral agents of the present, whether those be Livy's contemporaries, Renaissance political philosophers such as Macchiavelli, or modern students of Roman history. But this is not exactly what Livy says, and *rerum* and *exempli* are both genitives dependent on other nouns that are equally if not more crucial in his formulation. It is in the understanding of past events (*cognitione rerum*) that one finds evidence (literally, things that teach) of every sort of example (*omnis exempli documenta*). Understanding and evidence rather than history and examples constitute the path to moral instruction. Livy again draws attention to the teaching value of his work with the phrase *inlustri monumento*.[4] I take *monumento* as a reference to Livy's historical text in particular, like Horace's famous *monumentum* at *Carm.* 3.30, rather than to history more broadly or abstractly or, on the converse, to the characters within it.[5] He calls his text *tout court* a tool for advising (*monumento*) which is clear (*inlustri*) to boot, a pun that flatters Livy and points to the illuminating (educating) power of his history.

If the *res* and *exempla* are the raw materials, the content of Livy's work (we might call it the history), then the crafting of those materials into teaching and advising tools—*documenta, monumento, inlustri*—is the means whereby that material comes to the reader. We might call this means the historiography, which is the interface between the material and the learner. For this reason it is not the past that provides moral help to the contemporary moral agent but the apprehension (*cognitione*) of that past. The importance of *cognitione* and Livy's striking use of the second-person singular—*imitere, vites*—and the pronoun *te* assign Livy's reader a great deal of responsibility in learning from the lessons contained therein.[6] I note here too that vision is the primary means for readers to absorb Livy's content. We are to look (*intueri*) at and for *documenta* in this *monumento*. *Inlustri* likewise suggests a visual aspect. Given the usual meaning of *mon-*

---

4. See Jaeger 1997: 15–29, esp. 23–29; Miles 1995: 16–19; and Gowing 2005: 22–23 on history as a monument.

5. I agree with Ogilvie that to take *inlustri monumento* as referring to noteworthy historical characters is unsatisfying. In addition to the poor fit with the emphasis the preface places on history as a whole rather than on its individuals, the abstract singular *monumento* is awkward as a container for plural *documenta* of every sort of example. Yet where Ogilvie sees *monumento* as a reference to history, I see it as a reference to Livy's history.

6. See also Jaeger 1997: 23–24.

umentum—a physical monument[7]—looking at it seems the right thing to do, but we might ask, from what perspective?[8] For how long? How many times? Such questions will arise in the episodes I discuss in this chapter, and Livy seems to anticipate them here with the subjunctives *imitere* and *vites*. With the relative clause of characteristic ("the sort you might imitate or avoid"), Livy implies that we readers must decide which examples are which. Even *capias* puts the ball in our court: "from which you *might* take examples." And does *inde* lead back to *monumento* or *documenta*? Our work as readers grows.

My analysis here focuses on the gap between historical character (*exemplum*) and the reader or moral agent who would learn from it. The exchange between the *exemplum* and the moral agent through the interface of historiography has recently been explored, directly and indirectly, by several scholars of Roman culture. Most broadly, Matthew Roller posits a fourfold process: (1) event, (2) commemoration (textual or material), (3) interpretation of the commemoration, and (4) resulting action.[9] In *Spectacle and Society in Livy's History* (1998), Andrew Feldherr examines how, within Livy's own text, characters witness events in the text and act upon their interpretations—a process that is instructive to Livy's readers (recall *te . . . intueri*). Jane Chaplin's book *Livy's Exemplary History* (2000) scrutinizes instances in which Livy's historical figures themselves look to past *exempla* as models of behavior, or are self-conscious about the ways their actions may be read in the future.

We may return for a moment to Livy's preface, with its emphasis on learning, discerning, and individual appropriation of the past: *imitere* and *uites* are singular verbs, not plurals, further still from generalizing passives (including periphrastics). In the next section I explore the ways Livy's Tarpeia refuses to be pinned down as an *exemplum* with clear or universal meaning, and how Livy opens many paths for the reader to interpret and appropriate the story in different ways. This section focuses not on what Tarpeia herself means as an example in Livy's text, but how her story illustrates the process, or rather a process, of reading an example from the past.

---

7. *OLD* s.v. *monumentum* 1 and 2; and *TLL* s.v. *monumentum* B1 *oppida, loca sim* and B2 *aedificia, artificia sim.*

8. Jaeger 1997: 26 and Chaplin 2000: throughout, especially 50–72, both use the narratological concept of focalization to illuminate the complexities of *exempla*.

9. Roller 2004: 4–6.

LIVY'S EQUIVOCATIONS

Tarpeia's story appears in Livy as part of the Sabine cycle beginning with the Roman capture of Sabine brides and ending with the joint kingship of Romulus and Tatius. The rape sparked several skirmishes between Rome and her neighbors, none notable except the battle in which Romulus won and dedicated as *spolia opima* to Jupiter Feretrius the armor of the leader of the Caeninenses. Livy distinguishes the skirmish in which Tarpeia's treason plays a role as something different:

> Novissimum ab Sabinis bellum ortum multoque id maximum fuit; nihil enim per iram aut cupiditatem actum est, nec ostenderunt bellum prius quam intulerunt. Consilio etiam additus dolus. Sp. Tarpeius Romanae praeerat arci. Huius filiam virginem auro corrumpit Tatius ut armatos in arcem accipiat; aquam forte ea tum sacris extra moenia petitum ierat. Accepti obrutam armis necavere, seu ut vi capta potius arx videretur seu prodendi exempli causa ne quid usquam fidum proditori esset. Additur fabula, quod volgo Sabini aureas armillas magni ponderis brachio laevo gemmatosque magna specie anulos habuerint, pepigisse eam quod in sinistris manibus haberent; eo scuta illi pro aureis donis congesta. Sunt qui eam ex pacto tradendi quod in sinistris manibus esset derecto arma petisse dicant et fraude visam agere sua ipsam peremptam mercede. Tenuere tamen arcem Sabini . . . . (1.11.5–1.12.1)

The most novel war arose from the Sabines and it was by far the most serious. For nothing was done out of anger or greed, nor did they give any sign of war before they attacked. Deceit even supplemented their strategy. Spurius Tarpeius was in charge of the Roman citadel. His daughter, a virgin, Tatius tempted with gold so that she would let armed men into the citadel. She had, by chance, gone out of the fortress to fetch water for sacred rites. Once she accepted them they crushed her with their weapons, either so that it would seem that the citadel had been taken by force, or for the sake of a moral example, lest there evermore be any compact with a traitor. A story is added to this, that the Sabines commonly had golden armbands of substantial heft on their left arms and rings bejeweled with extraordinary beauty, and that she had bargained for what they had on their left hands. Then their shields were heaped upon her instead of the gold gifts. There are some who say that, from the agreement of handing over what was on their left hands, what she really sought was their weapons and that, having appeared to act in fraud, she was undone by her own "wage." At any rate, the Sabines got control of the citadel....

Let us start with Livy's inclusion of the word *exemplum* in this passage. It is the first use of the word in his narrative, and it is complicated in that her exemplarity is marked as only one possibility for interpreting Tarpeia's death. It is also ambiguous in itself, since at first blush the exemplary *proditor* is Tarpeia, but Livy soon makes clear that the Sabines also violated the spirit of their agreement. Chaplin notes how Livy's presentation of alternatives caps his narrative of the story and refuses to make a judgment, thus opening up Tarpeia's story to interpretation and allowing readers to valorize or condemn Tatius.[10]

Similarly, by including variants to his bare narrative, Livy also opens up other avenues for interpretation, including one that vindicates Tarpeia. He is careful to obscure his sources, though we know his main narrative follows Fabius Pictor and the alternative follows Piso Frugi as preserved in Dionysius of Halicarnassus 2.38–40 (see chapters 2 and 3). Rather, alternative traditions and possible additional details are marked by generalizing phrases. Just after requiring us to make a choice about Tatius's motive for having Tarpeia killed, Livy introduces a detail that might be relevant: the Sabines' habit of wearing golden armbands. Livy ascribes this detail to the crowd, to common belief: *additur fabula volgo*. *Habuerint* in the subjunctive further distances Livy from this belief. The erasure of agency makes the reader's work harder: who says this? How does this affect our judgment of Tarpeia's or Tatius's actions? Does it help to explain what precedes (the treason proper, Tarpeia's death) or what follows? For just after this detail Livy adds a strikingly different version—Piso's, but attributed again to an unnamed *sunt qui dicant*—in which Tarpeia was trying to trick (*fraude*) the Sabines out of their weapons. Again, Livy refuses to choose among these various points of view, and he moves on: *Tenuere tamen arcem Sabini*, "Whatever. The Sabines were in control of the *arx*."

AN *EXEMPLUM* IS FOR THE READER/VIEWER TO INTERPRET

Livy's presentation leaves much work for the reader to do. Roller's study (like Chaplin's) shows how the meaning of an example is not fixed or per-

---

10. Chaplin 2000: 17; see also Stevenson 2011.

manent, but changes over time and with context.[11] One core purpose of this book is to argue that Tarpeia's meaning is also not fixed or permanent, but exists in—and through—the exchange between teller and audience. One cannot predict how such exchanges will develop, or even how one's own commemoration will be read.

We can see the inconclusiveness of *exempla* not only in Livy's grander narrative, in which some characters use *exempla* to inspire their actions, others debate the applicability of *exempla*, and still others deny that an *exemplum* fits or they use an *exemplum* in order to argue the opposite of its apparent meaning.[12] But we can see openness in interpreting an *exemplum* even within Tarpeia's narrative. When Livy ascribes to Tatius the possible motive of making a moral example of Tarpeia (*prodendi exempli causa ne quid usquam fidum proditori esset*), the historian immediately makes such a hope moot since he tells an alternative version in which she is not a *proditor*; rather, she is a pro-Roman double agent.[13] Piso Frugi didn't read Tarpeia's death the way Tatius intended. We might phrase it thus: in the first motive ascribed to Tatius, Tatius wished to conceal Tarpeia's treachery (impossible once Livy outs the concealment). In the second Tatius wishes to reveal her treachery, even make a spectacle of it—impossible since Livy immediately gives us a counterexample that proves one can't control how later audiences will interpret a story. Similarly, in the most famous instance of a "negative example" in Livy's text, Lucretia takes the sword to herself lest any woman's *impudicitia* be justified by her precedent (*ego me etsi peccato absolvo, supplicio non libero; nec ulla deinde impudica Lucretiae exemplo vivet*, 1.58.10). Three witnesses interpret Lucretia's shame differently from this foreseen interpretation: her husband, her father, and their friend Brutus. Later in the first pentad, Verginius seems to take Lucretia's example as she intended, for he kills Verginia in order to prevent her from suffering *impudicitia*. In a further chain of disputed exemplary precedent, Livy tells us (3.48.8–9) that interpretation of Verginia's fate and its implications differed between men and women (*matronae . . . virorum*).[14]

---

11. Gowing 2005 offers a fruitful corollary to this idea, discussing "reading" monuments and histories in his fifth chapter ("Remembering Rome," pp. 132–59). Gowing notes that different meanings might be invested in monuments over time. The historical referent itself (the subject of a statue or sponsor of a building) is not the final arbiter of its own meaning.

12. Chaplin 2000 throughout, esp. 47–49.

13. Further, McCartney 1924 notes also that the Sabines, who used treachery themselves, were surely not interested in providing a moral example to posterity about treachery. McCartney sees Livy's fondness for paronomasia in *prodendi/proditor*.

14. Joshel's study of the Lucretia and Verginia episodes (1992) emphasizes this overlap of sameness (which would lead to exemplary relevance) and difference (which would hinder the applicability of the former situation to the latter). One key difference is that Lucretia speaks and tries to manipulate her own exemplary force, whereas Verginia is silent and must accept what those around

This same instability of the exemplary force of Tatius's and Tarpeia's actions points to a gap between the original action (and its intended perception) and how it is perceived by later audiences, no matter how later audiences may try to remain faithful to some perceived core meaning of the story.

One reason the moral of Tarpeia's story is so hard to pin down is that its characters are all engaged in deception. Livy takes pains to draw attention to this deception. I have mentioned the deception suggested in Tatius's first motive for killing Tarpeia: he wished to obscure the fact that he had relied on an insider's help to take the Capitol and to promote the idea instead that it had been taken by force. Livy has already introduced the idea of Sabine subterfuge. At the beginning of the Tarpeia digression at 1.11.5, the historian distinguished the Sabine attack from the other neighboring skirmishes by its scale (*multo maximum*) and because it was done on the sly, in a calculated manner. *Novissimum* here sharpens the point; it not only refers to the timing of this war in the sequence but hints at its artfulness in the sense of *novissimum* as "strange."[15] The Sabines were moved by no anger or greed—passions that cannot easily keep themselves hidden—and showed no sign of war before their attack (*nec ostenderunt bellum prius quam intulerunt*).[16] Livy's next sentence, *consilio additus dolus*, brings home the point, but its brevity and the use of the passive raise questions as well: who added the *dolus*? Did the Sabines seek out a traitor to exploit, who by chance (*forte*) ended up being Tarpeia? Or did the *dolus* initiate with her? Dionysius's exposition clearly identifies the origin of the compact with Tarpeia, who saw and desired the gold; her desire was Tatius's good fortune. Livy's compact sentence obscures the lines of responsibility, but the fact that Tatius is the subject and Tarpeia the object of the narrative's core sentence (*Tatius corrumpit filiam virginem*) suggests that the *dolus* arose in the Sabine camp first. But even in the Pisonian alternative in which Tarpeia is guilty of no treason, she is seen to be guilty of fraud (*fraude*), for she made a deliberately ambiguous promise, concealing her true intentions, as the Sabines had done when they were preparing for war.

Outright deception, present on both sides of this story, confounds

---

her find pertinent to say. The primary "audience" of these examples in Joshel's view is not Brutus, Collatinus, or even Verginius, but rather Livy and his contemporary Augustan elite audience, for whom disciplined female sexuality is a core factor in maintaining elite male integrity. I here note that the Lucretia/Verginia pair dramatizes the tension between women as objects (Verginia) and as subjects (Lucretia).

15. *OLD* s.v. *novus* entries 2 and 3.
16. Contrast the Roman counterattack later, done through *ira* and *cupiditas*, 1.12.1.

accurate understanding. But in Livy's narrative the difficulty in discerning goes deeper than the deliberate obfuscation of concealed intentions and double-dealing. There is also the challenge of interpreting what one sees. Livy's narrative of Tarpeia is full of words of showing, seeing, and seeming, which individually and together draw attention to the gap between appearance and reality. We have already seen that the Sabines did not show their intentions for war before they waged it (*nec ostenderunt*). The core physical meaning of *ostendo*, "to stretch out (i.e., for display),"[17] suggests that vision is important here. The Sabines did not put their war preparations on display. The way they looked was not the way they were. Their appearances were deceptive. One of Tatius's potential motives for killing Tarpeia was so that the Capitol would seem / be seen to have been taken by force—again, the fact that this may have been Tatius's intention does not dilute the difficulty of those who are trying to determine how the Capitol was taken. The rings the Sabines wear are described as being *magna specie*, with great appearance; *species* is almost always fraught with deception in the first book.[18] Like Vergil's Camilla, Tarpeia is lured by the luster of the jewelry into dropping her guard against less apparent dangers—here, the Sabines' shields and the possibility of their use as weapons against her.[19] Finally, in Livy's condensed Pisonian version, Tarpeia was punished by the Sabines because she had seemed / been seen to have acted in fraud (*fraude visam agere*).

---

17. *OLD* s.v. *ostendo* entry 1, p. 1274; see also TLL *praevalente notione originaria monstrandi* (sc. *offerendo obtutibus sive oculorum sive mentis*).

18. *Species*: *OLD* s.v. entry 5, p. 1799: "Outward appearance (opp. inner nature)," entry 6: "the semblance (of something other than is the actual case), illusory appearance, impression." I count eleven instances of *species*, including Tarpeia and Rhea Silvia. Outright deception or pretense occurs on five occasions: 1.3.11 (Rhea Silvia), 1.27.2 (Alban Mettius pretends alliance but intends treachery), 1.40.5 (a staged brawl to gain audience with the king), 1.41.6 (Servius Tullius pretends he is consulting King Tarquin, who is in fact already deceased), and 1.56.1 (the people are employed on projects that appear small but are labor-intensive). In four instances something's appearance (*species*) inspires deception in others: 1.11.8 (the rings whose appearance inspired Tarpeia), 1.7.4 (the beauty of Hercules' cows), 1.9.12 (Thalassius steals a particularly pretty Sabine woman), and 1.45.4 (the Sabine cow of exceptional mien is in effect stolen). In the two other instances *species* refers to something deceptive, elusive, or unprovable: 1.31.8 (Tullus Hostilius performs rites incorrectly and receives no vision [*species*] of the gods), and 1.55.6 (the appearance of a skull found on the Capitol betokens world empire for the Romans). In this last instance, Livy calls the portent clear (*haud ambages*) but then labels the interpreters (so said the soothsayers, both local and imported from Etruria).

19. Euryalus also falls into this trap in *Aeneid* 9. The temptation to greed is styled as a female weakness by Fabius Pictor in his Tarpeia fragment (see chapter 2) and by Pictor's contemporaries, such as the proponents of the *lex Oppia* (see Livy 34.1–4), but it may also simply characterize Tarpeia as immature or naïve. Her youth offers another twist on her perspective.

The combination in two of these instances of outright deceit and the subjectivity of seeing (*ostenderunt, videretur*) and the focus in two of these instances on the subjectivity of interpretation (*videretur, visam*) point to the challenges inherent in interpreting what one sees. The characters in the Tarpeia story suffer from these challenges, but so does the reader trying to understand Tarpeia's story as an *exemplum*. Here we may return to the studies of exemplarity mentioned above. Roller's study of exemplarity unveils a domino effect of visual interpretation: an event happens, it is witnessed, it is commemorated, the commemoration is witnessed, and so on. Each act of witnessing and commemoration involves interpretation, especially given the additional interpretive layer of Livy's prose as he describes the witnessed acts and the acts of witnessing.[20] Livy draws attention to the complexities by presenting so many interpretations of the original narrative kernel of Tarpeia's betrayal, that is, on the part on which everyone agrees: that she opened up the Capitol. Beyond that there is doubt.

To press the implications of witnessing a bit further, let us consider Feldherr's use of spectacle in Livy. Feldherr connects spectacle with group identity in Livy: groups of people watch events as a shared experience; their shared watching helps solidify common opinions and therefore build civic identity. Group interpretation can be seen in Livy's Tarpeia story as well, particularly in the phrases *sunt qui dicant* and *volgo*, which apply to later readers, and in *visam*, which obliquely draws in Sabine viewers who interpret Tarpeia's pact as fraud. If we extend this observation to Livy's text *writ large*, we readers constitute a group looking at (*intueri*) Livy's *documenta*. Recall, however, that in the preface Livy uses *te* as the subject accusative for *intueri*, rendering the phrase indefinite: "one may look."[21] This configuration emphasizes a key point in Livy's narrative strategy, for the indefinite *te* is both collective in the sense that it refers to any and every reader, and singular in that it refers to each reader's act of reading. Indeed, as we shall see, an individual seeing as part of a group might experience a rift or tension between those two (or more) perspectives.

The reader with access to the whole *monumentum* might be expected to fare better in the interpretive maze than the characters do. The labyrinth is a metaphor that Mary Jaeger has applied to Livy's history, in which characters must negotiate decisions without the benefit of the bigger, bird's-eye

---

20. In more subjective genres, such as love elegy, there is additional trouble because of the double-subjectivity of the witnessing "I" and the commemorating "I," a phenomenon that narratology has done much to explain.

21. Leumann-Hofmann-Szantyr 1972: 419. L-H-S maintain that a real person is in mind in the indefinite second person in Classical texts; in post-classical texts, "*keine reale Person denkbar ist*."

view available to the reader, who can see patterns in the larger image.²² In Tarpeia's case, Livy places himself in the maze-walker's position, confronted with the forks and paths of alternative traditions among which he may choose. By refusing to choose (*tamen*), Livy places the reader in the same position, faced with many choices and unaware where they may lead. In the next section I explore what can be gained from juxtaposing the indeterminacy of Tarpeia's anecdote with a bird's-eye view of the episode in the context of the whole first book.

WOMAN AS CONDUIT FOR OTHERNESS

Livy reveals to the reader the difficult process of interpreting the facts and meaning of Tarpeia's story, and in so doing he invites his reader to do the same sort of work. She is not thus so easy to characterize as a negative *exemplum* as it might seem. But this does little to explain what she means in his story, and any number of tales, as Chaplin, Jaeger, Connolly, and Feldherr show for Livy and Roller shows more broadly, present similar complications in perspective and interpretation.²³ I turn now to the other way Tarpeia is often described in Livy—as one of Livy's legendary women of Rome's rise. Rhea Silvia, Tarpeia, the Sabine women, Horatia, Tanaquil, Tullia, and Lucretia together exert a pressure on Livy's first book and on Rome's era of seven kings. In keeping with the distinction made above, these women function historically, as agents with greater responsibility during a monarchy than during the Republic,²⁴ and historiographically, as markers of disruption in the world of men.²⁵

My analysis also combines the historical with the historiographical. In this section I argue that Livy's women are especially memorable and rich characters—and especially vexed—in that they are "readability" personified. Their very position as women, acting in the world of men but with their own voices for the most part muted, situates them as objects of spectacle and thus of interpretation from various perspectives. These vari-

---

22. If *monumentum* in the preface refers to Livy's history as a whole, this confirms the reader's access to the broader view.
23. Chaplin 2000; Jaeger 1997; Connolly 2009; Feldherr 1998.
24. Glinister 1997.
25. Here fit the interpretations of Lucretia and Verginia as symbols of political malaise (Joplin 1990; Joshel 1992), and Milnor's 2009 study of women operating in the public sphere as an indication of men's failure to keep them at home. Consider also Tullia's willingness to be in the forum or senate house, Livy 1.48.5: her boldness is a symbol of Superbus's arrogant, transgressive power *and* a tip-off that the state is in disharmony (see particularly Milnor 2009: 282–83).

ous perspectives emerge from their role as "coin of the realm" in transactions between families and/or between communities; they come from one household and marry into another, thus bridging natal and marital families within a community, or even, as in many cases, linking one community to another. In the best cases (the Sabine women, Lucretia[26]), a woman bridges the gap between discrete identities solidly and seamlessly, the identities and her interests come to overlap, and she is interpreted unanimously. Tarpeia is not so lucky, nor is the heroine of one other extended tale in the book: Horatia. These two stories together reveal that unmarried women are especially vulnerable to divergent perspectives because, prone themselves to look beyond their fathers/fatherlands to the outside, they have not yet accomplished the assimilation of outside perspectives into the Roman consciousness, an assimilation that softens Roman expansion.

Twenty years ago, Gary Miles analyzed the story of the rape of the Sabine women.[27] Using resources from anthropology and from Roman law, Miles argued that this story re-enacts (or, rather, pre-enacts) the dynamics of the Roman marriage ceremony—not just specific practices in the marriage ritual, but also in some ideologies and tensions that underlie Roman marriage: the prowess and ingenuity of Roman men, both collectively and individually; the vulnerability of women to that ingenuity; and the resulting potential for abuses on both sides. This potential, for Miles, constitutes the difference between "good" *Sabinae* and "bad" Tarpeia in Livy's narrative. Miles concluded that woman's fundamental openness in Livy—her willingness to be persuaded—renders her helpful, if she is persuaded by the right people (*Sabinae*), and dangerous, if she listens to others (Tarpeia). I would characterize the difference differently: until her "openness" is closed off by marriage (or better still, absorbed and codified to the benefit of Rome via marriage), she remains much more sympathetic to other perspectives than is comfortable for Rome's foundational men. She is willing to read (or tell) a different story, to entertain possibilities that do not square with the interpretation her father and fatherland might ask of her. And so she is doubly indeterminate: first, in the ways she is read by various audiences, and second, in the way she reads differently from what is expected.

---

26. In the case of both Sabine women and Lucretia, not only are fathers and husbands aligned, but these overlap (or come to overlap) the needs of the state as well. The Sabine women's plea to husbands and fathers to cease their violence leads to an assimilation into one, stronger state and a joint kingship; Lucretia (1.58.5) has so blended her natal and marital families that she calls her father and husband to help her, and their subsequent actions benefit and strengthen the state.

27. Miles 1995: 179–219. He analyzes five versions: Cicero *de Republica* 2.12–14; Livy 1.9–13; Dionysius of Halicarnassus 2.30–47; Ovid *Fasti* 3.167–258; and Plutarch *Romulus* 14–20.

In some ways, then, the unattached woman acts as a model for Livy's own readers, who are put in a position to choose options that are not at all clear and who can see, then, that many perspectives pertain.

For my purposes, the myth of the rape makes vivid the role of women in mediating between families. Who can deny the power of the image of the Sabine women, holding their husbands and fathers apart with their very bodies, which constitute, in fact, not just the metaphorical but also the physical locus for the mingling of two bloodlines? The choice of the Sabine women for their new lives is telling in this context. To be sure, they are very diplomatic in their rhetoric and are careful to balance their affection for their husbands and fathers—but their argument, based on their children with the Roman men, identifies them as wives and mothers rather than as daughters, as members of their new bloodline rather than their old.

The result of their affection is, of course, that the Sabines and Romans unite into a common polity. Marriage blends family lines through children, who thereafter share in the common bonds of both families. The Sabine women make the fathers and other Sabines into Romans as well, inasmuch as those fathers become part of the new twinned Roman state (*geminata urbe*). Their marriage thus acts as a powerful metaphor not just for the specific, familial integration but also for integration on a larger community scale. The language of Livy's passage emphasizes their role as points of juncture, the meeting point at which self and other elide: *hinc patres, hinc viros, soceri generique,* and *viris ac parentibus* all stress separate identities (1.13.2–3); then *vestrum* and *unam ex duabus, consociant* and *conferunt* (1.13.3–5) show Sabines and Romans together; finally *geminata urbe* (1.13.5) reveals them to be indistinguishable.[28]

Not only the Sabine women, but all women in Livy's first book act as "foundational mothers" in Rome's rise, without whom the growth of Rome might have been quite different or even stunted. What they bring to Rome is the ability, and the means, to incorporate outsiders into the state, even at times at the expense of their fathers.[29] Livy's first book emphasizes women's roles as peaceful assimilators. Aeneas is, in Livy's account, the first outsider (*advenam*, 1.2.1; cf. 1.1.5 and 1.1.7) to blend into Rome. Livy's Lavinia is so attached to Aeneas or to the idea of him that she raises Aeneas's son Ascanius (Iulus) whether it is her son or Creusa's (1.3.1–3) and acts as good

---

28. The twin metaphor, which arises again below vis-à-vis Rhea Silvia, is a powerful device for exploring Rome's assimilation of other peoples. On twins as a marker of (troubling) symmetry, see Wiseman 1995: 17 and Konstan 1986: 202–4.

29. The practice of offering asylum to foreigners strives to accomplish the same goal; asylum, however, has more limitations than intermarriage as a means of assimilation. See now Dench 2005b.

regent for the boy until he is of age. Rhea Silvia was the conduit for the expansion and continuation of Numitor's line, despite the mandate of her father(land), which had consigned her to Vestal virginity (1.4). The Sabine women introduced, quite literally, Sabine blood into the Roman stock, to the benefit of their husbands rather than their fathers (since the Sabines transfer their power to Rome, *imperium omne conferunt Romam*, 1.13.4). Tarpeia looked to Tatius for alliance rather than seeing to the needs of her father Spurius Tarpeius and her fatherland. Horatia remained loyal to her fiancé rather than to her brother (i.e., her natal family), in a way that looked like treason, at least to her father and brother. The astounding Tanaquil first incorporated Priscus's Greek blood into the skeptical Etruscan state by marrying him (Lucumo is *aduena*, 1.34.5), then rejected her fatherland completely to advance her husband (*oblitaque ingenitae erga patriam caritatis dummodo virum honoratum videret*, she forgot her native affection toward her fatherland so long as she could see her husband honored, 1.34.5).[30] Tullia married the would-be Tarquinius Superbus despite the wishes of her father (1.46.9—*iunguntur nuptiis, magis non prohibente Servio quam adprobante*, they were joined in marriage, with Servius not forbidding it rather than approving it), and her affinity with her husband as against her natal family went so far that she did outright harm to her father, running over old Servius in the road. Though we do not know the wedding story of Lucretia and Collatinus, it is notable that she is Roman and he Etruscan, son of Egerius and grandson of Arruns (Tarquinius Priscus's brother), and that Collatia had only recently joined the Roman state (Livy 1.38.2).

All these women (save Lucretia), by rejecting their fathers/fatherland in favor of foreign men, strengthen horizontal rather than vertical ties.[31] Note that in some cases the girl is Roman (Rhea Silvia, Tullia, Tarpeia) while in others she is not (the Sabine women, Tanaquil, Priscus's mother). Horatia's category here is dubious since no one remembers which family was Roman and which was Alban (Livy 1.24.1). This horizontality is an interesting feature, since in the Republic heritage generally followed the father: thus Tullia's children would not have become Roman, nor Horatia's. All children in the examples above become Roman, no matter the ethnic heritage of their parents. Livy's myths of early Rome thus reveal a more liberal attitude toward belonging in the Roman state than did Republican law. Were ideologies changing? Did the regal period admit of greater

---

30. See Bitarello 2009 on Tanaquil and Tullia, Etruscan women who are able to sway their husbands.

31. See generally Hallett 1984.

ability to become Roman than we see attested in Republican laws? Or did Livy imagine a different set of values of inclusiveness for regal and Republican Rome? Perhaps we should take the approach of Suzanne Dixon, who argues that the imposition of a diachronic scheme to explain such anomalies undervalues the anomalies themselves.[32] Reality was likely to be looser than legal ideals, which were invoked only in the most extreme cases. As Dixon has shown, women often found ways to circumvent legal restrictions on inheritance and the like, leaving property to their children in a system that was vehemently agnatic. The Romanness of Livy's children can be read in a similar light.

So too may we evaluate the level of independence Livy's women demonstrate in their choices of allegiance and in their very willingness or ability to choose. The Sabine women, Horatia, Tullia, and Tarpeia all make the choice themselves to ally with their outsiders—even in the face of fatherly disapproval, and in the two cases involving marriage, even before the marriage.[33] The choice of the *sponsae* itself constitutes a paradox: her strong transfer of allegiance shows her subservience to her new husband, while her willingness to choose reflects more freedom and self-determination.[34] This, too, may synchronize a diachronic development in women's autonomy. Livy's women are situated at the point of conflict between these two ideologies—women as objects, as subjects—and not surprisingly the results are ambiguous: while fathers find themselves at risk in this tense situation, and daughters also often suffer, husbands (or their non-espoused analogues, i.e., Tatius) always come out ahead. In other words, individuals and families lose some ground, but the state broadens its citizen base.

That bears repeating. Individuals and families lose some ground, but the state broadens its citizen base. Because women's actions lead to the growth of the Roman state, in some sense their choice of husbands over fathers is also a choice of fatherland over fathers. In this way these women prefigure

---

32. Dixon 1992: 159 discusses the dynamic process of "the continual regrouping and redefinition that occurred over the individual and family life-span."

33. Hallett 1984: 138 sees Verginia and Cloelia as the antitheses to the "self-assertive and politically disloyal Tarpeia, Horatia, and Tullia of monarchic legend." She interprets these three as indicating that the support of a husband/lover that ends in "traitorous treatment of her father and his concerns point to a Roman belief that if a father's demands upon his daughter came into conflict with demands made on her by a sexual partner, the father's demands were supposed to receive precedence." An interesting corollary is offered by the declamatory themes on the rape of a woman, the legal remedy for which is that the woman may freely exercise her will to marry or have killed her rapist. See Kaster 2001 for a discussion of this aspect of female autonomy.

34. His tension is analogous to the tension between marriage *cum manu*, an earlier and stronger form of arrangement, and marriage *sine manu*, a later and looser bond allowing the wife more freedom. See Hersch 2010: 202; Treggiari 1991: 13–36.

Brutus's vivid choice to be a statesman rather than a father (2.5.8). In his earliest book Livy builds for his readers the notion that Rome's growth and success was a collective achievement. His women are part of that collective and add to that achievement. At the beginning of book 2 Livy summarizes that pledges of wives and children inspired the community feeling that enabled the state (*pignera,* 2.1.5). He means that genitive objectively—vows by men to their wives and children, but perhaps the genitive could also be interpreted subjectively: it was the wives' vows that made Rome great.

Finally, the force of these Roman myths comes into sharp focus when we compare them to similar stories from Greek myth. Greek myth is rich with tales of girls caught between their fathers and their lovers, but unlike their Roman analogues, loyalty swings both ways in the Greek stories. Medea and Scylla, for example, betray their fathers out of loyalty to their husbands or potential husbands, but the Danaids (except for Hypermestra), Procne, and Antigone choose their natal families over potential suitors. Contrast this with Roman Tullia, Horatia, Lavinia, and even Cloelia, who cleave to foreign men. Perhaps the difference lies in the ways these two cultures conceived of their origins: Greek communities rooted their identity strongly in the land they occupied; the Athenians and Thebans even sprang from that land itself. The Romans, on the other hand, had always been composed of someone else.

THE MIDDLE AS DESTABILIZING

Thus Livy's women are powerful means and instigators of horizontal ties, or agnatic relationships. Their external leanings lead to the incorporation of outsiders into Rome, and an expansion of "Romanness." Antony Augoustakis explores a similar phenomenon in Silius's *Punica,* in which assimilated foreigners both adapt to the values of the Roman center and expand that center, thus strengthening it and yet destabilizing some of the categories in which it trades, such as male and female, insider and outsider.[35] In Augoustakis's study, it is non-Roman mothers displaying Roman virtues who break open a closed notion of Romanness, but virtuous Roman women in Livy's narrative have also been shown to act as tokens of destabilization (and expansion) of normative categories.[36] Virtuous Veturia entering Coriolanus's camp, for example, betokens a crisis in the political system, in which men should be in control (Livy 2.39–40). For Livy, evil Roman

---

35. Augoustakis 2010: 197.
36. Milnor 2009.

forum-visiting Tullia indicates a similar crisis (1.48).[37] Everywhere women appear in Livy's history, they appear precisely for their impact on men's affairs. Lucretia spinning by night would never have been mentioned by Livy had her virtuous suicide not precipitated the fall of the Tarquin tyranny. These women acting like men, in a way, already blur a distinction between self (here, male) and other (female).[38] What do gender categories mean when one side bleeds into the other?

Horatia and Tarpeia further blur categories of self and other—here, Roman and non-Roman—by standing at the point when the non-Roman has not yet been assimilated, and Romanness has not yet been expanded to accommodate the men (and their allies) with whom they trade. I believe their not-yet-ness is related to the indeterminacy of these women's stories and the plurality of reactions to them, possible and actual, that Livy recounts. Both stories in a way recount a process of incorporation as much as an outcome (again, I am reminded of the interplay between historiography and history). One key difference between the two tales is that Livy's portrayal of Horatia's sad story in some measure exculpates everyone: Horatius and his father are vindicated by law, the king saves face, and Horatia garners sympathy from the crowd. The way he presents Tarpeia's tale, in contrast, flatters no one. As we shall see, this is because Tarpeia's story is interrupted before her death can be reconciled and understood in Roman terms, whereas Horatia's death and its legalistic aftermath restore harmony between the state and the individual.

Horatia's episode falls in the doldrums of the first book, between the fantastic stories of Rome's rise and the tragedy of Lucretia. The Albans and Romans have been itching for a fight and are moving toward open war against each other when Mettius, the Alban dictator, proposes an alternative: that the contest between the two states be resolved by single battle, or rather, triple battle, with a set of three brothers from each side standing in for his whole army. In the staged contest, the Alban brothers at first gain the upper hand, killing two of the Roman brothers. But then the remaining Roman combatant separates and kills all three of the Alban brothers. Fresh from his victory, he parades his spoils before his cheering, safe, victorious-by-proxy Roman comrades. When his sister sees the spoils and recognizes among them the battle cloak she had woven for one of the now-dead Alban

---

37. See Milnor 2009: 281 on Sempronia in Valerius Maximus 3.8.6: "Female virtue not only transcends civic immorality but transforms it, bringing back to the public sphere the integrity which its men have lost." See also Joplin 1990: 52 on Lucretia and Verginia as part of Livy's "causal link between female chastity and its destruction and the founding and preservation of Rome."

38. Hallett 1989 explores this tension more broadly in Roman sources.

brothers, to whom she had been betrothed, she laments and calls his name. Her Roman brother, upset at her allegiance to his defeated enemy, kills her on the spot. The crowd is horrified at his action yet hesitant to scorn its champion, and the matter comes before the king, who establishes a special court for adjudicating the case. The court pronounces the Roman soldier guilty and mandates his execution, whereupon the soldier's father intervenes, claiming he believes his son did the right thing, otherwise he would himself have killed the boy. The crowd and king are moved, the boy is subjected to a symbolic punishment, a sacrifice expiates any wrong, the Albans come join the Romans, and all ends well—except for the dead sister.

Andrew Feldherr has interpreted at length this episode's construction and deconstruction of civic identity, across the categories of self (Roman) and other (Alban), and family and state. His analysis traces the way these categories become distinct only to collapse into each other, and then to become again distinct. For example, the Albans are initially elided with the Romans through their common ancestor Aeneas. No one even knows which set of brothers were Roman and which Alban, so alike were they. Indeed they are so alike as to have produced and reared a set of triplet brothers, matched in age and strength to the enemy set (*trigemini fratres, nec aetate nec viribus dispares,* 1.24.1). But then, Alban and Roman separate into distinct categories and mutual (specious) hostility, except that they are aligned by their common motive for this hostility (desire for glory). The surrogate battle of the brothers again distinguishes Alban and Romans, both triplets and spectators, but then the peoples come to live together as one in Rome. In terms of family and state, the victory of the youngest Roman (named Horatius arbitrarily by Livy) is an honor for his family and his fatherland, and his murder of his sister Horatia serves to avenge her dishonor of both. But the crowd sees it differently, and sees his act as a violation of his family obligations and unjust punishment of Horatia's family ties. Feldherr links the instability of categories in this episode with a fundamental instability of sacrifice, in which the community must sympathize with both sacrificant and victim.

I cannot hope to improve upon Feldherr's reading of this episode. I wish, however, to linger on the particular instabilities that surround Horatia's death and to locate another source of instability, Horatia's not-yet-ness, so as to draw out in what ways she resembles Tarpeia. The key passage follows:

> Princeps Horatius ibat, trigemina spolia prae se gerens; cui soror virgo, quae desponsa uni ex Curiatiis fuerat, obvia ante portam Capenam fuit;

cognitoque super umeros fratris paludamento sponsi quod ipsa confecerat, solvit crines et flebiliter nomine sponsum mortuum appellat. Movet feroci iuveni animum comploratio sororis in victoria sua tantoque gaudio publico. Stricto itaque gladio simul verbis increpans transfigit puellam. "Abi hinc cum immaturo amore ad sponsum," inquit, "oblita fratrum mortuorum vivique, oblita patriae. Sic eat quaecumque Romana lugebit hostem." (1.26.2–4)

Horatius came first carrying his triple spoils in front of him. His maiden sister, who had been betrothed to one of the Curiatii, met him at the Porta Capena. When she recognized the cloak of her fiancé on the shoulder of her brother, which she had herself made for him, she loosens her hair and through her tears cries out by name for her dead fiancé. The lament of his sister, in the context of his own victory and such great public rejoicing, rouses the anger in the fierce young man, and so he drew his sword and uttered these words as he pierced the girl through: "Go away from here with your untimely love to your fiancé," he said, "heedless of your dead brothers and the one still living, heedless of your fatherland. Thus may any Roman girl go who mourns an enemy."

Horatia confuses self and other. As Feldherr notes, the Romans see her as one of them.[39] But not her brother, for whom her action is one of a non-Roman, "heedless of family and state," and Horatius kills her with almost the same verb Livy uses to describe his killing of the last Curiatius (Horatia: *transfigit*; Curiatius: *defigit*, 1.25.12). Yet Horatius equates her with the category "Roman girl" in his pithy precept *sic eat quaecumque Romana lugebit hostem*, a precept that also draws a distinction between Roman and enemy. Horatia is both. Livy places her carefully on the point where self meets other (sc. *obvia fuit*): the Porta Capena, Rome's southern entrance at the Appian Way. She is inside going out, and he is outside coming in. Horatius emphasizes as much at the edges of his speech, with the motion verbs *abi* and *eat*. We might also note that he too at this moment stands between identities. Though he is identified with the Romans, for whom his victory is the public joy, he arrives in the dress of his enemies, carrying their spoils and wearing the betrothed Curiatius's cloak (*cognito super umeros fratris paludamento sponsi*).[40] It is my fancy that Livy puts both *fratris* and *sponsi*

---

39. Feldherr 1998: 134.
40. Likewise, as Feldherr notes, the *tigellum sororium*, where he must later resubmit to his father's authority, is also the place where returning soldiers pass back into Roman civilians (1998: 144). See also Coarelli 1983: 111–17 and Platner and Ashby 1929: 538–39.

in the genitive to suggest the interchangeability of one with the other, with only their location in the sentence to distinguish them.[41] At the conclusion of the whole episode, Livy mentions—as if to remind us that Horatia is a marker of identity exchange—that she was buried on the spot where she died (*Horatiae sepulcrum, quo loco corruerat icta, constructum est saxo quadrato*, 1.26.14). Her tomb, placed at Rome's gate, is a *monumentum* to her position between communities.

It is not only Horatia's national identity that is confounded; she similarly resists familial and gender identification. Is she, or is she not, a part of her natal family? Her brother believes she still is and accuses her of being forgetful of it (*oblita*, cf. Tanaquil at 1.34.5, cited above, who had forgotten: *oblita ingenitae erga patriam caritatis*). This justifies his treating her as an outsider. But *oblita* implies that she has once been mindful of it, and evokes the idea that her identity has not been stable over time or perhaps cannot be stable because of her gender. When young Horatius is on the verge of public punishment, moreover, her father intervenes and firmly repositions her within his own family, calling her his *filiam* and asserting his right to do with her—and her brother—as he wishes (1.26.9).[42] What is more, the symbolic punishment bold Horatius Jr. must undergo is to pass beneath the *tigellum sororium*, so named for its proximity to Juno Sororia, "Juno of the Swollen Breast." The name must also evoke his sister, *soror*, and his passage under the "Sister's Beam" reverses in some sense the authority he showed over her earlier and marks them both subservient to their father. What is more, the *tigellum* is also adjacent to the shrine of Janus Curiatius; this cluster of monuments suggests liminality, transition, and perspective in two directions.

This last instance also draws attention to the elasticity of gender categories. Juno Sororia marks a moment in a girl's life when she passes from childhood to marriageability. Her very body is thus in flux and poised between two configurations of femininity. Just so is Horatia, old enough to be promised in marriage but not yet married. Indeed, Livy earlier calls her a *virgo* (1.26) in the rich collocation *cui soror virgo* (whose virgin sister), which itself places her in an uncomfortable tension: is she his sister, part of his family, or a *virgo*, which makes her available to other men? When Horatius forbids her—or any woman so caught between families—from mourning, he closes her off from one of the key duties of women: to mourn

---

41. Festus 380L, in a passage dependent on this one, is even more ambiguous: *morte sponsi sui fratris manu occisi*. The position of *sui* renders it attributable to *sponsi, fratris*, or both.

42. All the while, as Feldherr notes (1998: 142), the elder Horatius buttresses his family rights with words that evoke public authority (*iudicare, iure*).

the dead. That identity is no longer open to her. Finally, as if to sum up her place in the grey space between many categories, he refers to her love as *immaturo*. The adjective could as well describe her, her "not-yet-ness" rendering it impossible to assess her, include her, or exclude her in any meaningful, lasting way.

I will depart from Horatia with a final note, again drawn from Feldherr's observation but differently nuanced. We have seen how her identity is confounded, and this in turn renders indistinct the categories in which she might be classified and, therefore, the others who would be described by those categories. Feldherr connects the instability of roles in this episode (and in sacrifice, its more abstract real meaning to Feldherr) with the power of spectacle to inform identity. Those who watch the battle of triplets confirm their own identity by their reactions to the spectacle. Yet our identity depends on our perspective. The elder Horatius knows the crowd feels sympathy for Horatia, so he urges them to look at something else: the son returning victorious from battle:

> Inter haec senex iuvenem amplexus, spolia Curiatiorum fixa eo loco qui nunc Pila Horatia appellatur ostentans, "Huncine," aiebat, "quem modo decoratum ovantemque victoria incedentem vidistis, Quirites, eum sub furca vinctum inter verbera et cruciatus videre potestis? quod vix Albanorum oculi tam deforme spectaculum ferre possent. I, lictor, colliga manus, quae paulo ante armatae imperium populo Romano pepererunt. I, caput obnube liberatoris urbis huius; arbore infelici suspende; verbera vel intra pomerium, modo inter illa pila et spolia hostium, vel extra pomerium, modo inter sepulcra Curiatiorum." (1.26.10–11)

> Meanwhile the old man embraced his son and, pointing out the spoils of the Curiatii fixed in that place which is now called the Horatian Pillar, said, "Romans, you just saw this man honored and processing victoriously in ovation. Can you now bear to see him bound under the gallows and tortured with the lash? Even Alban eyes would scarce be able to bear such a perverted spectacle. Go, Lictor, bind the hands which just recently took arms to secure imperium for the Roman people. Go, veil the head[43] of the one who liberated this city. Hang him from a cursed tree, flog him within the *pomerium*, right there among the weapons and

---

43. This is the archaic formula, but Cicero connects it to the language for veiling the bride. Cf. Cicero *pro Rabirio perduellionis reo* 13. This can be read as more gender-overlap, inasmuch as punishing the young Horatius equates to making him into a bride.

enemy spoils he won, or outside the *pomerium,* among the graves of the enemy Curiatii he slew."

The father's emphasis on watching (*vidistis . . . potestis videre*) hints that the spectators too are torn among divergent perspectives, if they can see young Horatius triumph and fall with the same eyes. And he here addresses the onlookers as Romans, *Quirites,* but with the word most calculated to draw them closer to the Albans, whom Livy has just named *Curiatii*; not only does *curiatii* sound like *Quirites,* but *Quirites* indicates foreigners-become-Romans.[44] Horatius thus pegs their identity down and then connects that identity to a Roman way of looking that hints at the equation between Roman Quirites and Alban Curiatii.[45] His next comment further blurs the distinction between Roman and Alban by asserting some kind of universal perspective, for even Alban eyes could not tolerate such a sight. The sight of Horatius punished, even the potential of that sight, unifies the hostile people in a more subtle way than the overt conflict that had been resolved by the brothers. Thus the elder Horatius draws family, Rome, and Alba together into a unified perspective. Put differently, he expands Romanness and family and Alban so that they are coterminous with each other, and all of this based on the visual perspective of each. This recalls the beginning of the Alban conflict, in which the two sides hostile to each other were really more alike than different, each desiring war to further their glory but each putting forth petty spats as red herrings (*speciosa*, 1.23.7)[46] for the hostility. Livy shows separation on the surface, unity underneath; the appearance of difference, the reality of likeness.

Let us return to Tarpeia to recall the way appearance was linked with trickery and danger in that episode—the Sabines were peaceful on the surface but preparing war, both parties practiced some deceit, the rings themselves had a lovely appearance (*specie*) but proved Tarpeia's doom. I propose that here too Tarpeia dwells in the gap between appearance and reality, and between one identity and another, and therefore lends herself to multiple perspectives. In what follows we shall revisit some of the observations made

---

44. See Maltby 1991: 517 s.v. *Quirites,* which Livy 1.13.5 and Varro *DLL* 6.68 derive from *Curensibus,* Tatius's Sabines. A commentator on Lucan 5.32 even connects *curia* with *Curenses,* thereby rendering the connection between Curiatii and Quirites even closer. See also de Vaan 2008: 510 s.v. *Quirites.*

45. Similarly, the proximity of the *tigillum sororium* to the shrine of Janus Curiatius also links the Quirites and Curiates. Janus is, of course, a god who emphasizes plurality of perspective.

46. Cf. Cicero *Atticus* 16.7.6 and cf. *OLD* s.v. *species* entry 3, "fine-sounding, plausible, specious."

in the first section of this chapter, but with, I hope, a new understanding of the way those observations bring Tarpeia's not-yet-ness to bear on the indeterminacy of her tale.

Note how Livy introduces her and her story, literally framing her (*filiam virginem*) between her father (*Spurius Tarpeius*) and the outsider who would claim her allegiance (*Tatius*):

> Sp. Tarpeius Romanae praeerat arci. Huius filiam virginem auro corrumpit Tatius ut armatos in arcem accipiat.
> (1.11.6)

> Spurius Tarpeius was in charge of the citadel, whose virgin daughter Tatius corrupted with gold.

His word order reflects her dual roles, as the phrase *filiam virginem* also splits her in two—*filiam*, her familiar moniker, looking back to her father *Tarpeius* and *virginem*, the word that announces her availability, anticipating *Tatius* at the sentence's end (we recall here Horatia as *soror virgo*, sister virgin). The word order likewise mirrors a movement from father Tarpeius, through daughter (vertical tie), through virgin (horizontal availability), to potential husband Tatius. The fact that Livy does not name her specifically is no matter—Roman naming conventions render her Tarpeia, a name that connects her even more firmly to her father. There is no narrative need to mention Sp. Tarpeius—his position of authority doesn't seem to give Tarpeia any inside information about the citadel's defenses, and he does not appear blameworthy or at all involved after this incident.[47] He seems to simply explain who Tarpeia was. Indeed he serves no purpose in the story other than to identify Tarpeia as a daughter.[48] What Tatius entices Tarpeia to do is the political analogue of Roman marriage—to admit men into her home (as mentioned above, Livy's founding mothers enjoy matrilocal marriage; *he* follows *her* rather than the other way around).[49] And like Horatia, Tarpeia is explicitly a *virgo*. This descriptor implies Vestality, another "back-fill" detail to explain her presence in Rome—especially after Varro, who had connected the dots in the tradi-

---

47. Contra Plutarch, who expands a little on this character by claiming that he was tried for and convicted of treason after the fact (*Romulus* 17.5).
48. This is one of the most perplexing parts of her myth; if she is a daughter, why was there a need to steal the Sabine woman?
49. See Hersch 2010: 140–44 on the importance of the *deductio in domum mariti*, the usual movement, as a symbol of Roman marriage.

tion.⁵⁰ Livy seems to exploit our assumptions about her (that as a virgin she is a Vestal) even as he exploits her position as *filia virgo*.

The mixed perspectives Tarpeia generates by those who see her are intertwined with the notion of the Roman self and the invading (but to be incorporated) other. The two primary variants Livy names in his narrative—Tarpeia as Roman traitor (Pictor) or as Roman patriot (Piso) both locate Tarpeia between two peoples, Romans and Sabine invaders, but interpret her loyalty and identity in opposite ways. In Pictor's version her allegiance has shifted to the Sabines (or at least, to herself and her prize rather than to the Romans), and in Piso's version she remains attached to her natal community. It is possible to interpret the women in the middle either way, for as a *virgo* she is still connected to her father's *patria potestas* but is eligible for moving horizontally. Unlike Horatia, who calls out her fiancé's name and thus makes public her allegiance, Tarpeia is given no speech in Livy's account to reveal which direction she faces as she is perched between perspectives: inside Rome looking out (Piso), or outside looking in (Pictor). It is telling here that in Piso's version the Sabines interpret her endgame as *fraude*; a perspective which they do not share appears to them (*fraude visam agere*) as deceitful. This is a classic "us versus them" pose, only here the Romans are the fraudulent "them." But this pose is handed down by Roman Piso. Livy's brief mention of Piso's variant cannily exposes the messiness of Roman growth. Like Piso's version itself, which seeks to get inside Tarpeia's mind, Livy's mention of Piso's variant places his reader in the mind of the other (here, Piso). Again, history (Tarpeia, Romans, Sabines) and historiography (Livy, Piso, Pictor) collide. Which viewpoint—Roman, Other, or Middle—do his readers inhabit? The plurality of perspectives Livy offers suggests that it must be all three. "Roman" is big enough to accommodate difference, and just as no one knows which of the Horatii and Curiatii was Roman and which was Alban, no one can decide if Tarpeia was one of us or one of them. The scornful *tamen* that opens the next story shows that to Livy, it doesn't matter.

The Sabines' motives for killing Tarpeia also confound self and other. The key sentence is this: *accepti obrutam armis necavere, seu ut vi capta potius arx videretur seu prodendi exempli causa, ne quid usquam fidum proditori esset* (Once she accepted them they crushed her with their weapons, either so that it would seem that the citadel had been taken by force, or for the sake of a moral example, lest there evermore be any compact with

---

50. *DLL* 5.41; and cf. Martini 1998.

a traitor). First of all, the Sabines who kill her are now literal insiders, *accepti*. Their hostile presence on the *arx* suggests a multiplicity of perspectives even at the very center of the city. The first motive, that it should seem that the *arx* had been captured by force, again reveals a manifold perspective. So that it would thus seem to whom—to the Romans who had been invaded? To the other Sabine soldiers who weren't in the first wave, to the rest of the Sabines, or to non-Romans and non-Sabines watching from the outside?[51] The "captured by force" appearance would suggest a strengthened division between Sabines and Romans even as they cohabit the Capitol, for all hint of cooperation, or any point of contact between the two states, has been eliminated and, through violence, the distinction between us and them is maintained (and indeed rages on beyond this moment of entry).

The second, moralistic motive for killing Tarpeia (and the more exemplary one, given as it is to a summary judgment) suggests a moral category that transcends the division of self and other: *Ne quid, usquam,* and the existential *esset* ("lest any ever should be") extend the life of this moral to all people and all situations at all times. Sabines and Romans would not be so different from each other in this explanation, and Tarpeia's death would be interpreted as what must happen given her part in the opening of the *arx*. Pressing on this observation, one wonders whether there is a hierarchy of morals and behaviors. On lower levels we might see Sabines and Romans distinguished by their behavior, but on others they are united in perspective. The first motive violates and preserves a boundary between us and them, while the second motive zooms out to look at a bigger picture in which that boundary is meaningless.

As Livy's presentation confounds the distinction between the Roman self and the non-Roman other, he also problematizes perspectives within Rome by blurring the lines between family and state. Tarpeia is labeled as a Roman daughter and a virgin in one sentence, and in the next she is identified as the water-seeker for sacred rites. The obvious conclusion, and the one Varro makes explicit, is that she is a Vestal virgin. As Mary Beard has shown in two seminal articles (discussed in chapter 4), the Vestal priesthood is vexed with paradoxes of identification—she is a virgin yet a wife of the state, herself barren yet a guarantor of fecundity, and the like.[52] For Beard, these paradoxes are the point of the priesthood. In the context of

---

51. Cf. Mettius's suggestion at 1.23.8–9, in Horatia's story that hostile Etruscans were watching keenly what happened between Rome and Alba, and were waiting like vultures to finish off what the war left intact.

52. Beard 1980 and 1995.

the current exploration, I note that Tarpeia's Vestal priesthood renders her both more Roman, in that she is firmly connected to the fledgling state's institutions, and less familial, in that she is not to marry and no longer falls under her father's *patria potestas*.[53] In this way, describing her as the daughter of Tarpeius and a priestess *virgo*, Livy again positions Tarpeia in between—this time, in between her family and the state institution she serves. She is in between in another way, too; Vestals are wards of the state. The state *is* her family, so for her those two entities are no longer distinct.

Gender-wise, too, Tarpeia is in between. The Vestal's ritual chastity freezes her at a stage between unripe girlhood and fulfilled womanhood. In his analysis of Cloelia, Roller (2004: 38–42) notes that the heroine's virginity might ease some anxiety about her as a locus of contestation between male bloodlines. Cloelia's congress with the Etruscan Porsenna is not of such a sort as to allow him or his people to mingle, blood-wise, with the Romans.[54] Cloelia's virginity correlates to her *virtus*, a manly courage that is requisite to her heroic deed. Not so Tarpeia's virginity, which is allied with no manly courage or intention. On the contrary: she shows that the virgin might choose differently. Her virginity is really a place of exchange, a place of uncertainty and thus rife with anxiety. It is fitting that Tarpeia be buried by crushing, her body intact. The shields that cover her are the very weapon designed to protect the integrity of the fighter's body. Ovid's Caeneus would be another such character confounded in gender and eventually killed by crushing, unpenetrated by the sword.[55] Tarpeia's death is similar to the punishment meted out to transgressive Vestals, who were entombed alive (so as not to violate them even in their death). But it also forecloses any possibility that her body would be a point of reconciliation between Roman and Sabine, unlike Horatia, whose body, pierced by the same sword that had pierced Alban Curiatius, now admitted foreign blood.

LIVIAN TARPEIA

Tarpeia's refusal to be situated comfortably in any category—traitor or patriot, Roman or not, self or other, daughter, virgin, or bride—renders

---

53. Vestals and *patria potestas*: Gellius 1.12.9; and see also Staples 1998: 141–43 and Lorsch Wildfang 2006: 64–75.

54. Roller 2004: 39n82 mentions Tarpeia together with Tullia and Tanaquil. These three reveal tensions between endogamy and exogamy, since their bodies are vehicles for the convergence of bloodlines, whereas Cloelia's virginity alleviates some concern. See also Koptev 2005.

55. Ovid *Met.* 12.169–535.

her, in a way, an anti-example. If we are to read Tarpeia as an *exemplum*, either positive or negative, we must strip her story of its complexities and incongruities. Valerius Maximus (9.6.1) sanitizes her story in just this way, but its exemplary force remains problematic even in his exemplary text. When Livy's readers assess Tarpeia, they reveal the biases and contingencies of their own perspective. Livy puts us not only in the position of an onlooker with a broader view but also in the position of Tarpeia herself, pulled in two directions at least.[56] Livy positions his reader, that is, as both self and other at once.

Horatia's story, while it trades in tensions, resolves into harmony that blends family and state, women and men, other and self—with the first element of each pair joining and subordinating itself to the second element, which then expands to accommodate the addition. Cicero describes this harmony as a set of concentric circles.[57] Such harmony was also one of the goals and products of the Augustan regime, in which war would beget peace, the Republic and monarchy would align, and, most important for the current argument, the emperor as *pater patriae* would make all Rome into his own household, and through his marriage legislation insert the state's agenda into private lives.[58]

The refusal of Livy to circumscribe Tarpeia suggests how difficult it is to nest all the circles, for whatever shared space she occupies at the middle and at "not yet" is still riven by the many contradictory viewpoints from which she may be seen. Augustus's marriage laws may be seen as an attempt to clean up this messiness by prescribing who may marry whom, how many horizontal bonds there may be (no more than one per woman, thank you), how many vertical bonds (children) the state requires, and the like.[59]

Livy's foundational women all play out various scenarios of self and other. In closing, let us briefly consider Rhea Silvia, the first unwed Roman woman to be found in Livy's narrative (the first woman, Lavinia, was a good regent for Ascanius/Iulus until he was of age to rule). Rhea Silvia's openness is a matter of fear to her uncle Amulius. Wishing to usurp power

---

56. Solodow 1979 notes moral ambiguity inherent in providing multiple perspectives with respect to the Horatia episode.

57. *de Off.* 1.53: *Artior vero conligatio est societatis propinquorum; ab illa enim immensa societate humani generis in exiguum angustumque concluditur*, explored by Feldherr 1998: 118–20.

58. Milnor 2006: 140–85 examines Augustan marriage legislation as historiographical events, and Livy's representation of earlier events (such as the *lex Oppia*) as conditioned by "certain ideas and anxieties about the gendered relationship between public and private life which both reflect, and are reflected in, the moral legislation so closely associated with the age of Augustus" (143). Milnor's first chapter (47–93) treats the obverse, the Princeps' public performance of domesticity. See also Severy 2003: 44–56.

59. Raditsa 1980 offers a good overview of the law.

from his brother Numitor, Amulius closed off avenues for Numitor's successor that would in turn pose a threat to Amulius's occupation of the throne:

> Addit sceleri scelus: stirpem fratris virilem interimit, fratris filiae Reae Silviae per speciem honoris cum Vestalem eam legisset perpetua virginitate spem partus adimit. Sed debebatur, ut opinor, fatis tantae origo urbis maximique secundum deorum opes imperii principium. Vi compressa Vestalis cum geminum partum edidisset, seu ita rata, seu quia deus auctor culpae honestior erat, Martem incertae stirpis patrem nuncupat. Sed nec di nec homines aut ipsam aut stirpem a crudelitate regia vindicant: sacerdos vincta in custodiam datur, pueros in profluentem aquam mitti iubet. (1.3.11–1.4)

> He (Amulius) added crime to crime. He killed the male stock of his brother. As for his niece Rhea Silvia, when he named her a Vestal virgin (pretending it to be an honor) he destroyed all hope of offspring through her perpetual virginity. But the origin of such a great city as ours is indebted to the fates, the origin and the beginning of the greatest empire after the resources of the Gods. When the Vestal, having been taken by force, delivered twin sons, she named Mars as the father of her uncertain offspring, either because she believed it to be the case or because a divine instigator of her onus seemed more honorable. But neither gods nor men shielded the mother herself or the offspring from the king's cruelty; the priestess was bound and sent into custody, and the boys he ordered to be thrown into the running river.

Note in this episode two instances of the now familiar pairing of deception and the difficulty of seeming. First, Amulius made Rhea Silvia a Vestal virgin under the guise of honoring her, but his aim was really to prevent her from producing Numitor's heir. I draw attention to the fact that Rhea is a virgin precisely because Amulius wanted to close off any possibility that she reproduce; he wanted extreme control over the ways the larger family would be open to expansion. Like the other women we have considered here, Rhea Silvia "goes outside" to produce the first true Roman offspring. Livy speculates about Rhea's naming of Mars as the twins' father in a way that renders that paternity doubly suspect: either Mars was or was not the father but she thought it was so (*seu ita rata*); or he was not the father, she knew he was not, but she thought that naming him would lessen the burden of her culpability (*seu quia deus auctor culpae honestior erat*). This pair of possibilities is the first instance of "twinning" in the story about twins, and like the concept of twins it exploits the meeting point between similarity and difference. As further indication of Livy's equivocation he calls the babies *incertae stirpis*. These phrases together suggest just how powerful (and dangerous) the woman is in opening up a society to newcomers through her ability to incorporate external bloodlines. Exiled Romulus and Remus will turn out to have something regal in them that confirms, or at least suggests, their maternal regal heritage (*aetatem eorum et ipsam minime servilem indolem*, 1.5.6), but what proof can there be of their divine paternity? Even Rhea Silvia does not know.

What is more, Numitor's pretext of honoring Rhea Silvia with the priesthood is cast in terms that evoke the gap between appearance and reality: *Silviae per speciem honoris cum Vestalem eam legisset*. *Per speciem* "under the appearance" foreshadows the *magna specie* "(rings) with great appearance" in Tarpeia's narrative. Both uses of *species* point to the way appearances can be deceptive or lead to deception; as noted above, in the first book this word repeatedly evokes the danger that attends appearances.[60] In Rhea Silvia's case, what looks like an honor is actually a way to limit the family line.

Rhea Silvia, like Horatia and Tarpeia, exists in a gap, and at the same time they are that which constitutes the gap and the means by which that gap is bridged. Rhea Silvia is the point of connection between the Alban kings and Rome's rulers; Horatia is both Roman and Alban; and Tarpeia exists in the moment between complete Sabine hostility and Sabine cooperation. Livy's pluralistic Rome requires centripetal force, but the way Livy positions his founding women shows a centrifugal force to be operative as well. At the meeting place of these two forces, women may exert themselves toward or away from Rome, and may be pulled toward or away from Rome. The variety of positions they may thus occupy renders them individualistic even while they constitute a type.[61] They invite Livy's readers to reflect upon their own multiple stances, which brings new nuance to his moralistic salvo *hic illud est praecipue in cognitione rerum salubre ac frugiferum, omnis te exempli documenta in inlustri posita monumento intueri*. What if, in addition to the straightforward reading of *te* as the subject of *intueri*, it is its object? This, then, would be beneficial and fruitful—to scrutinize yourself as records of every sort of example set on display in the illustrious monument you are reading.

---

60. See note 18 in this chapter.

61. See Hinds 1998: 34–47 on *topoi* used both collectively/generally, and individually/idiosyncratically.

THE FRIEZE REPRISE

While I argue above that the Basilica Aemilia frieze was part of the restoration of the building begun at Julius Caesar's behest and funded by him (51–34 BCE), there is no doubt that the restored Basilica Aemilia of 14 BCE, undertaken by Augustus after the building had fallen to fire, was decorated with the extant narrative frieze of the Romulus cycle. Tarpeia was in the Augustan forum again, but the topographical context of this building was slightly different this time: on one side it was flanked by the Temple of Divine Julius, on the other by the Curia Iulia, across the Sacra Via was the Basilica Iulia. Augustus's restoration included a new portico fronting the Forum piazza, dedicated to his grandsons Gaius and Lucius. The area had become Dynastyland.

As discussed in chapter 4, during the years of Caesar's prominence and the decade after his death, when tried-and-true categories failed to contain or describe the new realities, the Basilica's Tarpeia challenged viewers to respond to the puzzle. Her reappearance in the Basilica might have functioned differently in the heady era of the moral legislation, the Ara Pacis, and Horace's Roman Odes. Like his adoptive father, Augustus's use of the frieze would have associated the Princeps and his restoration of Rome with the foundation and building of the original city—an association visible also on the Ara Pacis and in the Forum of Augustus. More forcefully, it built his heirs Gaius and Lucius, honorees of the new entrance hall, into the legends of Rome's urban founders. The building thus looked back in time and forward to Augustus's successors.

Kampen, who dates the frieze to this era,[62] suggests that the frieze spoke to the role of women in the renewed state, especially in the wake of the moral legislation of 18 BCE, which had sought to define and regulate exactly that role. Kampen's argument applies equally well to the reused frieze. The Sabine women and Tarpeia constitute two of the very few examples of women on civic monumental art of the Augustan age.[63] Their presence at the heart of the Forum, in a place marked by many kinds of public traffic, instructed Romans on the benefits of proper female behavior.

---

62. Kampen 1991. D'Ambra 1993: 80–86 supports Kampen's interpretation of the frieze's function in Augustan Rome. So too does Holliday 2005: 108–9, which sees the frieze as a working model for a cooperative model of *Romanitas* rather than a competitive glorification of a single man or *gens*. See also Kampen 1988.

63. The Ara Pacis is the other conspicuous example, and this lends support to Kampen's dating of the fragments to 14 BCE (Kampen 1991: 450). See also Kleiner 1978, who argues that the women on the Ara Pacis are represented in their traditional, familial roles.

When they behaved appropriately as wives, daughters, and mothers, Roman women acted as social mediators between men and even facilitated Roman expansion. Tarpeia's perfidy, on the other hand, represented the danger of unregulated female conduct. Kampen's analysis of the relief's resonance in the Augustan context squares well with my reading of Livy's Tarpeia above as a figure in a unique position to affect the stability of Rome through her position as a meeting point for men. We know, however, that Augustus would eventually draw a strong line between who was in and who was out in the case of his own daughter and granddaughter.[64] Dio Cassius attests that Julia's scandal was both political and amatory (55.10.15). In this Augustus would act like Tatius or the younger (or indeed elder) Horatius, punishing those who saw or strove for a wider circle than was permitted by those in control.

Augustus's response to Tarpeia might be visible in another artifact of his rule as Princeps. In 19 BCE, the moneyer P. Petronius Turpilianus issued a coin boasting Augustus on the obverse and Tarpeia buried under shields on the reverse (fig. 7). Turpilianus's coin, like his other coins that feature Liber and Feronia, attests his own Sabine background[65] and connects him to Tarpeia by punning on their names, Tarpeia and Turpilianus.[66] This would have served the moneyer's interest in the same way it had Titurius's in 90 BCE (see chapter 3). Augustus's authority is invoked on the obverse, and an up-and-comer advertises himself on the reverse. Wallace-Hadrill identifies this type as playful, in what he sees as an imaginative stage of coin design in the early Principate.[67] Might it not also speak to the evolving sense of the Augustan regime? Augustus takes the place of King Tatius on the coin, and the scene from Rome's foundational monarchy loops him into a cycle of Roman foundations and rebirth. The coin subtly suggests what he was recusant to assert outright: that he is a new Romulus. There is a further dimension. As he neared the end of his first decade as Augustus, the grandson of a baker (Suetonius *Aug.* 4) had accrued the powers of Rome's most important political offices and control of the rich provinces. Though several attempts were made on his life and reign, he never met the fate of Caesar. By the time Turpilianus struck his coin, Augustus had already executed three sets of men for treasonous plots: M. Aemilius Lepidus son of the

---

64. Holliday 2005: 109n6 also sees a connection between Tarpeia and Julia.
65. Morel 1962: 38.
66. This pun may be at work in Propertius's elegy, 4.4.1, *Tarpeium nemus et Tarpeiae turpe sepulcrum,* ([I will sing] the Tarpeian grove and Tarpeia's shameful grave). More on this pun in chapter 6.
67. Wallace-Hadrill 1986: 77.

FIGURE 7. Denarius of P. Petronius Turpilianus, 19–18 BCE. Augustus / Death of Tarpeia. Photo courtesy of the American Numismatic Society.

triumvir in 31 BCE (Dio 54.15.4), C. Cornelius Gallus and M. Egnatius Rufus in 26 BCE (Dio 53.23.5ff.), and Fannius Caepio and Licinius Murena in 23 BCE (Dio 54.3ff). A few more would be executed in 18 BCE, and then conspiracies would be rooted out and men punished in 15 BCE, 9 BCE, 2 BCE (the Julia scandal), and 6 CE. *Maiestas,* the charge under which most of the above were punished, was treason against the person of the emperor.[68] The coin of 19 BCE, with Augustus in the role of Tatius on the obverse, intimates that he is the punisher of treason and a monarch of Rome.[69]

It is no coincidence that the scene adjoining Tarpeia's on the frieze is a proper marriage scene;[70] the pair encapsulates the lesson succinctly: the *matrona,* not Tarpeia, is the model women should choose.

---

68. It is short for *maiestas minuta* or *laesa* (sovereignty diminished or injured). This appellation replaced the older technical term *perduellio,* which entailed armed action against Rome. Tarpeia's crime is usually called by the more general term *perfidia.*

69. Evans 1992: 128 makes a similar point, calling Tarpeia a political allegory in an uncertain time.

70. Carettoni 1961: 32–36 describes the marriage scene, without commenting on its resonance as an anti-model for Tarpeia.

CHAPTER SIX

ELEGIAC TARPEIA (WHO WON'T STAY PUT)

IN THIS SECOND PART of this book I have been exploring how, in the period of transition between Republic and Empire, Tarpeia emerges as a symbol for the interface of the individual and the community. In Varro's treatment of the words associated with her, this interface maps onto language itself. "Tarpeia" (and thus Tarpeia) originates as a linguistic anomaly—a singularity out of sync with rules and systems—but becomes subsumed into the broader rules that govern the Latin language. In the background of Varro's treatment is the personal singularity Julius Caesar, whose presence and person precipitated a new relationship between the individual Roman elite male and the state in which he lived. Livy's narrative of Tarpeia's story, written when the dust of the Caesarian upheaval was settling, renders this interface less abstract and more personal. Tarpeia, along with the other women of Rome's foundation, acts as an individual point of contact between communities (Romans and Sabines, Romans and Albans, etc.). Livy reveals the difficult position women occupy as subjects with their own wills and perspectives and as objects seen, interpreted, and acted upon by the communities in which they act.

The focus of this chapter is the continued exploration of this interface of individual and community in the poetry of Propertius, who devotes almost a hundred lines of elegiac verse to this troubled figure. My study finds Propertius's Tarpeia to be a poignant exploration of the challenge and the cost of reconciling self to state in the new order, that is, the challenge and cost of belonging.

Latin love elegy was a genre that flourished during Augustus's reign and all but died out when he did. Two influential yet very different scholarly approaches have connected this coincidence to the quickening of the tension between individual and collective during this time when a new sociopolitical order was forged. One approach is exemplified by Hans Peter Stahl, who in his 1985 book *Propertius: "Love" and "War": Individual and State under Augustus* traces in Propertius's poetry a recurring resistance on the part of the poet to the state and its demands; the poet lives, loves, and insists on being judged by a different set of standards from those espoused for Rome by its new first man Augustus.[1] The aitiological poems of the fourth book, of which the Tarpeia poem is a part, represent to Stahl an experiment with patriotism that ultimately fails. Two decades later the second approach emerged full force: in *Subjecting Verses: Latin Love Elegy and the Emergence of the Real* (2004), P. A. Miller identified elegy itself (rather than the elegist) as the expression of a crisis of identity caused by the Republic's collapse.[2] This set of events (called, in the Lacanian terms Miller uses, the Real) unsettled the relationship between the elite male's view of himself (Lacan's Imaginary) and the structures of authority, codes, and norms in which he operated (called the Symbolic). What I wish to do differently here and now is to explore what the application of this tension reveals about the mythic figure Tarpeia, and what Tarpeia can reveal about this tension in the Augustan age.

Propertius's Tarpeia is the most shocking entry in the development of Tarpeia's myth in Rome. Elegy 4.4, published around 16 BCE,[3] combines Varro's assertion that Tarpeia was a Vestal virgin with an erotic motivation for the girl's betrayal of Rome. This erotic element had been prevalent in Greek analogues to Tarpeia's myth but had only appeared in echoes in the Roman tradition thus far.[4] A further innovation in Propertius's poem is the fact that Tarpeia herself speaks in a long monologue embedded within the narrative.

---

1. Sullivan 1976 and Johnson 2009 participate in this approach.

2. See also Janan's Lacanian study (2001) of Propertius's fourth book, which brings feminist criticism also to bear.

3. 16 BCE, the year of the consulship of P. Cornelius Scipio mentioned at 4.11.65–66 (the brother of Cornelia who is the speaker of elegy 4.11), is the book's *terminus post quem* and the presumed publication date.

4. See the introduction to this volume, and chapter 8.

The combination of Vestality, erotic love, and subjectivity generates anxiety and suspense in the poem, as multiple perspectives, loyalties, and agendas collide. In the first section of this chapter I probe Propertius's elegiac Tarpeia as an embodiment of various tensions the poet sees in Roman life. Tarpeia's public priesthood bespeaks a special form of allegiance and responsibility to the Roman state, while her love for Tatius is a personal and private desire independent of the state, even antithetical to it, especially given her mandated chastity. The Augustan age is marked by the attempt to harmonize personal and public needs. Augustus's moral legislation and various other measures established guidelines and hierarchies for individual behavior so as to minimize the fragmentation and strife that had resulted from the unchecked liberty of the Republic's final decades. Tarpeia's conflict reveals this transition "on the ground" as it were. The form of the poem, in which Tarpeia's monologue is embedded within the poet's own frame narrative, further represents the tension between her personal voice and the public assessment of her that surrounds it. What is more, the outcome of Tarpeia's story and the embeddedness of her voice suggest the way the struggle between personal and public will go: her voice and desires will be subsumed within the state's need and assessment of her. This chapter's second section explores the interplay of Tarpeia's voice with the narrator's.

Propertius's Tarpeia poem is also unique in its emphasis on the lingering traces of Tarpeia's story in Roman place names. The poem, like many in the fourth book and in line with the book's aim to celebrate Rome's rites, days, and places, is an aetion for urban locations. This focus emerges in the poem's first couplet and is reinforced in the final couplet. The aetiological frame of the poem forges an explicit connection between Tarpeia's past and the reader's present-day experience, a connection that is to color our reading and cap it. The third section of this chapter addresses Tarpeia's topographical legacy as Propertius presents it. Three places are mentioned in these framing aetiological lines: the grove (*nemus*) of Tarpeia and her tomb (*sepulcrum*, 4.4.1–2), and the hill (*mons*, 4.4.83). The first two, those offered at the poem's opening, are otherwise unknown to modern readers. I believe they might have puzzled the ancient reader equally, who then struggles to reconcile what he knows of Tarpeian places in the city with what he reads in the poem. The same confusion closes the poem, but this time a recognizable and much-attested place (the *mons Tarpeius*) is glossed as a prize for an unnamed and unknowable addressee called a *vigil*, certainly Tarpeia but with disturbing echoes of Jupiter. The reader is left baffled once again.

The unresolved and unresolvable tension between Tarpeia's private desire and her public responsibilities and the destabilizing effect of the topographical *aitia* render Tarpeia's myth deeply troublesome, in a way different from the versions told by Q. Fabius Pictor and L. Cornelius Piso Frugi. Both those versions labored to contain the rupture in Roman identity caused by Tarpeia, the first by parsing out blame for the betrayal to Sabines and women, and the second by erasing blame entirely. In Propertius's text, conversely, the point is the uncontainability of the rupture. The factors that contribute to Propertius's presentation of Tarpeia—Greek literary precedents, Roman religious practice, a city mindful of its past, elegiac norms, Augustan-era politics—all complicate her message. There is no single moment or place at which she can belong to all the spheres that claim her.

A VESTAL IN LOVE

As explored in chapter 3, Varro's brief narrative of Tarpeia brought some sense and harmony to a tradition riddled with puzzles. Foremost, a Vestal Tarpeia removes the incongruity of a young girl's presence in Rome at a time when there were no women to wed. If Tarpeia was there, why could she not marry one of the Romans? As a Vestal, she was unavailable to be a bride. The antiquarian, almost clinical tone of his work also serves to sanitize the story—to render it distant, scholarly, remote, and therefore safe.[5] Yet as I argued in that chapter, Vestal Tarpeia, even as she erases some disquiet about her status in Romulus's day, generates further anxieties about gender roles in Rome.

Propertius was deeply steeped in the Varronian tradition. Throughout his fourth book he shows himself indebted to the great scholar's work and ideas. In many cases, Propertius's use of Varronian learning creates a new sort of "Roman Alexandrianism" in that it combines a predilection for esoteric details and arcana with Roman institutions and understanding. Often Varronian details in Propertius's poetry destabilize the status quo by suggesting alternative explanations or origins for certain phenomena. Thus for example the inclusion of a Varronian etymology for the Velabrum among many others given in elegy 4.9 on the origin on the Ara Maxima disrupts Varro's linguistic authority and its assumption of a recoverable and mean-

---

5. Wallace-Hadrill 1997: 14 discusses antiquarianism as subverting authority through research and learning, as authority shifted from the elite to the educated.

ingful past for words. A word etymologized in various ways, as we see in Propertius's poetry, smashes the notion of an objective truth that lies behind a word or phenomenon.

Propertius's adoption of Varro's Vestal Tarpeia functions in a similarly destabilizing way, for, like the etymologies in 4.9, his contextualization of Tarpeia among other possibilities and identities renders her priesthood and its role in Romulean Rome open to interpretation rather than settled. The Varronian tradition of Tarpeia as Vestal might put to rest some questions, namely those about the presence of a woman in womanless Rome and, given her presence, her unavailability for marriage. But in Propertius's treatment this rest becomes unrest when Tarpeia's desire is activated. As a desiring Vestal, is she really unavailable for the Roman marriage pool, and if so, why precisely? If Varro's answer to her awkward position is "she was constrained from marrying," Propertius's rejoinder to that position is "why, how, and to what end?"

VESTAL IN LOVE, ACT 1: A MESS

Propertius's Tarpeia is a woman with a public and a private identity. As a Vestal priestess she is consigned to chastity and to the performance of her duties on behalf of the state. So important is her priestly function that she is allowed, in the poem, to perform ritual duties despite personal risk. After opening the poem with an extended description of the locale of Tatius's camp (discussed later in this chapter), Propertius turns to Tarpeia's first encounter with Tatius. It is while Rome was being besieged by the Sabines, but Tarpeia was allowed to leave the Capitol:[6]

> hinc Tarpeia deae fontem libavit: at illi   15
>   urgebat medium fictilis urna caput.
> et satis una malae potuit mors esse puellae,
>   quae voluit flammas fallere, Vesta, tuas?
> vidit harenosis Tatium proludere campis
>   pictaque per flavas arma levare iubas: 20
> obstipuit regis facie et regalibus armis,
>   interque oblitas excidit urna manus.
> saepe illa immeritae causata est omina lunae,
>   et sibi tingendas dixit in amne comas:

---

6. I have relied on Barber's 1960 Oxford text. Several texts have since appeared, notably Heyworth's new Oxford edition (2007b) and Hutchinson's "green and gold" of book 4 (2006).

saepe tulit blandis argentea lilia Nymphis, 25
  Romula ne faciem laederet hasta Tati.
(4.4.15–26)

From this place Tarpeia drew libation at the fountain of the goddess, but the clay urn was pressing down on her head. And could one death be enough for the wicked girl who wished, Vesta, to destroy your flames? She saw Tatius performing maneuvers on the sandy plain, saw him lift his decorated weapons across the tawny mane. She stood agape at the sight of the king's face, and at his royal armor, and the urn slipped between her forgetful hands and fell. Often she cited omens of the moon as a pretext and she said she had to purify her hair in the river. Often she brought silvery lilies to the sweet nymphs, praying that Romulus's spear not harm Tatius's face.

This is the first mention of Tarpeia since the introductory couplet, and she is, at this entry-point moment, performing her Vestal duties (*libavit, deae*). As soon as Tarpeia-as-Vestal appears, however, she is guilty: before even describing her desire, or mentioning her first glimpse of Tatius, the poet judges her as evil (*malae puellae*) for cheating the goddesses' needs (*flammas fallere, Vesta, tuas*). Her cheat takes three forms. First, she drops her holy duties—literally dropping the urn she carries (*interque oblitas excidit urna manus*), and more metaphorically letting her priestly obligations slip from her consciousness (*oblitas manus*). Hutchinson here notes that the heavy meter of the pentameter's first half—spondees, long words—reflects Tarpeia's mind, and that the dropped urn "symbolizes Tarpeia's abandonment of the Vestal spirit."[7] Second, she uses her sacral duties or some version of them as pretexts to visit Tatius's camp (*saepe illa immeritae causata est omina lunae / et sibi tingendas dixit in amne comas*). Here, she imputes to the goddess the demand to wash her hair in the river (with the obligation housed in the gerundive *tingendas*); the moon is also a victim in Tarpeia's ploys (*immeritae*). Third, she supplicates the nymphs to keep her beloved from harm. Since Tatius is an enemy, her prayers on his behalf are a direct violation of the needs of the state that her priesthood protects. This violation might explain why she prays to the nymphs rather than to her tutelary goddess Vesta. In doing so, she violates chain of command and pits god against god. These real supplications to the wrong gods throw

---

7. Hutchinson 2006 *ad* 4.4.22.

into high relief the fake supplications to the right god she accomplishes in the couplet before.[8]

Thus, in the first lines describing her, Tarpeia has violated the spirit of her priesthood in the service of her love. Put another way, the needs of "Tarpeia desirous girl" are in conflict with the needs of "Tarpeia Roman priestess"; her love pulls more on her time, activity, and sentiment than does her public function. In these lines, the competition of demands and sentiments is a zero-sum game; she cannot be both lover and priestess, and cannot meet the needs of both her own heart and her duty to Rome.

In my previous work on this poem I explored Tarpeia's conflictedness between "what is good for the individual" and "what is good for the state" in terms of the Augustan marriage legislation. Augustus's legislation on marriage and adultery, passed in 18 BCE, spoke to the ability of women to undermine proper relationships between men. This set of laws on marriage and adultery sought to stabilize families via children, social classes via restricted intermarriage, and female conduct via the punishment for adultery. This legislation was but one aspect of a sweeping attempt at moral reform (in the guise of cultural renewal) during Augustus's Principate. One practical intention of the moral legislation was that more traditional family structures might be encouraged and rewarded, leading to stability and to more steady fecundity. These results would serve the state in turn by fostering peace and curtailing one avenue for social mobility (and transgression).[9] A broader implication of the moral program is that the personal is subsumed and harmonized with the public.[10] The laws established a new relationship between the individual and the state, subordinating private desires and personal liberties to public needs and state authority.

The moral program can be connected with a larger cultural shift discernible in this era, away from the valorization of individual *libertas/licentia, auctoritas,* and *dignitas* to the more circumscribed and enmeshed ties of *amicitia* and *concordia*.[11] This shift is discernible in literature, art and

---

8. Ibid. *ad* 4.4.25–26 is again eloquent: "Ritual is now actually performed, but with a personal and traitorous aim."

9. Raditsa 1980; della Corte 1982; Cohen 1991; Severy 2003; Milnor 2006.

10. Raditsa 1980: 282: "The effect of these laws was to make the private lives of all subjects a matter of 'public' concern . . . . They reflect in this effort to make private matters public the destruction of the public sphere, of freespoken speech, of the legislative and elective assemblies, of the sovereignty of the people—and with it the obliteration of the distinction between private and public."

11. Syme 1939: 149–61 is indispensable on the shifting meanings and co-option of the terms.

architecture, and topography.¹² The new ideal held that the state's and the individual's interests were coextensive. Individual choices were best and most sanctioned when they were seen as serving a societal rather than personal goal. Rather, societal *was* the personal.

This is not true for Tarpeia in Propertius's elegy. In her long monologue that forms the core of the poem, she reveals that her personal goal and the needs of the state do not overlap, much less support each other. She is not ignorant or naïve of their antithesis; she demonstrates that she is aware of the potential consequences of her desire and loath to do harm to the state. The opening lines of her speech highlight Tarpeia's inner struggle between her desire and the cost to her or to Rome of that desire:

> "Ignes castrorum et Tatiae praetoria turmae
>   et formosa oculis arma Sabina meis,
> o utinam ad vestros sedeam captiva Penatis,
>   dum captiva mei conspicer ora Tati!
> Romani montes, et montibus addita Roma,   35
>   et valeat probro Vesta pudenda meo:
> ille equus, ille meos in castra reponet amores,
>   cui Tatius dextras collocat ipse iubas!
> quid mirum in patrios Scyllam saevisse capillos,
>   candidaque in saevos inguina versa canis?   40
> prodita quid mirum fraterni cornua monstri,
>   cum patuit lecto stamine torta via?
> quantum ego sum Ausoniis crimen factura puellis,
>   improba virgineo lecta ministra foco!
> Pallados exstinctos si quis mirabitur ignis,   45
>   ignoscat: lacrimis spargitur ara meis."
> (4.4.31–46)

O fires of the camp, and headquarters of Tatius's squadron, and Sabine weapons lovely to my eyes, O, would that I might sit at your hearth as a captive, as long as I might gaze upon the face of my Tatius in captivity!

---

12. Some examples: Horatian satire, which is particularly concerned with the delicate balance between *libertas* and *amicitia*; the Ara Pacis's valorization of the peace and fecundity of the collective (de Grummond 1990; Zanker 1988: 175–83); reconciliation of Republican rivals in the Forum of Augustus by putting them all on harmonious display along its side walls; imperial building projects that harmonized the visual impact of places previously marked by monuments to Republican rivalry (Zanker 1988: 210–15, 5–31; Favro 1996: 53–60). Livia's temple to Concordia (Ovid *Fasti* 6.637–48, esp. 637–38, and see Severy 2003: 131–38, who discusses it as also representing/defining the role of "the matron of the family of state.").

Roman hills, and upon the hills, Rome, and you, Vesta, who must be shamed by my sin, fare well: that horse, that horse will carry my passions back into his camp, that horse whose mane Tatius himself smooths to the right. Why wonder that Scylla violated her father's hair, and her shining loins were changed into vicious dogs? Why wonder that the monstrous brother's horns were betrayed, when the twisted path lay revealed by a gathered thread? How great a crime am I about to commit for Italian girls, I, a sinful girl chosen to be minister to a virgin's hearth! If someone should wonder that the fires of Pallas have gone out, let him forgive me: the altar is wet with my tears.

For Tarpeia, public and private do not meet seamlessly. Her speech reveals, though, her understanding that, for her of all Romans, they *should* meet seamlessly. Consider her use of *Penatis* at 4.4.33. The phrase *ad vestros Penatis* indicates, of course, Tatius's home;[13] that she means his private home rather than the Sabine central hearth is confirmed by *mei ora Tati* in the following line, for she sees herself not only in his company but also as bound to him by her captivity—she is the captive, but he is hers. Yet the Roman reader knows that the Penates Tarpeia serves in Rome are not private but public, for the city's Penates, brought by Aeneas from burning Troy to preserve the new state, were kept in Vesta's temple.[14] Ideologically, her family *is* the state and the state *is* her family. Scholarship over the last three decades on the Vestal priesthood has sought to understand these contours of the Vestal's sexual, familial, and public status.[15]

Her mention of Scylla and Ariadne as analogous to (and precedent for) herself in her predicament further reveals the sick conflation of state and family that Tarpeia experiences. She mentions these girls' violation not of country but of family; Scylla violates her *patrios capillos* and Ariadne betrays her *cornua fraterni monstri* (4.4.39–40). The parallels she sees for herself thus reveal that Tarpeia equates family and state; indeed in this poem, unlike other sources,[16] there is no mention of her father Spurius Tarpeius, or even of the fact that she has a father. A little later in her speech she mentions another for whom state and family are one, though again in a way that she considers unsalutary:

---

13. Hanslik 1962: 242.
14. See, e.g., Dionysius 2.66.5 and cf. 2.65.2; Vergil *Aeneid* 2.296; Ovid *Fasti* 1.527–28; Cicero *Pro Scauro* 48, Livy 26.27.14.
15. See chapter 3 in this volume.
16. Fabius Pictor fr. 7 *FRH*; Livy 1.11; Valerius Maximus 9.6.1; and Antigonus in Plutarch *Romulus* 17 all call her a daughter.

> te toga picta decet, non quem sine matris honore
>   nutrit inhumanae dura papilla lupae.
> hic, hospes, patria metuar regina sub aula?[17] 55
>   dos tibi non humilis prodita Roma venit.
> si minus, at raptae ne sint impune Sabinae:
>   me rape et alterna lege repende vices!
> commissas acies ego possum solvere: nuptae
>   vos medium palla foedus inite mea. 60
> adde Hymenaee modos, tubicen fera murmura conde:
>   credite, vestra meus molliet arma torus.
>
> (4.4.53–62)

It is you the *toga picta* befits, not that one whom, without the honor of a mother, the harsh nipple of an inhuman wolf-bitch nursed. Here, stranger, will I be revered as queen in your country's palace? Rome betrayed comes as no humble dowry to you. Or, as punishment for the rape of the Sabine women, take me and settle the score by the law of retribution! I, as a bride, am able to resolve the battles that have begun. Enter into a treaty through my wedding gown! Hymenaeus, add your strains! Trumpeter, stop your wild sounds! Believe me, my marriage bed will soften your weapons.

Like Tarpeia, Romulus has no mother to speak of; the inhuman wolf, symbol of the state by Propertius's time, is his mother similar to the way the state is Tarpeia's family. Also similar to Tarpeia's situation, the elision of family and state in Romulus's case works to the detriment of both for, thus parented, Romulus is unfit to wear the *toga picta,* the sartorial indicator of a citizen's importance to the state worn by victorious generals and high magistrates. Tarpeia's refusal to say Romulus's name—she calls him *quem*—emphasizes her scornful assessment of him as a nonperson.[18] I would like to draw attention here to what I see as a very provocative novelty in Propertius's Tarpeia: the fact that she seeks advice and precedent in mythical and historical figures. She looks to Scylla,

---

17. This line is extremely vexed, and thus I do not make much of it here. I retain Barber's 1960 reading in order to be consistent, though Fedeli 1984, Hutchinson 2006, Heyworth 2007b, and Goold 1990 all offer good suggestions.

18. The Ohio State University Press's anonymous reader notes the similarity to Augustus, who unnamed his enemies in his *Res Gestae.* The connection between name and meaningful identity underscores the variety authors use in dealing with Tarpeia's own name, which they simply note (Pictor, Piso, Dionysius, Plutarch, Simylus), gloss (Propertius), analyze (Varro), or omit (Valerius).

Ariadne, and wolf-fostered Romulus as *comparanda* for herself and for her would-be lover. All three figures, like Tarpeia herself, occupy infelicitous positions within a community system that blends family and state. What is more, all three are antithetical to the human condition; Scylla is half-dog, Romulus is wolf-fed, and Ariadne is sister to a hybrid form and is herself saved from humanity by the god Dionysus.[19] For Tarpeia, her mythic analogues underscore and confirm the difficulty of her situation: that private needs do not mesh with public needs. Likewise wolf-fed Romulus, one of Rome's most prized myths, is inconsistent with what she finds valuable. Not only is she at odds with her state; she is at odds with its myths as well. The Augustan-era ideal of a state and its individuals all moving in the same direction, of *concordia* among people and among their various allegiances and identities, is not on display in this poem, in the myths she chooses to tell, or in her own myth.

Tarpeia's monologue reveals that, in her case, the intended harmony between personal and public fails. On one hand, she sees an either-or relationship in her verbal back-and-forth between her love and her duty. On the other hand, her speech reveals a perspective already aware of an overlap of the two—her private life *is* her public life—but neither is this overlap salutary, nor does it meet her needs or Rome's (ditto Romulus—blended, he is neither a person nor a statesman). Having laid bare her understanding of the conflictedness of her identity, Tarpeia seizes upon a potential solution that will bring her desire and her duty into proper alignment: marriage with Tatius. As the Sabine women would eventually do, Tarpeia envisions herself combining marriage and peacemaking. Her mention of dowry, the Hymenaeus, wedding dress, marriage bed, the reference to herself as *nupta* and her sexual pun in *molliet* all reveal Tarpeia's hope for a marriage with the Sabine king.[20] Her understanding of Rome as her dowry further elides state and family.

Indeed, she sees the solution that eventually does bring peace—the reconciliation brought about by the Sabine women through their marriage. Tarpeia wants to facilitate, not undermine, this process, an interesting comment since Tarpeia and the Sabine women are so often foils for each other in the sources, such as Livy's history and the relief sculptures in the Basilica Aemilia. Tarpeia's hopes for a treaty with the Sabines and an end to the war, seen in *solvere* and *foedus*, and encapsulated in the chiastic *arma torus* (ll.59,

---

19. I am indebted to Gabriella Moretti for this idea.
20. As DeBrohun 2003: 194 points out, Tarpeia's elision of her wedding clothes with her Vestal costume illuminates her own precarious situation and the uneasy mingling of *Amor* and *Roma* in book 4 generally. In her reading, *molliet* adds an elegiac touch to martial Tatius.

60, and 62, respectively), embody a hope of all Roman marriages: namely, that marriages blur the distinctions between families and strengthen the community, rather than sever community ties.[21] Tarpeia's hopes are noble. In envisioning a winning situation for all parties, the elegist's Tarpeia would become a positive example for all time.

VESTAL IN LOVE, ACT 2: NOT A WOMAN

But of course it is not so, because Tarpeia's Vestality prevents her from acting in this way. The Augustan moral ideal relied on men and women each fulfilling appropriate, and circumscribed, roles. Marriageable women were to marry appropriately, and other women—Vestal priestesses, prostitutes, and even *univirae*—would better serve the state by remaining unwed.[22] Propertius's poem draws attention to any number of other women who do not fit into the traditional categories desired and rewarded by the Augustan legislation. Before turning to these other women, it is important to note that Tarpeia herself steps out of a feminine role in asserting her plan to achieve a treaty through marriage with Tatius. Her language in that passage casts her at once as a bride and as a politician:

> si minus, at raptae ne sint impune Sabinae:
>   me rape et alterna lege repende vices!
> commissas acies ego possum solvere: nuptae
>   vos medium palla foedus inite mea.   60
> (4.4.57–60)

> Or, as punishment for the rape of the Sabine women, take me and settle the score by the law of retribution! I, as a bride, am able to resolve the battles that have begun. Enter into a mediating treaty through my wedding gown!

Her professed ability to end battles and to enact a treaty casts her as masculine; her use of the imperative also subtly suggests control in the exchange. Of course, in love poetry *foedus* had already been used to indicate mar-

---

21. See Miles 1995: 211–19, who discusses how the Roman myth of the Sabine women and the marriage legislation of Augustus promote marriage as an institution with greater societal than personal impact. See also Treggiari 1991: 90–94 for a more concrete expression of this desire.

22. Beard 1980 describes their attire as akin to the attire of the bride; their putative spouse would then be the cult or the state.

riage—and to appropriate the sanctity and permanence of political alliances to the realm of love.[23] In Catullus 109, for example, the word performs to Catullus's (male) audience the understanding that his relationship with Lesbia is the equivalent of the social and political bonds that men make with each other. In Tarpeia's mouth, the word shows her entering a sphere that is not normally woman's to enter (unless invited, like Lesbia).[24] Tarpeia's use of the lexicon of the male elite calls into question the stability of gender and political categories on which Concordia rests.[25] Her proposal further undermines the stability of the relationships and identities in that she is simultaneously enactor and object of the treaty. Propertius draws attention to this double role:

> hoc Tarpeia suum tempus rata convenit hostem:
> > pacta ligat, pactis ipsa futura comes.
> (4.4.81–82)

Tarpeia set this time to meet the enemy: she ratifies the deal, herself to be a part of the deal.

Women were normally not enactors but objects of treaties (cf. Lavinia, Sabine women). Tarpeia's double role creates a conflict of interest, rendering her and the treaty unstable. This instability is underscored by the poem's triple appearance of *foedus*'s lexical cousin *fidus/fides*, faith shored up at 4.4.8 (*fidaque suggesta castra coronat humo*), negated at 4.4.49 (*lubrica tota via est et perfida*), and betrayed near the poem's end:

> prodiderat portaeque fidem patriamque iacentem,
> > nubendique petit, quem velit, ipsa diem.
> at Tatius (neque enim sceleri dedit hostis honorem)
> > "Nube" ait "et regni scande cubile mei!"   90
> dixit, et ingestis comitum super obruit armis.
> > haec, virgo, officiis dos erat apta tuis.
> a duce Tarpeia mons est cognomen adeptus:
> > o vigil, iniustae praemia sortis habes.
> (4.4.87–94)

---

23. Cat. 109.6, 64.335; Prop. 2.9.35, 2.30.21, 25.
24. LaLonde 2012.
25. Arethusa and Cynthia also use the word. For LaLonde 2012 their appropriation of masculine language destabilizes the categories and assumptions on which political performance and identity rest. LaLonde also argues about women normally being the object of a treaty, not an agreeing participant in them.

> She handed over the trusteeship of the gate and her fatherland, spread out before him, and she asks what day he would like for their wedding. But Tatius (for not even as an enemy did he grant respect to a criminal deed) said "Here's your marriage; climb this bed of my kingdom." He spoke, and he overcame her, the weapons of his comrades heaped upon her. This, maiden, was the dowry fitted to your work. The hill took its name from its guide Tarpeia. O watchman, this is the prize you have for your unjust lot.

The impossibility of Tarpeia's *foedus* and her participation in it is marked by her syntactical return to her proper place as subordinate to men: Tatius now orders her in the imperative, and enlists his companions (*comitum*)—of which group she is pointedly not a part (cf. *ipsa futura comes*)—to overcome her with their shields. As Tatius did with his imperatives, the poet likewise twists Tarpeia's speech back to her discredit; she had suggested Rome as the dowry she would bring to her marriage, but the dowry given to the discredited Vestal is death (*haec, virgo, officiis dos erat apta tuis*). The final couplet reinforces Tarpeia's transgression of gender norms with the phrase *duce Tarpeia*[26] and enshrines it in an urban location that forever preserves her masculine dimension: the *mons Tarpeius*.

Duce Tarpeia caps another set of images that situates Tarpeia uncomfortably within normative Roman gender roles. Roman readers might recognize the phrase as a nod to Vergil's Dido, the *dux femina facti* of Carthage (*Aen.* 1.364) who is herself a woman acting as a man, and caught between her desires and a public role, as queen of Carthage, that limits her erotic freedoms. John Warden unpacked this resonance some thirty years ago in 1978, tracing the many evocations of Vergilian Dido in the Tarpeia elegy, particularly in the cluster of images that ends and immediately follows Tarpeia's soliloquy. There she prays for sleep and for pleasant dreams of Tatius, but is granted instead fuel for the fire of her passion:

> "et iam quarta canit venturam bucina lucem,
>   ipsaque in Oceanum sidera lapsa cadunt.
> experiar somnum, de te mihi somnia quaeram: 65
>   fac venias oculis umbra benigna meis."
> dixit, et incerto permisit bracchia somno,
>   nescia se furiis accubuisse novis.

---

26. Though *TLL* lists *dux* as masculine or feminine (v. 1, p. 2316, line 74), there is no doubt but that the phrase is jarring.

>   nam Vesta, Iliacae felix tutela favillae,
>   culpam alit et plures condit in ossa faces.   70
>   illa ruit,²⁷ qualis celerem prope Thermodonta
>   Strymonis abscisso pectus aperta sinu.
>   (4.4.63–72)

"Now the fourth chime heralds the coming sun, and the setting stars slip into the ocean. I will try to sleep, and I will pray for dreams about you. Do come as an encouraging spirit before my eyes." She spoke and relaxed her arms into fitful sleep, unaware that she was bedding with new furies. For Vesta, propitious guardian of the Trojan flame, feeds her sin and buries even more torches in her bones. She rushes forward like a woman of Strymon, with breast bared and cloak torn, along the side of swift-running Thermodon.

This passage, as John Warden has demonstrated, is richly resonant of Dido, who similarly succumbs to furies planted in her by a goddess.[28] The verbal resonances (*alit, nescia, furiis, sidera lapsa cadunt, somnia, culpa*) culminate in the image of Tarpeia raving like an Amazon or a Bacchant, just as Dido does throughout her tragic appearance in the *Aeneid*. The evocation not only shows Propertius's debt to Vergil and his skill at retooling the epic tradition for his own literary project. It also increases the list of ways Tarpeia does not fit the role of a bride she so desires and, more to the point, casts her as a threat to those roles and to the worldview they enable. Micaela Janan has drawn attention to the way Amazons and Bacchants "attest aspects of woman's desire that escape Man's calculation."[29] Neither Tarpeia nor Dido nor Amazons nor Bacchants are governable in the marriage legislation, nor are they able to live harmoniously within the Roman state.[30] Both Amazons and Bacchants are also antithetical to urban life; the former represent a sort of anti-civilization, and when they do enter Athens in the mythical record, their presence wreaks havoc and ends in death, and the latter perform their revelry in the wilderness. Janan goes on to note their topographical and cultural dualism: "The Bacchant originates inside

---

27. Heyworth 2007b and Hutchinson 2006 both suggest *furit* for *ruit*, an emendation congenial to the context and my analysis, but for consistency I retain Barber's 1960 reading.
28. The Amazon likeness also raises the specter of the Basilica Aemilia relief, though there Tarpeia is an Amazon frozen in a static moment of her death and here the poet emphasizes her movement and madness.
29. Janan 2001: 77.
30. Cf. Sharon James's argument (2003: 36–40) that the elegiac *puella* also stands outside of the strictures and surveillance of the Augustan moral regime.

the cityscape and goes outside its confines, while the Amazon dwells at civilization's borders but is drawn into war with those at its heart."[31] Tarpeia is also an insider who would leave Rome, yet who brings war right to the city center. Immediately after the double simile, Propertius cuts off the description of Tarpeia and turns to a cold description of the city celebrating the festival of its inauguration.

> urbi festus erat (dixere Parilia patres),
>   hic primus coepit moenibus esse dies,
> annua pastorum convivia, lusus in urbe,   75
>   cum pagana madent fercula divitiis,
> cumque super raros faeni flammantis acervos
>   traicit immundos ebria turba pedes.
> (4.4.73–78)

It was a holiday in the city (the elders called it the Parilia). This day was the first beginning for Rome's walls. It was a yearly feast for shepherds, a celebration in the city, when rustic plates dripped with delicacies, and when the country folk flung dirty feet over scattered heaps of burning hay.

The contrast between *abscisso pectus aperta sinu* and *urbi* is striking; we turn from a woman mad with passion, baring her breast, to the city and its men (*urbi, patres, moenibus, pastorum, urbe*). We are left with a sense of foreboding at the conflict to come. The poem moves to a speedy conclusion thereafter and, having defined Tarpeia as Vestal, lover, Scylla, Ariadne, man, Dido, Amazon, and Bacchant, leaves little doubt how the story ends.

WHOSE PERSPECTIVE?

Propertius's choice to give Tarpeia a voice in his poem is one of his most radical manipulations of the mythic material. In no other texts does she speak. Focusing the narrative through Tarpeia's perspective, Propertius portrays Tarpeia's love as compelling and her concerns as real. John Warden links the reader's sympathy for Tarpeia and understanding of her dilemma with the shift of focalization the poem offers;[32] readers understand, in the frame of the poem, that Tarpeia's love constitutes sacrilege, but through

---

31. Janan 2001: 77–78.
32. Warden 1980: 108–9, quotation from p. 109.

her monologue they come to "experience the vitality of Tarpeia's love." In what follows I hope to add some support to Warden's analysis that Tarpeia's monologue offers the reader an opportunity to sympathize with the girl, while the poem's framing narrative endorses her condemnation. The very presence of a sympathetic voice within the normative perspective complicates the moral value of her tale, for the state is seen to include a dissenting voice. I then wish, however, to go beyond Warden's assessment and trace some of the ways the poem complicates and elides even these two divergent perspectives. The result is a deeply riven assessment of Tarpeia, and one that leaves the reader torn about how to respond to the treasonous girl.

We have already seen how Tarpeia's own language presents her understanding of the difficult situation in which she finds herself. She convinces herself of a solution that suits her identity as a lover and as a Roman: marriage with Tatius.[33] Her monologue, however, is fantasy. The verbs she uses do not indicate but overwhelmingly hope, deliberate, project, urge, order, and suggest; thirteen verbs in her speech are indicative,[34] while twenty-five are subjunctive, future, or imperative.[35] By contrast, in the frame narrative fifty-one verbs are indicative and nine are subjunctive, future, or imperative.[36] The narrator also uses language that condemns Tarpeia outright; rather early in the poem (delayed only by a description of the locale), he implies condemnation of her:

et satis una malae potuit mors esse puellae,
    quae voluit flammas fallere, Vesta, tuas?[37]
(4.4.17–18)

---

33. Tissol 1997: 149 notes that Tarpeia, like Scylla in Ovid's *Metamorphoses*, uses language to deceive herself.

34. *Collocat, cum patuit, spargitur, ut ait, est, celat, decet, nutrit, venit, possum solvere, canit, cadunt, quid mirum*. Of these, *possum solvere* and *quid mirum* could perhaps be placed in the other list.

35. *utinam sedeam, dum conspicer, valeat, pudenda, reponet, facture, si mirabitur, ignosset, potabitur, cape, utinam nossem, tulisset, metuar/pariam, ne sint raptae, rape, repende, inite, adde, conde, credite, molliet, experiar, quaeram, fac venias*. In this list are two participles expressing expectation or futurity: *pudenda* (Tarpeia's expectation of how Vesta will react to her actions) and *factura* (describing what she intends). I do not include *venturam*, which modifies *lucem*, since this is not reasonably considered Tarpeia's perspective or wish.

36. The nine: *fabor, poturas, cum quateret, ne laederet, non patienda, future, quem velit, nube, scande*. Of these *poturas* seems a rather weak example (sheep go to drink), and *fabor* is the usual form of the verb (*fari* never appears in the first-person present; see Bettini 2008: 315). I counted *potuit esse* among indicatives, as I did in the inset speech above, but it could properly be added to this list of nine since it suggests potential.

37. Some editors have questioned the placement of this couplet, most recently Heyworth 2007b, but most retain it here in its manuscript position.

> Could one death be enough for this wicked girl who wished, Vesta, to deceive your sacred fires?

She is wicked (*malae*) and intentional (*voluit*) in her deceit (*fallere*). Just after this denunciation of her the poet offers an example of her deceit—her use of Vestal rites as pretexts to catch a glimpse of her beloved (4.4.23–26, *causata est* etc., discussed above). Indeed the poet's question is answered by his condemnation: one death isn't enough, and Tarpeia is executed every time someone reads the poem, or any version of her story, or any time someone is thrown from the rock as punishment. At the poem's close, too, the narrator affirms Tarpeia's punishment:

> at Tatius (neque enim sceleri dedit hostis honorem)
>   "Nube" ait "et regni scande cubile mei!"   90
> dixit, et ingestis comitum super obruit armis.
>   haec, virgo, officiis dos erat apta tuis.
> (4.4.89–92)

> But Tatius (for not even as an enemy did he grant respect to a criminal deed) said "Here's your marriage; climb this bed of my kingdom." He spoke, and he overcame her, the weapons of his comrades heaped upon her. This, maiden, was the dowry fitted to your work.

The reason for Tatius's harsh action is here given as an objective truth rather than as his perspective, or even as one possibility for his perspective as had been the case in Livy's account.[38] The girl got what was owed to her (*dos apta*), what is owed to anyone who commits such a crime (*sceleri*, sc. *prodiderat portaeque fidem patriamque iacentem* two lines above). The punishment and the moral are universal: *neque enim hostis* suggests any enemy and a self-evident truth.[39] On either side of Tarpeia's monologue, therefore, are clear statements of her guilt presented as fact. It is as if, like Tarpeia herself under the shields, her voice in the poem is buried under the weight of the narrator's condemnatory statements.

Yet as in the visual depictions of Tarpeia being buried—the coins, the frieze—in the poem readers are allowed to see the process of burying and

---

38. Livy 1.11 offers this explanation as one of two possible: the other is that he wished to lend the appearance that he took the Capitol forcefully. Livy includes the possibility that, if Tarpeia was a Roman patriot, in killing her Tatius only gave her what she deserved.

39. Allen and Greenough 1903: 324h ("*etenim* and the negative *neque enim* introduce something self-evident or needing no proof").

to acknowledge that someone disagreed and protested. As often as the poem executes her, it resurrects her. The presence of her divergent voice within the Roman state gives a strong sense of how important it is for Rome to define and cast out Tarpeia (and those like her) as the exception to the rule and as the "other" rather than the "self."[40] Her opposition makes more powerful the idea in this poem of the appropriate, in its usual sense of suitability (even Tarpeia is concerned with the language of decorum—*te toga picta decet* . . .) and in its more literal sense of belonging / "one's own."

I here note that the poem's first verb, *fabor* in the opening couplet, identifies what follows as the assessment of an individual speaker rather than an omniscient narrator. As Bettini has shown (2006), this verb itself blends two voices: that of the speaker who utters the words and that of the authority, whether divine or social, that inspires the words or guarantees their truth.[41] For Bettini, Propertius's use of *fabor* casts him as *vates,* a vehicle for the narrative rather than its creator. Propertius's reliance on divine or traditional authority would lend weight to his account of events that happened so long ago. In some instances in poetry it is clear where the intermediary speaker's prelude ends and the voice of the higher authority begins (Bettini cites the prophet Marcius relating Jupiter's sentiments on Cannae in Livy 25.12). In other cases it is less clear. In the poem at hand, one likely place would be between the first and second couplets: "I will tell of these things . . . there was a grove." But then line 9 presents a difficulty: "What was Rome back then . . ." followed by a meditation on the contrast of places then and now (lines 9–14). Reading divine authority behind the speaking *vates* does little to clear up the problem of perspective; in fact, it blurs it. What happens, then, when Tarpeia's perspective bleeds into that of the (two-voiced) narrator, and vice versa? Several features of the poem function in just such a blurring capacity. and these, more than the opposition of her voice to Rome's, serve to undermine the comfort with which the reader can accept her story as a clear-cut morality tale.

We have already explored the schism between what Tarpeia does (collect water and lilies) and what the narrator thinks she is doing (creating opportunities to see Tatius, praying that he not be harmed). Could these couplets not also reveal uncertainty in Tarpeia's mind? Perhaps when she washes her hair she really is seeking an excuse to see Tatius, or perhaps

---

40. See Hallett 1989 for the concept vis-à-vis Roman women.
41. See Bettini 2008.

she is trying to cleanse herself of impurity; what pain for her if her act of absolution also fueled her sin. When she prays to the nymphs, she may be seeking peace rather than war—a wish that would result in Tatius's safety. I do not think this is so, but I note that the narrator's description of her ritual actions, and his imputation of reasons for them, leaves room for doubt. We just don't know. Both the narrator's attempt to get inside her mind and her attempt (if it is such) to follow her cult's strictures while hiding her true motives display a propensity for double perspective.

This case of slippery perspective comes at the juncture between the objective narrative of Tarpeia's first encounters with the sight of Tatius and her subjective monologue. There is a similar blurring of perspectives at the same juncture near the close of the poem—just where Tarpeia ends her monologue and the narrator picks up again. Weary Tarpeia announces that she will try to sleep and dream of her beloved:

> "et iam quarta canit venturam bucina lucem,
>   ipsaque in Oceanum sidera lapsa cadunt.
> experiar somnum, de te mihi somnia quaeram: 65
>   fac venias oculis umbra benigna meis."
> dixit, et incerto permisit bracchia somno,
>   nescia se furiis accubuisse novis.
> nam Vesta, Iliacae felix tutela favillae,
>   culpam alit et plures condit in ossa faces.   70
> illa ruit, qualis celerem prope Thermodonta
>   Strymonis abscisso pectus aperta sinu.
> (4.4.63–72)

"Now the fourth chime heralds the coming sun, and the setting stars slip into the ocean. I will try to sleep, and I will pray for dreams about you. Do come as an encouraging spirit before my eyes." She spoke and relaxed her arms into fitful sleep, unaware that she was bedding with new furies. For Vesta, propitious guardian of the Trojan flame, feeds her sin and buries even more torches in her bones. She rushes forward like a woman of Strymon, with breast bared and cloak torn, along the side of swift-running Thermodon.

We have already seen how this passage confers on Tarpeia a problematic gender identity as Dido, as Amazon, and as Bacchant. I wish here to draw attention to how these couplets move from Tarpeia's perspective to the narrator's, without leaving us sure exactly where the break between the two falls. Emma Scioli's analysis of this passage in the context of other dream narratives draws attention to several features relevant to the current discussion.[42] First, Tarpeia's very intention to dream is framed in both subjective and objective terms; she seeks dreams of Tatius, suggesting she has some control over the dream, that it can arise from her subconscious. But in the very next line she bids him come as a benign shade, revealing the other understanding of dreams as shades that come from outside the mind, from the House of Sleep.[43] Second, Tarpeia's injunction highlights the visuality of the dream experience (*fac venias oculis meis*). As Scioli notes, the description of Tarpeia with arms relaxed evokes paintings and sculptures of dreamers; readers thus view Tarpeia as we might a work of art. We watch Tarpeia as she dreams of watching Tatius in a perspectival hall of mirrors. But what, then, is happening in the last couplet of this passage, in which Tarpeia rushes like an Amazon or a Bacchant (and like Dido, who also acts thus)? Scioli's final point is the most salient here: Propertius leaves the reader unsure whether that couplet is what she sees in her dream, or what we see when we watch her (i.e., she rushes madly upon waking). Scioli argues that it is the former, and I agree. Not only thus do we have a moment in the text at which it is unclear whose perspective is being offered—we also have an instance of the frame narrative getting inside Tarpeia's mind, thus eliding viewer and viewed. She sees herself as the condemning narrator sees her, as a dangerous woman antithetical to the world of men. If it is Tarpeia's dream, then she is viewing herself, occupying both subject and object positions, as she had in *quaeram somnia* and *fac venias benigna umbra*. The *aporia* is even more acute for the intervening couplet about Vesta fanning her flames. Is this Tarpeia's perspective or the narrator's? I have more to say on this below; here it suffices to conclude that the poet confounds Tarpeia's perspective and the narrator's at key moments in the poem, and positions the reader in each, both, and all perspectives at once.

This aporetic effect is borne out in the poem's lexicon, which reuses words in various contexts. We have just seen Tarpeia's use of *somnia*; it is paired with *somnum* in the previous line; it recurs later in the poem, when everything leads toward sleep (*Omnia praebebunt somnos*, 85). The *bracchia* she relaxes and stretches out in sleep (67) are the same arms she cuts climbing the brambly path up the Capitol (28). *Scand-* once refers to this climb (*ascensu*, 83), then later comes from Tatius's mouth scornfully

---

42. Scioli 2005: 315–23.
43. Ovid *Met.* 11.613–49 describes the shades and dreams Sleep can send.

inviting her to "climb" his marriage bed (90). Tatius's troops sound the tuba (*tubicen*, 9); Tarpeia wishes it silenced (*tubicen fera murmura conde*, 61), then Romulus decrees it silent (*tuba intermissa*, 80). Romulus decrees no guard (*Romulus excubias decrevit in otia solvi*, 79), but Jupiter decides otherwise (*Jupiter unus decrevit invigilare*, 85–86). Jove's threshold would be captured (*antiqua limina capta Iovis*, 2), and Tarpeia wishes to become Tatius's captive (*captiva*, 33).[44] Fire moves in many ways in this poem—Tarpeia wishes to deceive Vesta's flames, yet Vesta plants fires in Tarpeia's bones (lines 18 and 69–70). Tarpeia salutes the fires of the camps (*ignes castrorum*, line 31) then worries that it will be put out by her tears (*ignis exstinctos*, and catch the pun on *ignoscat*, 45–46). Fires spring up again in the Parilia, as they will every year in Rome's ritual rebirth (*faeni flammantis*, 77).

Perhaps the most perplexing reuse of a word comes at the poem's ending, the moment at which the point of the myth and of the aitiological poem seems to be clearest. Romulus has decreed a rest from the guard because of the Parilia, but Jupiter will stand guard:

> Romulus excubias decrevit in otia solvi
>   atque intermissa castra silere tuba.   80
> hoc Tarpeia suum tempus rata convenit hostem:
>   pacta ligat, pactis ipsa futura comes.
> mons erat ascensu dubius festoque remissus
>   nec mora, vocalis occupat ense canis.
> omnia praebebant somnos: sed Iuppiter unus   85
>   decrevit poenis invigilare suis.
> prodiderat portaeque fidem patriamque iacentem,
>   nubendique petit, quem velit, ipsa diem.
> at Tatius (neque enim sceleri dedit hostis honorem)
>   "Nube" ait "et regni scande cubile mei!"   90
> dixit, et ingestis comitum super obruit armis.
>   haec, virgo, officiis dos erat apta tuis.
> a duce Tarpeia mons est cognomen adeptus:
>   o vigil, iniustae praemia sortis habes.
> (4.4.79–94)

Romulus decreed that the guard be given leave for the night, and the camps were silent without the tuba's call. Tarpeia set this time to meet the

---

44. Miller and Platter 1999: 452 note this reversal and its configuration of Tarpeia as subject to object.

enemy: she ratifies the deal, herself to be a part of the deal. The mountain was difficult to climb and unguarded for the feast; without delay she slits the throat of the watchdog. Everything was urging on sleep. Jupiter alone decided to watch over his punishments. She handed over the trusteeship of the gate and her fatherland, spread out before him, and she asks what day he would like for their wedding. But Tatius (for not even as an enemy did he grant respect to a criminal deed) said, "Here's your marriage; climb this bed of my kingdom." He spoke, and he overcame her, the weapons of his comrades heaped upon her. This, maiden, was the dowry fitted to your work. The hill took its name from its guide Tarpeia. O watchman, this is the prize you have for your unjust lot.

Tarpeia chooses a moment during which she anticipates she will not be watched (*Romulus excubias decreuit in otia solui . . . hoc Tarpeia suum tempus rata*), but (*sed*) Jupiter decided to be watchful over the compensation owed him (*Iuppiter unus decrevit poenis invigilare suis*).[45] Presumably, his interest in Tarpeia's case stems from the consequence of her betrayal, the *antiqui limina capta Iovis* of line 2 (cf. *captiva* at line 33). Another noteworthy point is that, while everyone else is asleep, Jupiter alone remains awake (*Iuppiter unus*). But Tarpeia is awake as well, and she is the subject of the next couplet even though this is not made clear until late in the pentameter with *ipsa*. The following couplet shows Tatius is awake as well, for he responds with the cruel "Here's your marriage." The syntax of these three couplets shows an interesting relationship between these protagonists: everyone was asleep . . . **but** Jupiter (***sed** Iuppiter*) . . . Tarpeia did her deed . . . **but** Tatius (***at** Tatius*). Tatius acts as Jupiter's moral agent here, and the parallel makes sense; though all three are awake, both Jupiter and Tatius are opposed to Tarpeia.

The difficulty comes in the final couplet. The narrator makes his aitiological point—the Capitol took its name from Tarpeia—and then addresses the final line to an unnamed *vigil*: *O vigil, iniustae praemia sortis habes*. This must refer to Tarpeia, who had been wakeful and had looked out for an opportunity to admit Tatius, but the elision of her wakefulness and Jupiter's via *invigilare* is unsettling. Tarpeia and Jupiter have something else in common. They are both wakeful over the Capitol, which is his hill to protect (*antiqui limina capta Iovis,* line 2) and hers, as we see earlier in the poem:

---

45. Heyworth's translation of the poem in *Cynthia* understands that Jupiter decreed that Tarpeia would stand lookout for her own (opportunity for) punishment. I understand *decerno* + infinitive as "to decide to do . . ." and so I read the line differently.

> et **sua** Tarpeia residens ita flevit **ab arce**
>   vulnera, **vicino** non patienda **Iovi**.
> (4.4.29–30)

> And sinking back down from the Tarpeian citadel the bemoaned her wounds, wounds that her neighbor Jove would not permit.

Here Jupiter is just a neighbor.[46] The joint ownership of the Capitol—offended Jupiter, transgressive Tarpeia—is a crisp reminder of the impossibility of separating (the perspectives of) Rome and Tarpeia. They are one and the same.

The poem's final line, which is textually vexed, underscores the impossibility. *Iniustae sortis* is the problematic phrase, and Hutchinson and Heyworth, the two most recent commentators, have discussed and proposed alternatives (Heyworth 2007a: *iniusti amoris*; Hutchinson 2006: *ista tuae noctis* seems his preferred choice). The problem these and other editors see is that the line as transmitted makes little sense. But, given the reversals this text habitually enacts, could the text as transmitted be sound? The narrator had, in the previous couplet, called her death a fitting dowry for her duty (*officiis*). *Sortis,* on this reading, is thus the narrator's sarcastic interpretation of Tarpeia's deed, and her death is its sarcastic "prize" (*praemia*). *Iniustae*, though, softens the sarcasm a bit. As I have argued above and elsewhere, Tarpeia's "turn of duty" to the state as a Vestal virgin is unjust, in her view. This might be another instance in which the narrator's perspective and Tarpeia's interpenetrate.

This poem, like many in the Propertian corpus, is riddled with textual difficulties and corruptions, and editors must balance the evidence for and nature of possible errors with the need for sense and readability. Recently, criticism on Propertius has taken up the question of sense in terms of Propertius's poetry and other poetry. In 2004 Steven Green, using this poem and Ovid *Heroides* 1, argued that critics must account for the presence of idiosyncrasies within internal, embedded voices. He therefore defends two readings within Tarpeia's monologue (*purgabitur* in 47 and *pariamne tua* in 55, discussed above). I am not so much concerned with the specific textual choices here as with the rationale Green invokes to support them: Tarpeia's "consistently treacherous transgression of all norms" (p. 368) renders possible, even plausible, some shocking

---

46. If we accept Heyworth's 2007b emendation of *vicino* to *vicinae*, Tarpeia is the neighbor, but the sense remains the same.

textual turns. Similarly, Garth Tissol, in his 1997 book *The Face of Nature*, defends textual difficulty (rather than defends against it) by scrutinizing the poem's broader strategy of offering narrative red herrings, such as dizzying and unstable shifts of focus from plot to description and back, a choppy pacing that renders Tarpeia's death surprisingly perfunctory at the poem's end, and irony, including rhetorical questions. Propertius aims to mislead, says Tissol (p. 146), thus aligning the reader with the deceptions and self-deceptions inherent in Tarpeia's story. The most emphatic voice in this recent textual debate is that of Paul Allen Miller, who links textual uncertainty with a precarious and shifting understanding of what constitutes a speaking subject. Miller argues that our desire for sense emerges from our own critical preferences—for example, for a unified subject voice, or a poem with narrative flow, or consistency of character (whether a persona or the poet). Readings based on these preferences risk sweeping some meaning(s) under the carpet. As an alternative, Miller seeks to uncover the complexity of meaning:

> The effect produced by these multiple layerings of reference" is, on the one hand, undeniably intense. There is an extreme concentration of meaning. Yet, on the other hand, that meaning is neither totalizable under a single intention: aesthetic, erotic, homosocial, ironic, or confessional, nor by a single subject position: Propertius the lover, Propertius the reader of Hellenistic poetry, Propertius the crafter of self-conscious poetry books, Propertius the political subject, Propertius the *cliens*, Propertius the child of Umbria, Propertius the rival and imitator of Gallus. (2011: 338–39)

"Multiple layerings of reference" is another way to describe the phenomena I have elaborated above. I have argued previously that Tarpeia has much in common with Propertius the love poet (2005). She seems sometimes to be a character within the poem, and sometimes a mouthpiece for the poet. The phenomenon is similar to that of the chorus in Greek tragedy, which acts both as character within the drama and commentator on the drama.[47] The narrator too speaks at times like an individual and at times like a collective. Given how permeable both these voices are in the poem, is it any wonder that we try to control the textual chaos? Is one emendation enough for a wicked poem, reader, which wished to deceive your sensibilities? The poem

---

47. Fletcher 1999 investigates the distinctions/overlap in the chorus's role as both a character in the drama and the mouthpiece of the poet.

resists resolution into a smooth and harmonious whole just as the elegist and his Tarpeia resist integration into the regularity that the Augustan program sought to encourage.[48]

PLACES OUT OF PLACE

Recent studies of the landscape of Tarpeia's poem have found it to be troubling, foreboding, or downright oppressive. Most recently, Myrto Garani (2011) has seen in the landscape's watery elements echoes of philosophical (neo-Pythagorean/Empedoclean) notions of strife. Her argument is that, through intertextuality with other texts that espouse Empedoclean ideas, the poem is pervaded with a view of the world in which Love and Strife are at odds with each other and exist in a delicate balance that, once upset, runs amok. Such an understanding harks back to Dumézil's assessment of the myth of Tarpeia as the embodiment of a universal notion of three elements in balance (rulers, warriors, and producers).[49] The poem's slippery surfaces are at odds with the fires of Vesta and her priestess's love, a tension that results in the dousing, once and for all, of Tarpeia's fire ("Once water prevails over fire, Tarpeia's love for the Sabine king is doomed," p. 15). Micaela Janan sees a different sort of tension in the poem's watery landscape. For Janan, the water in Tarpeia's locale, and the pervasive water imagery in the poem, symbolizes Tarpeia's own femininity—fluid, changing, and difficult to contain. Janan too notes the Pythagorean resonance in this imagery, but in her analysis the philosophical slant is definitively gendered: watery Tarpeia cannot be contained, just as female desire proves to be uncontainable in a (male) worldview that favors definition and hierarchy.[50]

My own study of 2005 focused on the places in which Tarpeia moves and acts. Her nightly walk to spy on Tatius led her up and down the Capitol slope, an area treacherously slippery (*lubrica tota via est et perfida: quippe tacentis / fallaci celat limite semper aquas,* 49–50), filled with sharp brambles (*spinosi,* 48; cf. *hirsutis rubis,* 28), and hard to climb (*mons erat ascensu dubius,* 83). Both her point of origin—the Capitol—and her destination—the Forum valley—are areas occupied by men and destined to be places rich with masculine, patriotic resonance.[51] Tarpeia, I argued, is

---

48. The reference to La Penna's work (1977) is pointed and deliberate.
49. Dumézil 1947.
50. Janan 2001: 70–84.
51. Welch 2005: 75–76 for Tarpeia's liminality.

liminal to that masculine world both literally in her topographical situation and metaphorically in her conundrum as an erotic Vestal. Stahl's assessment of the matter is on target: "It is worth noting how once more Propertius chooses the scenic as a vehicle for the emotional."[52] In this cityscape, Tarpeia is doomed; on either side of her dangerous liminal area is even worse danger—a Capitol that constrains her desire and a Forum that spells her doom. The shape of the poem, in which her speech is framed by the narrator's voice, replays this doom. In that study I argued that Tarpeia's marginal position in Rome makes visible the moral pressure exerted by the city itself. Her voice and her place pose a durable "no" to this pressure.[53] In the context of this project, which seeks to understand the variables in Tarpeia's mythic tradition as focal points for areas of concern to individual tellers, I wish to explore the way Propertius renders variable, and therefore unstable, even the moralizing monuments associated with her in the Roman landscape.

Propertius begins his poem with an aetiological salvo common to this Alexandrian subgenre:

> Tarpeium nemus et Tarpeiae turpe sepulcrum
>   fabor et antiqui limina capta Iovis.
> (4.4.1–2)

> I shall tell of Tarpeia's grove, and Tarpeia's shameful grave, and how the threshold of ancient Jove was captured.

The grove of Tarpeia and her tomb are non-extant. The tomb of Tarpeia is attested in three sources. Two suggest it was not extant to them. Varro *DLL* 5.41 says she was killed and buried there, and that a monument of her name (*not* of her death, *cuius nominis monumentum relictum*) remains in the name *saxum Tarpeium*. Plutarch at *Romulus* 18.1 says she was buried on the Capitol, but her bones were removed by Tarquinius Superbus, and her name died out except for the infamous Tarpeian rock: τοὔνομα τῆς Ταρπηίας ἐξέλιπε· πλὴν πέτραν ἔτι νῦν ἐν τῷ Καπιτωλίῳ Ταρπηίαν καλοῦσιν, ἀφ' ἧς ἐρρίπτουν τοὺς κακούργους. L. Calpurnius Piso Frugi, preserved by Dionysius of Halicarnassus (2.40.3), mentions a monument at the site of her death on the Capitol at which Romans offered annual

---

[52]. Stahl 1985: 285; see also Scivoletto 1979 on Propertius's amatory landscape in books 1 through 3.

[53]. See Nau's *BMCR* review of my book (2006.06.17), which notes its (American) tendency to reduce "further voices" down to one dissonant voice.

libations; this certainly could be Tarpeia's tomb, but Dionysius had not seen it.[54] If it is Piso's monument at the burial site, in what sense and to whom is it shameful, especially since it is a place of annual devotion? Piso's solution to the conundrum was to exonerate Tarpeia from all blame by making her a double agent. Dionysius followed his lead; at least two ancient thinkers saw a disharmony between the myth as told and the urban places attached to it. Propertius raises the question with *turpe sepulcrum* without resolving it. The difficulty is compounded if the phrase is a complex pun on *se-pulcrum* as *se-pulchritudine* (an attested ancient etymology), which would then gloss *turpe* and *Tarpeia*.[55] Puns rely on linguistic slippage, on words' inability to stay put—just like Tarpeia's tomb, which likewise signifies two things at once.

The grove is no easier to fix in its potential meanings. No "grove of Tarpeia" exists outside this poem. This is one of the reasons editors have proposed emendation, most successfully of *nemus* to *scelus*.[56] The other is the difficulty of reconciling this *nemus* with the *lucus* of lines 3 through 6 or, indeed, with the rest of the poem. Both Heyworth and Miller explore in depth these difficulties:[57] is the *nemus* the same as the *lucus*? If Tatius has encircled the spring (4.4.7, *hunc fontem Tatius praecingit*), how did Tarpeia draw water from it (4.4.15, *hinc Tarpeia deae fontem libavit*)? Is it the same *fons* used by the warhorse (4.4.14, *bellicus ex illo fonte bibebat equus*)? How many springs are there anyhow (*hunc*, *ex illo*, *hinc*, cf. *nativis aquis* in 4.4.4)? Tissol (1997: 145) considers the grove as one of many strategies Propertius uses to deceive his audience. Hutchinson raises the problem that the *nemus* (which he believes can't be the tricky *lucus*) at any rate never comes into play in the rest of the poem, nor is it in any way described or better understood at the close of the aitiological poem.[58] I believe, though, that this is the point. The poem raises the specter of a grove, then lets it haunt the rest of the poem and the city that was built to golden splendor by Augustus's time. Later in the poem Tarpeia emphasizes Rome as an accretive space—a city built by adding:

---

54. "For she was honoured with a monument in the place where she fell and lies buried on the most sacred hill of the city and the Romans every year perform libations to her (I relate what Piso writes)," τάφου τε γὰρ ἔνθα ἔπεσεν ἠξίωται τὸν ἱερώτατον τῆς πόλεως κατέχουσα λόφον, καὶ χοὰς αὐτῇ Ῥωμαῖοι καθ' ἕκαστον ἐνιαυτὸν ἐπιτελοῦσι, 'λέγω δὲ ἃ Πείσων γράφει (Dionysius of Halicarnassus 2.40.3).

55. Boyd 1984; and see also Wallace-Hadrill 1986: 77, who notes that "Tarpeia could well be a punning reference to Turpilianus" (moneyer of 19 BCE who issued a denarius of Tarpeia).

56. E.g., Hutchinson 2006, Camps 1965, and Goold 1990. Fedeli 1984 retains *nemus*.

57. Heyworth 2007a *ad* 4.4.1–16, Miller 2011: 335–43.

58. Hutchinson 2006: *ad* 4.4.1

Romani montes, et montibus addita Roma . . .
(4.4.35)

Oh Roman mountains and Rome added to the mountains . . .

Rome is the sum total of the landscape and what has been added to it. But the lack of a formally attested "Tarpeia's grove" in the cityscape—indeed, its replacement by the Tarpeian rock, which is not mentioned in the poem and, truth be told, has nothing to do with her story or death, but remains the only memorable Tarpeian monument to this day—testifies to the city's ability to organize its myths according to its need. The Tarpeian rock, like the Basilica Aemilia and the tomb mentioned in 4.4.1, focuses attention on Tarpeia's punishment rather than her motivations or intentions. Propertius's Tarpeian grove, on the other hand, painted in pastoral terms, focuses attention on the girl's predicament. Tarpeia's grove can be seen as a "topographical crystallization point from which . . . Tatius and Tarpeia can now be measured . . . by reference to their attitude towards peaceful pastoral landscape."[59] For Tatius the *lucus* is a place to barricade. For Tarpeia it is a place for her love. His military-masculine use of the space would linger in the Roman Forum; hers would not be remembered. "Rome which was added to the hills" added the infamous rock and subtracted the grove.[60]

I have already proposed that the poem's end blurs the boundary between Tarpeia's perspective and others that the poem includes. It does so by proposing that the Capitol belongs to Jupiter (*antiqui limina capta Iovis*, line 2), to Tarpeia with Jove as neighbor (*sua . . . ab arce, vicino . . . Iovis*, lines 29–30),[61] and back again to Tarpeia (*a duce Tarpeia mons est cognomen adeptus*, line 93—and note here also the accretive element in **cog***nomen*). I concluded earlier that "the joint ownership of the Capitol—offended Jupiter, transgressive Tarpeia—is a crisp reminder of the impossibility of separating Rome from Tarpeia." So too, it is a reminder of the conterminousness of god and criminal at the heart of Rome.

Landscape is a powerful indicator of literary themes. It is prudent to recall here that Propertius's Tarpeian landscape is not entirely fictive. In her book *Representations* (1993), Ann Vasaly has explored Cicero's use of real

---

59. Stahl 1985: 282–83. He finds the same contrast between "(Julian) arms and (pastoral) lover" in 2.34, a poem that values Vergil's *Eclogues* higher than his *Aeneid* (p. 283).
60. See Miller 2011.
61. Also potentially to Tatius (*tu cape spinosi rorida terga iugi*, line 48) and to Tatius as his marriage bed (*regni scande cubile mei*, line 90).

places as rhetorical tools in his speeches. This tool brings with it opportunities—in Cicero's case, opportunities to tap into his audience's patriotism or fear of the outsider—but also constraints.[62] Cicero couldn't move a real place, for example, or rewrite its history entirely. She says, "He needed to make it appear to his audience that these images were an accurate reflection of reality. In (this) requirement, the orator parts company from the poet, the novelist, and the dramatist, for audiences allow the writer of fiction to create a world they know to be unreal, if only this world be compelling and internally coherent" (p. 132). Propertius's aetiological poem blends the possibilities of a fictive world with the constraints of his audience's lived experience. Propertius's Roman readers, at least, would have been able to see some Tarpeian place from many vantage points in the city. What Propertius's poem accomplishes is the destabilizing effect of letting them see from many vantage points at once.

THAT WAS AND IS AND IS TO BE

Propertius's juxtaposition of then and now renders perspectival flux acute for his contemporary readers. This poem brings past and present together prominently and overtly:

> quid tum Roma fuit, tubicen vicina Curetis
>   cum quateret lento murmure saxa Iovis?   10
> atque ubi nunc terris dicuntur iura subactis,
>   stabant Romano pila Sabina Foro.
> murus erant montes: ubi nunc est Curia saepta,
>   bellicus ex illo fonte bibebat equus.
> (4.4.9–14)

What was Rome back then, when the Sabine trumpeter was beating the nearby crag of Jupiter with a light murmur? And Sabine spears used to stand in the Roman Forum—the place where laws are now enacted for conquered peoples. The hills were our walls. The area where the Senate is now enclosed, the war horse used to drink from that spring.

These lines suggest a contrast between past and present, but the temporal relationship on closer reading emerges as more complicated. Again, the

---

62. See particularly the discussion at Vasaly 1993: 128–33.

words "blur," "elision," and "slippage" apply. The military force of Tatius's encampment back then replays itself every time laws are pronounced for subdued lands, for we know how they became subdued.[63] Back then the mountains were walls; just later, Tarpeia will talk of Rome added to the mountains (*Romani montes, et montibus addita Roma,* line 35). These two phrases refer to the same time; are the mountains the walls, or the foundations? Finally, the mention of the warhorse at the fountain cannot but recall the *Lacus Iuturnae,* at which Castor and Pollux watered their horses as they announced a great Roman military victory. Or does it recall the *Lacus Curtius,* where, later in this same Sabine war, the Roman soldier Mettius Curtius would sacrifice himself by plunging his warhorse (with him riding) into a chasm in the ground, thus fulfilling a prophecy and guaranteeing Rome's victory? Indeed, the notion of burying something valuable so as to preserve the state is not an idea antithetical to the myth of Tarpeia; my first chapter explores this phenomenon. At present, the key point is that the drinking warhorse refers to back then, a little later than back then, and a few hundred years down the line.

Past and present also come together in Tarpeia's spurious ritual actions (I intended this genuine pun). She visited the spring again and again in her attempt to catch a glimpse of her beloved, even perhaps to become his captive:

saepe illa immeritae causata est omina lunae,
    et sibi tingendas dixit in amne comas:
saepe tulit blandis argentea lilia Nymphis,
    Romula ne faciem laederet hasta Tati.
(4.4.23–26)

Often she cited omens of the moon as a pretext and she said she had to purify her hair in the river. Often she brought silvery lilies to the sweet nymphs, praying that Romulus's spear not harm Tatius's face.

The repetition of her action bespeaks circularity rather than progression. Hutchinson notes the elision of past and present in this passage in the use of religion to excuse women's movement (2006 *ad* 4.4.23–4). Indeed, Tarpeia's actions do mimic the habits of women in love in Propertius's day, habits about which elegies are wont to complain: women pretend to go to female-only sanctuaries and festivals, but this is merely their excuse

---

63. Vergil *Aen.* 6.853: *debellare superbos.*

to meet adulterers or to avoid the lover, or even his excuse to have stood her up (Tibullus 1.6, 1.3; Propertius 2.31 and 32, 4.8). Hutchinson goes on to note two couplets later (when Tarpeia returns to the Capitol at dusk) that "Propertius is blurring a movement from repeated actions in 23–6 to a single action in 29–30."[64] In this poem, it is difficult to sift past from present from future.

When, then, is Tarpeia? My answer is that she is at no time, and she is ever repeated. She thought her time had come on the Parilia:

> urbi festus erat (dixere Parilia patres),
>   hic primus coepit moenibus esse dies,
> annua pastorum convivia, lusus in urbe,   75
>   cum pagana madent fercula divitiis,
> cumque super raros faeni flammantis acervos
>   traicit immundos ebria turba pedes.
> Romulus excubias decrevit in otia solvi
>   atque intermissa castra silere tuba.   80
> hoc Tarpeia suum tempus rata convenit hostem:
>   pacta ligat, pactis ipsa futura comes.
> (4.4.73–82)

It was a holiday in the city (the elders called it the Parilia). This day was the first beginning for Rome's walls. It was a yearly feast for shepherds, a celebration in the city, when rustic plates dripped with delicacies, and when the country folk flung dirty feet over scattered heaps of burning hay. Romulus decreed that the guard be given leave for the night, and the camps were silent without the tuba's call. Tarpeia set this time to meet the enemy: she ratifies the deal, herself to be a part of the deal.

The Parilia, Propertius remarks, **began** to be the **first** day for the walls,[65] as an **annual** feast (i.e., repeated, habitual), and was celebrated in Propertius's day. It was then, now, and in between, every year repeating itself. Propertius's description is of a birthday celebration—a return, every year, to the beginning. Tarpeia deemed this her time (*hoc Tarpeia suum tempus rata*, line 81). Alas for Tarpeia, she too is caught in the circularity and repetition that marks the Parilia, and the poem's places. When the narrator asks, "Could one death be enough for such a wicked girl?" we know the

---

64. Hutchinson 2006: *ad* 4.4.27–28.
65. Further confusion: which walls—the walls added to the mountains, or the mountains?

answer is "no." It is ironic that the placement of this couplet in the poem is uncertain,[66] for it could go here, or there, or then, or now, or all of these. This does not mean we cannot attempt to place the couplet, only that temporal logic cannot be one of the arguments made in favor of or against any given placement.

Tarpeia's temporal problem is timely inasmuch as time—harnessed, recorded, frozen, and manipulated—was a key component of the evolving imperial ideology. The cyclicality of the Golden Age, the notion of Augustus as perfect *telos* of a linear march, and the return to old morals had implications for every aspect of culture, public and private. Vergil's *Eclogues* 4 boasts the return of a Golden Age with the birth of a mortal child; the *Aeneid* keeps its eye firmly on the end goal of Augustan Rome, and Propertius 4.1 (like the Tarpeia poem under scrutiny) juxtaposes then and now. In art and architecture the range may be felt in the Golden Age imagery on the Ara Pacis, the synchronicity of Roman heroes from various eras in the Forum of Augustus, and the giant *Horologium* that linked time, space, and the Princeps' own lifespan (it celebrated his birthday). Augustus's Mausoleum was built early but called to mind his death. Calendars were the object of scrutiny and interest in this period, and they were amended and expanded with new festivals, and even new months with new names (July, August). These real Fasti even sparked a poetic *Fasti* by Ovid that is similarly playful with time. Such broad changes certainly affected the way Romans identified themselves as Romans; if nothing else, the regularity of the calendar and its attachment to the city generated a stronger sense of shared identity.

Hunter Gardner has explored this shifting sense of time and its implications on subjectivity as foreground (see chapter 1) for a larger study on time in elegy, *Gendering Time in Latin Elegy* (2013). In her first chapter she identifies the impact on the life cycle of coming of age under a new and transcendent father (*pater patriae*); paying extra attention to generations, descent, and succession (think father Julius Caesar, grandsons and heirs Gaius and Lucius); and valorizing manhood, marriage, and parenthood (the *toga virilis*, the *leges Iuliae*), and having the example of Augustus's own accelerated adolescence and rush to a mature civic presence. Vis-à-vis elegy, Gardner traces the contraposition of an androcentric teleology, a notion of time that marches toward a goal (notably, sex with the beloved), and a gynocentric circularity, which includes repetition, delay,

---

66. Heyworth 200b puts 17–18 after 86; Goold 1990 after 92; Hutchinson 2006 square brackets it.

and reversion. Elegy presents then confounds the two times and genders, as the male *amator* is stuck in a relationship going nowhere, while he imagines the female beloved *puella* advancing in age and becoming an old woman. For Gardner, the blended temporalities bespeak the elegist's refusal to come of age and enter the social world of adult men, despite society's pressures to do so; the counterpressure a woman can exert to the teleological pull of adult manhood; and the man's attempt to resolve or cope with the temporal tension by projecting his beloved into the *telos* of old age. Gardner says, "The elegist's assignation of gendered temporal properties—and their shifting applications to lover and beloved—may also be understood as politically motivated, insofar as such properties are offered as an alternative way of constructing subjectivity at the birth of the Principate" (p. 24).

Like the arrested development of the elegiac lover in Gardner's reading, Tarpeia's development is also arrested. She may never mature to marriage. She remains unburied. She marks an ending and a beginning and a birthday. The combination of teleology, delay, and circularity does not find harmony in her case.

ONWARD TO OVID

I have been arguing that Propertius's poem on Tarpeia makes it difficult for the reader to draw a moral conclusion from her story. Not only does he present the girl in a sympathetic manner as someone whose personal desire clashes with the state's needs, but he even calls into question her identity as a woman. She cannot be accommodated within the new Augustan regime. Then, he complicates even this troubled identity by blurring her perspective with the narrator's perspective, so we are often unsure who is blaming or condemning her, or evaluating her in the poem. Finally, Propertius draws this uncertainty into our own time by emphasizing cyclicality and repetition. The reader thus occupies many, often conflicting, points of view, at once and in turn. While this sort of reading is consistent with the countercultural stance of elegiac poetry in general, I see it also as a symptom of the way Tarpeia herself can embody various problems and challenges to Roman identity. How can one be an individual in a harmonious Rome? Propertius's Tarpeia suggests one cannot.

Ovid's *Fasti,* a text with a design and expressed intention similar to Propertius's fourth book, includes a brief but tantalizing mention of Tarpeia that neatly distills the themes I have explored above. In the first book, Janus tells her story in indirect discourse in answer to the question of why his shrine sits where it does: the answer is that on the spot of her betrayal Janus sent a surprise spring of boiling waters to repel the Sabine invaders. Here is the precious little he has to say:

> ille, manu mulcens propexam ad pectora barbam,
>   protinus Oebalii rettulit arma Tati,   260
> utque levis custos, armillis capta, Sabinos
>   ad summae tacitos duxerit arcis iter.
> (1.259–62)

> He (Janus), stroking with his hand his beard that stretched down to his chest, told straightaway of the arms of Oebalian Tatius, how the fickle guardian, captivated by their armbands, led the silent Sabines to the path of the top of the fortress.

Carole Newlands (2002) traces the way Janus is an unreliable narrator in the *Fasti*. He offers mutually exclusive origins for his own shape; as a divine figure, whose domain is beginnings, and as the subject under study, he if anyone should be able to speak with certainty. Even in our little passage confusion rules the day. For example, which of his two beards is he stroking as he tells this kernel of Tarpeia's story? Janus of course had two faces and two beards, one facing forward (in time and space) and one back. Is the speaking face looking up to the citadel or down to the Forum? Back to Tarpeia's time, or forward to Augustus's? Janus is, indeed, a sort of personification of multiple perspectives. Immediately before these lines, Janus spoke in direct quotation in dialogue with the poetic interlocutor. This mimetic form of communication clearly marks speech acts as someone's perspective. Yet at just this point when he comes to Tarpeia, Ovid "indirects" Janus's narration (Ovid loves these narratological flips), which opens up a blur between an objective reality and a subjective experience or interpretation of it. The design of the lines renders Tatius's armor, the object of an indicative verb, closer to objective than Tarpeia's deed, which is given as an indirect question using the subjunctive. He told how she led the Sabines (how in fact *did* she lead the Sabines?). We can never know, from this presentation, what happened or how or why. Janus famously calls Tarpeia a fickle guardian—*levis custos*. *Levis* places Tarpeia in the elegiac mold in which Ovid found her; the word means "dainty" and "fickle," but also "trivial" and "gentle" and "unfaithful" and "nimble." How the contemporary reader might interpret Janus, or Janus's Tarpeia, or Tarpeia independent of any text, might just hinge on how that reader understands *levis*. But that depends on which dictionary she uses, which may—or may not—be the one Augustus used.

CHAPTER SEVEN

VALERIUS MAXIMUS ON REMEMBERING TARPEIA'S MEMORABLE DEED

IN CHAPTER 5 I explored how Livy, despite his adherence to the Fabian tradition, shapes his narrative of Tarpeia in ways that emphasize her contribution to the growth of the Roman state. Livy draws attention to Tarpeia's murky position as a woman caught between communities, a woman who must scrutinize conflicting allegiances and who is herself the object of scrutiny. Nameless Tarpeia is one of the many women in Livy's first book who help shape emerging Rome through the relationships between men they facilitate. Valerius Maximus, writing in Latin some thirty years later under Tiberius, takes the story in a new direction. His text, the *Facta et Dicta Memorabilia* (*Memorable Words and Deeds*), collects summaries of famous stories and arranges them thematically under headings such as "Friendship" or "Female lawyers" (sections 4.7 and 8.3). Valerius follows Livy's language closely but reshapes it subtly and recontextualizes it to further the aims of his text. As we shall see, Valerius's text works on Tarpeia in the following ways.

First, Valerius locates the moral of Tarpeia's story in *perfidia*—perfidy, or breaking faith—not in greed, as Fabius had done, or lust (love), as in Propertius. Second, the Tiberian writer strips the story of the complexities of context or motive. This is understandable for an exemplographer who has already identified the ethical focus of the story, which should therefore be clear and therefore uncomplicated by misunderstanding (i.e., of Tarpeia's motive as in Piso's or Propertius's versions) and unmitigated by attendant circumstances (such as Tatius's own double-dealing, as in Dionysius's and Pictor's versions). The concision of Valerius's narrative smacks of "and that's that." My third observation is related to the second. Despite the focus on *perfidia* as deceit in the preface, and the immediate and lean narrative about Tarpeia, Valerius fails to pinpoint precisely the perfidy in the story. Tarpeia seems to make her bargain straightforwardly—she means to trade treason for jewelry. If anything, in the Valerian narrative Tatius comes off as the perfidious one, though one must read between the few lines even for this assessment. Valerius's lack of clarity on the story's *perfidia* is quite striking, especially since his near-contemporary Dionysius of Halicarnassus would structure his own telling of Tarpeia's story around the nuances of double-dealing and deceit with both protagonists.

This terseness generates an interesting effect in Valerius's treatment of the myth. On one hand it relies on the reader's knowledge of Tarpeia's story and of her guilt to smooth over the missing complexities. Of course Tarpeia is guilty. She always has been guilty and always shall be. In this way Valerius's narrative depends on the tradition it seeks explicitly to preserve. On the other hand, Valerius draws attention to the problems inherent in accepting tradition, in this case or more broadly, by switching the terms of the debate at the end of her story where he asserts that the vice for which she is really condemned is not any *perfidia* to which she might contribute, but her *proditio,* her treason to the state, which must always be punished no matter what.

In what follows I explore Valerius's summary treatment of Tarpeia's guilt and demonstrate that Valerius positions this verdict as a by-product of the political milieu of an imperial system now established and unable to be unseated. The apparent indisputability of Tarpeia's guilt in Valerius reflects the book's pervasive rhetoric about the unanimity of the gods regarding proper morality, one aspect of which is their endorsement of Tiberius as right ruler of Rome. Because treason is a vice that undermines the divinely approved state and its divinely approved leader, its evil and its threat are worse than the personal failings of luxury, lust, avarice, and even perfidy. The capstone of Valerius's condemnation of *proditio* appears later in book 9, when Valerius is discussing more general examples of *dicta improba aut facta scelerata* (shameless utterances or wicked deeds). There, in the last example of pure evildoing in the book,[1] Valerius famously

---

1. The next sections treat unusual deaths, physical likenesses, etc.

denounces Sejanus's foiled attempt to unseat Tiberius from the throne. He does so without naming the guilty party and without any attempt at finding or listing explanations or mitigations for Sejanus's act.

I read this episode, as I read Valerius's text as a whole, not as a simple moral fable but as an invitation to contemplate the rules by which we form, offer, and evaluate *exempla*. In this sense Tarpeia's narrative is not so much a lesson about the morality inherent in *her* behavior, but a lesson about the morality inherent in *ours* as we read and write about her behavior. It strikes me that the moral of Tarpeia's story is debatable, and that Valerius gives us ammunition for that debate in his dense paragraph about her. This consideration offers some support for reading Valerius's text, as Bloomer does, as a handbook of exercises for *declamatio* or *controversiae*.[2] It does not, however, forestall readings such as Skidmore's or Mueller's, which assert that Valerius's aim is what he says it is: to provide examples for moral education. Instead, I argue that it is precisely the rhetorical nature of Valerius's text that makes it a suitable vehicle for moral education, for morality is contestable and contextual and is constructed out of the interplay of many sources: the gods' (perceived) will, a historical figure's innate character, social convention, and even the ideological needs of the emperor. Because Sejanus is guilty, Tarpeia must also be guilty. Yet the gap Valerius offers between Tarpeia's behavior and her guilt implicates Sejanus's story, too, and raises concern about what is missing there. By this I do not mean that Valerius questions Sejanus's guilt. Far from it. Rather, the relationship between Tarpeia's and Sejanus's story draws attention to how morality is constructed in an authoritarian time. In this way the text rather daringly opens up a space for moral discourse, reintroducing to the early Principate the opportunity for dialogue about history and legacy that was a hallmark of the Republic.

TATIUS'S PERFIDY, BUT TARPEIA'S GUILT

Perfidy is the transcendent rubric that governs Valerius's inclusion of Tarpeia's story. Valerius had already in his ninth book discussed the reprobate vices of luxury and desire, citing as examples Philip of Macedon, Clodius, and Catiline. Indeed, Valerius speaks about luxury and desire as if they are two sides of the same coin (*iungatur illi* [sc. *luxuriae*] *libido, quoniam ex iisdem vitiorum principiis oritur, neque aut a reprehensione aut ab*

---

2. Bloomer 1992, stated explicitly on pp. 1 and 255 and argued throughout.

emendatione separentur, gemino mentis errore co<ne>xae, 9.1.*praef*; let lust be joined to luxury, since it springs from the same origins of vice, nor can they be separated in censure or correction, connected as they are by a twin error of the mind). We have already seen collusion between lust and luxury in earlier Roman sources about Tarpeia—not only in the tradition *writ* large, in which she is either lusty or greedy, but even in individual sources.[3] These prior sources often placed Tarpeia's lust or love of luxury in tension with other qualities, such as patriotism, modesty, or religious shame. Valerius's organizational scheme, however, requires that he sift out one quality as a point of focus. Because he introduces this quality in general terms in the section's preface, and because Tarpeia's example follows this preface immediately, *perfidia* is expressly in the reader's mind. Livy, for example, structured her tale and placed it within his narrative so as to emphasize her position in her family and community. Valerius omits any such tension and boils down his narrative, as he usually does, to an opening device of transition or scene, followed by a condensed narrative, rounded off by a clever *bon mot* that captures the guiding moral. In the narrative portion of Tarpeia's tale—all but the last sentence below—the focus on the treasonous deed eclipses details that might complicate the story and precludes the need to attend to the tense or conflicting values by which the actors are constrained.[4] Any and all other values are extraneous to Valerius's intention:

> Romulo regnante Spurius Tarpeius arci praeerat. cuius filiam virginem aquam sacris petitum extra moenia egressam Tatius ut armatos Sabinos in arcem secum reciperet corrupit, mercedis nomine pactam quae in sinistris manibus gerebant: erant autem iis armillae et anuli magno ex pondere auri. loco potitum agmen Sabinorum puellam praemium flagitantem armis obrutam necavit, perinde quasi promissum, quod ea quoque laevis gestaverant, solv<er>it. Absit reprehensio, quia inpia proditio celeri poena vindicata est.[5] (9.6.1)

> During Romulus's reign, Spurius Tarpeius was in charge of the citadel. When his daughter had gone beyond the walls to fetch water for rites,

---

3. For the tradition in general, see the section "She has her reasons" in chapter 1. For the overlap in an individual source, see Fabius Pictor's ἔρως τῶν ψελλίων and chapter 2.

4. Maslakov 1984: 461–64 argues that the story is stripped of incidentals so as to make the moralism starker.

5. The text used is Shackleton Bailey's 2000 Loeb edition. Translations are my own, though it is difficult to improve upon his.

Tatius bribed her so that she would accept into the citadel the armed Sabine warriors and himself, having made a pact with the designation of recompense what they wore on their left hands; they wore on them bracelets and rings heavy with gold. When they seized control of the place, the company of Sabines killed the girl, who was demanding her payment, by overwhelming her with their weapons—just like they were fulfilling their agreement, because they also wore these on their left hands. May all blame for this be lacking, since impious betrayal was met with swift penalty.

A comparison with Livy, with like language in boldface type, makes clear exactly what Valerius leaves out and what he rearranges for emphasis:

> Novissimum ab Sabinis bellum ortum multoque id maximum fuit; nihil enim per iram aut cupiditatem actum est, nec ostenderunt bellum prius quam intulerunt. Consilio etiam additus dolus. **Sp. Tarpeius Romanae praeerat arci. Huius filiam virginem auro corrumpit Tatius ut armatos in arcem accipiat;** aquam forte ea tum sacris extra moenia petitum ierat. **Accepti obrutam armis necavere**, seu ut vi capta potius arx videretur **seu prodendi exempli causa ne quid usquam fidum proditori esset.** Additur fabula, quod volgo **Sabini aureas armillas magni ponderis brachio laevo gemmatosque magna specie anulos habuerint, pepigisse eam quod in sinistris manibus haberent; eo scuta illi pro aureis donis congesta.** Sunt qui eam ex pacto tradendi quod in sinistris manibus esset derecto arma petisse dicant et fraude visam agere sua ipsam peremptam mercede. (1.11)

As can be seen in the pale type, Valerius downplays some important threads in the tradition about Tarpeia. Gone is any attempt to determine her motive. What Livy mentions as an add-on to the tale (*additur fabula,* referring to her desire for bracelets) Valerius relates as essential, using participles rather than clauses to connect the detail more firmly into his account. Livy's narrative also admits some skepticism or distance from the tale, as seen in *additur fabula, volgo,* and *sunt qui dicant,* followed by indirect statement. Valerius does not draw attention to variants in this way.[6] Valerius omits entirely the possibility of a patriotic Tarpeia, or one engaged in more cunning diplomacy, such as Piso's maiden had been. Oddly, Piso's

---

6. Weileder 1998: 232–35 discusses this general difference between Livy and Valerius. Valerius's directness (which Weileder calls "Wahrheitsgehalt," 234) sometimes serves to lend coherence to the story and therefore to add point to the moral (*Musterbeispiel* 233–34).

Tarpeia, the one mentioned last by Livy and the one preferred by Dionysius, could be charged with perfidy because of the ambiguity of her promise to Tatius, but Valerius is silent as to this possibility. In fact, Valerius's Tarpeia is guilty of little other than religious piety (*aquam sacris petitum*) and vulnerability ([sc.*eam*] *Tatius . . . corrumpit*): the unnamed girl was seeking water for rites when she was corrupted by Tatius, and yet in some sources (Propertius, namely) her priesthood might be thought to heighten her guilt: for a Vestal to betray the state is even more heinous than for a person with no public function. Yet to underline the point of her passivity and vulnerability, Tarpeia is subject of no verbs in Valerius's brief narrative. She does govern a deponent participle—*pactam* (having made a bargain), but this is not breaking faith *per se,* especially since she keeps her pact with Tatius. If we read Tarpeia's perfidy as her breaking faith with the state, it is because of what we bring to the story, not because of what Valerius says.

On the other hand, Tatius even in this brief account can be accused of *perfidia,* for he violates the spirit if not the letter of his agreement with Tarpeia by exploiting the ambiguity of his promise: *armis obrutam necauit,* **perinde quasi promissum,** *quod ea* **quoque** *laevis gestaverant solvisset* ([the Sabine force] killed her by overwhelming her with their weapons, as if discharging the agreement since they also wore these on their left arms). Previous authors had struggled to make sense of Tatius's violent response to Tarpeia; it was either the result of innate Sabine trickery, named by Fabius and elaborated by Livy (*ut vi capta potius arx videretur*),[7] an appropriate response to her act of Roman partisanship (Piso, followed by Dionysius), predictably shrewd behavior by a self-interested sovereign (an option Plutarch suggests), or the only possible response to a traitor, a reason offered by Propertius (*neque enim sceleri dedit hostis honorem,* 4.4.89) and a possibility offered by Livy (*seu prodendi exempli causa ne quid usquam fidum proditori esset*). This last reason proposed by Livy is the one adopted by Valerius: *inpia proditio celeri poena vindicata est,* but it is important to note that Valerius reserves this judgment for the punch line that ends the section, whereas Livy had integrated it into the fabric of his narrative as *one* of the possible explanations for Tatius's actions. Especially to the reader familiar with Livy, Valerius's reservation of this sentiment until the end and his transformation of it into an assertion rather than a possibility stand out as beacons to the reader to pay attention and consider Valerius's strategies of organization.

---

7. Livy's Sabines are themselves tricky and deceitful, hiding their intention to attack until the moment of invasion (see chapter 5).

With this in mind, let us return to the abstraction *perfidia* that Valerius introduces at 9.6.*praef.*:

> Occultum iam et insidiosum malum, perfidia, latebris suis extrahatur. cuius efficacissimae vires sunt mentiri ac fallere, fructus in aliquo admisso scelere consistit, tum certus cum credulitatem nefariis vinculis circumdedit, tantum incommodi humano generi adferens, quantum salutis bona fides praestat. Habeat igitur non minus reprehensionis quam illa laudis consequitur. (9.6.*praef.*)

> And now let that hidden and insidious evil, perfidy, be dragged from its lair, whose most effective means are to lie and to deceive, and whose fruit consists in some sin being committed; and it is firm exactly at that point at which it encompasses credulity with its despicable bonds. It brings as much grief to humankind as good faith brings well-being. May it have no less reprehension, therefore, than good faith has praise.

One of Valerius's rhetorical devices is the repetition of words from the abstract preface of each section in the examples themselves. Several words from this preface recur in the six examples of perfidy he offers. To make the strongest point, *perfidia* or its cognates appears in five of the six: Servius Galba was the height of perfidy (*summae perfidiae*, 9.6.2); desire for glory rendered Cnaius Domitius perfidious (*perfidum coegit*, 9.6.3); the murder of Viriathus brought double accusation of perfidy (*duplicem perfidiae accusationem*, 9.6.4); the Carthaginians are the very font of perfidy (*perfidiae fontem*, 9.6.ext.1), and Hannibal waged war against faith itself with his lies and deceit (*adversus ipsam fidem . . . mendaciis et fallacia gaudens*, 9.6.ext.2). There are no words of perfidy in Tarpeia's story, but Tatius's *perinde quasi promissum* puts him uncomfortably close to lies and deceit (*mentiri ac fallere*). Finally, coming so close on the heels of the prefatory description of *perfidia*, which Valerius says explicitly should accrue a fair measure of censure (*habeat non minus reprehensionis*), Valerius's assertion that Tatius's action should be free of censure (*absit reprehensio*) reads like an apology. With due respect to Shakespeare's Gertrude, Valerius "doth protest too much, methinks."

WHERE DID TATIUS'S REPREHENSION GO?

In the introduction to *perfidia*, perfidy is itself a sort of creature, a treacherous beast hiding in its lair, ready to strike when least expected (*occultum *iam et insidiosum . . . latebris suis extrahatur . . . mentiri ac fallere . . . nefariis vinculis*). Though Valerius does not say so explicitly, his perfidy is like a snake ready to coil and strike—a tried and true symbol for deception in Roman discourse. Both foreign examples of *perfidia* are, unsurprisingly, Carthaginian; in Valerius's day, *Punica fides* (Carthaginian trustworthiness) had long been idiomatic for double-dealing.[8] These examples, read together, emphasize Valerius's strategy of startling the reader with an incongruous finale about *proditio* tacked onto a story ostensibly about *perfidia*.

The first example of *Punica fides* involves the Spartan Xanthippus, a Carthaginian ally in the Second Punic War whom the Carthaginians threw overboard, though they had promised him safe passage home on their ship (9.6.ext.1). Valerius wonders if the Carthaginians betrayed Xanthippus lest there be any partner in their victory (*ne victoriae eorum socius superesset*). This recalls Livy's question about Tatius's motive—he either acted so that it would seem he took the *arx* by force (the opportunistic motive similar to the Carthaginians'), or so that he could provide an example of the universal moral law against trusting traitors: *seu ut vi capta potius arx videretur seu prodendi exempli causa ne quid usquam fidum proditori esset* (whether [he did it] so that the citadel would seem to have been captured, or whether for the sake of providing an example that there would be no faith given to a traitor). For Tatius, Valerius recounts only the second of these motives, the one that positions Tatius on morally higher ground. For the Carthaginians, Valerius offers only the first motive, the one that is negative and opportunistic. Valerius's Tatius and his Carthaginians act similarly in punishing a traitor, but in one case this is a noble action and in the other it is calculated to protect the punisher's reputation.

The whitewashing of Tatius's reputation also becomes apparent when we scrutinize the second Carthaginian example of perfidy. At 9.6.ext.2, Hannibal's double dealings—suffocating enemies in the baths, or throwing them into wells—create for himself a legacy of a remarkable man with a tainted reputation (*quo evenit ut alioqui insignem nominis sui memoriam relicturus, in dubio maiorne an peior vir haberi deberet poneret*). Unlike that of Hannibal, whose perfidy tarnished the reputation of a man otherwise great, Tatius's reputation should not be in doubt: *absit reprehensio*, says Valerius about Tatius at the end of Tarpeia's narrative. When we read about Hannibal's reprehensible disingenuousness, we realize anew that the *reprehensio* resulting from disingenuousness should be there in Tatius's case as well.

---

8. See chapter 2 on *Punica fides* as a relic of the Punic wars.

The conclusion is that reprehension does not necessarily follow all perfidy; it depends on whose perfidy it is.

The thorny questions that vex the moral of this story—in what circumstances is *perfidia* justifiable? How does *perfidia* rate against *proditio*?—are solved by Valerius's appeal to *proditio* as *impia*. This descriptor suggests that Tatius acts as an agent of the gods themselves in punishing *proditio*. This comforting intervention of the gods appears in other thorny situations as well. In book 7, the consul Papirius Cursor is given a deliberately false omen by the keeper of the sacred chickens, the *pullarius,* who reported to the consul a positive omen about battle even though the chickens had behaved adversely to it. Cursor decided to regard the *pullarius*'s report rather than the chickens' behavior as the true omen. Having stationed the *pullarius* on the front line, Cursor fought the battle and won. The *pullarius* was killed. From this Cursor, and Valerius's reader, learn to trust the gods to enforce moral law, for they punish the *pullarius* and reward the consul's proper auspices. As Mueller discusses this episode, it confirms Valerius's reliance on and support of a traditional belief in the participation of the gods in human affairs, and in the efficacy of human respect for this participation.[9] The gods care, so we should act accordingly. But the episode leaves traces of disquiet, for Cursor punts moral judgment and responsibility to the gods (7.2.5, *ut haberent di cuius capite, si quid irae conceperant, expiarent,* [Cursor arranged it] so that the gods could have someone on whose head to exact punishment if they had taken offense). Valerius is not sure whether the gods did respond or whether the *pullarius* was killed by chance (*sive casu sive etiam caelestis numinis providentia,* whether by chance or by the providence of a god above). This *sive* pair opens the possibility that the morality of the tale is not as straightforward as might be wished. The *pullarius* might have died because he was guilty, or he might be guilty because he died. Valerius's plea *absit reprehensio* at the close of Tarpeia's tale leaves open a similar possibility, that we call Tarpeia guilty because she died rather than the other way around.

As Mueller has shown, Valerius's theology of virtue locates the impetus for moral good chiefly in the faithful heart rather than the head.[10] Rather than split hairs about which misdeed is worse, the gods work in human agents to promote an undefended right. Not that the Romans rejected legalistic arguments: on the contrary; they loved to debate and split hairs in religion, rhetoric, and law (cf. Cicero *de Haruspicum Responsis,* the elder

---

9. Mueller 2002: 111–30.
10. Ibid. 148–74 particularly. Mueller was kind enough to discuss this idea with me, for which I am grateful.

Seneca *Controversiae*). But they were willing to follow these debates to a variety of conclusions. In the case of the perfidious *pullarius* as in Tarpeia's case, Valerius presents the terms for a rhetorical debate and then, through a divine agent, obviates the need for a debate.

TARPEIA AND SEJANUS

Perhaps *proditio* is impious because it affects not just individuals, but communities, of which the gods are protectors. The valorization of the community is signaled in the preface to Valerius's work as a whole, in which the author immediately sets out his aim to lift up the worthy deeds and words of the city of Rome and of foreign peoples: *urbis Romae externarumque gentium facta simul ac dicta memoratu digna . . . constitui digerere* (*Praef.* 1.1). As Gowing asserts, this verbal move carefully sidesteps the possibility of exalting any individual other than The Individual, Tiberius, named in Valerius's second paragraph.[11] This Individual also appears in book 9, side by side with the gods, averting evil from the Roman state:

> Sed quid ego ista consector aut quid his immoror, cum unius parricidii cogitatione cuncta scelera superata cernam? Omni igitur impetu mentis, omnibus indignationis viribus ad id lacerandum pio magis quam valido adfectu rapior: quis enim amicitiae fide extincta genus humanum cruentis in tenebris sepelire conatum profundo debitae execrationis satis efficacibus verbis adegerit? Tu videlicet efferatae barbariae immanitate truculentior habenas Romani imperii, quas princeps parensque noster salutari dextera continet, capere potuisti? Aut te compote furoris mundus in suo statu mansisset? Urbem a Gallis captam, e trecentorum inclytae gentis virorum strage foedatum <amnem Cremeram et> Alliensem diem et oppressos in Hispania Scipiones et Trasimennum lacum et Cannas, bellorumque civilium domestico sanguine manantes mucrones amentibus propositis furoris tui repraesentare et vincere voluisti. Sed vigilarunt oculi deorum, sidera suum vigorem obtinuerunt, arae puluinaria templa praesenti numine vallata sunt, nihilque quod pro capite augusto ac patria excubare debuit torporem sibi permisit, et in primis auctor ac tutela nostrae incolumitatis ne excellentissima merita sua totius orbis ruina collaberentur divino consilio providit. itaque stat pax, valent leges, sincerus privati ac publici officii tenor servatur. qui autem haec violatis

---

11. Gowing 2005: 50–52.

amicitiae foederibus temptavit subvertere, omni cum stirpe sua populi Romani viribus obtritus etiam apud inferos, si tamen illuc receptus est, quae meretur supplicia pendit. (9.11.ext.4)

But why do I keep pursuing these doings, why do I linger on them, when I know that all crimes are superseded by the conception of a single parricide? So I am swept up toward castigating it with every impulse of my mind, and with the strength entire of my sense of moral rightness—with devotion more pious than strong. For who has words of the requisite contempt sufficiently powerful to cast to the deep that attempt, made by blotting out the bonds of loyalty, to bury humankind in gory shadows? Do you think you, more savage than the cruelty of wild beasts, could take the reins of Roman dominion, which our Prince and Parent holds fast in his safeguarding right hand? Could the world have remained in its state with you master of your madness? Our city captured by the Gauls, the river Cremera, fouled by the slaughter of three thousand men of renowned family, the *Dies Alliensis* when we remember the massacre by the Gauls, the Scipios overcome in Spain, Lake Trasimene and Cannae and the daggers of the civil wars dripping with homegrown blood—all these things you wanted to duplicate, even transcend, by the senseless enterprises of your recklessness. But the eyes of the gods stood guard, the stars kept their vigor, all altars, couches, and temples were fortified with the God in our midst, and nothing that ought to guard our Holy Chief and His fatherland relaxed into indolence. Foremost, the source and bulwark of our safety, by His divine guidance, forestalled the collapse of His most excellent merits in the ruin of the world entire. And so peace stands firm. Laws prevail. A firm grasp of private and public abides. The man who tried to overturn all this by violating all the bonds of friendship is trampled down by the might of the Roman people into the realm of the damned—if they will have him—along with his whole family tree.

Sejanus is unnamed here, as Tarpeia is earlier, but we all know the object of Valerius's rant.[12] The prefect's crime surpasses and caps all those listed in book 9, which seem now to Valerius to be a meaningless distraction (*quid . . . immoror*). As in Tarpeia's case, the outrage at Sejanus's crime (I hammed up the translation on purpose) is a pious reaction and therefore stems from the heart rather than the mind, or the law: *omni igitur*

---

12. Of course, Sejanus's erasure from memory was institutionalized in his *damnatio memoriae*, a move like *praeteritio* in its desire to erase and yet call to mind via the visibility of the erasure.

impetu *mentis, omnibus indignationis viribus ad id lacerandum* **pio** *magis quam valido* **adfectu rapior.** It is for this reason, perhaps, that words are not strong enough to address such a heinous crime (*satis verbis efficacibus*). Recall that in the introduction to the section on perfidy, Valerius drew attention to the compliance of words in this vice's operation: *efficacissimae vires sunt mentiri ac fallere, 9.6.praef.*).

Words are insufficient to deal with a Sejanus, and, twistable, they are the most effective contrivance of a Tarpeia. The very mutability and flexibility of language had been vitally important in the Republic. Romans understood the connection between political and verbal *libertas* and the value of public debate to the healthy working of the state, even though they disagreed about the shape of the connection.[13] Even Valerius explores this interdependency (6.2). How does verbal flexibility fit with the new non-Republic? Flexibility of language is also the turncoat's tool, as the *perfidus* exploits the gap between what is professed and what is really meant, or, what seems and what is. If we turn the question around, the risk of the gap is deceit/*perfidia,* but its benefits are debate, diversity of opinion, and *libertas.* Considering *perfidia* more literally as the disruption of an intended bond of *fides,* we begin to see how *fides* (like communication) is a relationship that is contestable, discursive, and far from monolithic. It is a relationship enabled precisely by the gap, or the flexibility of what is unspecified. When the relationship is with the state (as in Tarpeia's case), or with its sole leader (same thing, as in Sejanus's), there is no longer room for discussion. Any alternative interpretation or disparity of opinion about the relationship is *proditio.* Case closed.

From here let us return for a moment to *Romulo regnante,* the "throwaway phrase" that opens Valerius's Tarpeia example. I wonder whether this scant reference to monarchy serves to link Tarpeia's episode of treason even more closely to the recent threat against the new monarchy by Sejanus. In this way Valerius can turn old tales to new ends. Coudry has argued that Valerian anecdotes from the past reinforce moral codes of his own day, especially those regarding marriage and consumption.[14] I do not disagree, but the new moral I see Valerius supporting in the Tarpeia story is not a specific behavioral norm. Rather, Valerius promotes recognition and acceptance that a new moral code pertains.

The structure of Tarpeia's story—and of many others—supports the notion that one of Valerius's interests is the imposition of a new morality.

---

13. See most recently the extensive discussion by Arena 2013.
14. Coudry 1998: 45–53, and cf. Skidmore 1996, esp. 59–61 on marital relations.

As we saw above with the textual comparison between Livy's and Valerius's Tarpeia narratives, Valerius distills historical examples into concise narratives consisting of two or three sentences: an introduction, the narrative proper, and a summary *bon mot*. In the Tarpeia narrative the final epigram complicates the professed moral of the narrative, introducing a new situational ethics demanded by higher concerns—in this case as in some others, the needs of the new political milieu. The complicating moral conclusion suggests the fine line a moral agent must tread in the new era in which the needs of the Princeps could introduce a twist into any moral tale.[15] Because Tiberius's position (as Augustus's had been) would always be in danger from the threat posed by a Sejanus (or a Gallus, Caepio, or Murena), punishing *proditio* would trump all other moral concerns. Everything else is distraction (*quid immoror*, why am I wasting my time with other things, says Valerius as he introduces Sejanus).

Similar "new ethics" creep into the final epigrams of other *exempla*. I draw attention here to two examples to demonstrate the pattern. In book 9.3 on anger, Valerius offers the story of C. Figulus, a peaceful and moderate man made angry by the Republic's refusal to elect him consul:

> Ardentis spiritus virum et bellicis operibus adsuetum huc iracundiae stimuli egerunt. C. autem Figulum mansuetissimum, pacato iuris civilis studio celeberrimum, prudentiae moderationisque inmemorem reddiderunt: consulatus enim repulsae dolore accensus, eo quidem magis, quod illum bis patri suo datum meminerat, cum ad eum postero comitiorum die multi consulendi causa venissent, omnes dimisit, praefatus "[omnes] consulere scitis, consulem facere nescitis?" dictum graviter et merito, sed tamen aliquanto melius non dictum: nam quis populo Romano irasci sapienter potest? (9.3.2)

> Hither did the spurs of an ardent spirit compel that man, who was accustomed to war's workings: Gaius Figulus, on the other hand, was the gentlest of men, most renowned for his peaceful study of civil law. They made him forget his prudence and moderation: for he was grieved by the loss of the consular election, all the more because he remembered that the people had elected his father two times. When, on the day after the

---

15. Cf. Bloomer 1992: 258–59 on Valerian "indirection": "Mastery of the oblique and the ability to clothe and costume others' words and events in abstraction are skills for imperial service." Skidmore 1996 also admits amoral ambiguity in many Valerian passages and argues that such instances are not designed to convey outright condemnation or approval, but rather they seek moral guidance (rather than exhortation) (p. 68ff.).

election, many men sought him out for his advice on political matters, he dismissed them all, saying, "So you all know how to consult me but not how to make me consul?" This was said in earnest, and rightly—but nevertheless it should not have been said, for how could someone wisely grow angry with the Roman people?

The placement of this story under the heading "anger" suggests that Valerius is interested in the effects of competition and failure on a moderate temper. This interest is akin to the concern for "situation ethics," since it explores what happens to morality when a wildcard is introduced.[16] Figulus concludes this portion of the example with an epigram: *an nos consulere scitis, consulem facere nescitis?*, "so you know how to consult me but not how to make me consul?" The people's foolishness has aroused a moderate man's temper. But this is not the only moral issue in the story. Valerius ends his example with another thorny issue. When Figulus rails against the populace, Valerius calls the abuse just, yet better left unsaid (*graviter et merito sed tamen aliquanto melius non dictum*), for, cryptically, "who judiciously can be angry with the Roman people?" (*nam quis populo Romano irasci sapienter potest*). The conflict between the just and the judicious, especially when it pertains to a speech act regarding public office, points to the difficulties of free speech when one's position depends on the audience. Figulus's own epigram plays on the relationship between *consul* and *consulere*—and therefore it plays also on their divergence.[17] Puns rely on convergence of sound and divergence of meaning. We are not far here from Tatius's *perinde quasi promissum*, "just as if that was what he promised." Valerius recognizes the proximity of values in the punch line as well, for he admits it is only *somewhat* better (*aliquanto melius*) not to express anger against the *res publica*. The inability to challenge the state recalls Tarpeia's predicament. I quote three sentences that appeared just above: "When the relationship is with the state (as in Tarpeia's case), or with its sole leader (same thing, as in Sejanus's), there is no longer room for discussion. Any alternative interpretation or disparity of opinion about the relationship is *proditio*. Case closed."

---

16. Langlands 2011 brings the concept of situation ethics to bear on Valerius's text, though her focus is somewhat different from mine here.

17. Bloomer 1992: 250 speaks of the figure of *adnominatio* (a pun on a name or title) and connects it with the potential available in the gap. Here is it Figulus's rather than Valerius's technique. As Bloomer says, "his (sc. Valerius's) *adnominationes* succeed, as do his chapter headings for example, by stretching the applicability of words. Valerius thereby strives to contain and codify experience in verbal formulas." And, "Valerius is engaged in inquiry into the applicability of words" (256).

As my second example, at 7.4.3 in the section on stratagems, Valerius recounts how the besieged and starving Romans saved themselves by a cunning plan: they threw loaves of bread down upon their Gallic besiegers to simulate imperviousness to the siege. Livy, Valerius's source for this anecdote, is unapologetic about the deceit (*dicitur avertendae eius opinionis causa multis locis panis de Capitolio iactatus esse in hostium stationes. sed iam neque dissimulari neque ferri ultra fames poterat*); it is told that, for the sake of creating a different impression, the Romans in many places threw bread down from the Capitol onto the enemy camps, but their famine could neither be hidden nor further tolerated, 5.48.4–5). In contrast Valerius draws attention to the cunning ploy as problematic in theory but acceptable in practice:

> Illud quoque maioribus et consilio prudenter et **exitu** feliciter provisum: cum enim urbe capta Galli Capitolium obsiderent, solamque potiendi eius spem in fame eorum repositam animadverterent, perquam callido genere consilii unico perseverantiae irritamento victores spoliaverunt: panes enim iacere compluribus e locis coeperunt. Quo spectaculo obstupefactos, infinitamque frumenti abundantiam nostris superesse credentes, ad pactionem omittendae obsidionis compulerunt. misertus est tunc profecto Iuppiter Romanae virtutis, praesidium ab astutia mutuantis, cum summa alimentorum inopia proici praesidia inopiae cerneret. igitur ut vafro ita periculoso consilio salutarem **exitum** dedit. (7.4.3)

> This proviso also was both prudent in plan and felicitous in outcome for our ancestors. For when the city was captured and the Gauls were besieging the Capitol, they realized that their only hope of taking it lay in starving out the Romans. But the Romans stole from the victors their only reason to persevere, by the following clever type of plan: they began to throw loaves of bread down from various points on the Capitol. This compelled the Gauls, who thought we still had an infinite bounty of grain, to make an agreement to leave off the siege. At that time Jupiter indeed took pity then on our Roman valor, which borrowed protection from perspicacity, for he saw that, even though our lack of food was extreme, our safeguard against that lack was tossed aside. And so he granted a good outcome to a plan that was as dangerous as it was crafty.

Valerius twice stresses the outcome (*exitum*) as an important factor in the moral lesson, at the beginning and at the epigrammatic finale. The exemplographer's moral seems to be that the end justifies the means, a clever analogue to the exemplary structure of narrative → closural *bon mot*. Here we overlap with Tatius's punishment of Tarpeia, an action blessed because of its result (the elimination of a traitor) rather than its means (deliberate misunderstanding, a form of *fallacia*—that is, *perfidia*). There's a further twist in the "simulated plenty" example. Valerius places it under the rubric *strategemata*, a Greek word Valerius employs since, as he says, the Romans have no such concept (*Illa vero pars calliditatis egregia et ab omni reprehensione procul remota, cuius opera, quia appellatione vix apte exprimi possunt, Graeca pronuntiatione strategemata dicantur, 7.4.praef.*, but that part of cleverness is outstanding and far removed from all censure, whose deeds are called stratagems after the Greek word, since they are scarcely able to be expressed by fitting name [sc. in Latin]). Farrell (2001: 31–32) debunks the claim—Latin has an ample lexicon for tricks and ploys. The lexical feint allows Valerius simultaneously to prize Roman honesty and to appreciate a good ploy. Keeping in mind the Hellenicity of *strategemata*, Jupiter in the bread anecdote approves Greek cunning used in the service of Roman valor, the precise pairing that exonerates trickiness from reprehension. Embracing the same collaboration, Tiberius had co-opted cunning Odysseus as his personal mythic hero.[18] The choice was somewhat problematic, since Odysseus's reputation at Rome had suffered precisely because of his cunning. Valerius's story subtly affirms Tiberius's daring mythic association.

Valerius's anecdote about the thrown bread is a snapshot of the moral debate between intentions and outcomes. As in Tarpeia's story (whose punishment is swift), outcomes win and then the discussion is over. Or is it? Valerius's fascination with the bait-and-switch provides ample material for discussion.

AN EXAMPLE OF TREASON, AN EXAMPLE OF TRADITION

Valerius's narrative distills Tarpeia into an example. She is guilty of treason, and this is the only detail we need remember about her. In this way Valerius's text reproduces in literary form a feature that had prevailed in her visual iconography and her topographical namesake. Both coins depicting Tarpeia offer the moment of her punishment as the "shorthand"

---

18. Champlin 2006.

for her story.[19] The Basilica Aemilia frieze likewise shows Tarpeia at the moment of her demise, though this depiction admittedly at least places her story in the broader context of the building's other decorations. The Tarpeian rock is perhaps the best example of Tarpeia as an example, for it marks the punishment of traitors even though Tarpeia was punished neither on the rock, nor by being thrown to her death. The message transcends circumstances, both hers as she demonstrates it and ours as we receive it.

Roller's work on exemplary discourse elucidates the *way exempla* are transcendent.[20] Multiple viewers or audiences are to respond to *exempla* in similar ways—which responses come, through the process, to seem natural. The path to exemplarity is action → audience → commemoration → imitation. Applied to Valerius, we have Tarpeia's action, Tatius's response as audience, Valerius's commemoration, and our imitation. The elision of then and now is thus a crucial part of exemplary discourse. Or, put another way, exemplography requires that the example be separable from its original context and applicable to new contexts; this is the direction Rebecca Langlands is taking to understand exemplary flexibility in Valerius in particular.[21] In a movement toward abstraction, and therefore toward reassignment, the only clue to Tarpeia's historical context is the ablative absolute *Romulo regnante*, mentioned above. Her transgression is not linked to her gender, as it had been throughout the literary tradition.[22] In this way Valerius further universalizes her example: anyone may be guilty of *proditio*, and anyone of *perfidia*. It does not matter that Tarpeia might feel like an outsider, or might be on the margins of society—a feature that had been of central concern to Livy and to Propertius, and that, morphed into a critique of "insider-ness," would figure prominently in Dionysius's narrative of her story. Tatius's Sabinity is also no longer an excuse for his response to Tarpeia. He could be anyone, and is indeed an "insider" insofar as this story is listed among internal examples of perfidy. Context, affinity, partisanship, and even individuality are all absent to Valerius, because the moral is not contingent upon them. The exemplographer underlines this point in his final section, in which Tatius is stripped

---

19. Hölkeskamp 1996 traces the multiple ways (verbal, visual, ritual, theatrical, etc.) *exempla* are codified in Roman culture, and how they thus become *documenta* to promote a collective understanding of the *mos maiorum*.
20. Roller 2004, whose analysis springs from Hölkeskamp's observations.
21. Langlands 2011.
22. Pictor's maiden was corruptible as women are, Livy's protagonist requires the marginal status of a woman, Propertius's Tarpeia shows a perceived feminine weakness of will when faced with passion.

of his individual agency to allow the abstraction *proditio* to come through as the true subject of the anecdote, confirmed by another abstraction, swift punishment: *absit reprehensio, quia inpia proditio celeri poena vindicata est.* After all, as he had told us in introducing *perfidia,* this is an evil that poses a threat to the human race (*tantum incommodi humano generi adferens*).

The reduction of stories to widely applicable exempla in Valerius's text is emphasized in the preface to the work as a whole, in which he offers this explanation of and justification for his text:

> Urbis Romae externarumque gentium facta simul ac dicta memoratu digna, quae apud alios latius diffusa sunt quam ut breviter cognosci possint, ab inlustribus electa auctoribus digerere constitui, ut documenta sumere volentibus longae inquisitionis labor absit. nec mihi cuncta complectendi cupido incessit: quis enim omnis aevi gesta modico voluminum numero conprehenderit, aut quis compos mentis domesticae peregrinaeque historiae seriem felici superiorum stilo conditam vel attentiore cura vel praestantiore facundia traditurum se speraverit? (*Praef.*)

> I have decided to select from renowned authors and arrange those deeds and words of both the Roman city and of foreign peoples that are especially worthy of commemoration. These are scattered too widely among other authors to be able to be comprehended briefly. Thus may the hard work of long investigation be absent for those wishing to take up these teaching tools. Nor has some desire of treating everything come upon me. For who could contain the affairs of all time in a small number of volumes? Or who in his right mind could hope that he would hand down the sequence of domestic and foreign history, established already by the blessed pen of authors past, with closer care or smoother elegance than they?

Valerius characterizes his own work as a handbook for those wishing to avoid painstaking labor. Four times he draws attention to his act of redaction (*electa . . . digerere constitui; nec mihi cuncta complecti cupido incessit; quis . . . comprehenderit;* and *quis . . . speravit*), and twice to the reader's (perceived) desire for concision (*ut breviter cognosci possint* and *longae inquisitionis labor absit*).[23] Who is this reader, keen to speed-read his way

---

23. Marincola 1997: 43–47 does not mention Valerius but locates a similar aim in writers of the late Republic and early imperial period to package history in innovative ways, making it accessible and more appealing to a variety of readers. This posture can help the author dodge questions about originality and contribution.

into familiarity with traditional Roman material? For surely those nurtured in Rome's elite families already knew of Tarpeia's tale. By this measure Valerius's audience might be those new to Roman culture, or to Rome's culture of power. Bloomer's title for his analysis of Valerius's text reveals this sort of audience: *Valerius Maximus and the Rhetoric of the New Nobility.* On this understanding Valerius's text would therefore be one of the means for a newcomer to move inside, to come to belong to Rome. The cut-and-dried version of Tarpeia's story would make available to the new elite the message of consensus, of tradition, that Tarpeia's treason was a very bad thing, rightly punished.

On the other hand,[24] Valerius's opening statement, *Urbis Romae* **externarumque gentium** *facta simul ac dicta memoratu digna,* would seem to suggest that Valerius is opening up Roman outlooks to the examples provided by the other peoples now included in Rome's universal empire. It is not just about Rome any more. Other people had valid experiences too, and Romans could learn from them. Rather than present instances in chronological order, Valerius groups them by theme. The mixing and shuffling of historical *exempla* into categories of virtue and vice renders a diachronic set of incidences and persons into a synchronic whole, in which Tarpeia and Tatius may stand alongside Servilius Galba (*cos.* 144 BCE), Gn. Domitius (*cos.* 122 BCE), Q. Servilius Caepio (*cos.* 140 BCE), and Hannibal's Carthaginians (c. 215 BCE), their bedfellows in Valerius's section on perfidy. A result of this reshuffling is that, as with the omission of names, the original historical context of any one incident is downplayed, while the theme or moral (and Valerius's collection and arrangement of these) is made transcendent. By this measure Valerius's audience might well be Romans already on the inside of Rome's culture of power, and his text designed to widen their worldview as well as the category "Roman."[25] Skidmore assumes this sort of audience with his title *Practical Ethics for Roman Gentlemen.*

Need we choose between remedial cultural training for newcomers and subtle perspective-expansion for old-timers? No indeed, for in this brave new world (which by Tacitus's day would seem the only world; cf. *Annales* 1.1) everyone from freedman to bluest nobleman is learning new rules of comportment and hierarchies. Redacted, abstracted, and transcendent under Valerius's pen, these stories are for everyone. It fascinates me that Valerius's Maximus version of Tarpeia, so cut-and-dried, is also perhaps

---

24. This point I owe to conversation with Hans Friedrich Mueller.
25. This is the broad argument of Sarah Lawrence's 2006 dissertation on Valerius, an excellent study I hope to see published soon.

the most momentous moment in her story, when we see it being cut and dried—that is, when the stakes of Roman tradition and rhetoric are made visible. Much as tradition might sound comforting and closed, it is not. This book argues that Tarpeia represents anything but closure in the Roman tradition (etymologically, after all, tradition is treason's twin, a fact not much disguised by Valerius's use of *proditio* rather than *traditio*). Despite their, and our, efforts to explain her presence and her deed, even via the paradox of the *felix culpa,* she represents a fundamental openness, a rupture that both threatens and disturbs, and that allows for continuous input and interpretation. You and I are doing right now what Valerius, I believe, wants us to do—we are talking[26] about the rightness of Tarpeia's action and the rightness of Tatius's, and whether that rightness abides or is made obsolete when the emperor is listening.

---

26. Langlands 2008 makes a similar broad claim for Valerius's text using his examples of *severitas*.

PART THREE

TARPEIA FROM THE OUTSIDE IN

GREEK SOURCES AND THE ROMAN EMPIRE

CHAPTER EIGHT

HELLENISTIC TARPEIA IN THE ELEGY OF SIMYLUS

FABIUS PICTOR and L. Calpurnius Piso Frugi had written their histories of Rome in the Greek language, using the *lingua franca* of historiography and appealing to a broad and educated Mediterranean audience. Yet their perspective is wholly Roman; they look at Tarpeia as one of their own and seek to explain her to others. Conversely, Romans of the Republic's end and the Augustan age cast Tarpeia in the Latin language, writing to themselves and about concerns more domestic than international. In this third part I return to a Tarpeia written in Greek, though the voices who tell her story differ vastly from Rome's Republican annalists.

Three Greek authors found a voice to tell Tarpeia's story, and all three are authors who know Rome as either a rising or a risen imperial power in the Mediterranean. The poet Simylus, of unknown date, wrote a poem of uncertain length in elegiac couplets that includes Tarpeia's tale. In his version, quoted by Plutarch at *Romulus* 17, Tarpeia betrayed Rome's citadel, though this time to Gauls from the north, and out of love for their commander. Simylus's version marks the most significant departure in detail from the usual tradition about Tarpeia. Dionysius of Halicarnassus, the Augustan age's great Greek historian, includes a treatment of Tarpeia in the Romulus cycle of his *Roman Antiquities,* preserving lengthy portions of Fabius Pictor and Piso Frugi and adding his own assessment of the tale. Finally, Plutarch includes Tarpeia's tale in his *Romulus,* written a century later under Trajan's reign, when Roman rule was firm and stable. All three Greek authors (whose primary audiences I envision also to be Greek)[1] grapple with this Roman myth and, through it, with questions about Rome's centrality in the known world and Greece's increasing marginality in it. Read in chronological order (if Simylus is Hellenistic), these three Greek-authored Tarpeias present a compelling sketch of an evolution of responses to Rome. Simylus tries to fit Rome into a Greek framework; Dionysius asserts that Rome's and Greece's frameworks are one and the same; and Plutarch sees Greece fitting into a new Roman framework.

Plutarch's own assessment of this contribution to the Tarpeia tradition is discussed in greater detail in the Plutarch section below. Here I wish to probe what we can understand about this extraordinary version of Tarpeia's story. How bold Simylus was in assigning Tarpeia to the Gallic sack, we shall never know. Some historians find in Simylus's version the kernel of a very old tale, perhaps true, in which the Gauls in 390 BCE captured not just Rome's lowlands but the very Capitol itself.[2] Tarpeia's treason helped explain the Gallic possession; either the story of a treasonous girl was true, or it was invented on the spot to mask some other weakness in the Roman defenses, or it was borrowed from elsewhere (such as the Romulus cycle) to explain the possession. When the more flattering story of Manlius and the geese arose to explain the now non-sack, Tarpeia was (re)situated within the Romulus cycle.

It is not my project to determine whether the Gauls sacked the Capitol or not, or even if the story is a very old one. Indeed others consider Simylus's poem to be late because of its very focus on love; for such readers, greed is the earlier form of the Roman myth, replaced occasionally but never supplanted by the love-motive.[3] The hint of the greed motif in the phrase in Simylus's κόσμον ἔθεντο φόνον that ends Plutarch's quotation supports the priority of greed in the tradition. Which version came first—love or greed—is not possible to recover, given the extant sources. Nor,

---

1. It is of course impossible to ascertain this, especially for Simylus since nothing is known of the date or context of this poet. The apologetic tone of Dionysius's text convinces me that his audience is Greek, though it can be argued that he also aimed to educate Romans that their Greek subjects were not inferior. Plutarch's second-sophistic Greek lays firm claim to the Greek intellectual tradition and milieu: intellectual Greeks are his audience. The readership of these texts will appear in the discussions within the chapters.

2. Sources for this view are collected in Horsfall 1987, esp. pp. 68–71.

3. See, e.g., Horsfall 1987: 68–80 (love could be a spontaneous creation by Propertius and Simylus); Sanders 1904: 21 (love is Propertius's insertion, after the pattern of the Greek stories, though Sanders admits that even greed might not have been there in the earliest versions); and Dumézil 1947: 282, for whom "love replaces something more vile."

vis-à-vis love, is it possible to discover whether Simylus predates Propertius or the other way around.[4] But what is possible to recover is how Tarpeia functions in each of her appearances. Along those lines, I wish to understand the contours of Simylus's poem. Here it is important to note two key features. First, the embroidery Simylus adds to the tale—its framing in the Gallic rather than Sabine attack and its concern over intertribal marriage—place it in the Hellenistic poetic tradition. It is a poem for its own time and tastes, not for an earlier time and its tastes. Second, the "Tarpeia-in-love" motif stands in opposition to the dominant Roman form of the myth, made normative by Fabius Pictor and his followers and resisted among Roman tellers only by Propertius.

These details, I argue, fix Tarpeia in the milieu of the Hellenistic elite, in which movement and marriage combined to form cosmopolitan societies and complex networks of kinship. While this milieu offered opportunity and prosperity for women, and increased visibility into their lives, these were attended by a strong measure of concern over women's sexual and social agency. The dynastic intrigues of various wives and their children seen in the historical literature link ambition with marriage in a way similar to those we can read in Tacitus's pages; women at other levels of society can also be seen to exercise an uncomfortable degree of freedom and influence. Simylus's Tarpeia, willing to become the bride of Gallic chieftain Brennus, is comprehensible within this framework and, as we shall see, Brennus's Gallic allies respond to her action with nervousness. I suggest that these Gauls see Tarpeia's overture as an encroachment into their chieftain's family and a threat in the zero-sum game of influence and succession. Indeed, it is even possible to see some real Tarpeias within the dynastic families of the era, women who brought foreigners into their families, or did violence to their own people to further personal goals—in short, women whose intrigues threatened the integrity of their homes and states.

To close this chapter, I wonder what Simylus might have been after in writing about a Roman girl at all. The Gallic identity of Rome's attackers makes the Romans comprehensible to Greek Hellenistic audiences, since the Gauls had invaded various parts of Greece in the fourth and third centuries BCE. Other snippets of poetry survive in which Roman myths appear, and in which contemporary Greek events assume an air of mythology. Could Greek authors, by absorbing and crafting Roman myth, have

---

4. Sanders 1904: 22 sees Simylus as later than Propertius and deriving ultimately from him through Clitophon of Rhodes, but most others see influence going the other way.

been trying to reverse the flow of political and cultural imperialism that marks the relationship between Greece and Rome in the Hellenistic period?

SIMYLUS'S FRAGMENT

We cannot know Simylus's provenance and date given the evidence; it is surely not the new comic playwright Simylus, author of an *Ephesia* and perhaps also a *Megarike* (CAF 2.444 = PCG 7.591), nor the iambic poet (*Suppl. Hell.* 1.350 = fr. 726–28), but rather an independent composer in elegiac verse. In the *Romulus*, Plutarch records the following two fragments from this elegiac poet:[5]

> Σιμύλος δ' ὁ ποιητὴς καὶ παντάπασι ληρεῖ μὴ Σαβίνοις οἰόμενος, ἀλλὰ Κελτοῖς τὴν Ταρπηίαν προδοῦναι τὸ Καπιτώλιον ἐρασθεῖσαν αὐτῶν τοῦ βασιλέως. λέγει δὲ ταῦτα:
>
>> "Ἡ δ' ἀγχοῦ Τάρπεια παραὶ Καπιτώλιον αἶπος
>> ναίουσα Ῥώμης ἔπλετο τειχολέτις,
>> Κελτῶν ἣ στέρξασα γαμήλια λέκτρα γενέσθαι
>> σκηπτούχῳ, πατέρων οὐκ ἐφύλαξε δόμους."
>
> καὶ μετ' ὀλίγα περὶ τῆς τελευτῆς:
>
>> "Τὴν δ' οὔτ' ἄρ' Βοιοί τε καὶ ἔθνεα μυρία Κελτῶν
>> χηράμενοι ῥείθρων ἐντὸς ἔθεντο Πάδου,
>> ὅπλα δ' ἐπιπροβαλόντες ἀρειμανέων ἀπὸ χειρῶν
>> κούρῃ ἐπὶ στυγερῇ κόσμον ἔθεντο φόνον."
>> (*Rom.* 17)

And Simylus the poet is altogether absurd in supposing that Tarpeia betrayed the Capitol, not to the Sabines, but to the Gauls, because she had fallen in love with their king. These are his words:

> "And Tarpeia, dwelling next to the Capitolian crag, became the wall-destroyer of Rome. She, longing for the marriage bed with the scepter-bearer of the Celts, did not protect the homes of her fathers."

---

5. The text is quoted from Perrin's 1914 Loeb edition. The translations are mine.

And a little later, speaking of her death,

> "Here the Boii and the myriad tribes of Gauls did not, exulting, place on this side of the currents of the Po, but, hurling the shields from their belligerent arms upon the hateful maid they cast this 'decoration' to her doom."

It is clear that Plutarch is excerpting a fragment of a larger whole. Some lines of narrative obviously separated the two fragments the biographer quotes. Presumably the gap treated Tarpeia's compact with the king and her actual betrayal of the Capitol, yet Plutarch calls this gap "a little bit," which suggests that the poem in its brevity has an epigrammatic quality or that the Tarpeia episode is one "epigram" embedded in a longer, episodic poem. This latter inference is supported by the fact that Plutarch's fragment does not offer the beginning of the poem, for "δ'" would be odd at the start of a discrete poem.[6] It seems likely that Plutarch's quotation omits its end of the poem as well; his position of the second fragment "a little bit later" suggests a place further but not furthest in the source poem; if he was quoting the end, he could easily have said so. We have, therefore, two quatrains out of presumably at least five—with one missing before, between, and after the two we have. One wonders whether the intervening quatrain had something to say about the Celtic king's response, such as whether he had anything to do with the Celts' action or, indeed, their rejoicing.[7] One also wonders whether Plutarch's assessment that Tarpeia was in love (ἐρασθεῖσαν) was based on a missing earlier quatrain that described her ardor or whether it is an inference based on her desire to marry him (στέρξασα γαμήλια λέκτρα). Finally, Plutarch's introduction of the fragment suggests that he quotes only the bits that he finds wholly absurd—the identity of the enemy, and the potential death in the Po. It is reasonable to surmise that the missing bits, about the agreement and the opening of the Capitol, do not differ from the tradition as it survives.

I suggest that this fragmentary poem betrays unease about shifting identities, both ethnic and gendered, in Hellenistic society. Two features of

---

6. Denniston (1934) 1966: 162–84.

7. It is possible that the missing bit between the two fragments relates Brennus's response to her; οὔτ' normally occurs in pairs (Smyth [1920] 1984: 2942–50 notes that in poetry the first may be omitted), and this one seems to be the second of a pair rather than the first (what "nor" would follow Tarpeia's death?). If the missing middle fragment describes Brennus's rejection of her proposal, Plutarch might not have felt the need to reproduce it since it squares with the rest of tradition.

Hellenistic society contribute to such uneasiness, both relevant to Simylus's Tarpeia. The first source of uneasiness is the opening up of the world to travel and to migration.[8] Without the strong pull of a *polis*-centered identity, people could and did move about much more than before. Alexandria stood as the exemplar writ large of this phenomenon, but inscriptions in towns large and small attest a degree of movement and commerce thereto unremarked.[9] "Unremarked" is the key term here; Hellenistic individuals drew attention to their own displacement, replacement, and mobility in ways that advertise the importance of this phenomenon in understanding Hellenistic subjectivity. Gutzwiller's study of Hellenistic epigram shows this paradigmatic Hellenistic literary form to reflect the "new bonds—shifting, local, and pragmatic, and much altered from the earlier, inescapable and questionable web of relationships that enmeshed individuals in the cultural myths of their own polis."[10] The epigrammatic voice again and again reveals, in Gutzwiller's haunting description, "marginal, drifting, fragmentary, and fractured selves" that, because of their consistency, call out to be anthologized. Burton's study of Theocritus's urban mimes finds ample evidence of concern over shifting identities as people move from place to place and struggle to ratify their position in their new context.[11]

The unease about shifting identities emerges in the structure of the fragments. The first quatrain begins ἡ δ', and Tarpeia is the subject of the main verbs. The second begins τὴν δ' and indicates her as object. If we boil the fragments down to the verbs and participles that match her, the result makes clear the shift: "She, dwelling, became wall-destroyer; desiring, she did not guard," and "Her they did not establish exultingly but, throwing forward, they made adornment death." The shift in perspective from "she" to "they" is emphasized by the parallel structure of the two quatrains. Each contains two finite verbs, the first negated and the second positive; each introduces the subject in the first line and modifies that subject with a participle at the start of the second line, and an additional participle at the third line, one of which betrays a mood (ναίουσα and στέρξασα in the first quatrain, χηράμενοι and ἐπιπροβαλόντες in the next); each identifies the subject with a place: Tarpeia, the Capitol and the Celts, the Po. Therefore,

---

8. Van Bremen 2007: 317–19.

9. The naturalization inscriptions from Miletus (admitting Cretans to Miletan citizenship) show movement on a large scale (Rehm *Milet* 1.3 [1914]: 33–38); individual movement may be seen in a second-century BCE letter in which a wife commends a man for learning Egyptian while he is away traveling (*UPZ* 1.148 = Bagnall and Derow 2008 #139 p. 232).

10. Gutzwiller 1998: 13.

11. Burton 1995.

while we see Tarpeia first as acting subject then as passive recipient of the action, sharply divided from and opposed to the Celts, we also see her and the Celts as parallels. The poetry simultaneously likens and differentiates the two core players.

In his study of migration in Theocritean pastoral poetry, Burton further draws attention to various ways of demarcating ethnic identity, such as language difference, and to metaphors for such difference and permeability, such as roads and thresholds. Here it suits to recall the river Po in Simylus's poem, which acts as just such a marker between discrete identities. The Po is puzzling mostly since Tarpeia's deceit happened nowhere near that river. It might act as an erotic symbol, similar to other overlays of pastoral imagery and sexuality such as the "picking flowers" motif.[12] Another solution is that carrying her across the Po would indicate marriage inasmuch as she would then be in Gallic territory.[13] A third option suggests, based on comparanda, that crossing the river was part of the Gallic marriage ritual; the river in the poem is thus metonymic for marriage[14] in the same way our modern idiom "going down the aisle" is, and does not require Tarpeia to have been taken to or near the Po for it to make sense to a reader familiar with the practice. High Lloyd Jones and Peter Parsons, the editors of the *Supplementum Hellenisticum* (1983: 349), note these options but remain stymied, as does Plutarch and as do I, but I note that all explanations conflate movement and shifting identity. The Gauls' punishment of Tarpeia on Roman ground—that is, their refusal to bring her to or across the Po and kill her there—retains the maiden's former identity as a Roman and refuses her assimilation into their own culture. Strong reactions against newcomers are one by-product of mobility and permeability.[15] Whether the river means marriage or simply migration, the river as a physical boundary thus also becomes a social and symbolic boundary.

Two other features of Simylus's poem similarly suggest the tensions between self and other that result in a mobile society. First, Tarpeia's eager-

---

12. See Brenk 1979.
13. ἐντός functions in this understanding as does *cis-* in Latin (*LSJ* s.v. ἐντός I.2). This detail might illuminate Simylus's perspective or his audience's, for only to a non-Italian audience could ἐντός mean "on this side of" when speaking about the Po. In other words, to a Roman, the north of the river is *Trans*padane.
14. Müller 1963.
15. Burton 1995; see also *PColZen* II.66 (= Bagnall and Derow 2008: #137) and *UPZ* I.8 (= Bagnall and Derow 2008: #138), which address assaults on foreigners. Rome was not exempt from the backlash against newcomers: witness the late-Republican accusations of noncitizenship leveled at various members of Roman society (Archias, Balbus), and the heightened concern about citizenship and identity (Cicero's famous *duae patriae, Leg.* 2.5).

ness for alliance with someone else did not protect her fathers' homes (πατέρων οὐκ ἐφύλαξε δόμους). The use of "δόμους" conflates her public and domestic (rejected) identity and thus emphasizes the strong dichotomy between Tarpeia's exogamous desire and her natal loyalty.[16] She wishes to stake a claim to a new identity, and in doing so must renounce her former identity. Second, the Gauls themselves are described in terms that at once lump them together and distinguish them, one tribe from the other: τὴν δ' οὔτ' ἄρ' Βόιοί τε καὶ ἔθνεα μυρία Κελτῶν. Not only are the Boii somehow different from (but subsumed to) the Celts, but the Celts themselves are a mosaic of a thousand tribes, ἔθνεα. Indeed, Simylus's poem makes clear that Rome is not the only permeable, and thus vulnerable, community at stake in the Tarpeia myth. The breach in Rome's boundaries that Tarpeia's shifted allegiance brings about exposes the invader, too, to invasion of another sort.

The second source of uneasiness is a new gender dynamic in Hellenistic society. Women were already in an especially precarious position in this mobile society, because of the movement and displacement involved in marriage itself.[17] Yet as many scholars have shown, women's place was additionally made problematic by the very conditions of dynastic society, in which kinship and descent came to the fore as paths to power and status.[18] The soap opera plots of the Hellenistic dynasties reveal just how confused and confusing this new prominence of women was. As Ogden shows, serial monogamy among dynasts, which left children by various mothers (whom he calls "amphimetric children"), combined with unclear patterns of succession to lead to interfamilial strife as children tried to outdo, unsettle, or dethrone their half-siblings and rivals.[19] Because of the new importance of the woman in determining the status of her children, women came to (or came to be thought to) exert undue power over the men in their lives.[20] This power was reason enough for suspicion, and a

---

16. The description of Rome as Tarpeia's "fathers' homes" may offer some indication that Simylus's readership was Greek, for the Roman reader, aware that *patres* did not live on the Capitol, might have found the phrase perplexing. Indeed, Livy, who offers the most vivid surviving account of the Gallic sack, pointedly describes the *patres* refusing to ascend the Capitol for protection and remaining on their doorsteps in the valleys below. Our main Roman source for the sack therefore contrasts homes and Capitol, whereas Simylus conflates them.

17. See Loman 2004, and cf. Modrzejewski 2005 for details of several multiethnic marriages.

18. Ogden 1999 makes this case throughout. Roman perplexity about the maternity of Ascanius (Creusa or Lavinia?) and the possibility that Iulus is a separate child reflects similar difficulties, and Tacitus's depiction of Livia and Agrippina's machinations on behalf of their sons puts a fine point on the phenomenon.

19. Ogden 1999.

20. Ibid. 266ff.

new interest in women in family relationships can easily be detected in Hellenistic literature and art.[21] Anyte's epigrams, for example, relate the feelings of a mother for a deceased unwed daughter, or the tenderness between an unwed daughter, now deceased, and her father (5 Gow-Page and 7 Gow-Page, respectively), while the sculptures of the suicidal Gaul, or Niobe with her daughters, or the Montemartini woman with child capture such familial relationships and their emotions in visual form.

Tarpeia's desire for a marriage bed with the man in power (Κελτῶν ἢ στέρξασα γαμήλια λέκτρα γενέσθαι σκηπτούχῳ) underscores that her intentions are to insert herself into the chieftain's family. While the situation in Simylus's poem is decidedly different and no female rivals (or their children) exist, Tarpeia's murder not by the chieftain but by the Boii and countless tribes of Celts themselves, presumably of their own agency, invites speculation that she was perhaps killed by them as a rival or interloper rather than, as is explicit in the Augustan sources, for her breach of some universal moral code.[22] Their celebration at killing her (χηράμενοι) underscores the intensity of their rancor at her possible insertion into the chieftain's family.

The implications of Simylus's poem in the dynamics of Hellenistic gender run even deeper if her motivation is love.[23] Mobility and dynasty were two factors that contributed to a sort of gender revolution in the Hellenistic period, in which relationships were marked by a greater degree of sexual symmetry,[24] and women emerge as actively desiring selves rather than as mere objects of male desire. Nossis speaks for herself of her loves and its pleasures and pains (1 G–P and cf. Meleager's prefatory comment on the eroticism of her poetry), but male voices also preserve the sexually independent woman: to name just a few, Herodas presents Metro and Koritto seeking dildoes (Herodas 6), Theocritus's Simaetha narrates her love affair to the moon (*Idyll* 2) and his Galatea has a menu of lovers from whom to choose (*Idyll* 13), and Asclepiades' epigrams present a rich picture of desiring women and of men reacting to them.[25]

But women's independent eroticism was deeply unsettling when combined with notions of them as unstable and unable to rule their own pas-

---

21. See ibid. xxiv on family in Plutarch, and Pollitt 1986: 141 for Hellenistic art's emphasis on variety of experience.
22. Recall the triple appearance in the sources of this reason for Tarpeia's death: so that no honor should be given to a traitor (Livy 1.11; Propertius 4.4.89; and Valerius Maximus 9.6.1).
23. Plutarch mentions this at *Romulus* 17.5; the poem only talks of marriage.
24. Konstan 1994: 218–31, esp. 231.
25. Gutzwiller 131–40. To be sure, passive women and women as objects rather than selves also appear in Hellenistic literature; Callimachus's Cydippe is one such.

sions. The sensual female was a crisis in the making, especially in light of the new influence of women in family affairs. Love is especially dangerous in its ability to detach one from normal and normative relationships.[26] I note here the preponderance of Hellenistic sources for the treasonous girls discussed in chapter 1 and catalogued in the appendix to this book. For Francese,[27] trying to come to grips with Propertius's Tarpeia and her precedents in Parthenius's poetry, the recurring theme of the treasonous maiden in Hellenistic literature underscores two key fears of vulnerable Hellenistic communities: fear that it only takes one malcontent to undermine a community and fear that *eros* dissolves all national and familial ties. The characterization fits Simylus's poem as well. In this vein, Simylus pits Tarpeia's desire for a union with the enemy chief in direct opposition to her role in guarding her fathers' walls. The plural itself (πατέρων) elides the private, familial disorder she creates with the public destruction that results, especially if the audience recognizes this as *patres*, the Roman calque for senators. It is pointed that Simylus's language also casts her not as the subject of a verb of destroying, but as the destroyer itself (τειχολέτις), and destroyer of walls—that is, of city boundaries.[28] Her very person, her agency as a person, and her misuse of that agency spell doom for private and public alike.

Simylus's Tarpeia can thus be seen as a Roman girl caught up in Hellenistic Greek concerns, hopeful for but unsuccessful at achieving her own entry into another community, and further ill-starred in the threat she poses (or is perceived to pose) to her would-be hosts and homelanders alike. As a desiring woman she is all the more dangerous and endangered, to her own people and to others, for any upset in the balance of relationships—that is, any point of vulnerability and permeability (of an individual or of a community)—threatens to destabilize identities on both sides of the rupture.

HELLENISTIC POETRY AND HISTORY

Social trends of the Hellenistic era thus merge with literary concerns to shape Rome's greedy and vulnerable Tarpeia into a figure familiar to Hellenistic audiences. Her active and destructive love, with its attendant complications of object, dynasty, and rival tribes, assimilates her to the Greek experience. So too does the identification of her beloved as the

---

26. Burton 1995: 42
27. Francese 2001: 157–90.
28. See the discussion in chapter 1 of women on and as walls for a community.

Gallic chieftain. To be sure, the details in which Simylus differs—Tarpeia's motive and the ethnic identities involved (with the loyalties they entail)—are those where the tradition is most fluid. The Gallic besieger, though, is a surprising addition—absurd, even, in Plutarch's view (ληρεῖ). While this detail strikes the modern reader, steeped in Tarpeia's tradition, as incongruous, it might have been far more familiar to a Hellenistic Greek audience, and it is for Hellenistic readers that this poem's contours become clear. The Gallic invasion of Italy in 390 BCE stands firm in the Greek and Roman tradition, whether these Gauls sacked the Capitol or whether they were otherwise repelled (or bribed away) from its slopes (Livy 5.34–39; Plutarch *Camillus* 15–30; Diodorus 14.113–17; Polybius 2.18; Dionysius 13.6–12; Appian, etc.). Where tradition names a Gallic chieftain, it is Brennus (Livy; Silius 4.150). A Brennus with his Gauls had swept southward and attacked multiple states in Greece as well, some 100 years after Rome was sacked (Pausanias 10.12–23); after several victories in the north, they besieged Delphi in spectacular fashion. No great number of Greeks, however, repelled the attack with Apollo's help and the weather's (in the form of a thunderstorm that confounded their plans).

Simylus's choice to link Tarpeia's tale to the Gallic sack assimilates a Roman experience with a Greek experience and thus renders Roman affairs as parallel with Greek affairs. Indeed the Romans adopted the same sorts of adaptive techniques; as Williams has argued, Roman authors narrating their own Gallic sack emphasized the parallels between themselves as defenders of the holy Capitol and the Greeks who saved Delphi.[29] The glorious salvation of the Capitol from the Gallic attack was the outcome of the story, but along the way the conflict was almost resolved by a buyout—the Romans would give the Gauls a thousand pounds of gold to go away (Livy 5.48). It might be coincidental that gold also figured in the story of Brennus's sack of Delphi. According to Pausanias (10.19.8), this was Brennus's motive for attacking Apollo's sanctuary and, indeed, Greece. Others are more forgiving of the Gauls and attribute their movement into Greece to the overpopulation of their own land or to scarce resources.[30] Legend floated around that the Gauls did take the god's gold

---

29. Williams 2001: 158–70, especially 166–67; and cf. Dench 1995b: 69–70, on Roman propaganda after their defeat of Gauls at Sentinum in 295 BCE. Polybius 2.35, especially 2.35.7ff., draws explicit parallels between Romans vs. Gauls, Greeks vs. Gauls, and Greeks vs. Persians.

30. Justin's epitome of Pomponius Trogus's history (24.4) says they had exhausted their resources at home, while Memnon (*Heracleia* 8.8) says it was famine. Polyaenus (*Stratagemata* 7.35.2) attests that Brennus was not really after gold at Delphi; rather, he misled his soldiers about the amount of golden booty to be gained in order to spur them to battle.

and silver from the sanctuary, which loot was then cursed, deposited in a lake at Toulouse, later recovered by the Roman Q. Servilius Caepio (consul in 106 BCE), and responsible for his downfall (Strabo 4.1.13). Backfiring greed—Brennus's, his soldiers', Caepio's, and Tarpeia's—can certainly simply be a trope, but this is one more detail in which Simylus's elegy finds common ground between Greeks and Romans: the Celts made adornment Tarpeia's doom (κόσμον ἔθεντο φόνον).

This Gallic invasion had been a real threat to Greece and was accordingly commemorated in Hellenistic poetry by Callimachus (*Hymn to Delos* 4.171–87). Adrian Hollis has examined the Callimachus passage as part of a tendency in Hellenistic poetry to "mythologize the present."[31] Callimachus's hymn casts the Gauls as new Giants (actually called Titans, line 174[32]), repelled by the god Apollo and the god-to-be Ptolemy II Philadelphus (*Hymn* 4.165–70, 188–90).[33] Ptolemy II's own struggles against the Gauls (which amounted to quelling a rebellion of 4,000 of them whom he had hired as mercenaries for his own dynastic purposes) are thus overlaid with the Panhellenic victory of 279 BCE, and with the Gigantomachy (Titanomachy). The magnificent Pergamine Great Altar similarly overlaps two conflicts, one mythological and one historical, by combining in the artistic program sculpted Gauls and Gallika, and a frieze of the Gigantomachy in which the defeated Giants look just like Gauls.[34] Such mythologizing serves at times to glorify the reigning power, as in the participation of godlike Ptolemy II against the Gauls/Titans. It also interweaves topical concerns into the more learned fancies of Hellenistic poetry, thus not only putting myth and poetry to use in the service of kings and emperors[35] but also "aestheticizing" current events and people, rendering them more familiar to an audience attuned to art and artistry.

Myth and history also elided on the ground, as it were. There are even historical Tarpeias—treasonous women—in Hellenistic history.[36] Berenice II of Cyrene comes to mind; she killed her fiancé the Macedonian Deme-

---

31. Hollis 2003. The phrase comes from p. 9.

32. Mineur 1984 *ad* 4.174 argues that Callimachus meant Titans when he said Titans, but the elision of the two groups of anti-Olympians was so common in Hellenistic art and literature that it seems Giants are to be understood.

33. Elsewhere Callimachus mentions a Brennus and his Gauls, perhaps deriving them from the sea nymph Galatea (Fr. 379 Pfeiffer).

34. Mitchell 2007: 284–86; Marszal 2000; but see also Stewart 2000: 40 for other resonance in the Pergamine Giants' depiction.

35. This is Hollis's title (2003).

36. I am grateful for Kathryn Gutzwiller and Tony Corbeill for suggesting this line of thought.

trius the Fair, and thereafter married Ptolemy III Euergetes (and dedicated her famous lock; Catullus's poem mentions her crime as a *bonum facinus* at 66.27). The lurid tale of adultery between Demetrius and Berenice II's mother Apama/Arsinoe[37] does not altogether obscure the element of political intrigue; Apama had favored Demetrius's Macedonian alliance, whereas Berenice's father preferred the more local Ptolemy III Euergetes. Indeed there are two Tarpeias in this story: Apama/Arsinoe, who saw a potential alliance outside the ruling house, and Berenice II herself.

The overlay of historical topics and literary themes emerged from the flood of scholarship that came out of Alexandria, resulting in the cross-fertilization of branches of learning. Among many examples available, perhaps most relevant is Parthenius, who interweaves local history and myth and literature together to form his tales of love's sufferings, at times emphasizing political content (as in #30: Celtine, whose son by Hercules gave his name to the Celts), at times concentrating on the love motif (#17: Periander's mother, whose unnatural love for him caused the Corinthian tyrant's madness). Parthenius's stories, as Lightfoot argues, are shaped by the movement of stories from history into literature, and from poetry to prose and back.[38] Such movement can account for the portability of Tarpeia's tale from one historical context to another.

Simylus's poem reveals how a Roman myth might be comprehensible to a Greek audience. What must the Mediterranean's new master have looked like to the Greeks now under its sway? There is other evidence that other Hellenistic poets, beyond Simylus, sought to grasp Roman myth and naturalize it, as it were. Callimachus *Aitia* 106–7 Pf. tells of a mother encouraging her son Gaios, wounded in the thigh, that his wound would be a remembrance for all time of his bravery. This is likely a reference to the famous Horatius Cocles, legendary defender of Rome against the Etruscan Lars Porsenna.[39] This hero in some versions lost either a leg or an eye.[40] The "encouraging mother" motif is also attached to a Spartan soldier, to Spu-

---

37. Justin 26.3.

38. Lightfoot 1999: 301–2 and cf. 229–30 and 233–34: "The adaptation of myth to a new context, the lifting of motifs from one story and recasting them elsewhere, are clearly not confined to the Hellenistic period; but this is a particular type of borrowing and rewriting which is characteristic of that time, and reflects the copying of motifs between specifically literary sources" (234).

39. Most commentators agree that it is the Roman, but for a different view see Durbec 2011: 485, who concludes that he is a generic type rather than Cocles.

40. The wounded-eye version is cited by Plutarch *Poplicola* 16.7; the leg version appears in Plutarch *Poplicola* 16.10 and in Dionysius of Halicarnassus 5.25.1–3. There is an ancient etymology for Cocles as "without an eye" (see Roller 2004: 15 with note 30), and cf. Antigonas Monophthalmos (one-eyed), Alexander's famous general.

rius Carvilius, and to Philip of Macedon.[41] Greeks and Romans are not so unlike.[42] Callimachus's reference shows a passing interest in, if not devout adherence to, Roman myth, at least in his elegiacs. One Butas seems to have taken up the torch by writing a Roman *Aitia* in Greek elegiacs. Plutarch mentions this Butas also in the *Romulus,* in connection with a fantastic version of the Lupercalia (*Romulus* 21.6).[43] Callimachus, Butas, and Simylus taken as a group reveal Greek attempts to engage Roman material, but on rather free terms.[44] Perhaps the fact that all three authors wrote their Roman stories in elegiac meter is meaningful; the poetic casting of Rome's stories, into forms familiar in Hellenistic literature, asserts a Greek literary primacy and control over Roman tradition and authority.[45] The phenomenon is something of a reversal of Vergil's Roman mission from *Aeneid* 6, in which Anchises contrasts Greek arts to Roman imperialism. Here it is useful to note that Tarpeia's treachery happens against Rome, but the treasonous-girl motif is set in Hellenistic literature all over the known world, from Ephesus to Sardis to mainland Greece to Magna Graecia.[46] Rome itself is nothing special here; it is yet another Hellenistic city.

If this is the case, then Simylus's telling of Tarpeia's story participates in the larger endeavor I explore in this part of the book, of Greeks trying to understand and come to grips with Rome through Rome's history and myth. By blending the treacherous-girl motif with the Gallic sack, Simylus at once renders Rome more familiar (and somehow therefore less threatening) to a Hellenistic Greek audience, which had the same event in their past. A side effect of this interpretation of Simylus's elegy is that it is meant firmly for a Greek, not Roman, audience; even if a Roman audience of the Hellenistic period was still experimenting with a fluid tradition about Tarpeia, it is unlikely that Roman readers would tolerate a Capitol occupied by the Gauls.[47] Before Actium, a Greek audience still would.

---

41. Horatius Cocles's mother: Servius *ad Aen.* 8.646. Spartan soldier: Stobaeus 3.7.28. Philip: Plutarch *Par. Min.* 8, which compares Philip to Horatius Cocles directly and gives both a missing eye. Spurius Carvilius: Cicero *de Orat.* 2.249.

42. This is the prevailing theme that Acosta-Hughes and Stephens 2012 see in the episode; see pp. 175, 194–95, and 205–7.

43. Arnobius *Ad. Nat.* 5.18.3 mentions this Butas as well, as author of a story about the presence of wine jars and the absence of myrtle in the Bona Dea rites. It is highly unlikely that this elegist is the same as Cato Uticensis's freedman, mentioned at Plutarch *Cato* 70.2–5.

44. See Hubbard 1975: 121 on Butas.

45. Cf. Ovid's Greek source for Hersilia, which ignores Roman etymologies; see Wiseman 1983: 449–50.

46. Lightfoot 1999: 229–30.

47. Horsfall's chapter "From History to Legend: M. Manlius and the Geese" in Bremmer and Horsfall 1987: 63–75 is highly sensitive to this nuance of reception.

CHAPTER NINE

ON THE EDGE OF THE KNIFE IN DIONYSIUS OF HALICARNASSUS

DIONYSIUS OF HALICARNASSUS was a prolific historian and rhetorical theorist of the Augustan age. In addition to writing the grand *Roman Antiquities* (Greek: Ῥωμαϊκὴ Ἀρχαιολογία), tracing Roman history from the beginning to the present in twenty books, he authored a large handful of rhetorical treatises both abstract (such as the *Art of Rhetoric* and *On the Arrangement of Words*) and specific (such as the commentaries on Attic orators and on Thucydides). His narrative of Tarpeia, which appears in the Romulus cycle in *Roman Antiquities* book 2, is the longest extant treatment of her. Most of his text explicitly quotes or paraphrases the histories of Q. Fabius Pictor and L. Calpurnius Piso Frugi, but Dionysius does not hesitate to pass judgment on the divergent traditions. In chapters 2 and 3 I discuss the difficulty of sifting out Pictor's and Piso's quotations from the Dionysian context that preserves them. Here my focus is not on those quotations per se, but on those parts of Dionysius's narrative that appear to be his own contributions—those parts that knit together the chunks of Pictor and Piso that he cites and that contain Dionysius's own assessment of those prior accounts.

Dionysius's use of Pictor and Piso is indicative of his larger project of situating Roman culture into the world that includes, and always has included, Greeks. I deliberately do not say "situating Roman culture into a Greek world" or some such, because I believe Dionysius's most important contribution to ancient historiography is the way he intertwines the two throughout time and across genres. Neither Greek nor Roman emerges dominant over the other; indeed, neither can live without the other. Thus Dionysius's Greek world has always been, in a sense, Roman. His history of Rome finds Roman origins in Greece and Greek ethics still thriving in Rome. His rhetorical works revive for the Augustan age a formal, rhetorical Classicism that was highly congenial to—even central to—the Princeps' own cultural aesthetics.

I propose to examine Dionysius's Tarpeia in light of this larger project of cultural overlap. This is not to say that I shall locate Greek elements in the story. Despite several Greek precedents for the treasonous girl (see chapters 1 and 8) Dionysius does not try to make the story a Greek one. Rather, in Dionysius's hands Tarpeia's story is a laboratory for investigating common language as a point of intersection that can generate shared identity, or as a knife-edge that holds the possibility of cultural rift. Foremost in this exploration is Dionysius's use of words that convey several possible meanings, and even words whose meaning is "commonness of meaning." He also uses a varied lexicon to label individual elements of his story, some of them similes and some alternatives with shades of difference, a phenomenon that also evokes, in a different way, "commonness of meaning." The murky meaning of Tarpeia's verbal compact with Tatius mimics the girl herself, whose meaning cannot be pinned down precisely and who stands at a common point and dividing point between Roman and Sabine. Furthermore, the pact and Tarpeia both mimic Dionysius's *Roman Antiquities,* which also seeks to blur difference but is interpretable in divergent ways. Dionysius's preference for Piso's account is perhaps related to this feature of his narrative: Piso's version flatters everyone, which is fitting in a culture that now includes both Roman and Sabine. Dionysius's Greek-Roman history also flatters everyone, with perhaps the same longed-for outcome of assimilation and shared identity.

DIONYSIUS'S FAVORITISM FOR PISO

Dionysius prejudices his reader in favor of Piso's account of Tarpeia as patriot. Apart from Dionysius, this account had little truck in the surviving sources—indeed, Dionysius is Piso's only written champion[1]—but

---

1. Forsythe 1994: 156–57 explores the only other possible relic of Piso's patriotic version: a putative statue to her (Festus 496L s.v. Tarpeiae) that stood in Metellus's temple to Jupiter Stator.

despite skepticism about Piso's patriotic girl in the one other source that mentions it (Livy, *sunt qui,* "there are those who . . . ," 1.11), Dionysius seems convinced of Piso's trustworthiness. A primary reason for Dionysius's trust is that Piso's story is corroborated by (an interpretation of) monuments and ritual practice—a sort of corroboration especially valuable to this Augustan-age author when he deals with early sources.[2] Our historian is at times explicit about this evaluative tool (e.g., 2.66.4).[3] He also states outright that Piso's version seems more true to him because of the outcome (2.40.2, ἔοικε δὲ τὰ μετὰ ταῦτα γενόμενα τὴν Πείσωνος ἀληθεστέραν ποιεῖν ἀπόφασιν);[4] throughout his history Dionysius favors arguments based on likelihood, especially when faced with multiple versions. This "cart before the horse" logic may be compared with the overall thrust of his history, which maintains that early Rome must have been good and strong because Rome is now master of the known world.[5]

But Dionysius also uses more subtle ways of swaying his audience in Piso's favor. After presenting that kernel of the story on which everyone agrees, Dionysius parses out the Pisonian and Fabian traditions. The Pisonian explanations are given first with the connective γάρ or with the μέν half of a μέν–δέ pair.[6] He ends his exposition with Pisonian details and a conclusion endorsing Piso. This arrangement gives Piso's version some priority and leaves Piso's tale in the reader's mind as he moves on from Tarpeia's narrative. He also relates Piso's version at much greater length than he does Fabius's—roughly three to one.[7] What is more, he reduces the effectiveness of the canonical Fabian version by lumping together their

---

2. Schultze 2000: 9n11 contrasts Dionysius and Livy's approaches to early history in terms of the different ethnicity of their respective readership. See also Marincola 1997: 101n190, in which he contrasts Dionysius's boast of autopsy to convince his Greek readers with Livy's omission of such a boast, which would be unnecessary for Roman readers.

3. Andrén 1960 convincingly refutes the disparaging notion that Dionysius's evidence from monuments is a feature of armchair historiography. See p. 103: "He has no doubt acquainted himself with the topography and monuments of Rome and its vicinity, and in describing them he often shows himself to possess an observing mind, a good judgment, and a clear perception of the main features."

4. I have used Cary's 1937 Loeb edition. All translations are mine.

5. Gabba 1991 sustains this argument.

6. After the first point of comparison in which Dionysius prioritizes Pictor, Piso takes the lead. Piso is given priority at 2.39.1 (γάρ), where Pictor is given second place (δέ); at 2.40.1 with ὁ μὲν Πείσων and Pictor trailing with οἱ δὲ περὶ τὸν Φάβιον (2.40.2); then Dionysius finishes with Piso, whose account is vindicated by the cult of Tarpeia (on which see below).

7. Piso's version is given roughly three times as fully as Pictor's; I count 100 words of explicit reference to Pictor's version and 278 to Piso's. Not included in this count are those portions of the story on which everyone agrees.

many followers into the flat, even condescending, "those who follow Pictor and Cincius."[8]

Finally, Dionysius reveals his preference for Piso with a cross-linguistic wordplay. By repeatedly calling the historian "Πείσων" in this episode rather than "Καλπούρνιος" (which he elsewhere uses—Dionysius seems to use both forms equally),[9] the Greek historian indicates that Πείσων is "the one who will persuade," for Πείσων is both the Roman historian's name and the future active participle of the Greek verb πείθω, "to persuade." Dionysius had elsewhere constructed episodes around names with double meanings.[10] The "meaningful name" is not a pun *per se,* and it was a common device in history and myth. But it is important to note that the "meaningful name" crosses a linguistic boundary in the case of Piso/Peiso.

LANGUAGE AND CULTURE

Greek etymologies for Roman phenomena in Dionysius generally indicate trustworthiness of the Roman phenomena.[11] Greek names moreover suggest cultural continuity, for the Romans were after all originally Greek in Dionysius's mind.[12] Piso's name is an especially powerful indicator of Rome's original, and lingering, Hellenicity since this Hellenized name (Πείσων) of a very old Roman family (the Calpurnii Pisones, attested as early as the second Punic War) makes the Pisones Greek even before the Hellenization of Rome that swept Rome during Piso's own lifetime in the second century BCE. In this way Piso's Greekness ironically lends him clout on early (Greek) Rome, and helps Dionysius prioritize his version over the also-Greek-writing, but unfortunately Roman-named, Fabius Pictor.

I propose that the Tarpeia episode in Dionysius explores linguistic identity even more subtly than this. In both versions Tarpeia's guilt or innocence hinges on a double meaning in the pact she makes with Tatius. Dionysius

---

8. οἱ δὲ περὶ τὸν Φάβιόν τε καὶ Κίγκιον at 2.39.1, cf 2.40.2, οἱ δὲ περὶ τὸν Φάβιόν.

9. "Καλπούρνιος" doesn't appear in this episode at all but appears four times elsewhere in the history (alone at 1.7.3 and 12.4.2, Πείσων Καλπούρνιος at 1.3.4 and 1.79.4). In the Tarpeia episode Dionysius calls the historian "Πείσων" four times, never with "Καλπούρνιος": alone at 2.40.1 and 2.40.3, Πείσων Λεύκιος at 2.38.3 (and cf. 4.15.5), and Πείσων ὁ τιμητικός at 2.39.1 (and cf. 12.9.3). At 4.7.5 he is Λεύκιος Πείσων Φρῦγι.

10. Barnes 2005: 35–53 notes and discusses briefly the Πείσων pun in a much fuller discussion of episodes constructed around the punning names Meton and Philonides.

11. Schultze 2000: 36–37.

12. At 1.90.1 Dionysius identifies Aeolian Greek as the core ancestor of Latin. See de Jonge 2008: 60–65 for a full account of the linguistic continuity of the Greeks and Romans. See also the nuanced discussion in Gabba 1991: 98–113.

says, in his own voice and presumably telling a part of the story on which everyone agreed, that she made this bargain:

τὰς δὲ κλεῖς αὐτὴ φυλάττειν τῶν πυλῶν καὶ παραδώσειν αὐτοῖς τὸ ἔρυμα νυκτὸς ἀφικομένοις μισθὸν τῆς προδοσίας λαβοῦσα τὰ φορήματα τῶν Σαβίνων, ἃ περὶ τοῖς εὐωνύμοις εἶχον ἅπαντες βραχίοσιν. (2.38.4)

(She said that) she was guardian of the keys of the fortress, and she would hand over its defenses to them if they came at night, taking as her wage for this betrayal the cargo of the Sabines, which they all had on their left arms.

The crux is the word "φορήματα," literally "the things carried" on the Sabines' left arms. It could mean gold, or it could mean weapons. In Pictor's version, she intends it to mean their gold, but Tatius willfully misinterprets it to mean their weapons. Tatius therefore exploits an ambiguity in the meaning of the word, exploitation that Pictor calls "deceit" (ἀπάτην, 2.40.2). I discuss Pictor's deceptive Tatius at length in chapter 2. Here I wish to emphasize the shape of the deceit: manipulation of the meaning of words. In Piso's version, the verbal manipulation is Tarpeia's. Tarpeia's desired patriotic outcome—to deprive the Sabines of their shields, and thereby defeat them—depends also on the double meaning of φορήματα in the promise she gives Tatius. When she asks for the φορήματα, she intends for the Sabines to interpret the wage as their gold. They do thus interpret it, and are ready to hand it over to her (Σαβίνων τὸν χρυσὸν ἑτοίμων ὄντων διδόναι τῇ κόρῃ τὸν περὶ τοῖς ἀριστεροῖς βραχίοσι, 2.40.1) when Tatius intervenes. Dionysius/Piso is explicit that Tarpeia intends to capitalize on the ambiguity of the agreement (διὰ τῆς κοινότητος τῶν ὁμολογιῶν παρακρουσαμένη, 2.39.1). Her intention too is a cheat; παρακρουσαμένη, the middle voice participle of the verb παρακρούω "to strike aside," means "to cheat for one's own benefit." Notable here is the fact that the Greek word for "ambiguity" (κοινότης) that Dionysius/Piso uses is really "commonness," a word that also indicates linguistic commonality elsewhere in Dionysius's oeuvre (Thuc. 54 and Pomp. 2), or even universal quality. This word thus powerfully evokes a linguistic bond between Romans and Greeks and undergirds Dionysius's idea of Rome's archaic past as "universal history," the interconnectedness of all cultures and events.[13] Similarly, the word Dionysius employs for "agree-

---

13. See Schultze 2000: 18–19, but cf. Clarke 1999: 249–79 for whom Dionysius "fails to meet the strict criteria for universalism" (p. 251), and the subtle argument throughout Fox 1993 that

ment" is ὁμολογία, "same-speaking."[14] Translated literally, Tarpeia makes a cheat through the linguistic commonness of same-speaking.

One wonders, here as ever, how Roman Tarpeia and Sabine Tatius could communicate at all across their linguistic divide. How alike were Sabines and Romans? When Dionysius offers an ethnogenesis for the Sabines later in book 2 (2.48–49), he offers four possibilities he found in the sources: the Varronian tradition of aboriginal Sabines from Reate, descendents of the god Quirinus; Zenodotus's account of Umbrians displaced from Reate who changed their names to Sabines; Cato's version of Sabines, descended from Sancus son of Jupiter at Testruna, who moved to Reate; and the version in the "native histories" (2.49.4, ἐν ἱστορίαις ἐπιχωρίοις) that comparatively lax Spartan emigrants, having settled in Sabine territory, influenced the Sabines in their customs (whence Sabine severity). It is notable here that, even in the "Spartan explanation," the Sabines are not Greek *per se*.[15] Tatius would therefore not have an innate understanding of the nuances of Tarpeia's Latin (originally Greek) language. His inability is not, however, an indictment of his Sabine rusticity, for Dionysius does not subscribe to the characterization of Sabines as simpletons. Indeed, Dionysius's *filosabinismos* is palpable here and elsewhere, and he is the one to draw attention to their luxurious habits (2.38.3).[16] His Tatius is no fool. Rather, Tatius's failure to grasp the potential for fraud is simply a hallmark of his foreignness, and he proves to be a quick learner. "Commonness of same-speaking" is therefore a highly relevant collocation, given Dionysius's interest in ethnography and identity.[17]

Dionysius's treatment further probes and renders problematic the idea of linguistic unity. Linguists categorize all languages on a scale from perfect precision of expression, called monosemy, in which each word means exactly one thing and one thing only (the extreme of which would be a language so thoroughly parsed that no one could learn it), to perfect economy of expression, called polysemy, in which each word means many things dependent on context (the extreme of which is a language whose signifiers

---

Dionysius uses a different sort of universalism: a τέλος that organizes and influences all that precedes it.

14. *LSJ* s.v. ὁμολογία.

15. Earlier at 2.30.5, Romulus appeals to the Sabine women to let go their anger because woman-stealing was an old and illustrious Greek custom. Tellingly, Romulus casts the Greeks as external to both Sabines and Romans, but laudable in their apparent cultural superiority.

16. Musti 1970 suggests that in the Tarpeia episode Sabine duplicity is downplayed in comparison with Livy's account (p. 73 formulates this thought most concisely). For Musti this is a relic of the historians' sources, but I suggest that Dionysius's attitude here toward Sabines rusticity contributes to the exploration of linguistic identity.

17. Ancient authors worry about this problem, e.g., Aeschylus *Agamemnon* 1050–52.

are so vague that no speaker could understand another).[18] In Dionysius's preferred Pisonian narrative, Tarpeia and Tatius seem caught in the latter scenario, polysemy.[19] Tarpeia herself seeks to exploit the commonness of same-speaking to her own advantage, intending to use the linguistic signifier "φορήματα" in a way possible but unexpected. "Φορήματα" could mean the Sabines' bracelets, or it could mean their shields. To emphasize the ambiguity of the language, Dionysius says Tatius, faced with the duplicitous maiden, seeks a λογισμὸν (strategy) whereby he can evade payment in gold:

ἔπειτα πάλιν ὁ μὲν Πείσων φησὶ τῶν Σαβίνων τὸν χρυσὸν ἐτοίμων ὄντων διδόναι τῇ κόρῃ τὸν περὶ τοῖς ἀριστεροῖς βραχίοσι τὴν Τάρπειαν οὐ τὸν κόσμον ἀλλὰ τοὺς θυρεοὺς παρ' αὐτῶν αἰτεῖν. Τατίῳ δὲ θυμόν τε εἰσελθεῖν ἐπὶ τῇ ἐξαπάτῃ καὶ λογισμὸν τοῦ μὴ παραβῆναι τὰς ὁμολογίας. δόξαι δ' οὖν αὐτῷ δοῦναι μὲν τὰ ὅπλα, ὥσπερ ἡ παῖς ἠξίωσε, ποιῆσαι δ' ὅπως αὐτοῖς μηδὲν λαβοῦσα χρήσεται, καὶ αὐτίκα διατεινάμενον ὡς μάλιστα ἰσχύος εἶχε ῥῖψαι τὸν θυρεὸν κατὰ τῆς κόρης καὶ τοῖς ἄλλοις παρακελεύσασθαι ταὐτὸ ποιεῖν. οὕτω δὴ βαλλομένην πάντοθεν τὴν Τάρπειαν ὑπὸ πλήθους τε καὶ ἰσχύος τῶν πληγῶν πεσεῖν καὶ περισωρευθεῖσαν ὑπὸ τῶν θυρεῶν ἀποθανεῖν. (2.40.1)

But then again, Peiso says that, when the Sabines were about to give her the gold on their left arms, she demanded not their adornment but their shields. But anger rose up in Tatius because of the deceit, and some strategy whereby not to default on the agreement. So he decided to hand over his weapons, just as the child asked, but to do so in such a way that she could make no use of them after she received them, and immediately reaching out with all his strength he cast his shield at her and bid the others to do the same. Thus being struck on all sides Tarpeia fell under the number and strength of the blows, and, buried on all sides by the weapons, died.

The word "λογισμὸν" means a stratagem or device, but its linkage to "λογος" connects it closely to language: it is a linguistic trick, or, a means

---

18. This pair is nuanced by two other factors: homonymy, in which words of the same sound designate completely unrelated things (flour, flower), and synonymy, in which different signifiers label the same thing. We return to synonymy below.

19. Indeed, as de Jonge 2008 argues throughout, Dionysus's rhetorical theory writ large depends on variety of expression and the importance of context in producing and assessing nuance.

whereby multiple interpretations are allowable.[20] Thus he takes advantage of a different open-ended part of their agreement: he "gives" her the shields in a way unspecified and unanticipated by Tarpeia—he heaps them upon her. He exploits the signifier "δοῦναι" in the same way that she exploits "φορήματα." The same verbal pact thus legitimately gives rise to (at least) three valid interpretations (give your gold; give your shields; cast your shields). Both Tarpeia and Tatius have it in mind to use this indistinctness in their own favor. No such ambiguity exists in Pictor's version, according to Dionysius; for Fabius Pictor, Tatius was downright deceitful since, being obliged by the agreement, he intended to defraud it:

> οἱ δὲ περὶ τὸν Φάβιον ἐπὶ τοῖς Σαβίνοις ποιοῦσι τὴν τῶν ὁμολογιῶν ἀπάτην· δέον γὰρ αὐτοὺς τὸν χρυσόν, ὥσπερ ἡ Τάρπεια ἠξίου, κατὰ τὰς ὁμολογίας ἀποδιδόναι, χαλεπαίνοντας ἐπὶ τῷ μεγέθει τοῦ μισθοῦ τὰ σκεπαστήρια κατ' αὐτῆς βαλεῖν, ὡς ταῦτα ὅτε ὤμνυσαν αὐτῇ δώσειν ὑπεσχημένους. (2.40.2)

Those who follow Fabius place all the deception on the Sabines. They were supposed to hand over the gold, just like Tarpeia asked, according to their agreement, but they were aggrieved by the size of the price and cast their weapons upon her, as if they promised to give these to her when they swore.

In Pictor's rejected version the language of the pact wasn't ambiguous at all, or wasn't understood to be by the protagonists, who both understood the agreement to be about gold. The dispute therefore wasn't over that agreement but rather over whether it would be honored. It was not honored, and Pictor is far more judgmental of the Sabine capacity for deceit. Dionysius's preference for the version of the story that trades in ambiguity rather than deceit duplicates the larger dynamic of the story: whether Tarpeia's actions were nobly inspired, or not.

Someone might raise the objection that the knot of ambiguity, motive, and deceit is Piso's and Pictor's axe to grind, not Dionysius's. Yet by juxtaposing the two authorities so closely, especially vis-à-vis the knot just mentioned, Dionysius throws into higher relief the role of language as a uniting or dividing force. His own text, those parts of his lengthy narrative that do not purport to reproduce Pictor or Piso, confirm this interest. For example, when Tarpeia first sends an overture to Tatius in 2.38.4, she

---

20. *LSJ* s.v. λογισμὸν.

summons him to visit her "so as to discuss a matter of great magnitude and necessity" (ὡς ἐκείνῳ διαλεξομένη περὶ πράγματος ἀναγκαίου καὶ μεγάλου). Dionysius chose to use διαλέγω, a verb that implies, as does our "dialogue," a back-and-forth exchange of views rather than an exegesis or proposal or harmony. This verb, I suggest, indicates that Tarpeia is not the sole arbiter of her plan. Tatius must be involved. It also, interestingly, can indicate speaking in a dialect[21]—another indicator of impeded understanding. After they agreed, Dionysius says, they solemnized their pact, and Tarpeia pledged not to cheat the agreement (αὐτὴ δοῦσα τοῦ μὴ ψεύδεσθαι τὰς ὁμολογίας, 2.38.5). We know, however, that ὁμολογία, "same speaking," is tricky and lends itself to cheating.

What then shall we do with the fact that Dionysius reaffirms the unanimity of tradition with "thus far all the writers come together" but then says that "as to what happens next, they do not agree" (μέχρι μὲν δὴ τούτων συμφέρονται πάντες οἱ Ῥωμαίων συγγραφεῖς, ἐν δὲ τοῖς ὕστερον λεγομένοις οὐχ ὁμολογοῦσι, 2.39.1)? "Agreement," as we have seen, need not mean agreement. The root "ὁμο–" (same) arises again a section later at the start of 2.39.2 in a way that, in translation at least, gives space for differences within the agreement. There Dionysius resumes the undisputed part of the tradition thus: "regarding what follows, all again write likewise" (τὰ δ' ἑξῆς ἅπαντες πάλιν ὁμοίως γράφουσι). What follows this statement of "likewise" accounts is a list of events, some of which are not contestable: she admitted the Sabines into the gate, urged the Romans to flee, the Sabines took the Capitol, and Tarpeia demanded her payment. But some are contestable, for example two internal "events," both about Tarpeia's motive or expressed motive. First, she urges the Romans to flee since the Sabines were already masters of the place (ὡς κατεχόντων ἤδη τῶν Σαβίνων τὸ φρούριον). ὡς with participles indicates alleged reasons. Neither we nor Dionysius can ever know whether it was her real impression that the Sabines had taken the hill, and she intended to spare whatever Romans she could, or whether it was a pretext to clear out resistance to the Sabine invaders. Second, once the Sabines have the Capitol she demands her reward since she provided what she had contracted (ὡς τὰ παρ' ἑαυτῆς ὅσα συνέθετο παρεσχημένην). Again, ὡς + participle carries ambiguity. This could indicate what she felt, or what she told the Sabines. On the latter reading Tarpeia can be accused of some obfuscation. On the former she is genuine if misguided. The line between obfuscation and naïveté, which is thick but appears so thin, makes all the difference, and it

---

21. Polybius 1.180.6.

is not at stake merely in Piso's or Pictor's versions. Dionysius's explication of the story makes this distinction integral to every aspect of her story, even where everyone agrees.

TARPEIA'S AMBIGUITY AS A SIGNIFIER

Like the ambiguous words of her agreement with Tatius, Tarpeia is a signifier with at least two possible interpretations (traitor, patriot), a feature of her story that Dionysius's narrative highlights like no teller before him. It is curious, then, that the aspect of the story that confirms one interpretation for Dionysius—the monument at which libations were poured to Tarpeia each year—is perhaps the most ambiguous and perplexing part of her whole story. Dionysius supports Piso's version because to him it best explains Tarpeia's annual recognition at the monument where she was buried:

> τάφου τε γὰρ ἔνθα ἔπεσεν ἠξίωται τὸν ἱερώτατον τῆς πόλεως κατέχουσα λόφον, καὶ χοὰς αὐτῇ Ῥωμαῖοι καθ' ἕκαστον ἐνιαυτὸν ἐπιτελοῦσι, ('λέγω δὲ ἃ Πείσων γράφει) ὧν οὐδενὸς εἰκὸς αὐτήν, εἰ προδιδοῦσα τὴν πατρίδα τοῖς πολεμίοις ἀπέθανεν, οὔτε παρὰ τῶν προδοθέντων οὔτε παρὰ τῶν ἀποκτεινάντων τυχεῖν, ἀλλὰ καὶ εἴ τι λείψανον αὐτῆς ἦν τοῦ σώματος ἀνασκαφὲν ἔξω ῥιφῆναι σὺν χρόνῳ φόβου τε καὶ ἀποτροπῆς ἕνεκα τῶν μελλόντων τὰ ὅμοια δρᾶν. (2.40.3).

> She was given the honor of a tomb where she fell, holding the most sacred peak of the city, and the Romans carry out libations to her every year. I am saying what Piso writes. But if she died while betraying her fatherland to the enemy, she would have received none of these honors, neither from those she betrayed nor those who killed her. On the contrary: if there had been any remains of her body, they would have been dug up and cast out over time, out of fear and also as a protective measure for any others who would do something similar.

The antiquity of the practice of libation—it predates trustworthy, Hellenized Piso/Peiso, at the very least—lends this evidence more weight than more recent testimony.[22] But it is by no means conclusive. Greek precedent

---

22. 1.5.1, 1.6.3, 1.72.1. Schulze 2000: 33 writes, "(Dionysius) sometimes refers to an author's credentials: to belong to an early epoch (hence, of course, to be nearer to the historical events) or to have a claim to high personal status are the most important ones. The antiquity of a source is held as inherently important."

would suggest that annual libation at a tomb need not indicate an unmistakable heroine; Helen, a similarly problematic woman, was honored as a benefactress at shrines in Sparta and beyond, but not because of her patriotic deeds.[23] Rather, it was for her stance at the crux of inside and outside, Helen of Sparta and Helen of Troy at the same time.[24] Though Dionysius uses such a monument to confirm his interpretation of Tarpeia, the historian cannot erase the uncertainty that surrounds it:

ἔοικε δὲ τὰ μετὰ ταῦτα γενόμενα τὴν Πείσωνος ἀληθεστέραν ποιεῖν ἀπόκρισιν. φου τε γὰρ ἔνθα ἔπεσεν ἠξίωται τὸν ἱερώτατον τῆς πόλεως κατέχουσα λόφον, (2.40.2-3)

It seems that the events that followed these render truer the judgment of Piso . . . for she was thought worthy of a grave where she fell.

As Livy had been, but for different reasons, Dionysius is especially concerned with the difficulty of discernment in this story. The very beginning of the story bears this out well. When Tatius first approaches Rome he settles in the Forum valley and is at odds about what to do next: εἰς πολλὴν ἐνέπιπτεν ἀπορίαν, 2.38.1 (cf. ἀμηχανοῦντι in the following sentence, 2.38.2). Tarpeia's appearance was, as Dionysius calls it, a piece of good fortune contrary to appearances (παράδοξος εὐτυχία, 2.38.2). Since δόξα is legitimacy reliant upon appearance and/or agreement, παράδοξος evokes the senses of both "contrary to appearances" and "beyond agreement." Something in her undermines stable, or closed, signification. δόξα features again in her story, when Tatius agrees to her terms: εὐδοκοῦντος δὲ τοῦ Τατίου, 2.38.5 (cf. δόξαι, 2.40.1), or, seems to think they are good. The instability of this impression is immediately confirmed by the steps the two protagonists take to confirm this seeming—pledges through oaths not to falsify/misrepresent their same-speaking: εὐδοκοῦντος δὲ τοῦ λαβοῦσα τὰς πίστεις δι' ὅρκων παρ' αὐτοῦ καὶ αὐτὴ δοῦσα τοῦ μὴ ψεύδεσθαι τὰς ὁμολογίας (2.38.5). Neither of them honors the pact. Tarpeia sends a messenger girl to Tatius through a gate no one knows is open (2.38.4), then

---

23. Cf. Wiseman 1994: 37–48 (especially 48) that monuments need not imply praise. Gabba 1981: 60–61; and Rawson 1991: 582–98. See also the discussion of Aglauros, and the rites to Tarpeia, in the first chapter of this book.

24. See Scioli 2010, who sees in Helen's teichoskopeia in *Iliad* 3 a physical and narrative stance similar to Tarpeia's position looking out from the Capitol. This stance, in Scioli's interpretation, emphasizes Helen's liminality; not only does she narrate the Greeks to the Trojans, but she moves from inside her chamber (feminine space) to the city wall (masculine space), and from silence to speech.

after her betrayal she slips away unnoticed (ἔλαθε, 2.38.5). Another messenger betrays her trust; sent to make clear to Romulus her plans (δηλώσοντα, 2.39.1) this messenger does no such thing but acts on his own to betray her (αὐτομολήσαντα, 2.39.1). In this slippery story, her lone intention to make something clear backfires on her because of the intervention of another (mis)interpreter. Ironically, this messenger's "misinterpretation" of ambiguous Tarpeia's ambiguous instruction takes the form of making her intentions clear—to the wrong audience. In light of all this elusion, Dionysius invites his reader to decide for himself:

ἀλλ' ὑπὲρ μὲν τούτων κρινέτω τις ὡς βούλεται. (2.40.3)

But regarding these matters let each decide for himself as he thinks fit.

We might compare this to Livy's closural dismissal, *tenuere tamen arcem Sabini* ("At any rate, the Sabines held the citadel," 1.12.1). In Livy's narrative, which had presented in effect the same two traditions, the difficulty of assessing Tarpeia's story lay in the overlap and conflict among many modes of identity even within individuals. I suggest that in Dionysius's case it is the elusiveness of language itself, and therefore elusiveness of the identity that stems from language, that confounds his Tarpeia.

This elusiveness helps explain one of Dionysius's stylistic features, so prominent in this passage: the use of synonyms. Certainly in a tale this long Dionysius's varied lexicon breaks monotony, but also draws attention to the variety of ways one may say the same thing. Where do synonyms fall on the scale from polysemy to monosemy? True synonyms, which are extremely rare, violate both iconicity (the one-to-one relationship between a word and its referent that characterizes monosemy) and economy of expression (the maximization of the work one word may do that characterizes polysemy).[25] Much more common are words with slight differences in meaning that may work properly in a given context. Dionysius's synonyms, under even a little scrutiny, prove not to be true synonyms but rather words that indicate subtle differences, or that better fit a context. To illustrate this, we may examine the variety of referents used to describe Tarpeia. Tarpeia is first a παρθένος and θυγάτηρ ("maiden" and "daughter" respectively, 2.38.2), then a παρθένος (2.38.4, again mentioned in conjunction with her father), then a κόρη ("girl," twice in 2.39.1, twice in 2.40.1), then a παῖς ("child," 2.40.1). There is much overlap here. παρ-

---

25. Croft 2002: 359.

θένος and κόρη both indicate maidenhood and availability for marriage, and θυγάτηρ and παῖς both involve subjugation to a head of household. But they are not true equivalents. Curiously, Tarpeia is named and called a θυγάτηρ and παρθένος when she is the subject of a sentence or initiator of an action; these terms evoke her Romanness (θυγάτηρ) and social cachet (παρθένος). When she is the object of Tatius's consideration or perpetrator of treason she becomes κόρη and παῖς, both terms suggesting her youth, inexperience, or subordination. Such contradictory roles require different signifiers, all of which are incomplete but can come together in the multivalent name Tarpeia (Τάρπεια ὄνομα, 2.38.3).

This line of thinking might be at play also in Dionysius's synonyms for the Capitol: τὸ κράτιστον τῶν ὀχυρωμάτων, τὸ Καπιτώλιον, ὁ λόφος, ὁ τόπος, τὸ χωρίον, τὸ ἐχυρώτατον, τὸ φρουρίον. In this case, the use of many words for one place suggests a readership unacquainted with the site itself, since for the Roman reader "Capitol" is enough to signify all the topography plus the military function of the locale.[26] Likewise Dionysius uses both ἀριστεροῖς (2.38.3, 2.40.1) and εὐωνύμοις (2.38.4) for "left." The former is the regular word used as an indicator of which hand, but the latter more strongly conveys a sense of foreboding; since bad omens come from the left for Greeks, εὐωνύμοις functions apotropaically. The terms are not true synonyms, but lend nuance to Dionysius's point. The two instances that use the blander word ἀριστεροῖς describe the left arms as holding golden ornaments, whether straightforwardly as in Pictor's version (2.38.3) or in the Sabines' understanding of her desire in Piso's version (2.40.1). The more foreboding εὐωνύμοις labels the left arms when they are framed by Tarpeia's ambiguous intentionality, either for gold or shields. The sense of foreboding is pointed here, because this pact will not go well for Tarpeia despite her desire to do a good deed.

The richest example of Dionysius's word variation is the range of words he uses for pledge/pledging/agreement/pact. He calls this phenomenon πίστις, ὅρκος, ὁμολογία, ἀξίωμα, cf. σύγκειμαι, συγκειμένην, ἡ συνθήκη, συντίθημι, ἡ ὑπόσχεσις, ὄμνυμι, ὑπακούω, ἀξιουμένων. The number of these that express explicitly a relationship between two or more agents is striking: forms with συν, ὑπό, and ὁμο dominate, and indicate that, in Dionysius's account, arrangement is key. Caspar de Jonge's recent analysis of Dionysius's rhetorical theory shows that Dionysius's theory and practice of language favors arrangement of words over the individual constituent

---

26. Edwards 1996: 69–70 writes, "The term 'Capitol' is ambiguous, reflecting the ambiguity of Capitolium in ancient Roman usage."

words.²⁷ This arrangement is called, by Dionysius and other theoreticians, σύνθεσις.²⁸ Indeed, σύνθεσις and ὑπόκειμαι are two words Dionysius uses both for oaths and as technical rhetorical terms (the former means "arrangement," the latter "to underlie").²⁹ The emphasis on synthesis lends importance to context in generating meaning and beauty, and away from perfect iconicity of words in which there would be only one choice for each thing a person wants to say. In this way, synonymy shares two features of polysemy: an aversion to perfect one-to-one iconicity, and a reliance on context and arrangement to harness meaning. It is not surprising also that the relational words for oath-making, except for ὁμολογία, may all also apply to architecture, an art whose intimate linkages to rhetoric and philosophy were being exploited by Dionysius's contemporary Vitruvius.³⁰ As in buildings, and also in sentences, so too it is in oaths: any element gains meaning from its position in the whole.

This episode's referents refuse to be pinned down precisely; its emphasis on meaning that shifts in context speaks to the larger concerns of Tarpeia's narrative. The flexibility inherent in a polysemic system can also be a hindrance. Piso's name, common to Greek and Latin, might not thus be so easy to trust. The commonness of language can from one perspective persuade, but can from another perspective also deceive—this from the historian who suggests that one of the Romans' greatest strengths was their ability to talk, rather than fight, through stasis (7.66.3–5). Dionysius's Tarpeia narrative is rife with ambiguity that goes both ways—ambiguity as commonality, as a bridge between diverse perspectives or elements, and ambiguity as a means of deceit or inscrutability. Of course such ambiguity is at the core of Tarpeia's story itself: is she an insider or an outsider? Given Pictor's and Piso's versions, she, like her slippery pact, can be interpreted in different ways. Does she / her commonness (seek to, serve to) bridge the gap between Sabines and Romans, or reinforce their difference?

It is important to note here that the liminal figure is exactly the one who breaks the stalemate between Romans and Sabines. The messy mixing-bowl of meanings in common language is necessary for communication, just as messy, conflicted Tarpeia is necessary to bring about the union of Sabines and Romans, which Dionysius had hailed as the happy outcome of this story before he ever spoke of Tarpeia or even the Sabine invasion, back in 2.32.1 (τέλος εὐτυχές).

---

27. De Jonge 2008: 49–90.

28. *Comp.* is a treatise on synthesis. Cf. also Obbink 1995; and Walsh 1987: 59 writes, "Philodemus envisions a synthesis of matter as well as medium."

29. *LSJ* s.v. Σύνθεσις, ὑπόκειμαι.

30. Vitruvius 1.2.1–9; see also de Jonge 2008: 33–34 and Frith 2004.

Perhaps this feature is true of any insider/outsider, such as Dionysius himself—Greek and Roman at the same time. In his work he tries to reconcile the differences of these two identities, for himself and for others also caught between their intellectual and cultural heritage on one hand and the realities of the current political milieu on the other. This reconciliation would become a central concern of the Second Sophistic,[31] but recent scholarship on Dionysius reveals it also to be important to the historian and to his readers.[32] Were these readers native Greek speakers, adjusting to Roman social and intellectual norms?[33] For such readers, who seem to be Dionysius's primary audience, the *Roman Antiquities* palliates Roman rule by appealing to κοινότης, to that which the cultures have in common, and thereby to the idea that Greeks are not necessarily outsiders in this new world, but potentially insiders. In this way he adopts the perspective—and puts the reader into the position—of an outsider looking in. This perspective is that of Tatius, so to speak, foreign, shut out from the ruling power, seeking a way to climb the hill.

Or were Dionysius's readers Greek-speaking Romans (like Fabius Pictor and Piso had been), for whom the grand history, with its parallels between Greeks and Romans, softened the differences between the two cultures and thus rendered more palatable to Roman aristocrats the social, and perhaps political, advancement of Greeks, particularly in Hellenic parts of the empire?[34] Did his grand history work more broadly to emphasize to Romans the need for and value of classicizing thought?[35] In this case, if his readers are Romans, Dionysius and his readers occupy a position analogous to that of Tarpeia, a position on the inside looking out at a people who have something desirable to offer.[36]

Dionysius, like Tarpeia, like common language, is the polysemic medium through which these two audiences may meet.

---

31. See Pelling 2007: 244 on Dionysius as harbinger of Second Sophistic anxieties about conflicted identity, anxieties explored in such studies as Swain 1996; Gleason 1995; Whitmarsh 2005; Goldhill 2001; and Anderson 1993.
32. See Wiater 2001 and Schmitz and Wiater 2011.
33. See 1.5.1. Schultze 1986: 138–39.
34. Luraghi 2003 and a compromise position in Weaire 2007.
35. Wiater 2011: 204n525. De Jonge's (2008) discussion of Dionysius's Atticizing style fits in here as well; he concludes that it might have ingratiated Dionysius and his ideas to his educated Roman patrons, who had, in the Augustan age, re-embraced Atticism over the bombast of the Asiatic style that had infiltrated Roman rhetoric in the late Republic. See p. 17, with notes.
36. Habinek 1998: 3 (after Bourdieu) as "augmenting the symbolic capital of the Roman state by through expropriation of the cultural resources of recently colonized communities." See also Wiater 2011: 222 on Dionysius's classicism.

CHAPTER TEN

SONGWORTHY ATHENS, INVINCIBLE ROME

TARPEIA IN PLUTARCH'S *ROMULUS*

WHEN PLUTARCH approached the myth of Tarpeia, he was writing an altogether different sort of text: a biography of Romulus. His aim was not, therefore, to illuminate the succession of kings in early Rome or the role of women in Rome's development, nor to meditate on cultural stereotypes of Italic peoples new to Rome, nor to single out Tarpeia as a symbol of the pressure exerted on an individual by shared needs of the community. To appear in a biography of Romulus, Tarpeia must matter to Romulus's life story. Her inclusion could be justified by contingency alone: her treason happened during Romulus's life and therefore illuminates his milieu. Plutarch takes his narrative further than mere contingency, crafting a narrative that invites meditation on Romulus's leadership, on his role as Rome's founder, and on Rome's role in the world.

This chapter explores these invitations in turn. In the first section I trace how Plutarch shapes and embellishes Tarpeia's tale so as to contribute to his project of illuminating and studying Romulus as a man and leader. Plutarch follows the common version of a greedy Roman Tarpeia, but he mentions several variations to the tale that dwell on Tarpeia's connection to Romulus. As a result Romulus, though not a character in her story per se, emerges from it as a shrewd and savvy leader. What is more, in the middle of his tale, Plutarch pauses the tale to focus on her punishment at Tatius's bidding and to dwell on the general moral conundrum it poses: how to deal with a traitor when the treason is beneficial (*Rom.* 17.3). Plutarch universalizes the conundrum by citing other instances of leaders who had to decide how to handle bad but useful behavior. The result of Plutarch's focus, I argue, is a meditation on Rome's delicate relationship with those on its margins, those with some connection—but not a complete connection—to Rome. Tarpeia is one such figure, as are Tatius and his Sabines, and also Rome's client kings and other subjects.

I then move on to the relationship of Tarpeia's story with a passage late in the *Romulus* when Plutarch muses on the origins of the Nonae Caprotinae. He first explains this festival as a ritual commemoration of the public panic after Romulus's disappearance from the earth. Plutarch then lingers on a second explanation which is completely unconnected to Romulus (*Rom.* 29.2–11), as follows: After the Gallic sack, when Latins besieged the weakened Rome demanding Sabine-style intermarriage, the Romans instead followed a ruse proposed by the slave girl Philotis. She and other slaves would enter the camp tricked out as Roman brides, seduce and disarm the men, then invite by signal fire the Roman soldiers. It worked, and the Latin threat was repelled. In this scenario—discounted by Plutarch but told at much greater length—the annual festival of the Nonae Caprotinae re-enacts the Romans's excitement at the nocturnal invasion. The girl's stratagem, Rome besieged, and the explicit reference to the Sabine synoikism—not to mention Plutarch's earlier mention of a strand of the Tarpeia legend that situates her at the time of the Gallic sack—invite a comparison not only between Tarpeia and Philotis, but, more broadly, between Rome's founder and its re-founder Camillus—again, not for the first time in this biography. Like the meditation on the utility of traitors that appears within Plutarch's Tarpeia narrative, the linkage with Camillus via the Philotis digression also universalizes the events of Romulus's lifetime, and presents alternatives by which we may judge his actions.

The understanding of Romulus that we find through consideration of Tarpeia's inset tale is compounded and confounded when we consider her role in the larger unit of the paired Lives *Romulus-Theseus*. In the third section of this chapter I explore Tarpeia's functional and narrative counterpart in the *Theseus*: the Amazon invasion of Athens, a battle enjoined because of a stolen woman, fought in the Athenian cityscape, and commemorated, like Tarpeia's action, by women's graves (*Thes.* 27.1–9, cf. Tarpeia's monuments in *Rom.* 18.1). The graves are my point of departure. Unlike Tarpeia's urban legacy, which in Plutarch's account is uncontested, he mentions multiple monuments commemorating the Amazonomachy, and he notes conflicting interpretations about their precise connection to the war. Plutarch even observes that Amazon graves attest similar conflicts in places all around Greece (*Thes.* 27.2–6).

I argue that this difference between topographical certainty in Rome and uncertainty in Athens is a powerful symbol for the two dominant themes of this pair of Lives: the difference between history and myth, and the difference between Rome and Athens. We shall find that these two themes are mutually implicated, and that these Lives together with their synkrisis—that is, the evaluative synthesis Plutarch offers of the pair—help explain to Plutarch's audience Rome's succession of Greece in the Mediterranean and, in a way, help to justify it. Rome's success, like Romulus's and Camillus's, derives from a canny ability to exploit all resources, even the dangerous ones, to its own advantage.

THE STORY ITSELF

For the modern critic, one virtue of Plutarch's Tarpeia tale is the fact that he preserves three otherwise unknown versions of the myth and one version otherwise attested but not attributed securely. Indeed, Tarpeia's story is one of the richest in the *Romulus* in terms of the plurality and disagreement of named sources.[1] When recounting the canonical version of the story (Fabius Pictor's, fleshed out a bit), of which he approves, Plutarch cites no sources. He reserves his citations for sources with which he (and tradition) disagree. Plutarch's inclusion of these variants begs the question: why include them just to reject them? In the *Nicias*, Plutarch dismisses the notion that he is merely a collector of trivia, of useless pieces of information. Rather, he aims always to feed his character study:

> τὰ διαφεύγοντα τοὺς πολλούς, ὑφ' ἑτέρων δ' εἰρημένα σποράδην ἢ πρὸς ἀναθήμασιν ἢ ψηφίσμασιν εὑρημένα παλαιοῖς πεπείραμαι συναγαγεῖν, οὐ τὴν ἄχρηστον ἀθροίζων ἱστορίαν, ἀλλὰ τὴν πρὸς κατανόησιν ἤθους καὶ τρόπου παραδιδούς.[2] (*Nicias* 1.5)

And such things as escape the notice of most writers, and which are told

---

1. There are five variants offered for Tarpeia: the orthodox, unattributed version Plutarch prefers plus three named and one unnamed variant. Its variation is surpassed only at the very beginning of the *Romulus,* where Plutarch offers seven versions of the origin of Rome's name and four for Romulus's lineage. Most of the stories in the *Romulus* present two or three variants.

2. I am using Perrin's 1914 text for Loeb. All translations are mine.

sporadically in other men's writings, or appear on votive offerings, I shall bring together—not as a useless study of trivia, but providing an understanding of character and temperament.

Though the lesser-known anecdotes to which he refers here are about Nicias himself (e.g., the story of Nicias's response to a dressed-up slave at *Nicias* 3.3), it is fair also to look for such meaning or importance in the citations about Tarpeia's story. Two avenues, not exclusive of each other and perhaps even intertwined, suggest themselves. First, the variants add something to the study of Romulus's character and temperament. In fact, three of the four variants allow Plutarch to insert Romulus into the story where he is otherwise absent. Second, they powerfully demonstrate that there are no firm conclusions to be drawn about Rome's inaugural king.

Plutarch rejects the notion that some authors share (ὡς ἔνιοι λέγουσιν, *Rom.* 17.2) that Tarpeia was herself put in charge of the citadel rather than Tarpeius. The detail of Tarpeia's guardianship also appears in passing in Ovid, in Appian, and in Pseudo-Plutarch *Parallela minora* 15;[3] this latter version has an erotic motivation for our traitor and compares her to Demonike of Ephesus, who betrayed her town for love of Brennus the Gaul. Plutarch attributes the latter of these, a version with an erotic motivation for Tarpeia, to the *Italika* of Aristides Milesius, second-century BCE author of raunchy tales. This is a problematic attribution, and Aristides's version figures later in this chapter.[4] Plutarch rejects the "Tarpeia-as-guardian" version because it would make Romulus into a simpleton, (εὐήθη τὸν Ῥωμύλον ἀποδεικνύοντες). The unnamed source's authors (ἔνιοι) either believed such a decision on Romulus's part to be possible without censure, or didn't concern themselves with the implications for Romulus's character.[5] Plutarch cannot let that stand; he clearly does not find Romulus to be εὐήθης, whether that word is used positively (guileless, good-hearted) or negatively (foolish, simple-minded).[6] Here is a clear case

---

3. Ovid *Fasti* 1.261; Appian, preserved in the Suidas under σφραγὶς and Τάτιος dependent on an emendation from Ἀρριανὸς to Ἀππιανός (see Sanders on *Suidas* 1904: 21); *Parallela minora* 15 = Aristides Milesius *Italika*, see *FGrH* 286.

4. Sanders calls this attribution bunk (1904: 20–22): of the nineteen times that pseudo-Plutarch cites Aristides Milesius, only five find any support elsewhere; moreover, Sanders thinks it unlikely that Aristides wrote an Italian history. Whether or not this or any Aristides was Plutarch's source, it *is* possible that the tale was eroticized before Propertius's version of c.16 BCE.

5. The detail seems not to be a relic of an early and hostile tradition, but rather a later narrative choice to explain Tarpeia's presence at the crucial place and time. Other authors (Propertius 4.4.15–18, 36; Livy 1.11.6) suggest Tarpeia's access and freedom of movement were the result of her Vestal priesthood.

6. See *LSJ* s.v. εὐήθεια 1 and 2.

of Plutarch assimilating factual material to moral criteria, a phenomenon that is particularly useful in those Lives, such as *Romulus*, whose subjects inhabit a tradition mired in doubt and uncertainty.[7] I am not sure that Plutarch's assessment of Romulus is altogether flattering, but Romulus's shrewdness is a feature of the Roman king throughout the biography and a powerful point of contrast with his Greek counterpart Theseus.[8]

The three other discrepant sources, which appear at the end of the anecdote, are given names and more detail. Plutarch first cites a detail found in Sulpicius Galba, preserved by Juba. S. Sulpicius Galba is the grandfather of the emperor Galba of 69 CE. Grandfather Galba is said to have been a man "more renowned in learning than in rank" and author of an elaborate and probing history (*clarior studiis quam dignitate . . . multiplicem nec incuriosam historiam edidit*, Suetonius *Galba* 3.2).[9] Juba, who preserves the detail used by Plutarch, is Juba II, learned client king of Mauretania from 25 BCE to 23 CE. Plutarch cites him two other times in the *Romulus* as a source for the rape of the Sabine women (14.6, 15.3), and elsewhere calls him "the most erudite of kings" (*Sert.* 9.5).[10] He trusts the source. Tarpeia wasn't the only one to suffer, if Sulpicius Galba is right:

ἑάλω δὲ καὶ Ταρπήιος προδοσίας ὑπὸ Ῥωμύλου διωχθείς, ὡς Ἰόβας φησὶ Γάλβαν Σουλπίκιον ἱστορεῖν. (*Rom.* 17.5)

And Tarpeius was also convicted of treason when prosecuted by Romulus, as, Juba says, Sulpicius Galba relates.

Plutarch neither endorses nor rejects Sulpicius's detail, though the delay of the citation until after the detail leads to acceptance rather than rejection. Sulpicius Galba's variant, that Tarpeius was also prosecuted and convicted of treason by Romulus, hints at a wider guilt than Tarpeia's alone—perhaps even a conspiracy of the sort that was eventually thought to have organized the assassination of the king at *Rom.* 27.5. Or, it could reveal a proactive Romulus, unwilling to brook dissension in his own ranks. Either way, Plutarch again inserts the notion of a savvy or proactive Romulus into the tale, allowing Romulus some agency in a story in which he is most often the reagent.

---

7. Jones 1971: 88–89.
8. Larmour 1988 sketches the difference between shrewd Romulus and guileless Theseus.
9. Plutarch *Rom.* 17.5 = *HRR* ii.41 (Sulpicius Galba); only one other fragment survives.
10. Pliny the Elder (*HN* 5.16) and Athenaeus (3.83b) also compliment Juba's work. For Juba see Duane Roller's 2003 book on him and his literary output.

Plutarch is more disparaging of the third and fourth variants. The third variant he cites is that of an Antigonus, presumably the author of a history of Italy from the third to the second century BCE.[11] In Antigonus's version Tarpeia was a Sabine woman, Tatius's daughter no less, presumably one of those kidnapped by Romulus:

τῶν δ' ἄλλα περὶ Ταρπηίας λεγόντων ἀπίθανοι μέν εἰσιν οἱ Τατίου θυγατέρα τοῦ ἡγεμόνος τῶν Σαβίνων οὖσαν αὐτήν, Ῥωμύλῳ δὲ βίᾳ συνοικοῦσαν, ἱστοροῦντες ταῦτα ποιῆσαι καὶ παθεῖν ὑπὸ τοῦ πατρός· ὧν καὶ Ἀντίγονός ἐστι. (*Rom.* 17.5)

Regarding others who speak about Tarpeia, they are entirely untrustworthy who say that she was the daughter of Tatius, the Sabine general, and that she was living with Romulus by force. They say that she did these things and also suffered at the command of her father. Antigonus was one such writer.

Antigonus's Sabine Tarpeia lays emphasis on ethnicity in ways that resonated with an audience witnessing Rome's ascendancy within Italy and beyond. When mentioning this variant, Plutarch is careful to note that she was one of the Sabine girls living with Romulus by force. My sense is that Plutarch rejects this version primarily because it eliminates Tarpeia's treason altogether, thus vitiating the opportunity for moral exploration and commentary that Plutarch seizes in this episode, discussed below. But mentioning it allows the biographer to draw attention again to Romulus as architect of the rape, an affair in which Romulus comes off as shrewd by converting outrage into opportunity (14.2), but also as restrained and well-intentioned (14.6 and cf. *Syn.* 6.2). Even this rejected variant thus supports Plutarch's assessment of Romulus.

The fourth version Plutarch rejects is a poem by the otherwise unknown elegiac poet Simylus. Simylus offers a radical rewriting of Tarpeia's story, situating it later in Rome's history and tinkering with other details: presenting love as her motive rather than greed, Brennus the Gaul as her beneficiary rather than Tatius the Sabine, and the fourth century BCE as her historical context rather than Romulean Rome. The meaning and import of this perplexing text are the focus of chapter 8. Here I wish only to discuss Plutarch's inclusion of Simylus's poem. As with Antigonus's account,

---

11. *FGrH* 816. Other people named Antigonus writing at more or less the same time confuse the question of this author's identity; see Dorandi 1999 for arguments separating this Antigonus from the same-named author(s) of biographies of philosophers and treatises on art history.

Plutarch is careful to firmly prejudice our reading in advance : Σιμύλος δ' ὁ ποιητὴς καὶ παντάπασι ληρεῖ, "Simylus the poet is completely absurd in thinking . . ." (17.5). Plutarch's summary of Simylus's absurdity draws attention to two heterodoxies: Tarpeia's betrayal to the Gauls rather than Sabines (μὴ Σαβίνοις . . . ἀλλὰ Κελτοῖς), and her motivation to do so (love, ἐρασθεῖσαν). The fragments he quotes illustrate precisely these rejected points:

> Κελτῶν ἢ στέρξασα γαμήλια λέκτρα γενέσθαι σκηπτούχῳ, πατέρων οὐκ ἐφύλαξε δόμους. (*Rom. 17.5*)

> Longing for a wedding with the chieftain of the Celts, she did not protect the homes of her fathers.

Set during the Gallic sack, Simylus's poem allows Plutarch no opportunity for Romulean insertion or commentary. It must be dismissed. Just after the quotation Plutarch confirms his own (and the orthodox) chronological context for Tarpeia's story. At *Rom.* 18.1, he mentions that the Tarpeian rock is named for her grave on that site, and that this grave predates Tarquin, who moved it to make way for the temple of Jupiter. The Tarpeian rock is, to Plutarch, concrete proof that Simylus is wrong; to depart from the tradition too much requires rewriting what happens later. The Tarpeian rock, which (Plutarch is careful to note) still serves to punish criminals, also, to Plutarch's readers, witnesses both the veracity of Plutarch's account and the interconnectedness of distant past and present. This begs the question: why include Simylus's variant just to exclude it? One clue might be found in a citation of a different Greek elegiac poet later in the text. At *Rom.* 21.6, a certain Butas is discredited for his account of the Lupercalia, which Plutarch calls αἰτίας μυθώδεις ἐν ἐλεγείοις, "fabulous explanations in elegiac verse." The twin dismissals of Greek elegiac accounts of ancient Rome suggest that readers should proceed with caution when this genre turns its mischievous eye to Rome's past; while such poetic flights of fancy assert themselves against the canon of stories, so to speak, they cannot and do not account for that canon— in this case, Rome's history. At the same time they draw attention to the interplay between genre and narrative that highlights the biographical focus of Plutarch's text—in his tale, Tarpeia's story is about individuals and their choices.

The other detour Plutarch makes from his core narrative of Tarpeia also has implications for the life and character of his hero and for the continuity of past and present. Just after describing Tarpeia's motivation to betray (desire for gold bracelets) but before mentioning Tatius's punishment of her (killing her with shields), Plutarch offers other examples of the treatment of traitors:

> συνθεμένου δὲ τοῦ Τατίου, νύκτωρ ἀνοίξασα πύλην μίαν, ἐδέξατο τοὺς Σαβίνους. οὐ μόνος οὖν ὡς ἔοικεν Ἀντίγονος ἔφη προδιδόντας μὲν φιλεῖν, προδεδωκότας δὲ μισεῖν, οὐδὲ Καῖσαρ, εἰπὼν ἐπὶ τοῦ Θρᾳκὸς Ῥοιμητάλκου, φιλεῖν μὲν προδοσίαν, προδότην δὲ μισεῖν, ἀλλὰ κοινόν τι τοῦτο πάθος ἐστὶ πρὸς τοὺς πονηροὺς τοῖς δεομένοις αὐτῶν, ὥσπερ ἰοῦ καὶ χολῆς ἐνίων θηρίων δέονται· τὴν γὰρ χρείαν ὅτε λαμβάνουσιν ἀγαπῶντες, ἐχθαίρουσι τὴν κακίαν ὅταν τύχωσι. τοῦτο καὶ πρὸς τὴν Ταρπηίαν τότε παθὼν ὁ Τάτιος. (*Rom.* 17.3–4)

> Tatius agreed to her terms, and at night she opened one gate and admitted the Sabines. Antigonus wasn't alone in saying he loved the one betraying but hated the one who has betrayed, nor was Caesar Augustus, who, talking about the Thracian Rhoimetalces, said he loved the treason, hated the traitor. But this is a common feeling toward the wicked by those who need them, just as people need the gall and venom of wild beasts. They appreciate them when they have need of them, but they hate their evil when they've gotten what they want. Tatius felt this same way toward Tarpeia at that time.

It is unlikely that this Antigonus is Antigonus Carystius, cited as author of the "Tarpeia-as-Sabine" variant. First, the apothegm is an ill fit for that version even if Tarpeia acted and suffered at her father's behest (ποιῆσαι καὶ παθεῖν ὑπὸ τοῦ πατρός, 17.5). Second, if the two authors were the same, Plutarch's editorializing "Antigonus wasn't alone in saying . . ." makes no sense. Third and most serious, Plutarch's phrasing suggests either a gnomic statement or that Antigonus is reporting his own, not someone else's, feelings. A plausible alternative suggested by Ziegler in his 1970 translation is Antigonus Gonatas, Macedonian ruler and progenitor of the Antigonid dynasty in the late third century BCE. Ziegler notes that Antigonus Gonatas, unlike the historian Carystius, is a man who would be in a position to need and discard traitors and is a better partner for the second comparandum, Caesar (Augustus).[12] Augustus is said to have expressed this same sentiment to Rhoimetalces, a Thracian king who left Antony's party

---

12. Ziegler (1914) 1970 *ad loc.*, followed by Manfredini and Ampolo 1988 *ad loc.*

for the rising triumvir. Plutarch's readers may recall that Augustus's comment also appears in his *Apothegms of Leaders and Generals*, a compilation of snippets of leadership and wit organized leader by leader and dedicated to Trajan. In the section on Augustus, Plutarch relates the following:

> Ἐπεὶ δὲ Ῥοιμητάλκης ὁ τῶν Θρᾳκῶν βασιλεὺς ἀπ' Ἀντωνίου μεταβαλόμενος πρὸς αὐτὸν οὐκ ἐμετρίαζε παρὰ τοὺς πότους, ἀλλ' ἦν ἐπαχθὴς ὀνειδίζων τὴνσυμμαχίαν, προπιὼν τινι τῶν ἄλλων βασιλέων ὁ Καῖσαρ εἶπεν 'ἐγὼ προδοσίαν φιλῶ, προδότας δ' οὐκ ἐπαινῶ.' (*Apothegms* 207a)

> Rhoimetalces king of the Thracians, having defected from Antony to Augustus, when he did not practice moderation in drinking but made himself annoying by reproaching his new alliance, Augustus, drinking to one of the other kings who were present, said "I love treason, but I don't approve of the traitor."

The two versions of Augustus's apothegm are not strictly identical, and their disparity is highly suggestive of Plutarch's compositional methods. Plutarch did not copy one text directly from the other; rather, he relied on the same set of notes[13]—or even on his memory[14]—for each usage of the story. The difference between Augustus's apothegm in the *Romulus* and the version given in the *Apothegms* reveals the thrust of its appearance in the Tarpeia episode. In the *Apothegms*, the spotlight is on the traitor. Rhoimetalces seems to have earned the barb. The Thracian was an insolent drunk; Augustus was wise to keep him at a distance and justified in alerting him to that distance. Consequently, the *Apothegms*' Augustus comes off rather well.[15] In the *Romulus*, in contrast, Rhoimetalces doesn't insult, and Augustus's comment is as removed from its narrative framework as is the cryptic and uncontextualized comment by the unknown Antigonus. Plutarch even changes the Augustan verb, from ἐπαινῶ in the *Apothegms* to φιλεῖν in the *Romulus*, so that the two apothegms supporting Tatius's

---

13. Pelling 2002: 65–90 on the *Apothegms*' composition and on parallel composition of some Lives too. The side-by-side pairing of Antigonus Gonatas's and Augustus's apothegms in the *Romulus* lends support to Pelling's understanding of the compositional methods (2002: 65–90); Gonatas's *Apothegm* might have appeared in the preparatory notes for the Apothegms, but was left out because Gonatas was not one of the featured leaders.

14. Bowie 2000: 129–30.

15. Such an approach to the anecdote befits the *Apothegms*, a text designed to appeal and inspire by its brevity and its focus on a leader's successes; see 172e last sentence on the great men; Pelling 2002: 65–90 on the apothegms' purpose.

punishment of Tarpeia will match more closely and so that they will have a gnomic air. Stripped of their details, the two examples of the apothegm transfer emphasis from the traitor onto the powerful men who exploit them.[16] Plutarch's third take on the apothegm embraces anyone who uses treacherous measures (not just traitors) to serve his own ends. People, Plutarch elaborates, tolerate the wicked (πονηροὺς) while they're useful, then discard and abhor them when their usefulness is spent, just as they tolerate venomous animals when they need venom or gall (*Rom.* 17.3). We are not told to what ends one might need venom or gall, but the use that springs most quickly to mind is magic; whether the magic is benign or malign, it is a risky tool.

Nothing in the tradition approaches the digression the biographer offers to explain Tatius's response. To be sure, earlier authors had commented on the odd phenomenon that Tatius killed his benefactress,[17] but none of these broadens the killing of Tarpeia into a universal parable of opportunism in action. The earliest sources, discussed in chapters 2 and 3, erase or explain away the inconsistency of Tatius's action by connecting it to his Sabine identity. Either the Sabines were treacherous through and through, oath-breakers all (Fabius Pictor), or, Tatius, meeting a Roman Tarpeia trying to double-cross his people, simply punished a still-and-always enemy, who was then honored by the Romans for her service (Piso, followed by Dionysius). No inconsistency there.

Augustan-age sources note and express the inconsistency somewhat differently (see chapters 5, 6, and 7). Livy offers two suggestions. Tatius either kills Tarpeia so as to give the impression that the citadel was taken by force; here is a relic of the earlier "tricky Sabines" tradition that places blame in Tatius's hands for treating Tarpeia unfairly. Or, in a version that reflects the Sabines' later social and ideological status as honest countrymen, Tatius killed by way of example, lest there be any faith given to traitors (1.11). Propertius too implies Sabine morality; in his poem, "not even an enemy gives honor to a traitor" (*neque enim sceleri dedit hostis honorem*, 4.4.89). Valerius Maximus, in the section on treachery in his *Facta et dicta memorabilia* (9.6.1), explicitly absolves Tatius of all wrongdoing: *absit reprehensio, quia impia proditio celeri poena vindicata est* (Let there be no censure, since unholy treason was punished by swift reckoning). It is interesting to note that, in addition to rehabilitating the Sabines, the Augustan

---

16. One wonders whether, as successors of Alexander and Caesar who solidified and stabilized their dynasties, Gonatas and Augustus would have been a pair.

17. Of course, the visual renditions of Tarpeia's myth, focusing as they do on her punishment, invite reflection but offer no solutions.

age spawned such strong statements about the universal and transcendent guilt of the traitor (shades of Antony may be detected here); as I explored in the second part of this book, the Augustan age's predominant interest in Tarpeia was as a probe into questions about the individual's role and identity vis-à-vis the state.

Plutarch blames neither the traitor nor her punisher; rather, his digression on treason and its beneficiaries, and the tale it illumines, observe rather than judge the interaction between Tarpeia and Tatius. It is true that Plutarch's digression focuses more on Tatius's position than on Tarpeia's treason, but without the blame and the specific ethnic coloring he receives in the earliest written sources. His decision to kill Tarpeia is made as a leader, not as a Sabine. Plutarch's first two examples of treason-punishment reveal that such opportunism is a regal trait, and the second points more specifically to the emerging monarch; one could still defect from Antony. Tatius is also an emerging monarch, destined to rival Romulus in their eventual joint kingship but never to emerge because Romulus is more powerful and savvy.[18] Here I recall the passing references to Romulus that Plutarch inserts in the variants he records for Tarpeia's story. Rome's first king is present in Tarpeia's tale itself, and he is present in the digression about opportunism as the monarch who does emerge, rather than the weaker Tatius who is outshone in the list "Tatius-Antigonus-Augustus." In a way, those monarchs' apothegms become substitutes for Romulus's own missing remarks, lost to the centuries. The *Romulus* is strikingly poor in direct speech by the subject, and Romulus is not represented in the *Apothegms*.[19]

Some readers have seen in this biography Plutarch's moral disapproval of Rome's founder,[20] while others have seen a Plutarch more forgiving to the Roman king.[21] It is possible, though, not to have to choose between these extremes. The Lives, after all, are after something different, an exploration rather than exposition of morality.[22] Plutarch admits as much in the

---

18. Romulus's skillful navigation of the controversies surrounding Tatius's death shows his superiority to the Sabine king (*Rom.* 23.4). He had earlier, of course, outmaneuvered Remus (*Rom.* 9.5).

19. By way of contrast, Caesar and Cicero, both represented in the *Apothegms*, speak frequently in their Lives.

20. Larmour 1992: 4167 argues that in contrast to other depictions of Romulus's emotional state after the fratricide, "Plutarch's Romulus shows remarkably little sorrow at his brother's death." Also Larmour 1988: 371 discusses Plutarch's "blackening" of Romulus in his narrative.

21. Jones 1971: 88–94 for whom Plutarch gives voice to the bad tradition but generally prefers the generous one.

22. Pelling 2002: 237–49, especially 239, where he writes of Plutarch, "works can be ethically reflective and exploratory, without always producing conclusions which can be reduced to a simple expository imperative 'do that,' 'avoid this.'"

preface to the *Apothegms*, where he explains that, whereas the catalogue of sayings presents a leader at his best and most controlled, the Lives expand on this to present also a leader's responses to the contingencies of chance:

καίτοι καὶ βίους ἔχει τὸ σύνταγμα τῶν ἐπιφανεστάτων παρά τε Ῥωμαίοις καὶ παρ' Ἕλλησιν ἡγεμόνων καὶ νομοθετῶν καὶ αὐτοκρατόρων ἀλλὰ τῶν μὲν πράξεων αἱ πολλαὶ τύχην ἀναμεμιγμένην ἔχουσιν. (*Apothegms* 172D)

Indeed my book comprises also the Lives of the most notable, among Romans and Greeks alike, of rulers, lawgivers, and monarchs, but the majority of their actions have chance mixed in.

Tatius's decision is not a purely abstract position but real-life pragmatism, a portrait of a man in action. The syntax of the comparanda encapsulates this feature nicely; in Antigonus's formulation, the tenses of the participles illustrate the moment of and just after the decision (προδιδόντας ... προδεδωκότας), and their number indicates a repeatable situation, whereas the more abstract nouns of Augustus's formulation (slightly different from the one given in the *Apothegms*) elevates the principle to a sort of maxim (προδοσίαν ... προδότην).[23] The repetition of such decisions by leaders across cultures and times—eighth-century Sabine, third-century Greek, and first-century Roman—renders the observation applicable to any rising or risen monarch. The third example points the finger at Plutarch's readers as well,[24] and beyond; we all make such choices when faced with the need for a dangerous ally.

This episode and its digression on opportunism reveal in miniature a conclusion emerging in recent criticism on Plutarch's works: that they offer no easy moral lessons. The difficulty comes not only in the admixture of good and bad traits in all Plutarch's subjects, a notion supported by the scorecard technique of the synkrisis. It is also a feature of the ambiguity of virtue itself. Plutarch's Lives leave us with a number of questions and much food for thought: is virtue universal, or is it culturally bound?[25] Does it produce or is it the product of praise?[26] What balance of utility and justice

---

23. Pelling 2002: 95 explores this aspect.
24. See Larmour 1992: 4167: "Here the reader is actually brought into the selection process and encouraged to see the more probable version for himself."
25. See *Thes.* 6.4 and cf. Ingenkamp 2004: 71.
26. Ingenkamp 2004: 69: "Fame and praise are consequences of virtue."

is the best?[27] What are the relative merits of personal virtues versus national interests?[28] Or of ineffective good deeds versus effective bad deeds?[29] These sorts of questions do not arise in a cultural or intellectual vacuum, but are forged at the Second Sophistic's meeting of Academy, Lyceum, and Roman rhetorical practice.[30]

Plutarch forces more moral complexity out of Tarpeia's story than does any other author, for he reveals that hers is not the only morally ambiguous action. In fact, in Plutarch's version Tarpeia's action is no different from Tatius's except in its failure to achieve her goals. She, too, was willing to use dangerous means to achieve her ends. Tatius's opportunism itself is neither bad nor good; Plutarch is careful to withhold judgment on it. It simply is, and some people are better at it than others. He also refrains from judgment on Tarpeia's guilt; the closest he comes to moral evaluation is to imply that she is wicked when he says that people need then discard the wicked (πονηροὺς, "toilsome," a word that is not always pejorative),[31] and that her rock is still (ἔτι νῦν) the site for punishing malefactors (κακούργους, 18.1). His account is thus also thoughtful about the enduring power of her story at Rome. Why repeat and enshrine a tale so potentially embarrassing to Rome? The question certainly vexed Piso (see chapter 3). For Plutarch, it is that every part of Tarpeia's story is about turning, or trying to turn, dodgy circumstances to one's own advantage. For Plutarch, this is the Rome that conquered the nobler, but less durable, Greece.

I would like to draw brief attention to two interconnected ideas that emerge from the conclusions I have just outlined. First, Plutarch's choice of variants suggests something about Tarpeia's marginality, her position as an insider-outsider. It is necessary for the workings of the story—and the lessons it may impart—that she be a marginal figure. For her treason to work she must have inside information or access, and loyalty to the outside.[32] Plutarch rejects versions of the story in which she leans too much to one side or the other. She is not guardian of the gate; she would thus be too attached, and Romulus would not trust such a position of authority

---

27. Pérez Jiménez 1996; see also Roskam and Van der Stockt 2011, whose collected essays (especially those by Opsamer and Martin) make a case that in the end, utility and justice coincide.

28. Duff 1997; and cf. Larmour 1992: 4167, who discusses the "stark contrast" between Plutarch's depiction of his Romulus's grief after the loss of his brother and Theseus's grief after the loss of his father.

29. Duff 1997.

30. See the studies particularly of Pelling 2002: 1–2; Stadter 2002: 2–4; Ingenkamp 2004, etc.

31. πονηρὸς can qualify the victim of toils as well as their cause; see *LSJ* s.v. I–II.

32. See the discussion of Tarpeia as an insider-outsider in chapter 1.

to someone marginal.[33] Nor is she a Sabine wife; in this case she would be too detached. Indeed, the anatomy of treason inset into the tale similarly shines a spotlight onto the marginality of the traitor—and on a ruler's or society's need to keep them marginal, drawing them in when useful then casting them out when not. In this way the marginal figure both opens borders (literal and metaphorical) and reinforces them; Tarpeia gets out and then is shut out; the Sabine women are brought in then shut in.

Second, true to his promise in the *Nicias* 1.4, Plutarch presents obscure details and sources not found in the usual places. Of the four variants he lists to the narrative he accepts—one anonymous, one by Sulpicius Galba through Juba, one by Antigonus, and one by Simylus—only one (the anonymous variant) is found in any other sources before Plutarch. Another (Sulpicius Galba's) is corroborated after Plutarch's time. The two others—Antigonus's and Simylus's—appear nowhere else in the extant tradition. Plutarch's choice at once asserts the presence of rival versions to the canonical, unattributed version he supports, and makes apparent the power of that dominant tradition to suppress the others. All the rejected versions are by foreign—specifically Greek—authors; only Sulpicius Galba's detail is accepted as credible. On the other hand, the source he does accept is that of Fabius Pictor, a Roman through and through, followed also by Livy, Dionysius of Halicarnassus (in part), and Valerius Maximus. Roman tradition in this case has a great power to make rival versions— be they local histories or hostile interpretations—look like variants rather than like the real version. Perhaps it is because the Romans were willing to embrace an unflattering tradition as their own and make the most of it. In a sense, this is the same thing as befriending a traitor.

ZOOMING OUT: PHILOTIS

Romulus ends with Romulus's death—or, not quite; Plutarch finishes his biography with a discussion of a festival that arose from Romulus's death— or, not quite. The Nonae Caprotinae might instead have arisen in the time of Camillus two and a half centuries later, and Plutarch ends his biography of the first founder with an aition for that festival contextualized by the second founder. Plutarch discredits this aition but lingers over the tale in such a way as to draw attention to Romulus and Camillus as parallels, similar figures in a continuum of the Roman world.

---

33. A telling comparison is the too-attached Lucrezia Borgia, put in charge of the Vatican when her father, Pope Alexander VI, went on campaign. She was so attached that rumors of incest arose.

The aition powerfully recalls Tarpeia's story. Camillus had just repelled the Gallic threat of 390 BCE when the nearby Latins thought it best to seize the opportunity presented by Rome's weakened defenses to press their own advantage. They marched on Rome under Livius Postumius, halted near the city, and asked the Romans to renew their former alliance by sending Roman widows and virgins to be Latin brides (*Rom.* 29.4). The Romans were saved from acting on this proposal by a stratagem of the slave girl Philotis, who proposed to dress as a Roman bride, infiltrate the Latin camp with other decked-out slave girls, and betray it to the Romans by lighting a signal fire when the Latins were asleep. This Philotis did, successfully. The fig tree (*caproficus*) in which she lit the fire gave its name to the festival Nonae Caprotinae (July 7) and the material for the festival tents used to house the feasting women. During the festival, servant girls engage in rollicking play to commemorate their participation in the Roman victory (*Rom.* 29.6).

Parallels and conflations abound. Plutarch offers two possible origins for the Nonae: Romulean (29.2) or Camillan (29.3, 6). As a result there are two possible explanations for the name of this festival: Caprotinae (alternate spelling: Capratinae) from goat (*capra*) marsh (*Rom.* 29.2), or from a type of wild fig tree (*caprificus*, *Rom.* 29.6) whose fruit is edible to goats.[34] When discussing the Romulean setting for the Nonae Caprotinae, Plutarch pairs this festival with the Poplifugium, mistakenly even placing them on the same day (29.1).[35] In the Romulean context, the Poplifugium re-enacts the people's fear and flight at Romulus's mysterious death, while the Nonae re-enacts their departure from the city and sacrifice at the Goat's Marsh, shouting each other's names. Plutarch's description of the Camillan-era ritual at 29.3 seems to subsume the Poplifugium as well, even if it doesn't mention it specifically, since the Romans rushed out in great haste (ἐπείξεως ... καὶ σπουδῆς) to fight the Latins. Indeed, Varro does suggest a Camillan setting for the origin of the Poplifugium, attributing it to the people's flight from the Gauls (*de Ling.* 6.18). Two linked festivals, two potential historical origins for each of the two, two

---

34. Plutarch's spelling is matched by *CIL* IV.1555. Varro *de Ling.* 6.18, Macrobius *Saturnalia* 1.11.35–40, and Ausonius *de Fer.* 23.9 call the festival the Nonae Caprotinae; Bremmer 1981: 77 posits that Varro amended the festival name to link it with Juno Caprotina.

35. The Poplifugium fell on July 5 and the Nones on July 7; see Polemius Silvius at *CIL* 1.2.269. Wiseman 2004: 171 discusses the eventual inclusion of the Nonae Caprotinae within the Ludi Apollinares. As Bremmer points out (1981: 84–85), these festivals are unique in their calendrical placement, being the only two festivals on or before the Nones, and the only two in the long spell between June 12 and July 19.

founders of Rome, two wars with Latins, two traitoresses—even within the Philotis story there is a double, for she is called Philotis or, as some people say, Tutula. Finally, and most germane to the topic at hand, Philotis and Tarpeia are doublets—especially when the versions of Antigonus and Simylus are factored into the mix: Philotis is a "bride" living with the enemy just like Antigonus's Sabine Tarpeia, and a treasonous girl from Camillus's day just like Simylus's Tarpeia. Given this jumble it is easy to see how an author might wish to rationalize the myth (like Piso) or see fit to mix and match elements of the tradition (like Simylus). Plutarch's response is an offshoot of the latter. The Philotis episode is offered at the end of the *Romulus* deliberately as an analogue, or follow-up, to Tarpeia's episode earlier in the text. This narrative choice encourages a suggestive thesis about Romulus and Camillus, and about the use and reuse of Roman myth: using elements of a myth that is not flattering to them (Tarpeia), they craft one that is (Philotis). The Romans are masters at "new and improved."

A comparison with the version of the Nonae presented at *Camillus* 33 shows that Plutarch tailors the Philotis story in the *Romulus* so that it resonates with his Tarpeia episode..[36] In the *Camillus* version,[37] the Latins ask for Roman brides as a pretext for war, or because they really wanted intermarriage (*Cam* 33.2). The Romans' response shows that the Romans think it is a pretext. In contrast, in the *Romulus* the pretext motive is not mentioned, only desire to renew their old friendship. This slant recalls Plutarch's conclusion about Romulus's motives in asking for Sabine women; at *Rom*. 14.2, Plutarch dismisses the "brides as pretext" explanation and endorses the "true desire for brides" explanation. To make the parallel with the Romulean context more pointed, the Latin herald in the *Romulus* is explicit that such an alliance would repeat the one enjoyed by the Sabines so long ago (*Rom*. 29.3). The Sabine precedent for bride-exchange at the end of the *Romulus* acts to support Plutarch's earlier assessment of that rape, and places a sort of approval or acceptance of it in the mouths and minds of Rome's Latin neighbors. They believed/believe Romulus's story.

---

36. Buehler 1962 compares the two Plutarchan versions closely to conclude that the inset tale in the *Romulus* was composed before that in the Camillus; since the latter life was composed earlier than the *Romulus,* Buehler suggests that the Philotis episode was later added to the *Camillus.*

37. Macrobius *Saturnalia* 1.35–40 offers a version of the myth that closely follows that found in the Camillus. Since Macrobius can be shown to have followed Varro (he retains Varro's spelling of the festival name), it is likely that Plutarch too found his source in Varro's lost *Antiquitates.* See Coarelli 1997: 25–30. On the other hand, Polyaenus *Stratagemata* 8.30 seems to follow the *Romulus* in its particulars.

Mention of the Sabines also sends the reader back to that rape and, introduced even before any mention of Philotis occurs, inevitably colors the reader's perception of her stratagem with Tarpeian tones.

Tarpeia's presence in the background might help explain another element in the story: its lack of sexual content. Apart from naming the heroine Philotis, "Darling," Plutarch downplays any erotic element to the story or the festival to which it is connected.[38] Another author of the tale, Aristides Milesius as reported in Pseudo-Plutarch (*Moralia* 313A), revels in its raunchier aspects: Aristides's Gallic invaders demanded sex, not marriage, and, having gotten plenty of it from the slave girl Rhetana and her companions, were too exhausted to repel the Roman attack. Interestingly, this Aristides Milesius is the same one who, according to Pseudo-Plutarch, called Tarpeia the guardian of the rock (see above). Reconstructions of the ritual of the Nonae emphasize its ribald aspect.[39] Plutarch's de-emphasis of the sexual content of both ritual and aition is not simply, if even at all, a product of his civility.[40] Tarpeia's story is similarly sanitized in Plutarch's treatment; not only does he dismiss Simylus's lovelorn girl, but he omits to mention the tradition, which he surely knew, that Tarpeia was a Vestal virgin, which would make her crime, however motivated, *incestum* (unchastity).[41] Tarpeia's and Philotis's stories are stripped of their sexual content so as to downplay any erotic element in the *Romulus*. Plutarch

---

38. In *Camillus* she is called Tutula first; see Bremmer 1981: 84 for a discussion of possible sexual overtones of this name, and Coarelli 1997: 28–30 for the possibility of Tutula as an archaic figure reminiscent of Juno Sospita or Venus Victrix.

39. Wiseman 2004: 171–74 posits for the festival symbolic intercourse with a fig branch and a festival play re-enacting, in three acts, the sexual meeting between the Roman slaves and their new Latin "husbands." In Wiseman's interpretation, the sexuality of this festival represents one face of the Romans' Janus-like culture, brought into doubt and censure when the Romans sought in the Second Punic War to adopt the more austere Apollo, but ultimately unable to be purged. Cf. Wiseman 1998: 8–11, a fuller argument for a play focused on the Nonae ritual. Wiseman admits that his argument rests on an emendation of Varro *de Ling.* 6.18. Bremmer 1981: 83–86 and Coarelli 1997: 24–30 stress the ritual's Saturnalian reversal of norms which ultimately reinforces those norms, but see Coarelli 1997: 33–45 for a discussion of his departures from Bremmer's interpretation.

40. Bremmer 1981: 83 argues that Plutarch tried quite hard to recover female names, but that his sources preserved few of them.

41. *Numa* 10.1 names Tarpeia as one of the first Vestals, a new priesthood instituted by Numa according to Plutarch. Varro is the first extant author to have named Tarpeia the betrayer as a Vestal virgin (*de Ling.* 5.41; see chapter 4); Plutarch knew Varro's work and even cites him at *Rom.* 11.3. The raciest extant version is Propertius's, and I am not convinced that Plutarch did not know it; his phrase "the city was difficult to approach" seems to echo Propertius's "the hill was difficult to climb" (ἦν δὲ δυσπρόσοδος ἡ πόλις, *Rom.* 17.2 cf. *mons erat ascensu dubius,* Propertius 4.4.83); I can find no similar phrase in any of the other sources.

does not shy from erotic content elsewhere, even in the Lives,[42] so its deemphasis or even purging here suggests deliberate cant. As we find out in the comparative synkrisis to this pair of Lives, between the Greek and Roman founders, Theseus was the wandering hero with the wandering eye. Restraint in erotic affairs is the one criterion on which Romulus emerges as the clearly superior man in Plutarch's assessment (*Syn.* 5.2–3). By rewriting a nonsexual Philotis and Nonae at the finale of the *Romulus*, Plutarch buttresses the impression he has generated of Romulus and his Romans all along: they are pragmatic to the end, undistracted by those passionate pursuits that sometimes undermine their enemies.

Also unique to the Romulus version of Philotis's story is the amount of trust he encourages his readers to take in it. In the *Camillus,* Plutarch discredits Philotis's tale at the outset ("I'll tell you two stories about the war with the Latins, the first of which is bunk," περὶ τούτου τοῦ πολέμου διττοὶ λόγοι λέγονται· δίειμι δὲ τὸν μυθώδη πρότερον, *Cam.* 33.2). In the *Romulus* Plutarch refrains from casting doubt on the story until its end, and even then he only admits uncertainty about its connection with the Nonae. Having introduced the Philotis alternative with the neutral "some say" (ὡς δ' ἔνιοι λέγουσι), he ends the story by reaffirming that many writers believe it (29.7), ταῦτ' οὖν πολλοὶ προσίενται τῶν συγγραφέων. What Plutarch says next is extraordinary, especially so close to the end of the text: the details of the festival support the former story (i.e., the one connected with Romulus's death), unless, he suggests, the two events—Romulus's death and the Roman rout of the Latins under Camillus—happened to fall on the same day:

βαδίζοντας ἔοικε τῷ προτέρῳ λόγῳ προστίθεσθαι μᾶλλον, εἰ μὴ νὴ Δία τῆς αὐτῆς ἡμέρας ἐν χρόνοις ἑτέροις ἀμφότερα τὰ πάθη συνέτυχε γενέσθαι. (*Rom.* 29.7)

(The details) seem to fit the former story more, unless by Zeus both events happened to fall on the very same day in different eras.

The interjection εἰ μὴ νὴ Δία clearly shows Plutarch's skepticism at such a coincidence, but the fact that he mentions the possibility at all, and so prominently, as the penultimate thought in the whole *Romulus* followed only by the bald datum of Romulus's age at death, asks a little more of

---

42. See, e.g., the anecdote of Alexander's drunken public kiss of Bagoas at *Alex.* 67.8, or Antony's and Cleopatra's erotically motivated choices throughout the *Antony*.

his readers. The overlap of Philotis with Tarpeia and the similar doubling of Romulus and Camillus combine with the explicit mention of historic coincidence to invite the reader to contemplate the way these stories follow and fold upon each other. For me, this invitation leads to a consideration of the role that Roman history played in constructing and construing myth.

On one level, the presence of Camillus at all in the *Romulus* serves to liken the first founder to the later one, and to draw attention to similarities in their experiences, such as their inability to turn military excellence to use in quelling party strife.[43] Birds of a feather flock together. Camillus as a second founder thus accrues stories like those surrounding his predecessor. On another level, the Philotis digression reveals the Romans' ability to appropriate and recuperate the stories told about them, to their own advantage. We have already seen how, in the story, Plutarch's Latins (by Camillus's day much weaker vis-à-vis Rome) have accepted the pro-Roman version of the rape of the Sabine women: that it was purely for intermarriage. So too does Philotis's story rewrite Tarpeia, only now the traitoress is on Rome's side, and Rome becomes the aggressor rather than the victim, perpetrating on the Latins almost exactly what was done to them earlier by the Sabines. Philotis's identity cements this notion; from freeborn Tarpeia disloyal to her country, we now have a slave loyal enough to Rome to put herself at risk. It was even her idea. And she was Greek, no less a tricky Greek such as are sprinkled throughout Roman myth to marginalize and enfeeble any perceived Greek intellectual superiority.[44] Here lies the meaning of Plutarch's choice only in the *Romulus* to foreground her Greek name, Philotis. How must that detail have read to Plutarch's Greek audience?

The exposure of Roman myth as myth right at the end of this pair of Lives is a bold move, especially given Plutarch's explicit discussion of myth and history at the beginning of the *Theseus*.[45] There Plutarch expresses the difficulty of writing of such bygone heroes, whose lives lie beyond probable reasoning:

---

43. Pelling 2002: 132 and see also 194n57. The Romulus–Camillus parallel generates consistent themes across Lives and lends a sense of unity to Plutarch's broader biographical project.

44. See Sinon in Vergil's *Aeneid,* Pyrrhus, Odysseus, etc.

45. Pelling 2002: 365–68 sees the proliferation of versions and sources in the *Romulus* and in the *Theseus* as attempts to generate a sort of scholarly aura for these Lives, furthering the project of myth looking like history. For Pelling, this looks like Plutarch's diffidence rather than self-confidence. I agree that Plutarch steps back from his sources, but I think the end goal is slightly different: not the reader's trust in those sources, but a bird's-eye view of how many sources there are and how they shape each other.

εἴη μὲν οὖν ἡμῖν ἐκκαθαιρόμενον λόγῳ τὸ μυθῶδες ὑπακοῦσαι καὶ
λαβεῖν ἱστορίας ὄψιν, ὅπου δ' ἂν αὐθαδῶς τοῦ πιθανοῦ περιφρονῇ καὶ
μὴ δέχηται τὴν πρὸς τὸ εἰκὸς μῖξιν, εὐγνωμόνων ἀκροατῶν δεησόμεθα καὶ πρᾴως τὴν ἀρχαιολογίαν προσδεχομένων. (*Theseus* 1.3)

And so, may the mythic,[46] purified by me, submit to reason and take on the appearance of history. But where she daringly scorns the credible and admits no admixture of the likely, I shall beg for well-disposed readers who will receive my early history with a gentle temper.

Plutarch has not quite purified these myths for his readers as he promises. He could easily have explained away Philotis as a doublet for Tarpeia, or Simylus's or Antigonus's Tarpeias as back-readings based on Philotis's story. He does not do so, however; he leaves some of the cleaning up to us and offers rather a glimpse of how it might be done—a "before" snapshot (Tarpeia) and an "after" (Philotis). This is an ominous set of views at the birth of Rome.

WIDE ANGLE: TARPEIA AND THE AMAZONOMACHY

As I hope to have demonstrated in the first section of this chapter, Tarpeia's episode functions discretely as a parable of opportunism, especially that employed by Roman rulers or would-be rulers. Set more or less at the text's center, it encourages the reader to reassess those chapters of Romulus's early rule that precede the tale, and it colors the chapters on Tatius's rule and fall, and on Romulus's success and even his death. When paired with the Philotis episode at the end of the *Romulus,* as I explored in the second section, Tarpeia's story becomes part of a study of the use of myth in the Roman world. Philotis's story reworks Tarpeia's to Rome's advantage, with outsiders now wanting to become insiders through intermarriage, and with a loyal girl bringing about a victory, not a defeat, for Rome. The Tarpeia episode thus is not casually included but rather is powerfully integrated into the fabric of the *Romulus* as content and comment.

It would be inadequate to stop there and to ignore the fact that Romulus isn't primarily compared to Tatius, or Antigonus, or Augustus, or even Camillus, but to Theseus. *Romulus* is one of the paired Lives, endowed with a synkrisis and highly wrought throughout to enhance the connec-

---

46. Hardie 1991; Pelling 2002: 171–95 for this word's nuances.

tion between the Roman hero and his Greek counterpart. Plutarch makes explicit at the outset of the *Theseus* that the Athenian founder is an appropriate foil for the Roman one (*Thes.* 2.1). Major episodes in each man's life are tailored so as to evoke each other: the rumors of divine birth surrounding each, their similarly troubled childhoods exiled from their rightful homes and thrones, and their deaths and deifications.[47] Even minor episodes have been constructed so as to reinforce the parallel; Hercules makes some unprecedented appearances in the *Romulus* precisely because he is a leitmotif in the *Theseus*.[48]

Tarpeia's story, too, finds an analogue in the Theseus: the Amazonomachy fought at Theseus's Athens. The stories as Plutarch tells them are quite similar (*Thes.* 26–27, *Rom.* 14–19). In both cases, the episode begins with the hero's rape of a woman or women: Theseus's kidnapping of Antiope or Hippolyte on the one hand, the rape of the Sabines on the other. The rape provokes the women's people—Amazons, Sabines—to attack and press for their kinswomen's recovery. Both cities are very resistant to attack; Athens explicitly by its mettle, and Rome by its topographical situation. In both cases the fighting, when engaged, ranges to and through the center of the city. In both cases the raped women express alliance with their rapist: Antiope for Theseus, the Sabine women for their new Roman husbands. Finally, and most important for my purposes, both conflicts are inscribed upon the cityscape, not only by being fought in recognizable and named places such as the Athenian Pnyx and Roman Capitol, but by generating new monuments named for events and people of the battle, such as the Horcomosium, Theseum, and Amazoneum in Athens and the Lacus Curtius and temple of Jupiter Stator in Rome.

Robert Lamberton suggests that these "antiphonal topographies" make the cities themselves into silent witnesses of the events of so long ago.[49] In a pair of Lives introduced in *Theseus* with an apology for the material bordering on myth, such testament of monuments helps Plutarch meet his claim to submit myth to reason so as to give it the semblance of history (εἴη μὲν οὖν ἡμῖν ἐκκαθαιρόμενον λόγῳ τὸ μυθῶδες ὑπακοῦσαι καὶ λαβεῖν ἱστορίας ὄψιν, "and so, may the mythic, purified by me, submit to reason and take on the appearance of history," *Thes.* 1.3). Indeed Plutarch describes these most mythical of his Lives precisely in terms of geography, and he is a mapmaker:

---

47. Lamberton 2001: 75–77.
48. Larmour 1988: 363–64.
49. Lamberton 2001: 77–80. He refers also to Plutarch's notion that Theseus introduced coinage to Athens.

ὥσπερ ἐν ταῖς γεωγραφίαις, ὦ Σόσσιε Σενεκίων, οἱ ἱστορικοὶ τὰ διαφεύγοντα τὴν γνῶσιν αὐτῶν τοῖς ἐσχάτοις μέρεσι τῶν πινάκων πιεζοῦντες, αἰτίας παραγράφουσιν ὅτι 'τὰ δ' ἐπέκεινα θῖνες ἄνυδροι καὶ θηριώδεις' ἢ 'πηλὸς ἀϊδνής' ἢ 'σκυθικὸν κρύος' ἢ 'πέλαγος πεπηγός,' οὕτως ἐμοὶ περὶ τὴν τῶν βίων τῶν παραλλήλων γραφήν, τὸν ἐφικτὸν εἰκότι λόγῳ καὶ βάσιμον ἱστορίᾳ πραγμάτων ἐχομένῃ χρόνον διελθόντι, περὶ τῶν ἀνωτέρω καλῶς εἶχεν εἰπεῖν· 'τὰ δ' ἐπέκεινα τερατώδη καὶ τραγικὰ ποιηταὶ καὶ μυθογράφοι νέμονται, καὶ οὐκέτ' ἔχει πίστιν οὐδὲ σαφήνειαν.' (*Thes.* 1.1)

Just like in geographies, o Socius Senecio, scholars crowd those things fleeing their knowledge onto the outer parts of their maps, and they annotate thus: "What lies beyond is dry sand and full of wild beasts," or "blind marsh," or "Scythian frost," or "frozen sea," so to me, in the writing of my parallel Lives, passing beyond a time reachable by reasoned argument and traversable in the history of events, it's an option to say of the earlier periods, "What lies beyond is marvelous and worthy of the stage, which poets and fabulists treat, and it has no truck in credibility or clarity."

Plutarch's use of real monuments in the *Thes./Rom.* is more than evidentiary. Rather, Rome's and Athens's parallel monuments engage closely with the broader interpretive themes of this pair of Lives as set out in Plutarch's programmatic introduction and in the pair's synkrisis. I wish to focus on a matched set of monuments in Athens and Rome: the graves of the Amazons and Tarpeia's rock. These monuments engage each other particularly not only in that they are burials (unlike, say, the Theseum or the temple of Jupiter Stator) but in that, as such, they reflect the continued presence of the body of a threatening figure at the heart of the victorious city. Yet it is the differences between the two stories, and their resultant monuments, that do the real work in this pair of Lives. Plutarch's presentation of the graves of the Amazons and of Tarpeia reflects his examination of the difference between Theseus the consolidator and Romulus the father and, through them, the more profound and pervasive difference between songworthy Athens and invincible Rome (ἀοιδίμων ... Ἀθηνῶν ... ἀνικήτου ... Ῥώμης, *Thes.* 1.2).

Having spent time in Rome, Plutarch was perhaps familiar with the Basilica Aemilia reliefs in which Tarpeia appears bare-breasted in Amazon style.[50] Perhaps the pairing of her story with the Amazonomachy in his text

---

50. Propertius's poem is the literary source that brings to fullest fruit the portrait of Tarpeia

reflects an awareness of that feature of her myth in Rome. As discussed in chapter 4, the Basilica Aemilia sculpture cast Tarpeia as the outsider within: a dangerous version of the Roman self allowed to wreak havoc on the social and political order. Her threatening image in the Basilica Aemilia was, however, surrounded by much more reassuring scenes from the Romulus cycle, from wall-building to ritual preparations, and from the rape of the Sabine women to their eventual marriage with Roman men. Plutarch does not mention this artwork but focuses rather on Tarpeia's other monuments. Nevertheless, in his treatment of the story and its places, Plutarch reinforces the same sort of message: that Rome has been successful at containing Tarpeia.

Here is what Plutarch has to say about Tarpeia's monuments in Rome:

> τῆς μέντοι Ταρπηίας ἐκεῖ ταφείσης, ὁ λόφος ὠνομάζετο Ταρπήιος, ἄχρι οὗ Ταρκυνίου βασιλέως Διὶ τὸν τόπον καθιεροῦντος ἅμα τά τε λείψανα μετηνέχθη, καὶ τοὔνομα τῆς Ταρπηίας ἐξέλιπε· πλὴν πέτραν ἔτι νῦν ἐν τῷ Καπιτωλίῳ Ταρπηίαν καλοῦσιν, ἀφ' ἧς ἐρρίπτουν τοὺς κακούργους. (*Rom.* 18.1)

> At any rate since Tarpeia was buried there, the rise was named the Tarpeian hill until, after King Tarquin sanctified the place to Jupiter, her remains were moved and the name of Tarpeia faded away. Except even now they call "Tarpeian" that rock on the Capitol from which they hurl malefactors.

Tarpeia's burial place is now a place hallowed to Jove, and her name commemorates the lawful punishment of wrongdoers rather than the threat they pose. In other words, the threatening Tarpeia has been subsumed, or replaced, by the religious and legal strength of Rome.[51] This transformation of her monuments reflects that of the Sabine women from victims into wives, and more importantly, of the Sabines from foreign enemies into Roman citizens. These transformations were likewise accompanied by name changes (e.g., citizens into "Quirites" after a Sabine town, *Rom.* 19.7). Even the war itself follows suit: the temporary defeat brought about by Tarpeia's treachery turned into a lasting Roman success.

Theseus's war with the Amazons similarly is not decided militarily; hos-

---

as an Amazon; most scholars would reject the presence of Propertius in the background of Plutarch's parallel threatening women. It is also possible that Plutarch, the Basilica's designer, and Propertius all draw the Tarpeia–Amazon parallel from a now-lost source.

51. Cf. my analysis in chapter 4 of the transformation of "anomalous" Tarpeia into "analogous" Tarpeia in Varro's presentation of her story.

tilities end with a treaty enacted after three months of fighting (*Thes.* 27.4–5). Nevertheless, no assimilation of Amazons and Athenians followed. On the contrary: they would remain a firmly entrenched "other" throughout Athenian history, to become a symbol of any foreign, particularly Eastern, threat.[52] This despite the fact that there was an Amazon loyal, or at least not hostile, to Athens: Hippolyte/Antiope, the woman Theseus had kidnapped. It was she who, according to Cleidemus, brokered the treaty that ended the war (*Thes.* 27.4). She is pointedly the only Amazon in such an intermediary position; Plutarch goes on to mention the tradition in which the kidnapped queen, while fighting aside Theseus, was slain by one of her own, Molpadia.

The Roman story as Plutarch tells it dwells on the permeability of Roman identity. The Sabine rape stems from the desire to intermarry and mingle populations (τρόπον τινὰ συγκράσεως καὶ κοινωνίας ἀρχὴν, *Rom.* 14.2), a desire that eventually played out in the Sabine women's plea to remain united with their Roman husbands, even if they all must live in Sabine country (*Rom.* 19.3, 5). Tarpeia is the flip side of these outsider-insiders, in that she is an insider who would be out. Tellingly, each moment of progress or movement in the Roman conflict and its resolution is precipitated by an action designed to blur the boundary between Romans and others: rape, treachery, wives' intervention.[53] The same is not true in the case of the Amazonomachy. No part of that series of events aimed at inclusion or showed permeability, and the truce that ended the hostilities resulted in a reaffirmation of the peoples' separation rather than their assimilation.

Let us now return to the graves that punctuate the two narratives. Tarpeia's grave is presented at the end of the section of the story detailing her treachery (see above for text). Though Plutarch records disputes about her tale, he notes no such disputes about her monuments; he starts his topographical description with μέντοι "at any rate," a word that indicates the plain truth of what is to follow. The truth of the matter is conveyed also by the lack of cited sources or attributions in the topographical section. All the Tarpeian monuments, their names and changes over time, are presented simply as if they are, rather than as they are said or agreed to be. What is more, all the verbs in the topographical section are indicative. Whatever the veracity of the details of her story, the reader is not to doubt that she was buried on the Capitol and leant her name to the rock of punishment.

---

52. E.g., Tyrrell 1984; Merck 1978.
53. This aspect of Plutarch's *Romulus* resonates with Tarpeia on Roman coins, explored in chapter 3.

In contrast, graves commemorating the Amazonomachy at Athens are mentioned no fewer than three times, with conflicting interpretations about their precise connection to the war. At the first mention, before the narrative proper, Plutarch asserts that the names of places and the graves of combatants attest that a battle was joined within Athens:

> τὸ δὲ ἐν τῇ πόλει σχεδὸν αὐτὰς ἐνστρατοπεδεῦσαι μαρτυρεῖται καὶ τοῖς ὀνόμασι τῶν τόπων καὶ ταῖς θήκαις τῶν πεσόντων. (*Thes.* 27.2)

> That the women set up their battle line right at the heart of the city is witnessed by the names of places and the tombs of the fallen.

It is noteworthy that Plutarch foregrounds the monuments as witnesses to the past, to the extent that they even precede the narrative of the battle. With the reader's attention properly focused on graves, the narrative that follows becomes highly destabilizing and disturbing, for graves prove to be no secure indication of what happened but rather are the basis for conflicting interpretations. For example, Plutarch reports that Cleidemus the Atthidographer says that the Amazons set their battle formation along the line between the Pnyx and the place that would become the Amazoneum;[54] while the Athenians won ground near the former, fighting was fierce toward the latter, and the graves of the fallen still dot the area:

> καὶ τάφους τῶν πεσόντων περὶ τὴν πλατεῖαν εἶναι τὴν φέρουσαν ἐπὶ τὰς πύλας παρὰ τὸ Χαλκώδοντος ἡρῷον. (*Thes.* 27.3)

> And there are graves of the fallen on either side of the street leading (sc. from the Amazoneum) to the gate by the shrine of Chalcodon.

Cleidemus's conclusions are cast in doubt by Plutarch's introduction of him: "As Cleidemus writes, who wishes to split hairs..." (ἱστορεῖ δὲ Κλείδημος, ἐξακριβοῦν τὰ καθ' ἕκαστα βουλόμενος..., *Thes.* 27.3). Accordingly, after this introduction Cleidemus's topographical detail is given in indirect discourse only. Plutarch clearly does not believe such knowledge can be pressed from the topographical information. Put more strongly, Plutarch resists the close connection that Cleidemus draws between monument and history in this case. The third mention of an Amazon grave underscores his suspicion. This same Cleidemus suggests that, through

---

54. For Cleidemus (fourth c. BCE) see Meister 2012.

Hippolyte's (= Antiope's) agency, the Amazons and Athenians agreed to a truce after three months of fighting. Others refute this possibility, and topography is their witness:

ἔνιοι δέ φασι μετὰ τοῦ Θησέως μαχομένην πεσεῖν τὴν ἄνθρωπον ὑπὸ Μολπαδίας ἀκοντισθεῖσαν, καὶ τὴν στήλην τὴν παρὰ τὸ τῆς Ὀλυμπίας ἱερὸν ἐπὶ ταύτῃ κεῖσθαι. (*Thes.* 27.4)

But some say that she (i.e., Hippolyta) died fighting alongside Theseus, hit by a javelin by Molpadia, and that the stele next to the shrine of Olympia was placed there in her memory.

Once again the monument is mentioned in indirect discourse. With these instances so close together, Plutarch draws attention to the fact that the Athenian monuments do not help much in reconstructing or even understanding their past, since different tellers may point to different monuments to make their case. Of course, this option was available to Plutarch in the *Romulus* also; he could have pointed, like Piso had, to Tarpeia's worship or to the alternative—indeed, more common—versions of the *lacus Curtius* (the pit of Curtius).[55] Plutarch even elides the fact that Romulus vowed—but never built—the temple to Jupiter Stator; the building would await Regulus in 296 BCE and a second vow against the Samnites (Livy 10.36.16, 37.15–16). The Roman monuments in his treatment of this war admit no alternative or conflicting interpretations.

The Athenian monuments do, however, and immediately after noting the second monument-attested possibility for the war's conclusion, Plutarch apologizes for his inability to be accurate in this case. Certainty, he says, just isn't possible:

καὶ θαυμαστὸν οὐκ ἔστιν ἐπὶ πράγμασιν οὕτω παλαιοῖς πλανᾶσθαι τὴν ἱστορίαν . . . (*Thes.* 27.5)

And it is not astounding that history wanders about in events so very ancient . . .

---

55. Curtius's *praenomen* is often left out. In Plutarch's version, (Mettius) Curtius was an eminent Sabine warrior whose horse got stuck in the Forum's mud (*Rom.* 18.4 and cf. Livy 1.12.10; Varro *de Ling.* 5.149; Dionysius 2.42 and 24.11). The version most often repeated is that (Marcus) Curtius the Roman sacrificed himself there for the Roman good (Livy 7.6.1–6; Varro *de Ling.* 5.148; Val. Max. 5.6.2; Pliny *HN* 15.78; Festus 49). A third aition is that lightning struck there in the earliest days of the Republic and the place was consecrated by the consul (Caius) Curtius (Varro *de Ling.* 5.150).

Plutarch's metaphor—wandering about—speaks well to the point he has just been making. History does not stay put when its referents on the map keep moving around or are impossible to link firmly with historical events. His statement draws us back to the spatial image with which he began the *Theseus*: history of the earliest periods is fanciful and fringe, like the wild and unknown places off the edges of a map (*Thes.* 1.1). Historians and geographers must simply put early history somewhere and apologize for it, hoping for a generous and well-disposed reader (εὐγνωμόνων ἀκροατῶν δεησόμεθα καὶ πρᾴως τὴν ἀρχαιολογίαν προσδεχομένων, *Thes.* 1.3).

The uncertainty about the Amazonomachy's details in Athens pales when compared with what follows. Plutarch concludes his account of the Amazonomachy by drawing attention to similar monuments all over Greece, explaining these with the observation that the Amazons must have campaigned widely (*Thes.* 27.5–6). Plutarch defers these too to the authority of other tellers. "They say" that Amazon graves exist at Chalcis (φασὶ . . . καὶ ταφῆναί τινας ἐκεῖ περὶ τὸ νῦν Ἀμαζόνειον καλούμενον, *Thes.* 27.5). "The Megarians point out" a burial place of Amazons (δεικνύουσι δὲ καὶ Μεγαρεῖς Ἀμαζόνων θήκην παρ' αὐτοῖς, *Thes.* 27.6). "It is said" that some are buried in Chaeroneia (λέγεται δὲ καὶ περὶ Χαιρώνειαν ἑτέρας ἀποθανεῖν, καὶ ταφῆναι, *Thes.* 27.6); Plutarch's hedging here is striking given his surely certain knowledge of the graves there. Finally, "they appear" to have come through Thessaly too, where many graves "are pointed out" (φαίνονται δὲ μηδὲ Θεσσαλίαν ἀπραγμόνως αἱ Ἀμαζόνες διελθοῦσαι· τάφοι γὰρ αὐτῶν ἔτι καὶ νῦν δείκνυνται, *Thes.* 27.6).

Everyone tells the story that Amazons fought in their hometown, and everyone has the monuments to back up the claim. Plutarch's account raises the specter of the problem of appearances, of seeming and being seen (φαίνονται, δείκνυνται). His emphasis on the tellers (φασὶ, διελθοῦσαι, λέγεται) raises questions about the authenticity of the monuments and the stories they support in that it makes explicit the self-interest of the tellers. Plutarch elsewhere in the Lives draws attention to these very two problems of *Realien* as evidence: the difficulty of appearances and the bias or authority of the presenter. In Duff's analysis of images in the pair *Lysander-Sulla*, Plutarch exposes portrait sculptures as misleading, either because of their visual obfuscation of true personality or because of the use to which they are put—that is, the authority of the dedicator.[56] Plutarch's

---

56. Duff 1997.

use of monuments in the *Theseus* is similarly disconcerting, but to a different end.

The Amazon graves illustrate or obfuscate not the personality of Theseus, but of Greece itself. Plutarch's treatment makes visible a key difference between Athens and Rome. Though Athens would come to dominate the Greek imagination and would even become the symbol of Greek culture—Pausanias, Chariton, and others would enshrine this position[57]—it was in reality one of several city-states jockeying for position in the Greek world before Philip's conquest rendered such jockeying moot. Plutarch is careful to remind his readers about the sharp distinction between Greece's free but disparate past and its subject but unified present. When he mentions the Amazon graves at his homeland Chaeroneia, he reminds the reader that he discusses this also in his *Demosthenes* (19.2–3). In that text, Plutarch links together the so-called river Thermodon near Chaeroneia, a dire prophecy about the impending war with Philip, and a statue, found there by a soldier pitching his tent, of the river god Thermodon holding a dying Amazon—itself connected with a different dire prophecy about impending war. Immediately thereafter, Plutarch reports Demosthenes's confidence in the Greek troops aligning against Philip (*Demos.* 20.1). In the *Demosthenes,* the Chaeroneian biographer clearly wants to cast the later battle (against Philip) in the shadow of the earlier one (against Amazons); in the *Theseus* the reference to the *Demosthenes* establishes the same linkage between battles in reverse order. When we read of the Amazon graves in the *Theseus,* and Plutarch recalls his own *Demosthenes,* our minds jump forward to Philip's conquest one by one of the city-states of Greece. Fragmentation, not unity, was Greece's hallmark, and the same phenomenon that led to multiple Amazon graves all over Greece led to Greece's defeat at Philip's hands.[58]

There are many rival monuments of the Amazonomachy, but only one Tarpeian rock. To return to the geographical metaphor Plutarch uses at *Thes.* 1.1 to describe his antiquarian project: like places on a map, so too is the project of history through biography. Plutarch firmly locates Tarpeia's rock on the map of the past. But the urban relics of the Amazonomachy, in spite of the fact that Athenian writers worked hard to affix them to the center of the map, Plutarch repositions beyond its edges, so to speak, by revealing how many centers there are on a Greek map. In this way the rivalry

---

57. Lamberton 2001: 61–63. See Habicht 1999: 108–12 on Pausanias, and Smith 2007 on Chariton.

58. Pausanias would reach a similar conclusion but places the seeds or unraveling in the Peloponnesian War (Habicht 1999: 112).

between Tarpeia's rock and the many Amazonomachies mimics the project of the Lives as a whole, in which Roman and Greek confront each other through the pairings Rome-Athens, Rome-Sparta, Rome-Thebes, Rome-Syracuse, Rome-Macedon.[59] There are many avenues into Greek culture; there is only one Rome.[60]

This is a striking suggestion to make about and in the Lives, a project whose core assumption is that individuals define a culture rather than vice versa. But the individuals bear it out as well, and the profound difference between Greece and Rome that plays throughout the Lives as a whole is a powerful subtext of the *Theseus/Romulus*. In the synkrisis to this pair, Plutarch judges Romulus to have been the more effective founding father, on several counts. Though Theseus comes across a little less ruthless than his Roman counterpart, his achievement with Athens is lesser than Romulus's with Rome. For in launching Athens, Theseus merely consolidated nearby towns—all transplants, as he was (μετοικισταί)—into one dwelling place, whereas Romulus started Rome from scratch (οἰκισταὶ πόλεων, *Syn.* 4.1–2). Whereas Theseus's rapes led to conflict and dissent, Romulus's one rape (of the Sabine women) led to oneness and joint rule (*Syn.* 6.1–3). Whereas Theseus left Athens on the road to a democracy (*Syn.* 2.1) that would ultimately self-destruct because of the competing identities and agendas it enabled, Romulus left Rome an autocracy (*Syn.* 2.2), a system with singular purpose and authority, a straighter path to greatness, that would compose and order, like Plato's Demiurge,[61] not only its own past but the chaotic Greek world as well.

Like Romulus and Theseus, who are individuals to be studied both for their own sake and for the light they shed on the larger questions of Greek and Roman culture and dominance, Tarpeia is interesting to Plutarch both for her own sake, as someone whose choice has perplexing moral implications, and for the opportunity she presents to explore Rome. Though Plutarch does not dwell on Tarpeia as a moral agent per se, he surrounds her with details and commentary that lend moral complexity and weight to her story. Tarpeia presents a dangerous—and not entirely aboveboard—opportunity to Tatius, which he seizes to advance his cause against the

---

59. Pelling 2002: 171–73.

60. This technique is opposite the one found recently to be at play in the *Greek and Roman Questions,* in which Greek questions admit generally one answer but Roman questions are met with many possibilities (see Preston in Goldhill 2001). Greek culture thus comes off as natural and knowable to Plutarch's Greek audience, whereas Rome comes off as constructed and unknowable. The Lives' project—and its audience—is different.

61. Dillon 1997: 235–40.

Romans. Any monarch worth his salt—Antigonus, Augustus—would do the same. So, the suggestion is, would Romulus too, and the *Romulus* is full of instances in which Romulus carefully navigated the difficult opportunities that arose for him, and the dangers they posed (Remus's death, Tatius's death, the rape of the Sabine women). In fact, legends of early Rome are rife with incidents and outcomes not entirely flattering to the Romans. Plutarch is quick to remind us that such calculated ruthlessness is not simply Roman, and not simply regal. We are implicated, too, both in this self-serving morality and in the mythmaking that naturalizes the behavior. We all sometimes have need of something dangerous.

Tarpeia's story thus does some work in the *Romulus* to illustrate its moral themes, but its importance in the text does not end there. The parallel with Philotis at the end of the *Romulus* reveals what happens to myth after it has grown up and become entrenched. The marginal figure—here, Philotis the Greek slave woman—so fully embraces Rome's mission that she is willing to play Tarpeia in its service. Plutarch's inclusion of Philotis offers an object lesson in how myths evolve and become enmeshed with each other to construct a sense of Rome's past, its character, and its destiny. The parallel Plutarch draws between Tarpeia's story and the Amazonomachy in the *Theseus* continues and caps this lesson, for it reveals a Rome masterful at winnowing down the potential stories as it includes more and more tellers of its one story, whereas Greece favored plurality and liberty, even at its own eventual expense.

It is clear from the beginning of the *Theseus* that Plutarch wishes his readers to think about the differences between myth and history. Is there any difference between the two, except in the belief? As the *Theseus-Romulus* seems to suggest, one man's history is another man's myth.

CONCLUSION

IN THE SECOND OR THIRD century CE, someone in Roman Britain took a copy of the Tarpeia coin minted originally by Turpilianus, *triumvir monetalis* under Augustus (this coin is discussed in chapter 5) and transformed it into a testimony to the rock-birth of the sun-god Mithras.[1] The obverse, which had depicted Augustus in profile, was rubbed out completely and reinscribed with the words Μίθρας Ωρομάσδης in a circle surrounding the word Φρήν, that is, "Mithras" the bull-killing god of a popular mystery cult, "Oromasdes" the Zoroastrian chief god equated with Zeus in the Hellenistic period, and "Phre," an Egyptian personification of the sun (fig. 8). The reverse still shows the small figure half-covered with round shields, but the legend on the reverse, which had read "Turpilianus IIIvir," has been scraped or rubbed off (fig. 9). The coin is understood to be a token for entry into a sanctuary or perhaps a personal amulet.[2] Female has become male, human has become god, Roman has become Persian or Egyptian, and death has become birth. For this worshipper or community of worshippers, Tarpeia was meaningful only for the handy visual model her death provided. As a less likely alternative, on the off chance the Mithraist knew her story, Rome's founding non-mother was less important to him than his local and personal affiliations.

1. RIB vol 2. #248.2 = CIMRM 827.
2. Beck 1984: 2049 emphasizes the medallion's idiosyncrasy. See also Clauss 2001: 63.

CONCLUSION

FIGURE 8
Obverses (left) and reverses (right) of Petronius Turpilianus'
coin of Tarpeia and its re-use as a Mithraic token.
Photos courtesy of the Verulamium Museum, St. Albans.

This extreme example indicates the extreme malleability of her myth. Who was Tarpeia, really, and why did she approach the Sabines? Did the ancients surmise correctly, when they surmised at all, about the range of her emotions, or was something entirely different driving her story—jealousy, fear, remorse, political dissent? To ask these questions is to assume she was a real girl with real interactions, as the Romans and Greeks did when they always made space for her in Rome's foundational narrative. The crux of that narrative, variously told, seems always to slip from "what she did" to "what they did with her." She is not so much a person as an invitation to a response.

But this has been my point throughout the preceding pages. It has not been the intention of this book to illuminate the girl, but rather to reveal how and what she illuminates for those who take up her story. The patient reader will have gained perspective on the power and flexibility of Tarpeia's myth in the ancient world. In these pages I have argued that Tarpeia was useful to the ancient authors and artists who told her tale. Her story speaks to ethics, gender, ethnicity, political authority, language, conquest, and tradition. Thus she would be attached to the birth of Latin literature, a phenomenon that emerged to give voice to the evolving Roman elite class, as in Fabius Pictor's *Annales* where her actions and her demise set clear boundaries on proper behavior for Romans and those who would be Romans. She would witness the various crises engendered by that elite class—the pushback of the lower classes against elite privilege and the renewal of social strife under Piso's day, the rebellion in the Social War of Italian allies still marginalized by Rome's elite, and ultimately the chaos and internecine war triggered by Caesar's simultaneous use and rebuke of elite moral standards. Tarpeia would see Rome through the sea change of culture and politics between Caesar's death and the certainty of autocracy under Tiberius. In this framework, she would act as a type—the woman whose presence knits society together, and as an individual struggling to define herself against a wave of expectations that the new settlement required. At the end of this shift, with Rome's autocracy secure and with Rome's place in the world secure, Tarpeia could become a point of reconciliation between Greece and Rome, or an entry point for Greece into Rome, if you will, similar to the way generations earlier she was the entry point into Rome for Tatius and his Sabines.

Would the same be true of any myth recycled? Yes and no. The analysis of any myth told and retold would reveal similar usefulness to its tellers. It must; else, why retell? But it is interesting to consider that the Romans did not dwell on mythic matricides or evil stepmothers, like Greek authors did, nor on hybrid creatures such as centaurs or demigods, nor descent to the underworld. The cluster of themes listed above—ethics, gender, ethnicity, political authority, language, conquest, and tradition—reveal that Tarpeia's myth is not primarily about what it means to be human, but what it means to be Roman. This is why her story spans centuries, distance, genres, and modes of communication: because Rome did. No Greek city-state could admit such continuity, and Greece itself was never so constant. In this way, though Tarpeia has a dozen Greek cousins whose stories are similar to hers, hers is a powerfully Roman myth. Even the Greeks who told her tale considered it to be a Roman myth. She is a token, totem, and symbol of Rome.

Rome is itself a token, totem, and symbol for the known world. Catharine Edwards's 1996 book *Writing Rome* explores many of the themes my analysis has taken up as they pertain not to the girl, but to her city. The Rome of Roman letters, argues Edwards in her chapter "The City of Memories," was a repository of Rome's cultural past and a means to preserve and perpetuate the glories and mores of that past. Varro's, Propertius's, and Valerius Maximus's verbal engagement with Tarpeia's tale and the Basilica Aemilia's visual representation all trade on the blurred distinction between past and present, and thus the way Romans of their day can absorb, respond to, honor, and better their roots. Edwards's Rome is "The City of Exiles," from mythical Aeneas to very historical Cicero. For Roman authors, the city of Rome was not only a way to express longing for home, but a way to explore the alienation that attends belonging in a cosmopolis. Tarpeia too is a figure of longing and alienation, especially in the texts of Pictor, Piso, Livy, Dionysius, and Simylus and on the coins that bear her imprint. Above all, the seven hills constitute "The City of Empire," or rather, one hill does: the Capitol, and it was Tarpeia's hill before it was the Head Hill.

Tarpeia, as Capitol, as Rome, is a token, totem, and symbol of modern global humanity confronted with the task of being together while being different. Some sixty-five years ago in the wake of World War II, when the world had been galvanized into an "us" and a "them," two European scholars undertook studies of the legendary Roman traitoress Tarpeia. For Georges Dumézil, the famous French comparative philologist of the twentieth century, Tarpeia's story encapsulated a triad of sacral-martial-economic elements that permeates all Indo-European cultures. This triad relates myth to social class, and Tarpeia, in Dumézil's 1947 book *Tarpeia: Essais de philologie comparative indo-européenne,* represents the economic element in that her treason results in the incorporation of Sabine wealth into the Roman state. Dumézil considered Tarpeia the functional equivalent to the Icelandic mythic figure Gullveig, a duplicitous woman in the midst of a war between a rich group (the Vanir) and a more modest group (the Æsyr). For Dumézil the equivalence of these stories stems from a common Indo-European ancestor. The meaning of the myth is therefore universal to all descendants of that ancestor.

In 1949 the Polish classicist Zofia Gansiniec published a monograph entitled *Tarpeia: The Making of a Myth.* Her title betrays her aim, stated on page 8: "The proper study of the historian is to find out the original source and prototype of the myth within the centre of culture which formed this very legend and to detect the special motives leading to its formation." She therefore surveys the evidence for Tarpeia and concludes that the myth arose from a victory dedication of foreign spoils on the Capitol, a monument form called τρόπαιον (trophy) in Greek. This monument became sacred and accrued rites and this, combined with imagination and Greek stories, gave rise to the myth of Tarpeia. All this happened in the third century BCE.

Dumézil saw Tarpeia as transcendent and universal; Gansiniec saw her as specific to a time and place. For one the dominant interpretive axis was social structure, for the other cultural cross-pollination. It is interesting to note that both scholars hail from countries occupied by the Nazis during the war. Dumézil has been charged with sympathy for fascism, and some critics have seen this sympathy at the heart of his work on comparative mythology;[3] he refuted the claim, but the debate abides.[4] Gansiniec wrote in an era of renewal for Classical studies in Poland after the devastations the academy suffered in the war. Gansiniec would eventually edit the popularizing Classical journal *Filomata.* The communist regime, through the Polish Academy of Sciences, supported new departments, publications,

---

3. Arvidsson 2006: 1–10; Lincoln 1991: 231–43; within Classics, see famously Momigliano 1984.
4. Eribon 1992 led the counterattack; most recently see Garcia Quintela 2002–5 for a study that links prosopography with questions of scholarly ideology and the academy. Garcia Quintela calls the criticism of Dumézil "a witch hunt tinged with political correctness" (199).

and outreach. The new Poland was claiming for itself a linkage with the Classical past.[5]

These two scholarly responses to Tarpeia's myth reveal the attraction it holds: it is a story about military occupation, side-taking, and ultimately cultural reconciliation. Perhaps the political and cultural crises of the twenty-first century prompt my study as well. So too might the current professional milieu in Classics. Marginality and otherness are now firmly rooted interests in Classics, as our discipline absorbs and responds to current academic work in postcolonialism (a focus on issues of identity arising from conquest), transnationalism (an approach that emphasizes plurality rather than essentiality in cultural identity), and subaltern studies (the study of anyone of inferior rank or status), and to such political issues as naturalization and nationhood. The myth of Tarpeia speaks to the creation, perpetuation, and expansion of the Roman state. Through her we may confront one of the grand paradoxes of a(ny) dominant ideology: that the sorts of figures or ideas it places at the margins—women, foreigners, homosexuals, the elderly, the young, the disenfranchised—are actually central to its operation and self-understanding.

In this context it is not surprising to see Dumézil's and Gansiniec's studies of Tarpeia emerge in post–World War II Europe, nor, uncomfortably enough, my own study at this time and in this place. Her myth helps us ask, Who are we in the world? Who are they? What do we have in common with others, and what keeps us separate? These are the questions that kept Tarpeia alive two millennia ago, and that keep her alive today.

---

5. Natunewicz 1967; Kumaniecki 1967. It is likewise fascinating that in the 1960s two articles appeared in English detailing and supporting the tradition of Classics in Poland.

APPENDIX

OTHER TREASONOUS GIRLS

Aglauros may be considered a loose parallel. One of the daughters of Cecrops, she opened the forbidden box in which the autochthonous baby Erichthonius was kept. She went insane and leapt to her death from the Acropolis, where she had a temple and was connected with the annual ritual in which new soldiers took an oath of loyalty. Like Tarpeia's, her action might have been shameful or, in some versions, patriotic: she threw herself from the cliff as an offering so that Athens would be victorious at war.[1]

Antiope was an Amazon queen who, according to one version of her myth, fell in love with Theseus and betrayed her people to him (Pausanias). In another version, she was kidnapped by Theseus and became his bride, whereupon the Amazons attacked Athens to retrieve her (or to avenge Theseus's abandonment of her for Phaedra). She is thus analogous to Tarpeia and to the Sabine women, an analogy Plutarch exploits in his paired Lives of *Theseus* and *Romulus*.[2]

Arne, of Paros, betrays Siphnos to Minos for gold. Her name is also a toponym, and her ethnic origin (Siphnian or Karian), like Tarpeia's, is vexed.[3]

Briseis is the famous Trojan prisoner of war who causes the rift between Achilles and Agamemnon. Though a captive of the Achaeans, she expresses love for Achilles

---

1. Pausanias 1.18.2; Apollodorus 3.14.2–6; Hyginus *Fab.* 166; Hesychius s.v. Ἄγραυλος.
2. Pausanias 1.2.1; Apollodorus 4.1.16; Diodorus 4.16; Hyginus *Fab.* 30; Ovid *Her.* 4.
3. Ovid *Met.* 7.465–66; Huxley 1982: Bömer 1977 *ad loc.* connects her to Tarpeia and others on this list.

in the *Iliad* and in her appearance on vase paintings can be interpreted as helping him.[4]

Comaetho was a princess of Taphos. When Taphos was at war with Thebes, Comaetho fell in love with the Theban commander Amphitryon and betrayed her city by cutting off the magical lock of hair from her father, king Pterelaos. This rendered him mortal and he fell to Amphitryon, who then killed Comaetho.[5]

Demonike of Ephesus is the closest parallel to Tarpeia, and interestingly, like Tarpeia, she is set in the historical rather than mythic record. When Brennus king of the Gauls was besieging Ephesus, Demonike fell in love with him and promised to betray the city to him in exchange for the Gauls' gold and jewels. Brennus took her help then threw the ornaments upon her, crushing her to death.[6]

Dido, at least in Vergil's account. Dido, queen of Carthage, scorned marriage with the local man Iarbas in favor of the foreigner Aeneas. Iarbas calls Aeneas another Paris, likening Dido to Helen, and Dido herself discusses the way her love affair with Aeneas undermines the success of her state.[7]

Dorcia of Achaea, a town in Ialysus on Rhodes that Iphiclus was besieging. The Achaeans had an oracle that their town would not fall until crows flew white and fish appeared in their wine bowls. Dorcia fell in love with the besieger Iphiclus and helped orchestrate a ruse whereby someone smuggled fish into a drinking bowl and painted crows with gypsum. Achaea made terms for peace.[8]

Eriphyle was also married—to the seer Amphiaraus of Argos, one of the seven against Thebes. He had been persuaded to enter this famous battle by his wife, who had been bribed: Polyneices (the leader of the seven) offered Eriphyle the enchanted necklace of Harmonia if she would persuade her husband to join the attack. Eriphyle succeeded in her wiles, Amphiaraus joined the battle though he had foreseen his death; he did indeed die, and his sons avenged him on their mother Eriphyle.

---

4. In addition to Homer *Iliad* (primarily books 1 and 19), Briseis appears in Bacchylides 13.131–38; Dictys of Crete 2.17, 33, and 49, 3.12 and 4.15; Apollodorus 4.1, 3, and 7; Ovid *Her.* 3; Quintus of Smyrna 3.551–76; Hyginus 106; and Proclus's summary of *Cypria*. See Dué 2002: 115–19 for more sources; her book sees in Briseis a complexity similar to that I am exploring with Tarpeia.

5. Apollodorus, 2.4.7; Tzetzes on Lycophron 930–35 with Tzetzes' commentary; Pausanias 7.19.1–9; Euphorion (*Suppl. Hell.* 415 col.ii.14ff.); Ovid *Ibis* 360.

6. Clitophon of Rhodes = *FGrH* 293.1 = (Plut) *Par. Min.* 15; cf. Stobaeus Flor. 10.70–71.

7. Vergil *Aeneid* 4.198–218 and 4.319–25. In earlier sources, Aeneas is not the problem, but Dido remains caught between her loyalty to her city and to her dead husband, and the demands of her suitor Iarbas.

8. Polyzelus's *History of Rhodes*, given in Athenaeus *Deipn.* 8.360E–361C = *FGrH* 513 F1.

Helen of Sparta/Troy may herself be considered a member of this type. Her erotic preference for the outsider Paris over her husband Menelaus led to the Trojan War. Like Tarpeia, ancient sources debated her level of responsibility and her allegiance. She too looks down on the besieging enemy—the famous *teichoskopeia* of *Iliad* 3—but, opposite Tarpeia, she sees not a foreigner whom she loves but her own whom she has dismissed.

Herippe was from Miletus but was kidnapped by Gallic forces and, not ransomed in time, was taken to Gaul as the bride of a Gallic captain. Her husband from Miletus, Xanthus, came to ransom her. She, however, was now in love with her captor and encouraged him to kill Xanthus. The Gaul, disgusted at her disloyalty to her husband, killed her and sent Xanthus home. She is also called Euthymia.[9]

Leukophrye a maiden from Asia Minor. When Menander of Pherae was attacking the city Magnesia, which had resisted his efforts to establish a Pheran colony there, Leukophrye fell in love with him and betrayed her city to him. Her fate is unknown.[10]

Medea might be the most famous maiden who falls for a foreigner against the interests of her country. She helps the Greek Jason acquire the golden fleece, thus betraying her father Aeetes and her homeland Colchis. She flees with Jason and becomes a notorious and dangerous sorceress in Greece.

Nanis, daughter of Croesus. She betrayed Sardis to Cyrus for the (unfulfilled) prize of marriage to Cyrus. Like Tarpeia, her name is a toponym.[11]

Pedasa is the name given to a maiden from the town of Monenia in the Troad, which Achilles was besieging during "The Great Foray." This maiden fell in love with Achilles and sent him a message, inscribed in iambs on an apple, that her town would fall soon due to thirst. Achilles thus continued the siege until the city fell; the town was renamed Pedasus.[12]

Peisidice. When Achilles was besieging the city of Methymna on Lesbos, the princess Peisidice fell in love with him and agreed to undermine the fortifications if he would marry her. Achilles took the city through her aid, then ordered that she be stoned to death, resulting in her burial under a rock heap.[13]

---

9. Parthenius 8 with Lightfoot 1999 *ad loc.*; and Aristodemus of Nysa = *FGrH* 22, who names her Euthymia.

10. Only at Parthenius 5.6; see Lightfoot 1999 *ad loc.*

11. Parthenius 22 with Lightfoot 1999 *ad loc.* (who details the discovery of a new text on Nanis); Licymnius *PMG* 772; and Hermesianax fr.6 Powell. See Bremmer 2008: 269 for the toponym.

12. Briseis is said by Dictys of Crete to be from Pedasa; Dué 2002: 61–62 links the two stories, among others of this type (see 49–65). Pedasa's sources are the Homeric scholia, which ascribe the story to Hesiod or to Demetrius (see Dué 2002: 61n47).

13. Parthenius 21; Apollonius Rhodius fr.12 Powell; and see Lightfoot 1999: 496–98.

Polycrite of Naxos was a maiden from Naxos. When the Milesians waged war on Naxos to avenge the rape of Neaira, a man named Diognetus, commander of the Erythreans who allied with the Milesians, fell in love with Polycrite. She used his love to the advantage of her native Naxians; she bargained that she would be his if he would consent to her wishes. Bound by oath, he undermined the offensive allies, and the Naxians prevailed in the war. They thanked the daughter of their native soil by giving to her all sorts of gold and ornaments; she was buried under the weight of them and died. A monument marked her place of death.[14]

Scylla is the daughter of Nisus; she betrays her hometown Megara out of love for King Minos, whom she, like Tarpeia, espied from Megara's fortification. Her delivery of Megara was a direct violation of her father, who had a magical lock of hair that would keep him invincible. She cut the lock and delivered it, and therefore Megara, to Minos. He, disgusted, rebuked her and she changed to a bird.[15]

Theano was a member of a priestly family in Troy, wife of Antenor. She and her family advocated that Helen be given back to the Greeks, which disposition was considered treasonous by some. Antenor might have opened Troy's gates to the Greeks, who spared his life. The Greeks left Theano alive at the sack, and she left with Aeneas and later, with Antenor, founded Padua.[16]

Cf. **Rahab,** a woman of Jericho, helped Joshua capture the city for the Israelites. In return for her help Joshua's men did not kill her. Like Tarpeia, she is villainized in some sources as a prostitute.[17]

Cf. **Tharbis** was a princess of the Kush, a region of Ethiopia. When Moses was besieging Meru at the command of Egyptian forces, according to Josephus, Tharbis saw him from the city walls and fell in love with him. She promised him the city, delivered it, and he married her. She later forgot her love for him and remained in Kush when he returned to Egypt.[18]

---

14. Parthenius 9; Polyaenus *Stratagemata* 8.36; Plut. *De Mul Virt* 17 = Mor 254c–f; Aulus Gellius *Noctes Atticae* 3.15; Andriscus = *FGrH* 500.1; Theophrastus 626.

15. Scylla's is a complex tradition with tens of references, among which are Callimachus *Hecale* fr. 90H; Ovid *Met.* 8.1–151 and *Ciris*; Apollodorus 3.15.8; Aesch. *Cho.* 612–22; and the scholia to Dionysius Periegetes 420 = SH 637a. See Lyne 1978 for a full discussion.

16. Homer *Iliad* 6.297–310; Lycophron 340–47 with Tzetzes' commentary; Pausanias 10.27.3; Servius *ad Aen.* 1.242.

17. Joshua 2.1 and the Septuagint translators; Josephus merely calls her an innkeeper (5.1.2). Cf. Joshua 6:17, 23, and 25; James 2:25; Hebrews 11:31.

18. Josephus *Jewish Antiquities* 2.252–53; Numbers 12:1.

BIBLIOGRAPHY

Acosta-Hughes, B., and S. A. Stephens. 2012. *Callimachus in Context: From Plato to the Augustan Poets.* Cambridge: Cambridge University Press.

Albertson, F. 1990. "The Basilica Aemilia Frieze: Religion and Politics in Late Republican Rome." *Latomus* 49: 801–15.

Allen, J. H., J. B. Greenough, G. L. Kittredge, A. A. Howard, and B. L. D'Ooge, eds. 1903. *Allen and Greenough's New Latin Grammar for Schools and Colleges.* Boston: Ginn & Co.

Anderson, G. 1993. *The Second Sophistic: A Cultural Phenomenon in the Roman Empire.* New York: Routledge.

Andrén, A. 1960. "Dionysius of Halicarnassus on Roman Monuments." In *Hommages à Léon Hermann.* Collection Latomus 44: 88–104.

Arena, V. 2013. *Libertas and the Practice of Roman Politics in the Late Roman Republic.* Cambridge: Cambridge University Press.

Arvidsson, S. 2006. *Aryan Idols: Indo-European Mythology as Ideology and Science.* Chicago: University of Chicago Press.

Arya, D. 1996. "The Figural Frieze of the Basilica Aemilia: A New Perspective in Building Context and Pentelic Marble." Master's thesis, University of Texas at Austin.

———. 2000. "Il fregio della Basilica Paulli (Aemilia)." In *Roma: Romolo, Remo e la fondazione della città,* edited by A. Carandini and R. Cappelli. Rome: Museo Nazionale Romano, Terme di Diocleziano. 303–19.

Augoustakis, A. 2010. *Motherhood and the Other.* New York: Oxford University Press.

Ax, W. 1996. "Pragmatic arguments in morphology. Varro's defence of analogy in book 9 of his *de lingua Latina.*" In *Ancient Grammar: Content and Context,* edited by P. Swiggers and A. Wouters. *Orbis. Supplementa* 7. Leuven: Peeters. 105–19.

Babelon, E. 1885. *Description historique et chronologique des Monnaies de la Republique Romain.* Vol 2. Paris: Rollin et Feuardent.

Badian, E. 1968. *Roman Imperialism in the Late Republic.* Oxford: Basil Blackwell.

Bagnall, R. S., and P. Derow, eds. 2008. *The Hellenistic Period: Historical Sources in Translation.* Oxford: Blackwell.

Baier, T. 1997. *Werk und Wirkung Varros im Spiegel seiner Zeitgenossen von Cicero bis Ovid.* Hermes einzelschriften 73. Stuttgart: Franz Steiner.

———. 1999. "Myth and Politics in Varro's Historical Writings." *EMC* 18: 351–67.

Balot, R. 2001. *Greed and Injustice in Classical Athens.* Princeton, NJ: Princeton University Press.

Barber, E. A., ed. 1960. *Sexti Properti Carmina.* Oxford: Oxford University Press.

Barchiesi, A. 1997. *The Poet and the Prince: Ovid and Augustan Discourse.* Berkeley: University of California Press.

Barnes, C. L. H. 2005. *Images and Insults: Ancient Historiography and the Outbreak of the Tarentine War.* Stuttgart: Steiner.

Bartel, H. and A. Simon. 2010. *Unbinding Medea: Interdisciplinary Approaches to a Classical Myth from Antiquity to the 21st Century.* London: Legenda.

Bauer, H. 1988. "Basilica Aemilia." In *Kaiser Augustus und die verlorene Republik : eine Ausstellung im Martin-Gropius-Bau, Berlin, 7 Juni-14 August 1988*, edited by M. Höfter et al. Mainz: Von Zabern. 200–12.

Beard, M. 1980. "The Sexual Status of Vestal Virgins." *JRS* 70: 12–27.

———. 1993. "Looking (Harder) for Roman Myth: Dumézil, Declamation and the Problems of Definition." In *Mythos in mythenloser gesellschaft: das Paradeigma Roms*, edited by F. Graf. Stuttgart: Teubner. 44–64.

———. 1995. "Re-reading (Vestal) Virginity." In *Women in Antiquity: New Assessments*, edited by R. Hawley and B. Levick. London: Routledge. 166–77.

———. 2007. *The Roman Triumph.* Cambridge, MA: Harvard University Press.

Beck, R. 1984. "Mithraism since Franz Cumont." *ANRW* 2.17 (4): 2002–15.

Berti, M. 2013. "Collecting Quotations by Topic: Degrees of Preservation and Transtextual Relations among Genres." *Ancient Society* 43: 269–88.

Bettini, M. 2006. "*Mythos/Fabula:* Authoritative and Discredited Speech." *HR* 45: 195–212.

———. 2008. "Weighty Words, Suspect Speech: *Fari* in Roman Culture." *Arethusa* 41: 313–75.

Bianchi Bandinelli, R. 1970. *Rome, the Centre of Power: Roman Art to AD 200.* London: Thames & Hudson.

———. 1971. *Rome, the Late Empire: Roman Art, AD 200–400.* London: Thames & Hudson.

Bieber, M. 1973. "The Development of Portraiture on Roman Republican Coins." *ANRW* 1.4: 871–98.

Biss, E. 2009. *Notes from No Man's Land: American Essays.* St. Paul, MN: Graywolf Press.

Bitarello, M. 2009. "Etruscan Otherness in Latin Literature." *GR* 56: 211–33.

Bloch, René. 2011. *Moses und der Mythos: die Auseinandersetzung mit der griechischen Mythologie bei jüdisch-hellenistischen Autoren.* Supplements to the *Journal for the Study of Judaism* 145. Leiden: Brill.

Blondell, R. 2010. "'Bitch That I Am': Self-Blame and Self-Assertion in the Iliad." *TAPA* 140: 1–32.

Bloom, H. 1994. *The Western Canon: The Books and School of the Ages.* New York: Harcourt Brace.

Bloomer, W. M. 1992. *Valerius Maximus and the Rhetoric of the New Nobility.* Chapel Hill: University of North Carolina Press.

Bömer, F. 1969. *P. Ovidius Naso: Metamorphosen.* Heidelberg: C. Winter Universitätsverlag.

Borbonus, D. 2014. *Columbarium Tombs and Collective Identity in Augustan Rome.* Cambridge: Cambridge University Press.

Bourdieu, P. 1993. *The Field of Cultural Production.* Edited and introduced by R. Johnson. New York: Columbia University Press.

Bowie, E. L. 2000. "Athenaeus' Knowledge of Early Greek Elegiac and Iambic Poetry." In *Athenaeus and His World*, edited by D. Braund and J. Wilkins. Exeter: Exeter University Press. 124–35.

Boyd, B. W. 1984. "Tarpeia's Tomb: A Note on Propertius 4.4" *AJPh* 105: 85–86.

Braund, S. M. 2004. "*Libertas* or *licentia*? Freedom and Criticism in Roman Satire." In *Free Speech in Classical Antiquity*, edited by I. Sluiter and R. Rosen. Leiden: Brill. 409–28.

Bremmer, J. 1981. "Plutarch and the Naming of Greek Women." *AJPh* 102: 425–26.

———. 1983. "Scapegoat Rituals in Ancient Greece." *Harvard Studies in Classical Philology.* Vol 87. 299–320.

———. 2008. *Greek Religion and Culture, the Bible and the Ancient Near East.* Leiden: Brill.

Bremmer, J. N., and N. M. Horsfall, eds. 1987. *Roman Myth and Mythography.* BICS Supplement 52.

Brenk, F. E. 1979. "Tarpeia among the Celts: Watery Romance, from Simylus to Propertius." In *Studies in Latin Literature and Roman History, I*, edited by C. Deroux. *Collection Latomus.* 166–74.

Brilliant, R. 1973. Review of *Rome, the Centre of Power* by R. Bianchi Bandinelli and *Rome: The Late Empire* by R. Bianchi Bandinelli. *The Art Bulletin* 55: 282–85.

Briquel, D. 1991. *L'Origine lydienne des Étrusques. Histoire de la doctrine dans l'Antiquité.* École Française de Rome.

Broughton, T. S. R. 1951. *Magistrates of the Roman Republic.* Oxford: Oxford University Press.

Brunt, P. A. 1965. "Italian Aims at the Time of the Social War." *JRS* 55: 90–109.

———. 1980. "On Historical Fragments and Epitomes." *CQ* 30: 477–94.

Buehler, W. 1962. "Die doppelte Erzaehlung des Aitions der Nonae Caprotinae bei Plutarch." *Maia* 14: 271–82.

Buonocore, M. (Rome). 2012. "Vestini." *Brill's New Pauly.* Antiquity volumes edited by H. Cancik and H. Schneider. Brill Online, August 11, 2012. http://www.encquran.brill.nl/entries/brill-s-new-pauly/vestini-e1220243o.

Burkert, W. 1979. *Structure and History in Greek Mythology and Ritual.* Berkeley: University of California Press.

———. 1985. *Greek Religion.* Translated by John Raffan. Cambridge, MA: Harvard University Press.

———. 1993. "Mythos—Begriff, Struktur, Funktionen." In *Mythos in mythenloser Gesellschaft*, edited by F. Graf. Stuttgart: Teubner. 9–24.

Burnett, A. M. 1998. "The Coinage of the Social War." In *Coins of Macedonia and Rome: Essays in Honour of Charles Hersh*, edited by A. M. Burnett and R. Witschonke. London: Spink and Son Ltd. 165–72.

Burton, J. B. 1995. *Theocritus's Urban Mimes: Mobility, Gender, and Patronage*. Berkeley, CA: University of California Press.

Burton, P. 2004. "*Amicitia* in Plautus: A Study of Roman Friendship Processes."*AJPh* 125: 209–43.

Butler, H. E. 2004. *Post-Augustan Poetry*. Whitefish, MT: Kessinger.

Calame, C. 2009. *Greek Mythology: Poetics, Pragmatics, and Fiction*. Cambridge: Cambridge University Press.

———. 2011. "The Semiotics and Pragmatics of Myth." Translated by K. Dowden. In *A Companion to Greek Mythology*, edited by K. Dowden and N. Livingstone. Oxford: Wiley Blackwell. 507–24.

Camps, W. A. 1965. *Propertius Elegies Book IV*. Cambridge: Cambridge University Press.

Carettoni, G. 1961. "Il fregio figurato della basilica Emilia: rinvenimento, dati tecnici, collocazione." *RIA* 10: 5–78.

Cary, E. 1937. *Dionysius of Halicarnassus: Roman Antiquities*. Cambridge, MA: Harvard University Press.

Cassola, F. 1962. *I gruppi politici romani nel III secolo a. C.* Trieste: Università, Istituto di Storia Antica.

Cavazza, F. 1981. *Studio su Varrone etimologico e grammatico: La lingua latina come modello di struttura linguistica*. Firenze: La Nuova Italia.

Champion, C. B. 2004. "Material Rewards and the Drive for Empire." In *Roman Imperialism: Readings and Sources*. Malden, MA: Blackwell. 30–46.

———. Forthcoming. "Livy and the Greek Historians from Herodotus to Dionysius: Soundings and Reflections." In *Blackwell's Companion to Livy*, edited by B. Mineo. Oxford: Wiley-Blackwell.

Champlin, E. 2006. "Tiberiana 2: Tales of Brave Ulysses." Working Papers in Classics. Princeton University (PDF online).

Chaplin, J. 2000. *Livy's Exemplary History*. Oxford: Oxford University Press.

Clarke, K. 1999. "Universal Perspectives in Historiography." In *The Limits of Historiography: Genre and Narrative in Ancient Historical Texts*, edited by C. S. Kraus. Leiden: Brill. 249–79.

Clauss, J. J., and S. Iles Johnston, eds. 1996. *Medea: Essays on Medea in Myth, Literature, Philosophy and Art*. Princeton, NJ: Princeton University Press

Clauss, M. 2001. *The Roman Cult of Mithras: The God and His Mysteries*. Translated by R. Gordon. London: Routledge.

Coarelli, F. 1983. *Il Foro Romano: Periodo Arcaico*. Rome: Quasar.

———. 1997. *Il Campo Marzio: dalle origini alla fine della Repubblica*. Roma: Edizioni Quasar.

Cocchi, E. Ercolana. 2004. "*Aeternitas* e il crescente lunare in etàrepubblicana, ovvero: la riabilitazione di Tarpeia." In *La Tradizione Iconica come Fonte Storica,* edited by M. C. Caltabiano et al. Reggio Calabria, Italy: Falzea. 47–73.

Cohen, D. 1991. "The Augustan Law on Adultery: The Social and Cultural Context." In *The Family in Italy: From Antiquity to the Present,* edited by D. Kertzer and R. Saller. New Haven, CT: Yale University Press. 109–26.

Colish, M. (1985) 1990. *The Stoic Tradition from Antiquity to the Early Middle Ages.* Studies in the History of Christian Thought 34. Leiden: Brill.

Collart, J. 1954. *Varron Grammairien Latin.* Paris: Les Belles Lettres.

Connolly, J. 2009. "Virtue and Violence: The Historians on Politics." In *The Cambridge Companion to Roman Historians,* edited by A. Feldherr. New York: Cambridge University Press. 181–94.

Corbeill, A. C. 1996. *Controlling Laughter: Political Humor in the Late Roman Republic.* Princeton, NJ: Princeton University Press.

Corbier, M. 1995. "Male Power and Legitimacy through Women: The Domus Augustua Under the Julio-Claudians." In *Women in Antiquity: New Assessments,* edited by R. Hawley and B. Levick. London: Routledge. 178–93.

Coudry, M. 1998. "La deuxième guerre punique chez Valère Maxime." In *Valeurs et Mémoire à Rome: Valère Maxime ou la vertu recomposée,* edited by J.–M. David. Paris: de Boccard. 45–53.

Crawford, M. 1969. *Roman Republican Coin Hoards.* London: Roman Numismatic Society.

———. 1974. *Roman Republican Coinage.* Vol. 1. Cambridge: Cambridge University Press.

———. 1985. *Coinage and Money Under the Roman Republic: Italy and the Mediterranean Economy.* Berkeley and Los Angeles: University of California Press.

Croft, W. 2002. "Typology." In *The Handbook of Linguistics,* edited by M. Aronoff and J. Rees-Miller. Oxford: Blackwell. 337–68.

Culham, P. 1982. "The Lex Oppia." *Latomus* 41: 786–93.

Curti, E. 2001. "Toynbee's Legacy: Discussing Aspects of the Romanization of Italy." In *Italy and the West: Comparative Issues in Romanization,* edited by S. Keay and N. Terrenato. Oxford: Oxbow Books. 17–26.

D'Ambra, E. 1993. *Private Lives, Imperial Virtues: The Frieze of the Forum Transitorium in Rome.* Princeton, NJ: Princeton University Press.

Dahlmann, J. H. 1932. *Varro und die hellenistische Sprachtheorie.* Berlin: Weidmann.

———. "Varro." *RE* Suppl. 6 (1935) col. 1172–84, *Paulys Real-Encyclopädie der classischen Altertumswissenschaft.* Supplement. Stuttgart. Edited by August Friedrich von Pauly, Georg Wissowa, Wilhelm Kroll, and K. Witte, 16 vols. Stuttgart: J. B. Metzler, 1903–78.

Daremberg, C., and E. Saglio, eds. 1873. *Dictionnaire des Antiquités Grecques et Romaines.* Paris: Hachette.

David, J-M. 1984. "Du Comitium à la Roche Tarpéienne: sur certains rituels d'exécution capitale sous la République, les règnes d'Auguste et de Tibère." In *Du Châtiment dans la Cite. Supplices corporels et peine de mort dans le monde antique,* edited by Y. Thomas l'École française de Rome 79, Rome. 131–75.

———. 1996. *The Roman Conquest of Italy.* Oxford: Oxford University Press.

———, ed. 1998. *Valeurs et Mémoire à Rome. Valère Maxime ou la vertu recomposée.* Paris: de Boccard.

De Angelis, F., J.-A. Dickmann, F. Pirson, and R. von den Hoff, eds. 2012. *Kunst von unten? Stil und Gesellschaft in der antiken Welt von der "arte plebeian" bis heute.* Palilia 27. Wiesbaden: Rochert Verlag.

de Grummond, N. T. 1990. "*Pax Augusta* and the *Horae* on the *Ara Pacis Augustae.*" *American Journal of Archaeology* 94: 663–77.

de Jonge, C. 2008. *Between Grammar and Rhetoric: Dionysius of Halicarnassus on Language, Linguistics and Literature.* Mnemosyne Supplement 301. Leiden: Brill.

de Sanctis, G. 1964. *Storia dei Romani.* Firenze: Nuova Italia.

de Vaan, M. 2008. *Etymological Dictionary of Latin and the Other Italic Languages.* Leiden: Brill.

DeBrohun, J. 2003. *Roman Propertius and the Reinvention of Elegy.* Ann Arbor: University of Michigan Press.

Degrassi, A. 1954. *Fasti Capitolini recensuit: praefatus est, indicibus instruxit Atilius Degrassi* Corpus scriptorum Latinorum Paravianum. Turin: Paravia.

———. 1963. *Inscriptiones Italiae, Vol. XIII—Fasti et elogia, fasc. II—Fasti anni Numani et Iuliani.* Rome: Istituto Poligrafico dello Stato.

della Corte, F. 1982. "*Le leges Iuliae e l'elegia romana.*" *ANRW* 2.30 (1): 539–58.

Dench, E. 1995. *From Barbarians to New Men: Greek, Roman, and Modern Perceptions of Peoples of the Central Apennines.* Oxford: Clarendon.

———. 1998. "Austerity, Excess, Success, and Failure in Hellenistic and Early Imperial Italy." In *Parchments of Gender: Deciphering the Bodies of Antiquity*, edited by M. Wyke. Oxford: Oxford University Press. 136–41.

———. 2005a. "Beyond Greeks and Barbarians: Italy and Sicily in the Hellenistic Age." In *A Companion to the Hellenistic World*, edited by A. Erskine. Malden, MA: Blackwell. 294–310.

———. 2005b. *Romulus' Asylum. Roman Identities from the Age of Alexander to the Age of Hadrian.* Oxford: Oxford University Press.

Denniston, J. D. (1934) 1966. *Greek Particles.* 2nd ed. Oxford: Clarendon.

Devoto, G. (1940) 1991. *Storia della lingua di Roma.* Bologna: Cappelli.

———. 1958. "La leggenda di Tarpea e gli Etruschi." *Studi Etruschi* 26: 17–25.

Dillery, J. 2009. "Roman Historians and the Greeks, Audiences and Models." In *Cambridge Companion to Roman Historiography*, edited by A. Feldherr. Cambridge: Cambridge University Press. 77–107.

Dillon, J. 1997. "Plutarch and the End of History." In *Plutarch and His Intellectual World*, edited by J. Mossman. London: Duckworth. 169–88.

Dixon, S. 1992. *The Roman Family.* Baltimore: Johns Hopkins University Press.

Dorandi, T., ed. 1999. *Antigone de Caryste. Fragments.* Paris: Les Belles Lettres.

Dosse, F. (1991) 1997. *History of Structuralism, Volume I: The Rising Sign, 1945–1966.* Translated by D. Glassman. Minneapolis: University of Minnesota Press.

Dougherty, C. 1998. "Sowing the Seeds of Violence: Rape, Women, and the Land." In *Parchments of Gender,* edited by M. Wyke. Oxford: Oxford University Press. 267–84.

Dué, C. 2002. *Homeric Variations on a Lament by Briseis*. Lanham, MD: Rowman and Littlefield.

Duff, T. 1997. "Moral Ambiguity in Plutarch's Lysander-Sulla" In *Plutarch and His Intellectual World*, edited by J. Mossman. London: Duckworth. 169–88.

Dumézil, G. 1947. *Tarpeia: Essais de philology comparative indo-européenne*. Paris: Gallimard.

———. 1970. *Archaic Roman Religion*. Translated by P. Krapp. Chicago: University of Chicago Press.

———. 1973. *Mythe et épopée*. Paris: Gallimard.

DuQuesnay, I. M. 1984. "Horace and Maecenas: The Propaganda Value of *Sermones* I." In *Poetry and Politics in the Age of Augustus*, edited by T. Woodman and D. West. Cambridge: Cambridge University Press. 19–58.

Durbec, Y. 2011. "Individual figures in Callimachus." In *Brill's Companion to Callimachus*, edited by B. Acosta-Hughes, L. Lehnus and S. A. Stephens. Leiden: Brill. 468–86.

Edwards, C. 1993. *The Politics of Immorality in Ancient Rome*. Cambridge: Cambridge University Press.

———. 1996. *Writing Rome: Textual Approaches to the City*. Cambridge: Cambridge University Press.

Elkins, N. 2009. "Coins, Contexts, and an Iconographic Approach for the 21st Century." In H.-M. von Kaenel and F. Kemmers, eds., *Coins in Context I: New Perspectives for the Interpretation of Coin Finds* = *SFMA* 23: 25–46.

Elsner, J. 1996. "Naturalism and the Erotics of the Gaze: Intimations of Narcissus." In *Sexuality in Ancient Art*, edited by N. B. Kampen. Cambridge: Cambridge University Press. 247–61.

Eribon, D. 1992. *Faut-il brûler Dumézil? Mythologie, science et politique*. Paris: Flammarion.

Ertel, C. et al. 2007. "Nuove indagini sulla Basilica Aemilia nel Foro Romano." *AC* 58: 109–42.

Evans, J. D. 1992. *The Art of Persuasion: Political Propaganda from Aeneas to Brutus*. Ann Arbor: University of Michigan Press.

Farney, G. D. 2007. *Ethnic Identity and Aristocratic Competition in Republican Rome*. New York: Cambridge University Press.

Farrell, J. 2001. *Latin Language and Latin Culture from Ancient to Modern Times*. Cambridge: Cambridge University Press.

Favro, D. 1996. *The Urban Image of Augustan Rome*. New York: Cambridge University Press.

Fedeli, P., ed. 1984. *Sexti Properti: Elegiarum Libri IV*. Stuttgart: Teubner.

Feldherr, A. 1998. *Spectacle and Society in Livy's History*. Berkeley: University of California Press.

Fletcher, J. 1999. "Choral Voice and Narrative in the First Stasimon of Aeschylus *Agamemnon*." *Phoenix* 53: 29–49.

Forsythe, G. 1990. "The Tribal Membership of the Calpurnii Pisones." *ZPE* 83: 293–98.

———. 1994. *The Historian L. Calpurnius Piso Frugi and the Roman Annalistic Tradition*. Lanham, MD: University Press of America.

———. 2006. *A Critical History of Early Rome: From Prehistory to the First Punic War*. Berkeley: University of California Press.

Fox, M. 1993. "History and Rhetoric in Dionysius of Halicarnassus." *The Journal of Roman Studies* 83: 31–47.

———. 1996. *Roman Historical Myths: The Regal Period in Augustan Literature.* Oxford: Oxford University Press.

———. 2011. "The Myth of Rome." In *A Companion to Greek Mythology, Part III: New Traditions,* edited by K. Dowden and N. Livingstone. Chichester: Wiley Blackwell. 243–63.

Francese, C. 2001. *Parthenius of Nicaea and Roman Poetry.* New York: Peter Lang.

Frank, T. 1933. *An Economic Survey of Ancient Rome.* Vol. 1 of *Rome and Italy of the Republic.* Baltimore: Johns Hopkins University Press.

Franko, G. F. 1995. "*Fides,* Aetolia, and Plautus' *Captivi.*" *TAPA* 125: 155–76.

Frede, D., and B. Inwood, eds. 2005. *Language and Learning: Philosophy of Language in the Hellenistic Age.* New York: Cambridge University Press.

Freeble, D. S. 2004. *The Other Greeks: Metaphors and Ironies of Hellenism in Livy's Fourth Decade.* PhD diss., The Ohio State University.

Freudenburg, K. 2001. *Satires of Rome: Threatening Poses from Lucilius to Juvenal.* Cambridge: Cambridge University Press.

Freyberger, K. S. et al. 2007. "Neue Forschungen zur Basilica Aemilia auf dem Forum Romanum." *Römische Mitteilungen* 113: 493–552.

Freyburger, G. 1986. "*Fides.* Étude sémantique et religieuse depuis les origines jusqu'à l'époque augustéenne." *IL* 36: 70–73.

Frier, B. W. (1979) 1999. *Libri Annales Pontificum Maximorum: The Origins of the Annalistic Tradition.* Ann Arbor: University of Michigan Press.

Frith, S. 2004. "A Primitive Exchange: On Rhetoric and Architectural Symbol." *Architecture Research Quarterly* 8: 39–45.

Fuhrer, T. 2012. "*Teichoskopia*: Female Figures Looking on Battles." Paper presented at the Colloquium Balticum XI Lundense, Lund.

Gabba, E. (1973) 1976. "The Origins of the Social War and Roman Politics After 89 BC." Translated by P. J. Cuff. In *Republican Rome: The Army and Allies.* Berkeley and Los Angeles: University of California Press. 71–130.

———. 1981. "True History and False History in Classical Antiquity." *JRS* 71: 50–62.

———. 1991. *Dionysius and the History of Archaic Rome.* Berkeley: University of California Press.

———. (1994) 2008. "Rome and Italy: The Social War." In *The Cambridge Ancient History.* Vol. 9, *The Last Age of the Roman Republic, 146–43 BC,* edited by J. A. Crook, A. Lintott, and E. Rawson. Cambridge: Cambridge University Press. 104–28.

Gallo, L. 1984. *Alimentazione e demografia della Grecia antica. Salerno: P. Laveglia Editore. presentazione di Giuseppe Nenci.* Salerno: P. Laveglia Editore.

Gansiniec, Z. 1949. *Tarpeia: The Making of a Myth.* Wratislaviae: Kazimierz Majewski.

Garani, M. 2011. "Revisiting Tarpeia's Myth in Propertius (IV, 4)." *Leeds International Classical Studies* 10(3): 1–22.

García Quintela, M. 2002–2005. "Dumézil, Momigliano, Bloch, Between Politics and Historiography." *Studia Indo-Europaea* 2: 187–205.

Gardner, H. H. 2013. *Gendering Time in Augustan Love Elegy.* Oxford: Oxford University Press.

Gardner, S. 1986. *Women in Roman Law and Society.* Routledge: London.

Gelzer, M. (1933) 1964. "Römische Politik bei Fabius Pictor." *Kleine Schriften* vol. 3, edited by H. Strasburger and C. Meier. Wiesbaden: Franz Steiner Verlag. 51–92.

Gelzer, M., and R. Seagar. 1969. *The Roman Nobility.* Oxford: Basil Blackwell.

Gergel, R. A. 2004. "Agora S166 and Related Works: The Interpretation of the Eastern Hadrianic Breastplate Type." In *Charis: Essays in Honor of Sara Immerwahr*, edited by A. P. Chapin. Princeton, NJ: Princeton University Press. 371–410.

Gibbon, J. 1938. *Canadian Mosaic: The Making of a Northern Nation.* Toronto: McClelland and Stewart.

Gleason, M. W. 1995. *Making Men: Sophists and Self-Representation in Ancient Rome.* Princeton, NJ: Princeton University Press.

Glinister, F. 1997. "Women and Power in Archaic Rome." In *Gender and Ethnicity in Ancient Italy*, edited by T. Cornell and K. Lomas. London: Accordia Research Institute, University of London. 115–28.

Goetz, G., and F. Schoell. 1910. *M. Terentii Varronis De Lingua Latina quae supersunt.* Leipzig: Teubner.

Goldberg, S. M. 2005. *Constructing Literature in the Roman Republic: Poetry and Its Reception.* Cambridge: Cambridge University Press.

Goldhill, S., ed. 2001. *Being Greek under Rome: Cultural Identity, the Second Sophistic and the Development of Empire.* Cambridge: Cambridge University Press.

Goold, G. P., ed. 1990. *Propertius: Elegies.* Cambridge, MA: Harvard University Press.

Gowing, A. 2005. *Empire and Memory: The Representation of the Roman Republic in Imperial Culture.* Cambridge: Cambridge University Press.

Graf, F. 1997. "Medea, the Enchantress from Afar: Remarks on a Well-Known Myth." In *Medea: Essays on Medea in Myth, Literature, Philosophy and Art*, edited by J. J. Clauss and S. Iles Johnston. Princeton, NJ: Princeton University Press. 21–43.

———. 1993. *Greek Mythology: An Introduction.* Translated by T. Marier. Baltimore: Johns Hopkins University Press.

Grassigli, G. L. 2002. "Un'insospettabile afonia creativa in Giotto. Considerazioni sommarie (e non fondamentali) sulla migrazioni di schemi e soggetti." *Ostraka* 11: 157–65.

Green, C. M. C. 2007. *Roman Religion and the Cult of Diana at Aricia.* Cambridge: Cambridge University Press.

Green, S. 2004. *Ovid, Fasti* 1: A Commentary. *Mnemosyne,* Suppl. 251. Leiden: Brill.

Grimal, P. 1951. "Etudes sur Properce, II: César et la légende de Tarpeia." *REL* 29: 201–14.

———. 1953. "Les intentions de Properce et la composition du libre IV des Elegies." *Latomus* 12: 5–53.

Gruen, E. S. (1974) 1995. *The Last Generation of the Roman Republic.* Berkeley: University of California Press.

———. 1984. *The Hellenistic World and the Coming of Rome.* Berkeley and Los Angeles: University of California Press.

———. (1984) 2004. "Material Rewards and the Drive for Empire." In *Roman Imperialism:*

Readings and Sources, edited by C. B. Champion. Malden, Oxford, and Carlton: Blackwell Publishing. 30–46.

———. (1990) 1996. *Studies in Greek Culture and Roman Policy.* Berkeley and Los Angeles: University of California Press.

———. 1992. *Culture and National Identity in Republican Rome.* Ithaca, NY: Cornell University Press.

Gumpert, M. 2001. *Grafting Helen: The Abduction of the Classical Past.* Madison: University of Wisconsin Press.

Gutzwiller, K. 1998. *Poetic Garlands: Hellenistic Epigrams in Context.* Hellenistic Culture and Society 28. Berkeley: University of California Press.

Habicht, C. 1999. *Pausanias' Guide to Ancient Greece.* Berkeley: University of California Press.

Habinek, T. 1997. "The Invention of Sexuality in the World-City of Rome." In *The Roman Cultural Revolution*, edited by T. Habinek and A. Schiesaro. Cambridge: Cambridge University Press. 23–43.

———. 1998. *The Politics of Latin Literature: Writing, Identity, and Empire in Ancient Rome.* Princeton, NJ: Princeton University Press.

Hall, J. M. 2002. *Hellenicity: Between Ethnicity and Culture.* Chicago: University of Chicago Press.

Hallett, J. 1984. *Fathers and Daughters in Roman Society: Women and the Elite Family.* Princeton, NJ: Princeton University Press.

———. 1989. "Women as Same and Other in Classical Roman Elite." *Helios* 16: 59–78.

Hanslik, R. 1962. "Textkritisches in Properz Buch IV." *RhM* 105: 236–52.

Hardie, P. R. 1991. "Plutarch and the Interpretation of Myth." *ANRW* 2.33 (6): 4743–87.

Harris, W. V. 1979. *War and Imperialism in Republican Rome, 327–70 BC* Oxford: Clarendon.

———. (1971) 2004. "On War and Greed in the Second Century BC." In *Roman Imperialism: Readings and Sources*, edited by C. B. Champion. Oxford: Blackwell. 17–29.

Herbert-Brown, G., ed. 2002. *Ovid's Fasti: Historical Readings at Its Bimillenium.* Oxford: Oxford University Press.

Hersch, K. 2010. *Roman Wedding: Ritual and Meaning in Antiquity.* New York: Cambridge University Press.

Hetzner, U. 1963. *Andromeda und Tarpeia.* Meisenheim am Glan: A. Hain.

Hexter, Ralph. 1992. "Sidonian Dido." In *Innovations of Antiquity*, edited by R. Hexter and D. Selden. London. 332–84.

Heyworth, S. J. 1999. "Propertius: Division, Transmission, and the Editor's Task." *PCPhS* Suppl. Vol. 22: 165–85.

———. 2007a. *Cynthia: A Companion to the Text of Propertius.* Oxford: Oxford University Press.

———. 2007b. *Sexti Properti Elegi.* Oxford: Oxford University Press.

Hinds, S. 1998. *Allusion and Intertext.* Cambridge: Cambridge University Press.

———. 2006. "Venus, Varro, and the Vates: Toward the Limits of Etymologizing Interpretation." *Dictynna* 3. http://dictynna.revues.org/206.

Hölkeskamp, K.-J. 1996. "*Exempla* und *mos maiorum*: Überlegungen zum kollektiven Gedächtnis der Nobilität." In *Vergangenheit und Lebenswelt: Soziale Kommunikation, Traditionsbildung und historisches Bewußtsein,* edited by H.-J. Gehrke and A. Möller. Tübingen: G. Narr. 301–38.

Holleman, A. W. J. 1984. "Considerations about the Tomb of the Claudiand at Cerveterii." *Historia* 33: 504–8.

Holliday, P. 2005. "The Rhetoric of '*Romanitas*': The Tomb of the Statilii Frescoes Reconsidered." *MAAR* 50: 89–129.

Hollis, A. S. 1970. *Ovid Metamorphoses Book VIII.* Oxford: Oxford University Press.

———. 2003. "Myth in the Service of Kings and Emperors." In *Mitos en la literatura griega helenística e imperial,* edited by J. A. López Férez. Madrid: Ediciones Clásicas. 1–14.

Holscher, T. 1988. "Historische Reliefs." In *Kaiser Augustus und die verlorene Republik: Eine Ausstellung im Martin-Gropius-Bau, Berlin, 7 Juni-14 August 1988,* edited by M. Höfter et al. Mainz: Von Zabern. 351–400.

Horsfall, N. M. 1987. "From History to Legend: M. Manlius and the Geese." In *Roman Myth and Mythography,* edited by J. Bremmer and N. M. Horsfall. *BICS* Supplement 52. 63–75.

———. 1993. "Mythological Invention and poetica licentia." In *Mythos in mythenloser gesellschaft: Das Paradeigma Roms,* edited by F. Graf. Stuttgart: Teubner. 131–41.

Hoyos, D. 2007. "The Age of Overseas Expansion (264–146 BC)." In *A Companion to the Roman Army,* edited by P. Erdkamp. Oxford: Blackwell. 63–79.

Hubbard, M. 1975. *Propertius.* London: Duckworth.

Hutchinson, G., ed. 2006. *Propertius: Elegies, Book 4.* Cambridge: Cambridge University Press.

Huxley, G. L. 1982. "Arne Sithonis." *CQ* 32: 159–61.

Ingenkamp, H. G. 2004. "How to Present a Statesman?" In *The Statesman in Plutarch's Works.* Vol. 1, *Plutarch's Statesman and His Aftermath: Political, Philosophical, and Literary Aspects,* edited by L. de Blois et al. *Mnemosyne* Supplement. Leiden: Brill. 67–86.

Isaac, B. 2004. *The Invention of Racism in Classical Antiquity.* Princeton, NJ: Princeton University Press.

Jacoby, F., ed. 1957. *Die Fragmente der griechischen Historiker.* Leiden: Brill.

Jaeger, M. 1997. *Livy's Written Rome.* Ann Arbor: University of Michigan Press.

James, S. L. 2003. *Learned Girls and Male Persuasion: Gender and Reading in Roman Love Elegy.* Berkeley: University of California Press.

Janan, M. 1999. "Beyond Good and Evil: Tarpeia and the Philosophy of the Feminine." *CW* 92: 429–43.

———. 2001. *The Politics of Desire: Propertius IV.* Berkeley: University of California Press.

Jenkyns, R. 2015. *God, Space, and City in the Roman Imagination.* Oxford: Oxford University Press.

Johnson, W. R. 2009. *A Latin Lover in Ancient Rome.* Columbus: The Ohio State University Press.

Johnston, P. A. 1980. "*Poenulus* 1, 2 and Roman Women." *TAPA* 110: 143–59.

Jones, C. P. 1971. *Plutarch and Rome.* Oxford: Clarendon.

Jones, P. 2001. "Saving Water: Early Floods in the Forum." In *Between Magic and Religion: Interdisciplinary Studies in Ancient Mediterranean Religion and Society*, edited by S. Asirvatham, C. O. Pache, and J. Watrous. Lanham, MD: Rowman and Littlefield. 35–46.

Joplin (Klindienst), P. 1990. "Ritual Work on Human Flesh: Livy's Lucretia and the Rape of the Body Politic." *Helios* 17: 51–70.

Joshel, S. 1992. "The Body Female and the Body Politic: Livy's Lucretia and Verginia." In *Pornography and Representation in Greece and Rome*, edited by A. Richlin. New York: Oxford University Press. 112–30.

Kampen, N. B. 1988. "The Muted Other." *Art Journal* 47: 15–19.

———. 1991. "The Reliefs of the Basilica Aemilia: A Redating." *Klio* 73: 448–58.

———. 1996. "Gender Theory in Roman Art." In *I, Claudia: Women in Ancient Rome*, edited by D. Kleiner and S. Matheson. New Haven, CT: Yale University Art Gallery. 14–25.

Kaster, R. 2001. "Controlling Reason: Declamation in Rhetorical Education at Rome." In *Education in Greek and Roman Antiquity*, edited by Y. L. Too. Leiden: Brill. 317–37.

Keegan, P. M. 2002. "Seen, Not Heard: *Feminea Lingua* in Ovid's *Fasti* and the Critical Gaze." In *Ovid's Fasti: Historical Readings at Its Bimillenium,* edited by G. Herbert-Brown. New York: Oxford University Press. 129–53.

Kent, R. G. 1938. *Varro on the Latin Language*. Cambridge, MA: Harvard University Press.

Kermode, F. 1983. *The Classic: Literary Images of Permanence and Change*. Cambridge, MA: Harvard University Press.

Kennedy, D. 1992. "Augustan and Anti-Augustan: Reflections on Terms of Reference." In *Roman Poetry and Propaganda in the Age of Augustus*, edited by A. Powell. London: Bristol Classical. 26–58.

King, R. 2006. *Desiring Rome: Male Subjectivity and Reading Ovid's Fasti*. Columbus: The Ohio State University Press.

Kleiner, D. E. 1978. "The Great Friezes of the Ara Pacis Augustae: Greek Sources, Roman Derivatives, and Augustan Social Policy." *MEFRA* 90: 753–85.

Knox, B. 1950. "The Serpent and the Flame: The Imagery of the Second Book of the *Aeneid*." *AJP* 71: 379–400.

Kolbas, E. D. 2001. *Critical Theory and the Literary Canon*. Boulder, CO: Westview.

Konstan, D. 1986. "Narrative and Ideology in Livy Book 1." *ClAnt* 5: 198–215.

———. 1994. *Sexual Symmetry: Love in the Ancient Novel and Related Genres*. Princeton, NJ: Princeton University Press.

Koptev, A. 2005. "'Three Brothers' at the Head of Archaic Rome: The King and His 'Consuls.'" *Historia* 54: 382–423.

Krappe, A. H. 1929. "Die sage von der Tarpeia." *RM* 78: 249–67.

Kumaniecki, K. 1967. "Twenty Years of Classical Philology in Poland." *Greece and Rome* 14: 61–76.

Kuttner, A. 1995. *Dynasty and Empire in the Age of Augustus: The Case of the Boscoreale Cups*. Berkeley and Los Angeles: University of California Press.

La Penna, A. 2000. "Le Sabinae di Ennio e le Fenicie di Euripide." *SIFC* 18: 52–54.

LaLonde, D. 2012. "Tarpeia's Peace Treaty in Propertius 4.4." Paper presented at the Annual Meeting of the American Philological Association Conference, Philadelphia, PA, January 6.

Lamberton, R. 2001. *Plutarch.* New Haven, CT: Yale University Press.

Lambropoulou, V. 1995. "Some Pythagorean Female Virtues." In *Women in Antiquity: New Assessments,* edited by R. Hawley and B. Levick. London: Routledge. 122–34.

Langendoen, D. 1966. "A Note on the Linguistic Theory of M. Terentius Varro." *Foundations of Language* 2: 33–36.

Langlands, R. 2006. *Sexual Morality in Ancient Rome.* Cambridge: Cambridge University Press.

———. 2008. "'Reading for the Moral' in Valerius Maximus: The Case of *Severitas.*" *CCJ* 54: 160–87.

———. 2011. "Roman *Exempla* and Situation Ethics: Valerius Maximus and Cicero *de Officiis.*" *JRS* 101: 1–23.

Larmour, D. H. J. 1988. "Plutarch's Compositional Methods in the Theseus and Romulus." *TAPA* 118: 361–75.

———. 1992. "Making Parallels: Synkrisis and Plutarch's 'Themistocles and Camillus,'" *ANRW* 2.33.6: 4162–74.

Larson, J. L. 1995. *Greek Heroine Cults.* Madison: University of Wisconsin Press.

Latte, K. (1960) 1967. *Römische Religionsgeschichte.* München: C. H. Beck.

Lawrence, S. J. 2006. *Inside Out: The Depiction of Externality in Valerius Maximus.* PhD Thesis, University of Sydney.

Lazenby, J. F. 1996. *The First Punic War: A Military History.* Stanford: Stanford University Press.

Leumann, M., J. B. Hofmann, and A. Szantyr. 1977. *Lateinische Syntax und Stilistik.* München: C. H. Beck.

Lightfoot, J. L., ed. 1999. *Parthenius of Nicaea: The Poetical Fragments and the Erotica Pathemata.* Oxford: Clarendon.

Lincoln, B. 1991. *Death, War, and Sacrifice. Studies in Ideology and Practice.* Chicago: University of Chicago Press.

Littleton, C. S. 1974. "'Je ne suis pas . . . structuraliste': Some Fundamental Differences between Dumezil and Levi-Strauss." *The Journal of Asian Studies* 34: 151–58.

Littlewood, R. J. 2006. *A Commentary on Ovid: Fasti Book VI.* New York: Oxford University Press.

Lobur, J. A. 2008. *Consensus, Concordia, and the Formation of Roman Imperial Ideology.* Studies in Classics. New York: Routledge.

Lockyear, K. 2013. *Coin Hoards of the Roman Republic Online,* version 1. New York: American Numismatic Society. Data retrieved from <http://numismatics.org/chrr> on May 8, 2014.

Loman, P. 2004. *The Mobility of Hellenistic Women.* PhD Thesis, University of Nottingham.

Lombardo, M. 1983. "*Habrosyne* e *habra* nel mondo greco arcaico." In *Forme di contatto e processi di trasformazione nella società antiche.* Pisa/Rome: Scuola Normale Superiore / École Française de Rome. 1077–1103.

Loraux, N. (1987) 1991. *Tragic Ways of Killing a Woman.* Translated by Anthony Forster. Cambridge, MA: Harvard University Press.

Lorsch Wildfang, R. 2006. *Rome's Vestal Virgins: A Study of Rome's Vestal Priestesses in the Latest Republic and Early Empire.* New York: Routledge.

Luce, T. 1968. "Political Propaganda on Republican Coins: Circa 92–82 BC." *AJA* 72: 25–39.

———. 1977. *Livy: The Composition of His History.* Princeton, NJ: Princeton University Press.

Luraghi, N. 2003. "Dionysios von Halikarnassos zwischen Griechen und Römern." In *Formen römischer Geschichtsschreibung von den Anfängen bis Livius,* edited by U. Eigler et al. Darmstadt: Kontexte. 268–86.

Lyne, R. O. A. M. 1978. *Ciris.* Cambridge: Cambridge University Press.

Maltby, R. 1991. *A Lexicon of Ancient Latin Etymologies.* Leeds: Francis Cairns.

Manfredini, M., and C. Ampolo 1988. *Plutarco: Le vite di Teseao e Romolo.* Milan: Mondadori.

Marincola, J. 1997. *Authority and Tradition in Ancient Historiography.* Cambridge: Cambridge University Press.

———. 2010. "The Rhetoric of History: Allusion, Intertextuality, and Exemplarity in Historiographical Speeches." In *Stimmen der Geschichte: Funktionen von Reden in der antiken Historiographie,* edited by D. Pausch. Berlin and New York: De Gruyter. 259–89.

———. 2011. "Intertextuality and *Exempla.*" *Histos* Working Papers No. 2011.3. http://research.ncl.ac.uk/histos/documents/2011WP03MarincolaIntertextualityandExempla.pdf (accessed May 2014).

———, ed. 2007. *A Companion to Greek and Roman Historiography.* 2 vols. Malden, MA: Blackwell.

Marszal, J. 2000. "Ubiquitous Barbarians: Representations of the Gauls at Pergamon and Elsewhere." In *From Pergamon to Sperlonga: Sculpture and Context,* edited by N. de Grummond and B. S. Ridgway. Berkeley: University of California Press. 191–234.

Martini, C. 1998. "Il fatto di Tarpeia. Virgo Vestalis *ante litteram.*" In *Due studi sulla riscrittura annalistica dell-etàmonarchica a Roma. Collection Latomus* 245: 9–42.

Maslakov, G. 1984. "Valerius Maximus and Roman Historiography: A Study of the *Exempla* Tradition." *ANRW* 2.32 (1): 437–96.

Mastrorosa, I. 2006. "Speeches pro and contra Women in Livy 34, 1–7: Catonian Legalism and Gendered Debates." *Latomus* 65: 590–611.

McCartney, E. 1924. "An Irrelevant Moral (Livy 1.11)." *CJ* 19: 567–68.

McDonnell, M. 2006. *Roman Manliness:* Virtus *and the Roman Republic.* Oxford: Oxford University Press.

Meineke, A. 1839–1857. *Fragmenta Comicorum Graecorum. Volumes I–IV.* Berolini: G. Reimeri.

Meister, K. 2012. "Cleidemus." In *Brill's New Pauly,* edited by H. Cancik and H. Schneider. *Brill Online.* http://www.paulyonline.brill.nl/entries/brill-s-new-pauly/cleidemus-e614840.

Merck, M. 1978. "The City's Achievements: Patriotic Amazonomachy and Ancient Athens." In *Tearing the Veil: Essays on Femininity,* edited by S. Lipshitz. London: Routledge. 95–115.

Miles, G. 1995. Livy: *Reconstructing Early Rome.* Ithaca, NY: Cornell University Press.

Miller, P. A. 2004. *Subjecting Verses. Latin Love Elegy and the Emergence of the Real.* Princeton, NJ: Princeton University Press.

———. 2011. "What Is a Propertian Poem?" *Arethusa* 44: 329–52.

Miller, P. A., and C. Platter. 1999. "Crux as Symptom: Augustan Elegy and Beyond." *CW* 92: 445–54.

Milnor, K. 2006. *Gender, Domesticity, and the Age of Augustus: Inventing Private Life.* Oxford: Oxford University Press.

———. 2009. "Women in Roman Historiography." In *Cambridge Companion to the Roman Historians,* edited by A. Feldherr. Cambridge: Cambridge University Press. 276–87.

Mineur, W. H. 1984. *Callimachus, Hymn to Delos.* Leiden: Brill.

Mitchell, S. 2007. "The Galatians: Representation and Reality." In *A Companion to the Hellenistic World,* edited by A. Erskine. Malden, MA: Blackwell. 280–93.

Mitchell, S., and G. Greatrex. 2000. *Ethnicity and Culture in Late Antiquity.* London: Duckworth / Classical Press of Wales.

Modrzejewski, J. M. 2005. "Greek Law in the Hellenistic Period: Family and Marriage." In *The Cambridge Companion to Ancient Greek Law,* edited by M. Gagarin and D. Cohen. Cambridge: Cambridge University Press. 343–56.

Momigliano, A. 1938. *Tre figure mitiche: Tanaquilla, Gaia Caecilia, Acca Larenzia. Miscel. della Facoltà di lettere di Torino.* Torino: Bona.

———. 1984. "Georges Dumézil and the Trifunctional Approach to Roman Civilization." *History and Theory* 23: 312–30.

Mommsen, T. 1886. "Die Tatius-legende." *Hermes* 21: 570–87.

———. 1893. *Corpus Inscriptionum Latinarum.* Berlin: Georgium Reimerum.

Moore, T. 1993. "Morality, History, and Livy's Wronged Women." *Eranos* 91: 38–46.

Morel, J.-P. 1962. "Thèmes sabins et themes numaïques dans le monnayage de la république romaine." *MEFRA* 74: 7–59.

Morford, M. P. O. et al. 2011. *Classical Mythology.* 9th ed. New York: Oxford University Press

Mossman, T. 1886. "Die Tatiuslegende." *Hermes* 21: 570–84.

Moxon, I. S., J. D. Smart, and A. J. Woodman, eds. 1986. *Past Perspectives: Studies in Greek and Roman Historical Writing.* Cambridge: Cambridge University Press.

Mueller, H.-F. 2002. *Roman Religion in Valerius Maximus.* London: Routledge.

Müller, K. 1825. *Prolegomena zu einer wissenschaftlichen Mythologie.* Göttingen: Vandenhoeck und Ruprecht.

———. 1963. *Zu Plutarch, Romulus 17, 7. MH* 20: 114–18.

Musti, D. 1970. "Tendenze nella storiografia romana e greca. Studî su Livio e Dionigi d'Alicarnasso." *QUCC* 10.

Natunewicz, C. 1967. "The Classics in Post-War Poland." *CW* 60: 271–72, 275–80, 282, 307–8.

Nau, F. 2006. Review of *The Elegiac Cityscape,* by T. S. Welch. *Bryn Mawr Classical Review* 2006.6.17.

Negri, M. 1992. "La lingua di Numa." In *Historical Philology: Greek, Latin, and Romance,* edited by B. Brogyanyi and R. Lipp. *Current Issues in Linguistic Theory* 87: 229–66.

Nenci, G. 1983. "Truphe e colonizzazione." In *Forme di contatto e processi ditrasformazione nelle società antiche.* Atti del Convegno di Cortona, maggio 1981. Pisa. 1019–1031.

Newlands, C. 1997. "The Metamorphosis of Ovid's Medea." In *Medea: Essays on Medea in Myth, Literature, Philosophy and Art,* edited by J. J. Clauss and S. Iles Johnston. Princeton, NJ: Princeton University Press. 178–210.

———. 2002. "*Mandati Memores*: Political and Poetic Authority in the *Fasti.*" In *The Cambridge Companion to Ovid,* edited by P. Hardie. Cambridge: Cambridge University Press. 200–216.

Nobles, M. 2000. *Shades of Citizenship: Race and the Census in Modern Politics.* Stanford, CA: Stanford University Press.

Oakley, S. P. 2005. *A Commentary on Livy Books VI–X.* Oxford: Clarendon.

Obbink, D., ed. 1995. *Philodemus and Poetry: Poetic Theory and Practice in Lucretius, Philodemus, and Horace.* New York: Oxford University Press.

Ogden, D. 1999. *Polygamy, Prostitutes and Death: the Hellenistic Dynasties.* London: Duckworth with the Classical Press of Wales.

Ogilvie, R. M. 1965. *A Commentary on Livy: Books 1–5.* Oxford: Clarendon.

———, ed. 1974. *Titi Livi Ab Vrbe Condita.* Oxford: Oxford University Press.

Pagán, V. 2004. *Conspiracy Narratives in Roman History.* Austin: University of Texas Press.

Pais, E. 1905. *Ancient Legends of Roman History.* Translated by M. Cosenza. New York: Dodd, Mead.

Parker, H. N. 2004. "Why Were the Vestals Virgins? Or the Chastity of Women and the Safety of the Roman State." *AJPh* 125: 563–601.

Parker, R. 1983. *Miasma, Pollution and Purification in Early Greek Religion.* Oxford: Oxford University Press.

Pasco-Pranger, M. 2002. "A Varronian vatic Numa? Ovid's *Fasti* and Plutarch's *Life of Numa.*" In *Clio and the Poets,* edited by D. Levene and D. P. Nelis. Leiden: Brill. 291–312.

Pelling, C. B. R. 2002. *Plutarch and History: Eighteen Studies.* London: Classical Press of Wales.

———. 2007. "Greek Historians on Rome: Polybius, Posidonius and Dionysius of Halicarnassus." In *A Companion to Greek and Roman Historiography,* edited by J. M. Marincola. Oxford: Blackwell. 244–58.

Pérez Jiménez, A. 1996. "La asociación de ideas como criterio formal en las *Vidas Paralelas.*" In *Estudios sobre Plutarco: Aspectos Formales,* edited by J. A. Fernández Delgado and F. Pordomingo Pardo. *Actas Del IV Simposio Español Sobre Plutarco.* Salamanca, 26 a 28 de Mayo de 1994. Sociedad Española de Plutarquistas Sección de la International Plutarch Society. Ediciones Clásicas, Universidad de Salamanca. 257–66.

Perrin, B. 1914. *Plutarch Lives: Theseus and Romulus, Lycurgus and Numa, Solon and Publicola. Volume I.* Cambridge, MA: Harvard University Press.

Peter, H. (1906) 1914. *Historicorum Romanorum Reliquiae.* Vol. I2. Leipzig: Teubner.

Picard, G. 1957a. *Les Trophees romains.* Paris: de Boccard.

———. 1957b. "Le châtiment de Tarpeia (?) et les frises historico-légendaires de la basilique Aemilia, à Rome." *Revue Archéologique* 49: 181–88.

Platner, S. B., and T. Ashby. 1929. *A Topographical Dictionary of Ancient Rome.* London: Oxford University Press.

Platt, V. J. 2011. *Facing the Gods: Epiphany and Representation in Greco-Roman Art, Literature, and Religion.* Cambridge: Cambridge University Press.

Pobjoy, M. 2000. "The First Italia." In *The Emergence of State Identities in Italy in the First Millennium BC,* edited by K. Lomas and E. Herring. London: Accordia Research Institute. 187–211.

Pollitt, J. J. 1986. *Art in the Hellenistic Age.* Cambridge: Cambridge University Press.

Pomeroy S. B. 1975. *Goddesses, Whores, Wives and Slaves: Women in Classical Antiquity.* New York: Schocken.

Poole, R. S., ed. 1873. *A Catalogue of the Greek Coins in the British Museum: Italy.* London: The Museum.

Porter, J. 1965. *The Vertical Mosaic: An Analysis of Social Class and Power in Canada.* Toronto: University of Toronto Press.

Poucet, J. 1967. *Recherches sur la légende sabine des origins de Rome.* Kinshasa, Congo: University of Lovanium.

Powell, B. 2012. *Classical Myth.* 7th ed. Upper Saddle River, NJ: Prentice Hall.

Przeworski, A. 1991. *Democracy and the Market.* Cambridge: Cambridge University Press

Purcell, N. 1993. "*Atrium Libertatis.*" *PBSR* 61: 125–55.

Raditsa, L. F. 1980. "Augustus' Legislation Concerning Marriage, Procreation, Love Affairs, and Adultery." *ANRW* 2.13: 278–339.

Rawson, E. 1985. *Intellectual Life in the Late Roman Republic.* Baltimore: Johns Hopkins University Press.

———. 1991. *Roman Culture and Society: Collected Papers.* Oxford: Clarendon.

Rehak, P. 2006. *Cosmos and Imperium: Augustus and the Northern Campus Martius.* Edited by J. Younger. Madison: University of Wisconsin Press.

Rehm, A. 1914. *Das Delphinion in Milet.* Berlin: G. Reimer.

Rei, A. 1998. "Villains, Wives, and Slaves in the Comedies of Plautus." In *Women and Slaves in Greco-Roman Culture: Differential Equations,* edited by S. R. Joshel and S. Murnaghan. London: Routledge. 92–108.

Reinach, S. 1912. *Cults, Myth, and Religion.* Translated by E. Frost-Knapmann. London: D. Nutt.

Reitz, B. 2012. "*Tantae molis erat*: On Valuing Roman Imperial Architecture." In *Aesthetic Value in Classical Antiquity,* edited by I. Sluiter and R. Rosen. Leiden: Brill. 315–44.

Resinski, R. 1997. "Constituting the Adorned Female Body—From Pandora to Livy's *Lex Oppia.*" *Diotima.* http://www.stoa.org/diotima/essays/resinski.shtml.

Rich, J. 1993. "Fear, Greed and Glory: The Causes of Roman War-Making in the Middle Republic." In *War and Society in the Roman World,* edited by J. Rich and G. Shipley. London: Routledge. 38–68.

Richardson, J. S. 1987. "The Purpose of the Lex Calpurnia de Repetundis." *JRS* 77: 1–12.

Richardson, L. 1979. "Basilica Fulvia, modo Aemilia." In *Studies in Classical Art and Archaeology: A Tribute to Peter Heinrich von Blanckenhagen,* edited by G. Kocke and M. B. Moore. Locust Valley, New York: J. J. Augustin. 209–15.

———. 1992. *A New Topographical Dictionary of Ancient Rome.* Baltimore: Johns Hopkins University Press.

Richlin, A. 1997. "Towards a History of Body History." In *Inventing Ancient Culture: Historicism, Periodization, and the Ancient World*, edited by M. Golden and P. Toohey. London: Routledge. 16–35.

Rissanen, V-M. 1997. "Some Aspects of Cicero's Conception and Use of Analogy." In *Utriusque linguae peritus. Studia in honorem Toivo Viljamaa*, edited by J. Vaahtera and R. Vainio. *Annales Universitatis Turkuensis. Ser. B. Tom. 219. Humaniora*. Turku: Turun Yliopisto. 120–25.

Robert, J.-N. 2003. "La Legendaire Misogynie de Caton L'ancien." In *Hommages à Carl Deroux* 3, edited by P. Defosse. *Collection Latomus* 270: 376–83.

Rosenstein, N. 2010. "Aristocratic Values." In *A Companion to the Roman Republic*, edited by R. Morstein Marx and N. Rosenstein. Oxford: Blackwell. 365–82.

Roskam, G., and L. Van der Stock. 2011. *Virtues for the People: Aspects of Plutarchan Ethics*. Leuven: Leuven University Press.

Roller, M. 1997. "Color-Blindness: Cicero's Death, Declamation, and the Production of History." *CP* 92: 109–30.

———. 2004. "Exemplarity in Roman Culture: The Cases of Horatius Cocles and Cloelia." *CP* 99: 1–56.

———. 2009. "The Exemplary Past in Roman Historiography and Culture." In *The Cambridge Companion to the Roman Historians*, edited by A. Feldherr. Cambridge: Cambridge University Press. 214–30.

Rowland, R. J. 1966. "Numismatic Propaganda under Cinna." *TAPA* 97: 407–19.

Rumpf, A. 1951. "*Armillae*." *JHS* 71: 168–71.

Sanders, H. 1904. "The Myth about Tarpeia." In *Roman Historical Sources and Institutions*, edited by H. Sanders. New York: Macmillan. 1–47.

Scardigli, B. 1995. *Essays on Plutarch's Lives*. Oxford: Clarendon.

Schepens, G. 1997. "Jacoby's *FGrHist*: Problems, Methods, Prospects." In *Collecting Fragments: Fragmente Sammeln*, edited by G. Most. Göttingen: Vandenhoeck and Ruprecht. 144–72.

Schlegel, C. 2005. *Satire and the Threat of Speech*. Madison: University of Wisconsin Press.

Schneider, R. M. 2012. "The Making of Oriental Rome: Shaping the Trojan Legend." In *Universal Empire: A Comparative Approach to Imperial Culture and Representation in Eurasian History*, edited by P. F. Bang and D. Kolodziejczyk. Cambridge: Cambridge University Press. 76–129.

Schneider-Herrmann, G. 1996. *The Samnites of the Fourth Century BC: As Depicted on Campanian Vases and Other Sources*. London: Institute of Classical Studies, School of Advanced Study, University of London and Accordia Research Centre.

Schmitz, T. A., and N. Wiater, eds. 2011. *The Struggle for Identity: Greeks and Their Past in the First Century BCE*. Stuttgart: Steiner.

Schultze, C. 1986. "Dionysius of Halicarnassus and his Audience." In *Past Perspectives: Studies in Greek and Roman Historical Writing*, edited by I. S. Moxon, J. D. Smart, and A. J. Woodman. Cambridge: Cambridge University Press. 121–41.

———. 2000. "Authority, Originality and Competence in the 'Roman Archaeology' of Dionysius of Halicarnassus." *Histos* 4: 6–49.

Sciarrino, E. 2011. *Cato the Censor and the Beginnings of Latin Prose: From Poetic Translation to Elite Transcription*. Columbus: The Ohio State University Press.

Scioli, E. 2005. *The Poetics of Sleep: Representing Dreams and Sleep in Latin Literature and Roman Art.* PhD diss., University of California at Los Angeles.

———. 2010. "*Incohat Ismene*: The Dream Narrative as a Mode of Female Discourse in Epic Poetry." *TAPA* 140: 195–238.

Scivoletto, N. 1979. "La città di Roma nella poesia di Properzio." *Colloquium Propertianum* 2: 27–38.

Scullard, H. 2002. *Scipio Africanus: Soldier and Politician.* Oxford: Oxford University Press.

Semioli, A. A. 2010. *Tarpeia e la presenza sabina di Roma arcaica.* Rome: Bulzoni.

Severy, B. 2003. *Augustus and the Family at the Birth of the Roman Empire.* New York: Routledge.

Shackleton Bailey, D. R. 2000. *Valerius Maximus: Memorable Doings and Sayings. Volumes I and II.* Cambridge, MA: Harvard University Press.

Short, W. 2005. "Tenuere tamen arcem Sabini: Tarpeia, Ethnic (Re)Imagination, and the Social War." Paper presented at the University of Virginia Classics Colloquium, 2005. http://www.virginia.edu/classics/colloquium2005/abstracts.html#Tenuere. Accessed March 14, 2015.

———. 2008. "*Clipeos an armillas?* Ambiguity in the Riddling of Tarpeia." In *Papers on Ancient Literatures: Greece, Rome and the Near East,* edited by E. Cingano and L. Milano. Padua: Università Ca' Foscari Venezia. 511–28.

Simon, E. 1966. "Die Fragmente vom Fries der Basilica Aemilia." In *Führer durch die öffentlichen Sammlungen klassischer Altertümer in Rom,* edited by W. von Helbig; updated by H. Speier. 4th ed. Tübingen: Wasmuth. 834–43.

Skidmore, C. 1996. *Practical Ethics for Roman Gentlemen: The Works of Valerius Maximus.* Exeter: University of Exeter Press.

Skutsch, O. 1985. *The Annals of Q. Ennius.* Oxford: Clarendon.

Smith, C. 2011. "Thinking about Kings." *BICS* 54: 21–42.

Smith, D. 2007. *Greek Identity and the Athenian Past in Chariton: The Romance of Empire.* Groningen: Barkhuis.

Smyth, H. W. (1920) 1984. *Greek Grammar.* Cambridge, MA: Harvard University Press.

Solodow, J. 1979. "Livy and the Story of Horatius, 1.24–26." *TAPA* 109: 251–68.

Spencer, D. *Varro's Guide to Being Roman: Citizen Speech and de Lingua Latina.* Unpublished manuscript.

Stadter, P. 2002. "Introduction: Setting Plutarch in his Context." In *Sage and Emperor: Plutarch, Greek Intellectuals, and Roman Power in the Time of Trajan (98–117 AD),* edited by P. Stadter and L. Van der Stockt. Leuven: Leuven University Press. 1–26.

Stadter, P. A., and L. Van der Stockt, eds. 2002. *Sage and Emperor: Plutarch, Greek Intellectuals, and Roman Power in the Time of Trajan (98–117 AD).* Leuven: Leuven University Press.

Stahl, H.-P. 1985. *Propertius: "Love" and "War": Individual and State under Augustus.* Berkeley: University of California Press, 1985.

Stanford, W. B. 1982. "Astute Hero and Ingenious Poet: Odysseus and Homer." *Yearbook of English Studies* 12): 1–12.

Staples, A. 1998. *From Good Goddess to Vestal Virgins.* New York: Routledge.

Steel, C. E. W., and H. van der Blom, eds. 2013. *Community and Communication: Oratory and Politics in Republican Rome*. Oxford: Oxford University Press.

Steiner, G. 1984. *Antigones*. Oxford: Oxford University Press.

Stevenson, T. 2011. "Women of Early Rome as *Exempla* in Livy *Ab Urbe Condita*, Book 1." *Classical World* 104: 175–89.

Stewart, A. 2000. "*Pergamo Ara Marmorea Magna*: On the Date, Reconstruction, and Functions of the Great Altar of Pergamon." In *From Pergamon to Sperlonga: Sculpture and Context*, edited by N. De Grummond and B. S. Ridgway. Berkeley: University of California Press. 32–57.

Strobel, K. 1991. "Die Galater im hellenistischen Kleinasien: Historische Aspekte einer keltischen Staatenbildung." In *Hellenistiche Studien*, edited by J. Seibert. Munich: Bengston. 101–34.

Stroup, S. 2010. *Catullus, Cicero, and a Society of Patrons: The Generation of the Text*. Cambridge: Cambridge University Press.

Sullivan, J. P. 1976. *Propertius: A Critical Introduction*. Cambridge: Cambridge University Press.

Swain, S. 1996. *Hellenism and Empire: Language, Classicism, and Power in the Greek World AD 50–250*. Oxford: Clarendon.

Sydenham, E. A. 1952. *The Coinage of the Roman Republic*. London: Spink and Son.

Syme, R. 1939. *The Roman Revolution*. Oxford: Oxford University Press.

Takács, S. 2010. *Vestal Virgins, Sibyls, and Matrons: Women in Roman Religion*. Austin: University of Texas Press.

Taylor, D. 1974. *Declinatio: A Study of the Linguistic Theory of Marcus Terentius Varro*. Amsterdam: John Benjamins.

Taylor, L. 1960. *The Voting Districts of the Roman Republic: The Thirty-Five Urban and Rural Tribes*. MAAR 20. Rome: American Academy in Rome.

Thesleff, H., ed. 1965. *The Pythagorean Texts of the Hellenistic Period*. Helsinki: Abo, Abo Akademi.

Thein, A. G. 2002. "*Area Capitolina/Capitolii*." In *Mapping Augustan Rome*, edited by L. Haselberger. JRA Supplement 50. http://digitalaugustanrome.org Map #116. Accessed June 2014.

Thiel, J.-H. 1994. "*Punica fides*." In *Studies in Ancient History*, edited by H. T. Wallinga. Amsterdam: Gieben. 129–50.

Tissol, G. 1997. *The Face of Nature: Wit, Narrative, and Cosmic Origins in Ovid's Metamorphoses*. Princeton, NJ: Princeton University Press.

Tomei, M. A., ed. 2010. *Memories of Rome: The Aemilii and the Basilica at the Forum*. Milano: Electa.

Toynbee, J. M. C. 1956. "Picture Language in Roman Art and Coinage." In *Essays in Roman Coinage Presented to Harold Mattingly*, edited by R. A. G. Carson and C. H. V. Sutherland. Oxford: Oxford University Press. 205–26.

Treggiari, S. 1991. *Roman Marriage: Iusti Coniuges from the Time of Cicero to the Time of Ulpian*. Oxford: Oxford University Press.

Tyrrell, W. B. 1984. *Amazons: A Study in Athenian Mythmaking.* Baltimore: Johns Hopkins University Press.

Van Bremen, R. 2007. "Family Structures." In *A Companion to the Hellenistic World,* edited by A. Erskine. Malden: Blackwell. 311–30.

Vasaly, A. 1993. *Representations: Images of the World in Ciceronian Oratory.* Berkeley and Los Angeles: University of California Press.

Verboven, K. 2002. *The Economy of Friends: Economic Aspects of Amicitia and Patronage in the Late Republic. Collection Latomus.*

———. 2011. "Friendship among the Romans." In *The Oxford Handbook of Social Relations in the Roman World,* edited by M. Peachin. New York: Oxford University Press. 404–21.

Vermeule, C. 1959. *The Goddess Roma in the Art of the Roman Empire.* London: Spink and Son.

Veyne, P. 1988. *Did the Greeks Believe in Their Myths? An Essay on the Constitutive Imagination.* Chicago: University of Chicago Press.

Vishnia, R. F. 1996. *State, Society and Popular Leaders in Mid-Republican Rome, 241–167 BC.* London: Routledge.

Walbank, F. 1957. *A Historical Commentary on Polybius.* Oxford: Clarendon.

———. 2005. "The Two Way Shadow: Polybius among the Fragments." In *The Shadow of Polybius: Intertextuality as a Research Tool in Greek Historiography,* edited by G. Schepens and J. Bollansée. Studia Hellenistica 42. Leuven: Peeters. 1–18.

Waldherr, G. H. 2000. "'*Punica fides*'—das Bild der Karthager in Rom." *Gymnasium* 107: 193–222.

Wallace-Hadrill, A. 1986. "Image and Authority in the Coinage of Augustus." *JRS* 76: 66–87.

———. 1989. *Patronage in Ancient Society.* Leicester-Nottingham Studies in Ancient Society 1. London: Routledge.

———. 1997. "*Mutatio morum*: The idea of a Roman cultural revolution." In *The Roman Cultural Revolution,* edited by T. Habinek and A. Schiesaro. Cambridge: Cambridge University Press. 3–22.

Walsh, G. B. 1987. "Philodemus on the Terminology of Neoptolemus." *Mnemosyne,* 4th ser. 40: 56–68.

Ward, A. W. 2004. "How Democratic Was the Roman Republic?" *NECJ* 31: 101–19.

Warden, J. 1978. "Another Would-Be Amazon: Propertius 4.4.71–72." *Hermes* 106: 177–87.

———. 1980. *Fallax Opus: Poet and Reader in the Elegies of Propertius.* Toronto: University of Toronto Press.

———. 1982. "Epic into Elegy: Propertius 4.9.70f." *Hermes* 110: 228–42.

Weaire, G. 2007. "Dionysius of Halicarnassus' Etruscans and the Politics of Cultural Determinacy." Paper presented at Annual Meeting of the American Philological Association, San Diego, CA, January 5.

Weileder, A. 1998. *Valerius Maximus. Spiegel kaiserlicher Selbstdarstellung* Münchener Arbeiten zur Alten Geschichte 12. München: Editio Maris.

Welch, K. 2003. "A New View of the Origins of the Roman Basilica: The Atrium Regium, Graecostasis, and Roman Diplomacy." *JRA* 17: 5–34.

Welch, T. S. 2001. "*Est locus uni cuique suus*: City and Status in Horace Satires 1.8 and 1.9." *CA* 20: 165–92.

———. 2004. "Cultural Inclusion in Roman Myths and Roman Marriage." Paper presented at the annual meeting of the Classical Association of the Middle West and South, St. Louis, MO, April 17.

———. 2005. *The Elegiac Cityscape: Propertius and the Meaning of Roman Monuments.* Columbus: The Ohio State University Press.

Whitmarsh, T. 2005. *The Second Sophistic.* Cambridge: Cambridge University Press.

Wiater, N. 2001. *The Ideology of Classicism: Language, History, and Identity in Dionysius of Halicarnassus.* Untersuchungen zur antiken Literatur und Geschichte 105. New York: De Gruyter.

Williams, C. A. 1995. "Greek Love at Rome." *CQ* 45: 517–39.

Williams, J. H. C. 2001. *Beyond the Rubicon: Romans and Gauls in Republican Italy.* Oxford: Oxford University Press.

Williamson, G. 2005. "Aspects of Identity." In *Coinage and Identity in the Roman Provinces*, edited by C. Howgego, V. Heuchert, and A. Burnett. Oxford: Oxford University Press. 19–28.

Wiseman, T. P. 1971. *New Men in the Roman Senate, 139 BC–AD 14.* Oxford: Oxford Classical and Philosophical Monographs.

———. 1979. "Topography and Rhetoric: The Trial of Manlius." *Historia* 28: 32–50.

———. 1983. "The Wife and Children of Romulus." *CQ* 33: 445–52.

———. (1989) 1994. "Roman Legend and Oral Tradition." In *Historiography and Imagination: Eight Essays on Roman Culture*, edited by T. P. Wiseman. Exeter: University of Exeter Press. 23–36.

———. 1994. *Historiography and Imagination: Eight Essays on Roman Culture.* Exeter: University of Exeter Press.

———. 1995. *Remus.* Cambridge: Cambridge University Press.

———. 1998. *Roman Drama and Roman History.* Exeter: University of Exeter Press.

———. 2004. *The Myths of Rome.* Exeter: University of Exeter Press.

———. 2009. *Remembering the Roman People. Essays in Late Republican Politics and Literature.* Oxford: Oxford University Press.

Wissowa, G. 1912. *Religion und Kultus der Römer. Handbuch der Altertumswissenschaft* 5:4. München: C. H. Beck.

Witschonke, R. 2012. "The Use of Die Marks on Roman Republican Coinage." *RBN* 158: 65–86.

Wong, L. 2008. "Multiculturalism and Ethnic Pluralism in Sociology: An Analysis of the Fragmentation Position Discourse." *Canadian Ethnic Studies Journal* 40.1: 11–32.

Wyke, M. 1987. "The Elegiac Woman at Rome." *PCPhS* 33: 153–78.

———. 1999. *Parchments of Gender: Deciphering the Body of Antiquity.* Oxford: Oxford University Press.

Zakeri, M. 1998. "Arabic Reports on the Fall of Hatra to the Sasanids: History or Legend?" In *Story-Telling in the Framework of Non-Fictional Arabic Literature*, edited by S. Leder. Wiesbaden: Otto Harrassowitz.

Zanda, E. 2011. *Fighting Hydra-Like Luxury: Sumptuary Regulation in the Roman Republic.* London: Bristol Classical, 2011.

Zanker, G. 2003. *Modes of Viewing in Hellenistic Poetry and Art.* Madison, WI: University of Wisconsin Press.

Zanker, P. 1988. *The Power of Images in the Age of Augustus.* Translated by A. Shapiro. Ann Arbor: University of Michigan Press.

Zetzel, J. E. G. 1996. "Poetic Baldness and Its Cure." *MD* 36: 73–100.

Ziegler. (1914) 1970. *Plutarchi Vitae parallelae.* Leipzig: Teubner.

Zimmerman, R. 1996. *The Law of Obligations: Roman Foundations of the Civilian Tradition.* Oxford: Oxford University Press.

Zorzetti, N. 1990. "The *Carmina Convivalia.*" Paper presented at the First Symposium on the Greek Symposion, Balliol College, September 4–8, 1984. In *Sympotica: A Symposium on the Symposion,* edited by O. Murray. Oxford: Clarendon. 289–307.

———. 1991. "Poetry and Ancient City: The Case of Rome." *Classical Journal* 86: 311–29.

Zweig, B. 1999. "Euripides' *Helen* and Female Rites of Passage." In *Rites of Passage in Ancient Greece: Literature, Religion, Society,* edited by M. W. Padilla. Lewisburg, PA: Bucknell University Press (Associated University Presses). 158–80.

INDEX LOCORUM

CIL
    1(2) p. 258: 38
    1(2) p. 269: 268
    4.155: 268
    6.67988: 82
PColZen
    2.66: 231
RDGE
    33.1.12: 68
Rehm *Milet*
    1.3.33–388: 230
SEG
    36.1123: 47, 63
SIG
    3.593 l.12: 68
Thesleff
    143.28ff: 71–72
UPZ
    1.8: 231
    1.148: 230

Aeschylus
    Ag. 918–19: 62
    Ag. 1050–52: 244
    Choeph. 612–22: 292
    Pers. 41: 62
Andriscus
    FGrH 500.1: 292
Appian *Bellum Civile*
    2.26: 125
Arnobius
    Ad. Nat. 5.18.: 238
Anyte
    5GP: 233
    7GP: 233
Apollodorus
    2.4.7: 290
    3.14.2–6: 289
    3.15.8: 23, 292
    4.1: 290
    4.1.6: 289

4.3: 290
4.7: 290
Apollonius Rhodius
   3.1–266: 27
   3.275–79: 27
   3.648–64: 27
   3.681–92: 27
   F12 Powell: 291
Appian
   Hann. 27: 48
   Hann. 49: 74
   Hann. 109.1: 57
Aristodemus of Nysa
   FGrH 22: 291
Aristotle
   Pol. 6.35, 1320b: 69–70
Athenaeus
   3.836: 258
   8.360e–361c: 290
   12.522d–f: 70
Aulus Gellius
   1.12.9: 160
   3.15: 292
   9.18.18: 36
Ps. Aurelius Victor
   de Vir. Ill. 47: 53
Ausonius
   de Fer. Rom. 23.9: 268

Bacchylides
   13.131–38: 290
Butas
   Aetia: 238

Caesar
   de Anal.: 119
Callimachus
   Aet. 106–7: 237
   Hecale F90H: 292

Hymn 4.171–87: 236
Fr.379Pf: 236
Calpurnius Piso Frugi
   FRH 7: 85–90
   FRH 36: 88
   FRH 44: 88
Cato the Elder, Fragments
   FRH 8: 96
   ORF (4) 8: 193
Catullus
   29: 113
   64.335: 179
   66.27: 237
   109: 178
Cicero
   Acad. 1.9: 108, 124
   ad Att. 4.16.8: 125, 130
   ad Att. 13.12.3: 109
   ad Att. 16.7.6: 156
   ad Fam. 9.8: 109
   ad Fam. 15.20.1: 82, 90
   Brut. 27.106: 88
   Brut. 258: 116, 118
   de Har. Resp.: 211–12
   de Inv. 1.94: 25
   de Leg. 2.5: 231
   de Nat. Deorum 2.69: 114
   de Off. 1.38: 66
   de Off. 1.53: 161
   de Off. 2.21.75: 88
   de Orat. 2.249: 238
   de Rep. 2.12: 96
   de Rep. 2.12–14: 146
   de Rep. 2.14: 78
   de Sen. 39–41: 71
   in Verr. 3.84.195: 88
   in Verr. 4.25.56: 88
   pro Archia: 94
   pro Rab. 13: 155

pro Scauro 48: 175
pro Scauro 19.42: 66
Cincius Alimentus
  FRH 51: 78
Ciris
  205: 31
  481–83: 31

Dictys of Crete
  2.17: 290
  2.33: 290
  2.49: 290
  3.12: 290
  4.15: 290
Dio Cassius
  14.24: 66–67
  49.42: 125
  53.23.5ff.: 166
  54.3ff.: 166
  54.15.4: 165–66
  55.22.2: 36
  55.15.3: 36
  65.17.3: 65
Diodorus Siculus
  4.16: 289
  14.113–17: 235
  32.1.4: 65
Dionysius of Halicarnassus
  RA 1.3.4: 242
  RA 1.5.1: 248, 253
  RA 1.6.3: 248
  RA 1.7.3: 242
  RA 1.72.: 248
  RA 1.79.4: 242
  RA 1.90.1: 242
  RA 2: 239
  RA 2.4.11: 279
  RA 2.30–47: 146
  RA 2.30.5: 96, 244

  RA 2.32.1: 252
  RA 2.38.1: 249
  RA 2.38.2: 26, 249–50
  RA 2.38.3: 242, 244, 251
  RA 2.38.4: 243–47, 249–51
  RA 2.38.5: 247, 249–50
  RA 2.39.1: 49, 56, 241–43, 247, 250
  RA 2.39.2: 247–48
  RA 2.40.1: 241–43, 245–46, 249–51
  RA 2.40.2: 241–43, 246
  RA 2.40.2–3: 249
  RA 2.40.3: 37–38, 108, 131, 193–94, 242, 248–50
  RA 2.42: 279
  RA 2.49.5: 73
  RA 2.50.3: 101
  RA 2.65.2: 75
  RA 2.66.4: 241
  RA 2.66.5: 175
  RA 2.75.3: 65
  RA 4.7.5: 242
  RA 4.15.5: 242
  RA 4.26: 101
  RA 5.25.1–3: 237
  RA 7.66.3–5: 252
  RA 10.14.1–2: 39
  RA 12.4.2: 242
  RA 12.9.3: 242
  RA 13.6–12: 235
  RA 15.5: 73
  Thuc. 54: 243
  Pomp. 2: 243

Ennius
  Ann. 209 Sk.456: 73
Euphorion
  Suppl. Hell. 415 col.2: 290
Euripides
  Med. 477: 27
  Med. 527–28: 27

Fabius Pictor
    FRH 7: 26, 49–50, 56, 59, 61, 64, 78, 114, 175, 206
    FRH 8: 47
    FRH 13: 60–62
    FRH 24: 61–62, 89–90
Festus
    49L: 279
    246L: 101
    296L: 101
    364L: 36–37, 114
    496L: 39–42, 240
    380L: 154
Florus
    1.2.3: 34
Fronto
    221N: 116

Hebrews
    11.31: 292
Herodas
    6: 233
Herodotus
    1.94: 62
    8.53.1: 35
Hermesianax
    F6 Powell: 291
Hesiod
    Theog. 560–612: 26
    W&D 60–105: 26
    F214 MW: 20
Homer
    Il. 1: 290
    Il. 2.688–93: 8
    Il. 3: 24, 249
    Il. 6: 20, 24
    Il. 6.297–310: 292
    Il. 19: 290
    Il. 19.282–300: 28
    Od.: 69

Horace
    Carm. 3.16.1: 25
    Carm. 3.30: 137
    Epist. 2.1.156–57: 89
Hyginus
    Fab. 30: 289
    Fab. 106: 290
    Fab. 166: 289

James
    2.25: 292
Josephus
    Ant. Iud. 2.252–53: 292
    Ant. Iud. 5.1.2: 292
    Bell. Iud. 7.153–57: 36
Joshua
    2.1: 292
    6.17: 292
    6.23: 292
    6.25: 292
Justin
    24.4: 235

Licymnius
    PMG 772: 291
Livy
    Praef. 10: 136–38, 144, 163
    1.1.5: 147
    1.1.7: 147
    1.2.1: 147
    1.3.1–3: 147
    1.3.11: 143
    1.3.11–1.4: 161–63
    1.4: 148
    1.5.5: 143
    1.5.6: 163
    1.7.4: 143
    1.9: 96
    1.9–13: 146

INDEX LOCORUM

1.9.12: 143
1.11: 34, 56, 114, 115, 119, 139–40, 141–44, 147, 156–60, 175, 184, 207–8, 233, 241, 257, 263
1.11.6: 157
1.11.8: 143
1.12: 40
1.12.1: 145, 250
1.12.10: 279
1.13.2–3: 147
1.13.3–5: 147
1.13.4: 148
1.13.5: 147, 156
1.13.8: 82
1.19: 102
1.21–26: 151–53
1.21.4: 65
1.23.8–9: 159
1.24.1: 148, 152
1.25.12: 153
1.26: 154
1.26.2–4: 153–55
1.26.4: 155
1.26.9: 154
1.26.10–11: 155–56
1.26.14: 154
1.27.2: 143
1.31.8: 143
1.34.5: 148, 154
1.38.2: 148
1.40.5: 143
1.41.6: 143
1.45: 101
1.45.4: 143
1.46.9: 148
1.48: 151
1.48.5: 145
1.56.1: 143
1.58.5: 146
1.58.10: 141

2.1.5: 150
2.5.8: 150
2.39–40: 150
3.48.8–9: 141
3.55.67: 56
5.48: 235
5.48.4–5: 217
6.20.1–12: 40
7.1: 118
7.6.1–6: 279
9.40: 73
10.36.16: 279
10.39: 73
21.19.5: 65
21.63: 53
22.1.17–18: 57
22.1.18: 57
22.7.1–3: 57
22.49.15: 57
22.56.4–6: 57
22.57.2: 58
22.60.3: 58
22.61.1–4: 58
22.61.3: 55
23.11: 48
23.31.2: 53
23.48.4ff: 53
24.18.13–14: 54, 58
25.2.9–10: 58
25.12: 185
26.27.14: 175
27.15.4–16: 74
27.15.10: 75
27.37.9–10: 58
28.40–44: 53
29.14.5–14: 58
34.1–8: 53
34.4.9: 53
34.4.14: 55

34.4.14–15: 55
34.5.10: 54
34.6.14: 54
34.6.16: 54
34.7.1: 55
34.7.2: 55
34.7.4: 54
34.7.7: 55
34.7.6: 56
34.17.13: 55
34.76.5: 54
37.15–16: 279

Lucretius
  2.61: 65

Lycophron
  340–47: 292

Macrobius
  1.11.35–40: 268

Meleager
  Garl., Praef.: 233

Memnon
  Herac. 8.8: 235

Nepos
  Hamil. 32.3.3: 67

Nossis
  1GP: 233

Numbers
  12.1: 292

Obsequens
  128: 65

Orosius
  4.13.6: 68
  4.20: 53

Ovid
  Ars 1.101–34: 78
  Ars 3.13–14: 25
  Fasti 1.259–62: 201–2
  Fasti 1.261: 257
  Fasti 1.527–28: 175
  Fasti 3.167–258: 146
  Fasti 4.179–372: 58
  Fasti 6.637–48: 174
  Her. 1: 190
  Her. 3: 290
  Her. 4: 289
  Ibis 360: 290
  Met. 7.465–66: 289
  Met. 8.1–151: 292
  Met. 12.169–535: 160
  Tr. 2.259: 91
  Tr. 2.424: 91

Parthenius
  5.6: 291
  8: 291
  9: 292
  17: 237
  21: 291
  22: 291
  30: 237

Pausanias
  1.2.1: 34, 289
  1.18.2: 289
  7.19.1–9: 290
  10.12–23: 235
  10.19.8: 235
  10.27.3: 292

Plato
  Rep. 580c2–581a1: 29
  Rep. 590a: 26

Plautus
  Aul. 500–503: 55
  Aul. 526–531: 55
  Capt.: 66
  Epid. 226–88: 55

Pliny the Elder
   HN 5.16: 258
   HN 7.120: 58
   HN 15.78: 279
   HN 19.87: 73
   HN 34.26: 72
   HN 34.34: 68
Plutarch
   Apothegms 172d: 265–66
   Apothegms 172e: 262
   Apothegms 207a: 262–63
   Caes. 29.3: 108, 125
   Cam. 15–30: 235
   Cam. 33.2: 269, 271
   Cato 70.2–5: 238
   de Mul. Virt. 17: 34, 292
   Demos. 20.1: 281
   Fab. 16.9: 57
   Fab. 18.3: 48
   Fab. 21: 74
   Fab. 21.2: 75
   Mor. 313a: 270
   Nicias 1.4: 267
   Nicias 1.5: 256–57
   Nicias 3.3: 257
   Numa 10: 107
   Numa 10.1: 41, 270
   Numa 16.1: 65
   Numa 21: 85
   Numa 21.2: 85
   Par. Min. 8: 238
   Par. Min. 15: 257, 290
   Popl. 16.7: 237
   Popl. 16.10: 237
   Quaest. Rom. 86: 32
   Rom. 9.5: 264
   Rom. 14–19: 274
   Rom. 14–20: 146
   Rom. 14.2: 259, 269, 277
   Rom. 17: 175, 228–29
   Rom. 17.2: 257–58, 270
   Rom. 17.3: 255, 263
   Rom. 17.3–5: 261–66
   Rom. 17.5: 40, 157, 233, 258–61
   Rom. 18.1: 36, 193, 255, 260, 266, 276
   Rom. 18.4: 279
   Rom. 19.3: 275
   Rom. 19.5: 277
   Rom. 19.7: 276
   Rom. 21.6: 238, 260
   Rom. 23.4: 264
   Rom. 27.5: 258
   Rom. 29.2–11: 255
   Rom. 29.1: 268
   Rom. 29.2: 268
   Rom. 29.3: 268–69
   Rom. 29.4: 268
   Rom. 29.6: 268
   Rom. 29.7: 271–72
   Sert. 9.5: 258
   Synk. Th-R. 2.1: 282
   Synk. Th-R. 2.2: 282
   Synk. Th-R. 4.1–2: 282
   Synk. Th-R. 5.2–3: 271
   Synk. Th-R. 6.1–3: 282
   Synk. Th-R. 6.2: 259
   Thes. 1.1: 274–75, 280–81
   Thes. 1.2: 275
   Thes. 1.3: 273–74, 280
   Thes. 2.1: 274
   Thes. 6.4: 265
   Thes. 26–27: 274
   Thes. 27.1–9   255
   Thes. 27.2–6   256
   Thes. 27.2: 278
   Thes. 27.3: 278
   Thes. 27.4: 277, 279
   Thes. 27.4–5: 277

Thes. 27.5: 279–80
Thes. 27.5–6: 280
Thes. 27.6: 280
Polyaenus
   7.35.2: 235
   8.14.3: 74
   8.25.1: 39
   8.36: 292
Polybius
   1.7.8: 65
   1.11.1–15: 68
   1.11.2: 68
   1.20.1: 68
   1.180.6: 247
   2.18: 235
   2.29.8: 68
   2.35: 235
   3.8.1: 69
   3.8.1–3.9.5: 69
   3.29.8: 65
   3.117.4: 57
   12.4b: 63
   FGrH F70: 74
Proclus
   Cypr.: 290
Propertius
   2.9.35: 179
   2.6.29: 25
   2.30.21: 179
   2.30.25: 179
   2.31: 198
   2.32: 198
   2.34: 195
   3.13.57–58: 25
   4.1: 199
   4.1.61: 91
   4.4: 115, 168–97
   4.4.1: 114, 165, 185, 195
   4.4.1–2: 169, 193–94

   4.4.2: 188–89, 195
   4.4.4: 194
   4.4.7–18: 183–84
   4.4.7: 194
   4.4.8: 179
   4.4.9: 188
   4.4.9–14: 185, 196–97
   4.4.14: 194
   4.4.15: 194
   4.4.15–18: 257
   4.4.15–26: 171–73
   4.4.18: 188
   4.4.23–24: 197
   4.4.23–26: 184, 197–98
   4.4.27–28: 198
   4.4.28: 91, 187, 192
   4.4.29–30: 188, 190, 195
   4.4.31: 188
   4.4.31–46: 174–75, 177
   4.4.33: 188
   4.4.35: 195, 197
   4.4.45–46: 188
   4.4.47: 190
   4.4.48: 192, 195
   4.4.49–50: 192
   4.4.53: 185
   4.4.53–62: 176–78
   4.4.55: 190
   4.4.57–60: 178–79
   4.4.61: 188
   4.4.63–72: 180–82, 186–87
   4.4.67: 187
   4.4.69–70: 188
   4.4.73–78: 120, 182
   4.4.73–82: 198–99
   4.4.77: 188
   4.4.79: 188
   4.4.79–94: 188–90
   4.4.81–82: 179

4.4.83: 169, 187, 192, 270
4.4.85: 187
4.4.85–86: 188
4.4.87: 184
4.4.87–94: 179–80
4.4.89: 208, 233, 263
4.4.89–92: 184
4.4.90: 187–88, 195
4.4.93: 114, 195
4.9: 170
4.9.49: 91
4.10.20: 91
4.11.65–66: 168

Quintus of Smyrna
   3.551–76: 290

Sallust
   Bell. Iug. 108.3: 66
   Hist. F2.94: 82
Sappho
   140.1: 62
Seneca the Elder
   Cont. 1.3: 36
   Cont. 1.2.23: 110
Servius
   ad Aen. 1.242: 292
   ad Aen. 8.646: 238
Silius Italicus, 150
   4.150: 235
Simylus
   Elegy: 40, 47, 230–36
Solinus
   1.126: 58
Statius
   Theb. 2.265–305: 26
Stobaeus
   3.7.28: 238
   10.70–71: 290

Strabo
   4.1.13: 236
   4.2: 100
   5.1.1: 97
   5.3.2: 100
   5.4.12: 73
Suetonius
   Galba 3.2: 258
   Iul. 49–52: 113
   Iul. 52.2: 113
   Tib. 61.4: 36

Tacitus
   Ann. 1.1: 221
   Ann. 3.34: 53
   Ann. 3.72: 125
   Ann. 6.19: 36–37
   Ann. 6.41: 37
Theocritus
   2: 233
   13: 233
Tibullus
   1.3: 198
   1.6: 198
Theophrastus
   626: 292
Thucydides
   1.6: 62

Valerius Maximus
   Praef.: 220–21
   3.8.6: 151
   4.3.5: 73
   4.3.10: 88
   5.6.2: 279
   6.2: 214
   7.2.5: 211
   7.4.*praef.*: 218
   7.4.3 217–18

9.1 *praef.*: 205–6
8.15.1: 58
9.1.*praef.*: 29
9.1.3: 53
9.3.2: 215–16
9.6.*praef.*: 208–10, 214, 220
9.6.1: 110–11, 161, 175, 206–8, 209, 214–16, 219–20, 222, 233, 263
9.6.2: 209
9.6.3: 209
9.6.4: 209
9.6.*ext*.1: 209–10
9.6.*ext*.2: 209–11
9.11.*ext*.4: 212–15

Varro *de Lingua Latina*
de Ling. 5.1.1: 109
de Ling. 5.20: 113
de Ling. 5.37: 113
de Ling. 5.40: 122–23
de Ling. 5.41: 109–12, 112–16, 119–23, 157–58, 193, 270
de Ling. 5.42: 34, 37, 39, 101, 122–23
de Ling. 5.43: 101
de Ling. 5.55: 82
de Ling. 5.68: 101
de Ling. 5.74: 101
de Ling. 5.148: 279
de Ling. 5.149: 279
de Ling. 5.150: 279
de Ling. 6.4: 125
de Ling. 6.18: 268, 270
de Ling. 6.68: 156
*de Ling.*8.5: 17–18
de Ling. 8.9: 116–18
de Ling. 8.18: 120–21
de Ling. 9.1: 117
de Ling. 9.34: 120–21

Vergil
Aen. 1.364: 180
Aen. 2.296: 175
Aen. 4.198–218: 290
Aen 4.319–25: 290
Aen. 6: 238
Aen. 6.853: 197
Aen. 9: 143
Aen. 11.656: 41
Ecl. 4: 199

Vitruvius
1.2.1–9: 252
9.17: 108

Zonaras
8.26.14L 53
9.8: 74
9.17.1: 53

GENERAL INDEX

Adornment: 10–11, 25–26, 46, 54–56, 71–72
Aetiology: 168–69, 193
Aglauros: 25, 35, 289
Albans: 151–52, 156
Amazonomachy: 17, 255, 274–75, 277–78, 280–81
Amazons: 1, 13, 17, 34–35, 105–6, 131–32, 181–82, 274–75, 277–78, 280–81, 289; graves of: 255–56, 275, 278, 280–81
Antigonus (Historian): 107, 109, 114, 175, 259, 261, 265, 267, 269, 273
Antigonus Gonatas: 17, 261–62, 263, 283
Antiope: 23, 34, 274, 277, 279, 289
Antiquarian / Antiquarianism: 9, 39, 115, 124, 170, 281
Apollonius: 27
Ariadne: 26, 30, 175, 177, 182
Arne: 23, 34, 289
Athens: 35, 52, 181, 255–56, 274–75, 277–78, 280–82
Augustus/Octavian: 17, 109, 115, 130, 161, 164–66, 168, 173, 176, 215, 261–62, 263, 265, 273, 283, 284; and moral legislation: 14, 161, 164, 168, 173, 178; and urban buildings / monuments: 40, 124, 164–66, 174, 194, 199

Bacchants: 181–82, 186–87
Bigae: 11, 76–77, 93, 94–95
Brennus, Gallic Chieftan: 16, 227, 229, 235–36, 257, 259, 290
Briseis: 28, 34, 289–91
Butas: 16, 238, 260

Caesar: 12–3, 67, 82, 105–6, 109, 113, 115–16, 118–20, 124–25, 129–31, 164–65, 167, 199, 263, 264, 285
Callimachus: 16, 233, 236–38, 292
Camillus: 17, 255–56, 267–73
Carthaginians: 66–67, 69, 209–10, 221
Cato the Elder: 6, 46, 54–56, 67, 84–85, 89, 94
Cato the Younger: 238
Catullus: 26, 113, 179, 237
Cicero: 25, 66, 71, 78, 82, 88, 90, 108–9, 114, 116, 118, 124–25, 130, 146, 155, 161,

175, 195–96, 211, 231, 238, 264, 286

Cincius Alimentus: 26, 45, 51, 78, 242

Ciris: 26, 30–31

Class (social, political, etc.): 48, 52–53, 55–56, 69, 72, 80–81, 83, 91, 93, 95, 99, 118, 173, 285–86

Cloelia: 149, 150, 160

Coinage: 2, 10, 47, 73, 76, 78–82, 94–95, 96–98, 98–102, 218, 274; ideological uses: 79, 91–93, 94–102, 65–66

Comaetho: 23, 290

Crushing, death by: 1, 25–26, 30–33, 41, 100, 107, 160, 290

Deception: 65, 142–43, 156, 162–63, 191, 209, 243

Declamation: 5, 110, 149, 205

Demonike: 23, 31, 37, 257, 290

Dido: 180–82, 186–87, 290

Dionysus of Halicarnassus: 8, 10, 15–6, 26, 37–39, 48–51, 56, 60–61, 64, 73, 85, 87, 101, 108, 110, 123, 140, 142, 146, 176, 193–94, 204, 208, 219, 225–26, 237, 239–53, 267, 286

Dorcia: 23, 290

Elegy: 9, 24, 144, 165, 168–69, 174, 178–79, 197–98, 199–200, 238, 260

Eriphyle: 23, 25, 290

Ethnicity: 2, 10–11, 56, 73–74, 80, 82, 83, 92, 95, 131–32, 156, 285–86; Roman vs. Sabine: 91, 93, 96, 98–100, 159, 255; and conquest: 94–95; and marriage: 16, 96, 146–48, 233, 269, 272; and migration: 229–31; and religion: 101–02

Etruscans: 41, 47, 61–63, 67, 85, 97, 148, 159, 160, 237

Euripides: 27

Exempla and exemplarity: 5, 14, 25–26, 106, 115, 135–38, 140–45, 161, 203–5, 214–15, 217–21

Fabius Pictor: 7, 10–11, 13, 14, 26, 38, 45–75, 84, 89, 107, 114, 140, 143, 158, 170, 176,

204, 206, 219, 225, 239, 241, 242–43, 246, 251–53, 256, 263, 267, 285

Family: 13, 21–23, 56, 82–83, 92, 97, 108, 111, 114, 135, 147–49, 152–54, 156, 159–63, 173, 175–77, 206, 227, 233–34, 292

Felix culpa: 69, 130, 222

Festivals and rites: 37–38, 57, 131, 182, 197–98, 199, 255, 267–71; *Nonae Caprotinae*: 255, 267–68; *Parentalia*: 38, 131; *Parilia*: 38, 120–21, 123, 188, 198; *Poplifugium*: 268

Festus (grammarian): 36, 39–41, 101, 114, 154

Fides and πίστις: 65–67, 70, 179, 210, 214, 251

Focalization and perspective: 23, 99, 133, 135, 138, 159, 182; blurring of: 187–88, 191, 195; of Italians: 95–96; of narrator: 184, 187–91; *Teichoskopeia*: 23–24, 28, 249; and time: 197–98

Gauls: 16, 28, 39–40, 45, 47, 58, 68, 227, 231–33, 235–36, 260, 268, 290–91; Gallic Sack: 2, 7, 39–40, 225–26, 235, 238

Gender: 2, 12–13, 16, 37, 54, 80, 93, 100, 119, 124, 132–33, 151, 154–55, 160, 170, 179–80, 192, 198–200, 219, 229, 232–33, 240, 285–86; androcentric: 22, 27–8, 157, 198–99; and greed: 57–59, 143; masculinity: 17, 73–74, 179; roles: 12–13, 16, 69, 105–6, 111–12, 114–15, 129, 131–32, 170, 233; patriarchy: 12–13, 22, 27–8, 141, 145, 149

Genre: 2–4, 8, 49, 50, 144, 168, 193, 240, 260, 286

Greed: and bribery and acquisitiveness: 1, 10, 14, 25–27, 29, 45–59, 108, 114, 142, 143, 203, 226, 234, 236, 259; accusations of against Romans: 67–70; originating abroad: 89

Greece and Greeks: 16–17, 20, 29, 34, 62–63, 66, 69, 88, 226–27, 235–36, 238, 240, 256, 280–83, 285–86; language: 10–11, 47, 239–40

Hannibal: 10–11, 45–46, 48, 52–60, 65–66, 69, 74–75, 107, 209–10, 221

Helen of Sparta/Troy: 5, 9, 24, 26–28, 30, 249, 291

Hellenistic: and Roman myth/history: 16, 226, 237–38, 253, 259–60, 272, 282–83; culture and identity: 63, 89–91, 133, 229–30, 234; literature: 16, 20, 26, 227, 232, 235–36, 238; politics/Dynastic politics: 8, 16, 65, 227; women: 227, 232–33

Herippe: 28, 291

Historiography: 11, 46, 136–38, 145, 158, 239–41; as diplomacy: 47–48; quoting/fragments: 48–50;

Horatia: 136, 145–46, 148–60

Identity: 2, 69, 74–75, 81, 92, 95–98, 105–6, 112–14, 154–56, 200, 231–32, 239–40, 244, 250, 264; and belonging: 8–9, 12–4, 30, 46, 81, 167–68; cross-cultural: 2, 15–17, 72–74, 89, 156, 171, 186; Greek: 149–50; insider-outsider: 21, 121, 253, 277; Italian: 63, 90, 97–98; "not-yet-ness": 152–56, 161; and place: 125; Roman: 2, 15–7, 47–48, 81, 90, 93, 105, 149–50, 156, 158, 170, 198–99, 239–40, 277; self-perception/identification: 2, 70, 100, 136, 144; self and other: 151–54, 158–61, 177, 185, 227, 231–32, 277

Italy: 10–1, 15, 46–48, 52, 56, 60, 63, 70–71, 75, 79–82, 91, 94, 97–98, 100, 235

Janus: 76, 154, 156, 201–2, 270

Kalon kakon: 26

Ktisis: 20

Landscape and topography: 2, 12–13, 35–37, 39–42, 113–14, 174, 192–94, 196, 251, 254–56, 270–280

Language, linguistics, power of words: 3, 13, 16, 41, 47, 62–63, 93, 106, 109, 115–23, 132, 136, 167, 178, 183, 214, 225, 231, 234, 239–40, 242–48; ambiguity of: 16, 214, 243, 247; analogy and anomaly: 13, 115–19, 124–25; etymology: 5, 113–14, 120, 125, 170, 194, 237, 242; monosemy and polysemy: 244–45, 250–52; as politics: 12–3, 115–16, 118, 124–25; puns: 137, 165, 177, 188, 194, 216, 242

Leukophrye: 23, 291

Livia: 174, 232

Livy: 6, 8, 12–13, 33, 38, 45, 50, 53–54, 66, 73–74, 78, 89, 102, 114, 123, 135–66, 167, 177, 184, 203, 206–8, 210, 215, 217, 219, 232, 241, 244, 250, 257, 263, 267

Love, *eros*, and sexuality: 1, 14, 16, 25–29, 32, 34, 36–37, 45, 51, 75, 112, 114–15, 149, 150, 155, 168, 171–73, 177, 182–83, 192, 195, 197, 206, 226–27, 229, 233–34, 237, 250–51, 270–71, 289–92

Lucretia: 141, 141–42, 145–46, 148, 151

Luna/Diana/the Moon: 76, 101–2, 172, 253

Luxury and anti-luxury: 10–11, 26, 47, 54–56, 60, 62, 65, 67–68, 70, 73–73, 84–85, 87–89, 102, 204, 205–6

Lydians: 62–63

Marriage: 11, 16, 19, 57, 75, 80–81, 93, 112, 126, 132, 135, 146–49, 166, 157, 161, 170–71, 173, 177–78, 180, 199, 214, 227–29, 231–32, 251, 269, 272, 273, 276

Medea: 9, 26–28, 30, 35, 150, 291

Melting pot: 81, 93, 95–100

Mithras: 284

Monumentality/Monuments: 6–7, 13, 17, 25, 34–35, 37, 40, 72, 113–14, 131–32, 133, 137–38, 141, 144, 154, 164, 193–95, 241, 248–49, 255, 274–81, 287

Morality and ethics: 10, 17, 27, 29, 59, 72, 88, 93, 110, 113, 185, 204–5, 211, 214–16, 218, 240, 263, 264, 265–66, 285–86

Mos Maiorum 5, 218

Mosaic (ethnicity), 81, 93, 98–101, 232

Myth/Methodologies of Myth Studies: 2–4, 5–6, 285–88

Nanis: 23, 34, 291

Neoteric literature: 26

"Noble savage": 91

Ovid: 26–27, 58, 78, 160, 183, 190, 199, 200–202, 238, 257

Parthenius: 20–1, 26, 234, 237
Patriotism/Tarpeia as Patriot: 1, 11, 24, 32–33, 37–38, 67, 85, 94, 109–10, 115, 168, 192, 196, 207, 240–42
Pax Romana: 15
Pedasa: 23, 34, 291
Peisidice: 23, 26, 31, 291
Perfidia: 14, 66, 203–4, 206, 208–11, 214, 219–20
Philotis: 17, 255, 267–73, 283
Piso Frugi (L. Calpurnius): 10–11, 13, 32, 37–38, 49, 64, 84–90, 93–94, 99, 107–10, 114, 141–43 158, 193–94, 207–08, 225, 239–43, 245–46, 252, 266, 279, 285–86
Plautus: 55, 57, 65–66, 74
Plutarch: 8, 15–7, 32, 34, 36–37, 41, 45, 74–75, 78, 107, 125, 146, 157, 193, 225–26, 229, 235–38, 254–83
Polybius: 47, 49, 52, 57, 63, 65, 68–70, 74, 89
Polycrite: 25, 31–32, 34, 292
Principate: 12,14, 165, 167–69, 200, 205; public vs. private in: 167–69, 173–74, 177
Propertius: 8, 12–4, 25, 27, 38, 78, 99, 108, 114–15, 120, 123, 130, 165, 167–204, 208, 219, 226, 227, 234, 263, 270, 275–76
Punica fides: 66, 210
Pythagoreanism: 70–72, 192

Rahab: 25, 292
Rape: 1, 11, 28, 78–80, 95–100, 125 -6, 131, 139, 146–47, 149, 258–59, 269–74, 282–84
Reader and audience: 13–14, 24, 27, 48, 63, 136, 137–38, 140–45, 158, 161, 163, 169, 180, 187, 200–202, 206, 210, 220–21, 226, 232, 235, 238, 241, 251, 253, 260, 264–65, 271–73, 278, 280–81

Religion and god(desse)s: 101–2, 197, 211
Republic, Roman: 9, 12, 15, 52, 88, 83, 105–6, 149, 174, 214–15, 220; elite competition: 45–46, 52, 53, 55, 72, 113; ethnic plurality: 74–75, 93, 97–102, 158; as international power: 2, 10, 46, 66–70; reaction to Hannibal: 53, 56; rebellion in: 81, 84; self-positioning: 45, 46, 48, 133; and upheaval of identity: 105, 113, 168
Rhea Silvia: 143, 145, 147–48, 161–63
Rome: Ara Pacis: 129, 164, 174, 199; Basilica Aemilia (frieze): 12–13, 40–41, 106, 125–34, 164–65, 177, 181, 195, 219, 275–76, 286; Capitoline or Mons Tarpeius: 7, 12, 19, 34–40, 45, 65, 91, 101, 106, 107, 109–10, 112–13, 119, 121, 123, 130, 132, 142–44, 159, 171, 184, 187, 189, 192, 193, 195, 198, 217, 226, 229, 230, 232, 235, 238, 247, 249, 251, 274, 277, 286, 287; Forum: 22, 40, 72, 124–26, 130, 132, 134, 145, 151, 164, 174, 192–93, 195–96, 201, 249, 279; Porta Pandana: 35, 39–40, 101, 122; Statue of Tarpeia: 35, 40–41, 240; Tarpeian grove: 14, 114, 165, 169, 185, 193–95; Tarpeian Rock: 13, 17, 34–37, 40, 78, 107, 109, 112, 114, 119, 121, 132, 184, 193, 195, 219, 260, 266, 275–77, 281–82, 284; Tarpeian tomb/grave: 14, 17, 35, 37–38, 40, 72, 78, 87, 107, 114, 131, 154, 165, 169, 193–95, 248–49, 255–56, 260, 275, 277
Romulus: and Camillus: 267–73; death: 255, 267–68, 271, 273; early life: 163, 176–77; qualities as a ruler: 3, 17, 79, 83, 125, 131, 139, 139, 177, 254, 256–58, 264, 266, 271, 282, 283; and the rape of the Sabine women: 96, 244, 258–59, 269, 282; and Roman places: 101, 120–21, 123, 130, 279; Romulus cycle: 48, 78, 164, 225–26, 239, 276; in warfare: 40, 119, 126, 139

Sabines: as austere: 11, 47, 60–61, 65, 73, 89, 93, 110, 263; enfranchisement and belonging: 17, 39–40, 69–70, 83, 99–

01, 110, 147–48, 158–60, 167, 177, 244, 252, 255, 267–70, 272, 274, 276–77, 282, 286; identity and value of: 56, 82–90, 96; as luxurious: 10–11, 60, 61–63, 65, 67, 70, 73, 84, 89–90, 110, 140; women: rape of: 28, 80, 96–100, 125–26, 139, 146–48, 178, 258–59, 269, 274

Samnites: 72–73, 97, 279

Scapegoat: 29, 32–33, 38

Scylla: 23, 26–7, 30–31, 108, 150, 175–77, 182–83, 292

Second Sophistic: 8, 15, 226, 253, 266

Sejanus: 14, 205, 212–16

Simylus: 9, 15–16, 26, 40, 47, 78, 225–38, 259–60, 267, 269–70, 273

Social War: 11, 79–80, 91, 94–99, 101, 285

Spectacle: 144–45, 155

Spoils: dedication of: 7, 287

Spurius Tarpeius: 34, 41, 139, 148, 157, 175

Stockholm syndrome: 28

Sumptuary laws: 46, 54–55, 107

Tarentum: 70–74

Tarpeia: as Amazon: 13, 105–6, 131–32, 181–82, 187–87, 275–76; as elite: 69; as guardian: 181, 186, 201–2, 257, 266–67, 270; historical parallels: 74–75, 236–37; the name Tarpeia: 41, 114, 113–14, 121, 165, 194; origin of myth: 7, 114, 287; as process personified: 3, 102, 106, 124, 136; as roman patriot: 13, 32–33, 37–37, 45, 85, 109, 115, 134, 158, 160, 184, 207, 240–41, 243, 248; and/as Roman places: 35–42, 106, 112–4, 125–34, 164–65, 169, 192–96, 275–77, 281, 286; and Sabine women: 11, 28–9, 76–79, 99–100, 130–31, 164, 170, 177–78, 267, 276–77; as Sabine: 25, 109, 114, 259, 269; as Vestal: 1, 12–14, 33, 105, 107–15, 132, 157–60, 168–69, 170–73, 175, 177, 178, 180, 184, 190, 193, 208, 257, 270; worship of: 35, 37–40, 78, 87, 89, 108, 113, 249, 279

Tatius: king of Sabines: 17, 64, 76, 82–83, 89–91, 95, 98, 101, 119, 133, 140–43, 148, 157–58, 165–66, 184, 187–89, 195, 204, 208–1, 218–19, 222, 243, 247–49, 251, 253–54, 259, 262–66, 273, 282–83

Tharbis: 23, 292

Theano: 25, 292

Theseus: 30, 34–35, 258, 266, 271, 273–77, 280–82, 289

Tiberius: 12, 14, 36, 203–5, 212, 216, 218, 285

Titurius Sabinus (L.), 10, 76, 80, 82–84, 90–91, 98

Tragedy: 4, 29–30, 191

Treason and *proditio*: 7, 14, 17, 23, 34, 40, 51, 75, 132, 141, 148, 157, 165–66, 204, 218–20, 222, 234; benefiting from: 17, 255, 259, 262–65, 267; punishment for: 30–31, 36–37

Treasonous girl mytheme: 9, 16, 19–35, 234, 289–92

Valerius Maximus: 14–15, 203–22, 263

Varro: 12–13, 33, 105–24, 167–68

Vestal virgin: 12, 23, 107–8, 110–12, 159–60; as man: 111; punishing of: 32–33, 57–58, 107, 110–11

Virginity: 100, 110–12, 148, 154, 157, 159–60, 162, 170–71

Virtus: 132, 160

Women and girls: 20–5, 29, 57–58, 131–32, 145–50, 163–65, 167, 178–79, 197, 219, 227, 255, 275–76, 288; agency of: 20, 27, 29, 58–59; as benefit to men: 21–2, 55, 58; as city: 23–24, 33–35; as conspirators: 22–23; as facilitators for change: 20; and greed: 57–60, 73, 143; as mediators: 147–48, 164–65; motivations of: 25–29; as objects and subjects: 135, 142, 145–47, 149–50, 167; and perspective: 23–24; and religion: 57–58; and Roman expansion: 147–50, 164–65; as weakness: 21–28; and wealth/power: 53–59, 131–32